'An Angel Amongst Strange Bears'

DEDICATED TO

The other John in my life, my beloved husband, and to the best production of my life, my daughter Francesca aka Roo.

ৡয়

I have read your book and am full of admiration for the scholarship, the depth of research and the easy to read style of your writing. I enjoyed the book very much and am so grateful that I have been introduced to an ancestor who has previously been in the distant past. You have really brought him to life for me. He was obviously a man of character and strength as well as remaining at heart a family man to his daughters.

Lord Lothian

Throughout the text you will find QR codes that will take you to music pertinent to the subject.

Front Cover: John Hobart by Thomas Gainsborough.

'An Angel Amongst Strange Bears'

John Hobart
2nd Earl of Buckinghamshire
Blickling Hall, Norfolk

Joy Beresford Frye

POPPYLAND
PUBLISHING

Designed and typeset in 10.5 on 13.5 pt Gilgamesh Pro.

Printed by Halstan.

Picture credits:

Allen County Public Library Genealogy Center, 45*
Arkesteijn J., front cover*
Davies, K., 189
Heritage Fine Art, 43*
Heritage Image Partnership Ltd / Alamy Stock Photo, 17
Library of Congress, 69*, 144*, 175*, 225*, 242*, 247*
Linwood, J., 24*
Lord Belmore collection, 220, 239, 262
Lord Lothian collection, 260, 261
Metropolitan Museum of Art, 36*, 270*
Mike Page photography, 60, 187
Miller, C., 136*
National Museum of Ireland, 215
National Trust, 245
National Trust / Sue James, 285
New York Public Library, 21*, 57*, 211*
Norfolk Record Office, 10, 142, 281
Odesa Art Museum, 63*
Pettitt, M., 129*
Poppyland Ltd. collection, 13
Philadelphia Museum of Art, 27*
Red Zebra, back cover
Sotheby's, 56
Victoria and Albert Museum, 156
Ward. I., 9, 178, 294, 289, 290, 291, 292
Wellcome Collection, 29*, 85*, 227*
Yale Center for British Art, 20*, 309*, 38*
unknown, 82*, 89*, 94*, 100*, 113*, 125*, 150*, 153*, 209*, 219

*public domain or Creative Commons Licence.

Every attempt has been made to ensure that images are correctly attributed, we apologise for any inadvertent errors.

Contents

Acknowledgements

My heartfelt thanks to Maria Morris and Ges Ashby for their extraordinary kindness when the plague prevented me from visiting Scotland in person. This biography could not have been completed without their invaluable help.

Special thanks to my first draft readers Linda Fullegar and Gerri Way.

I am indebted to the late Peter Marson for his wise and witty guidance.

My thanks to all at the Norfolk Record Office, especially Gordon Blacklock, Ian Palfrey, Jenny Watts, Alison Barnard and Vaughan Griggs.

Thank you to Jenny Barley at the National Horseracing Museum, Newmarket, and to Rupert Baker at The Royal Society.

Thanks to Peter F. French and Martin Hardy-Shepherd for advice on all things Masonic.

Thank you to my family and friends, especially Chris Gavin, Gerri Way, Heather Staff, Pat Crowder, Lynne Day, Mary Rezlik, my pyramid pals Jan Cole and Linda Fullegar; Debs Hicks, Kevin and Lynn James, Sarah Holmes, and everyone else who encountered me during the research for this book who listened patiently to me rabbiting on about 'my' 2nd Earl.

Thanks to all my friends at Blickling, with special mentions to Chuck Weigand, Megan Dennis and Bethan Edmunds, and to Gerald Peachey at Red Zebra for the mugshot.

Thanks to Ian Ward for his fabulous photographs.

Many thanks to the brilliant Tracy Borman, and to Lord Lothian of Monteviot House and Lord Belmore of Castle Coole for their kindness in allowing images from their private collections to be reproduced in this book. Thanks to Eva Ewart, Archivist at Castle Coole and Susan Elliot at Monteviot House for their assistance.

Finally, thanks to Gareth and Janet Davies at Poppyland Publishing without whom, dear reader, you would not be reading this.

Joy Beresford Frye, 2023.

Bibliography

Borman, T., *King's Mistress, Queen's Servant*, Vintage, 2010.

Correspondence of Emily, Duchess of Leinster, @irishmanuscripts.ie.

Despatches and Correspondence of John, Second Earl of Buckinghamshire Ambassador to the Court of Catherine II of Russia 1762-1765, Vols. 1 and 2, *(ed.)* Royal Historical Society, 1902.

Grenville Papers: being the correspondence of Richard Grenville Earl Temple, K.G., and The Right Hon: George Grenville, Vol. 3, John Murray, 1853. —archive.org.

Letters to and from Henrietta, Countess of Suffolk, and her second husband, the Hon. George Berkeley: From 1712 to 1767, Vol. 2, John Murray, 1824.

Lewis W. S. (ed.),*Horace Walpole Correspondence* (Yale Edition), Yale University Press, 1937-1983.

Marson, P., *Belmore: The Lowry-Corry Families of Castle Coole*, Ulster Historical Foundation, 2012.

Massie, R. K., *Catherine the Great, Portrait of a Woman*, Random House, 2011.

Report on the Manuscripts of the Marquess of Lothian, preserved at Blickling Hall, NRO MC3443/3/4.

Scarfe, N. (ed. trans.), *A Frenchman's Year in Suffolk, 1784* by Francois de La Rochefoucauld, Vol. XXX, The Boydell Press / Suffolk Records Society, 1989.

Stirling, A. M. W., *The Hothams: being the chronicles of the Hothams of Scarborough and South Dalton from their hitherto unpublished family papers*, Jenkins, H., London, 1918.—archive.org.

ABBREVIATIONS

NRO   Norfolk Record Office

NRS   National Records of Scotland

NLI   National Library of Ireland

PRONI   Public Record Office Northern Ireland

Franz Joseph Haydn's String Quartet No.30 in E-Flat Major, Op.33 No.2. Hob.III:38 "The Joke": 1. Allegro moderato.

This delightful music reflects Buckingham's character perfectly and I listened frequently whilst writing his biography. It is light, playful and tender, and I always think of it as his 'theme tune'.

Introduction

Although I had walked with various dogs on the Blickling Estate for several years, none of us paid much attention to the Pyramid which appears unexpectedly to startle and perplex the casual passerby. Except on the first sighting which, on my part at least, provoked wonderment as pyramids are in rather short supply in Norfolk; none of the dogs, however, seemed surprised. We, or rather I, paused to puzzle over the inscription, but it made little sense. Some time later, as a volunteer guide of tours to the Mausoleum, for that's what the pyramid is, I became intrigued as to why John Hobart came to be interred within such an unusual structure, flanked by his first and second wives. This seemed a strange arrangement, so I resolved to find out more.

John Hobart's distinctive voice speaks to us through his letters and I make no apology for reproducing them here in some quantity. They convey his keen sense of humour and optimistic outlook, yet in rare introspective moments we witness him acknowledging his flaws and expressing a desire to eradicate them. We follow his growth from naive adolescent, through his courting years, evolving into an adept politician and accomplished diplomat. The trials of his political life and the tribulations of his private life are laid bare.

The Mausoleum at Blickling, August 2019.

As is most often the case with political careers, his met with degrees of success and failure, the verdict of which was determined by whether a colleague or an opponent pronounced judgement; but it speaks volumes that at home, in Europe, Russia and in Ireland, he inspired lasting affection amongst a great many of the people he encountered. Speaking of volumes, there are two densely packed books of letters solely devoted to his mission in Russia, which was principally to conduct two Treaty negotiations with that country, of Alliance and of Commerce. He witnessed dramatic events at the Court of the Empress Catherine and his first hand accounts are fascinating. His tenure as Viceroy of Ireland similarly produced copious amounts of intense letter writing. I have chosen excerpts that illustrate many of the difficulties and some of the

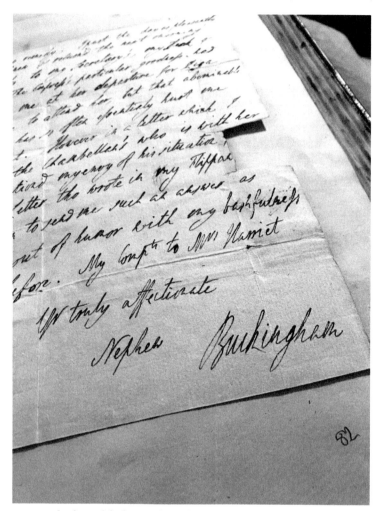

An example of one of the letters John Hobart sent to his aunt.

pleasures he encountered in those locations.

As for the other characters involved in the 2nd Earl's life, especially those of his wives, there is relatively little written correspondence extant, but where there is, and in combination with their painted portraits, glorious glimpses of their personalities are revealed. A welcome exception is found in the numerous letters exchanged between John Hobart and his aunt, Henrietta, Lady Suffolk, who was more mother to him than aunt and who was the most influential person in his life.

But to understand how John Hobart came to be an Earl in the first place, it is necessary to begin with his grandfather, Sir Henry Hobart. This is fortunate, because no history of Blickling Hall would be complete without the story of the duel.

Sir Henry the Hot-Head

Sir Henry Hobart, the 4th Baron of Blickling was an impetuous, rather belligerent fellow and it would not be unfair to say that his life ended as a direct result of his stubborn and headstrong nature. The young Henry was knighted at the tender age of thirteen by King Charles II who visited Blickling as part of his Grand Tour of the Realm in 1671. This bestowing of a knighthood was a deliberate and generous act of reconciliation on the King's part as Henry's father Sir John Hobart, the 3rd Baronet, in concert with almost all the nobility of Norfolk, was stubbornly republican and had not supported the Stuart cause. Furthermore, Sir John's wife Mary was a daughter of John Hampden, one of the leading parliamentarians involved in challenging the authority of King Charles I, which had precipitated the English Civil War and lost Charles his head. It was even intended, so his enemies said, that Hampden would sit in Oliver Cromwell's projected Upper House.[1] Perhaps understandably in the circumstances, Charles chose not to stay overnight at Blickling, preferring instead the company of the staunchly loyalist Paston family at nearby Oxnead Manor, perhaps stopping on the way at Aylsham's Blackboys Inn to quaff some restorative Norfolk ale.

Thirteen years later Sir Henry inherited the Blickling Estate when its fortunes were in considerable decline, largely because his father had managed to shrink the acreage by three quarters during his tenure. Sir John had fought several elections which cost him dear and the estate was now encumbered to a large degree.

Despite Sir Henry's efforts to reduce the debts by selling parts of the property and despite even the considerable £10,000 fortune his wife Elizabeth Maynard brought with her on their marriage in 1684, he remained in considerable financial trouble. Whilst his career as a Whig MP undoubtedly suited his argumentative temperament, running election campaigns also meant huge expenditure which drastically drained his resources and, moreover, the very little patience he possessed. To compound matters he also had a persistent and compulsive habit of feuding with his neighbours. Humphrey Prideaux, Dean of Norwich, commented:

> I wish Sir Henry instead of persecuting his neighbours would think of
> paying his debts, which he takes no care of, but uses his privilege to protect
> him. There is a lady of one of the best families in the country who hath
> all her fortune in his hands, and he hath not paid her any interest these
> several years whereby she is put to great hardship. The case of several
> others of ye like nature will come against him next sessions, and I hope the
> House will not think fit to protect him.[2]

In the general election of 1698, to his considerable chagrin, Sir Henry lost not only his Norfolk seat to Sir William Cooke, his old Tory rival, but also the prospect of a seat in St Ives where he had an interest through his wife. His last hope of a position in the House was to gain Thetford after the imminent resignation of the holder Sir Joseph Williamson, but subsequent events would make this an impossibility.

Sir Henry left Westminster for Blickling in high dudgeon, humiliated, furious, and with his debts further increased after the massive and ultimately fruitless expense of the election campaign. With his customary inability to blame himself for failure, a target at which to unleash his fury announced itself from an unlikely quarter. Word reached him that Oliver Le Neve, a Tory neighbour at Great Witchingham, was spreading a rumour that Sir Henry had acted in a cowardly fashion at the Battle of the Boyne. Sir Henry had attended William III in his capacity as a Gentleman of the Horse and had in fact acquitted himself well, but this was a battle fought a full nine years earlier. Nevertheless, he convinced himself that it was this ugly lie that had cost him the election and in Reepham market place publicly demanded a duel. Le Neve, an amiable individual who had recently married for the second time, and whose blameless pursuits included hunting, fishing, reading and gardening, maintained his innocence. But when Hobart refused to accept his written protestations Le Neve bravely wrote:

> Honoured Sir, I am very sorry that I was not at Reepham yesterday when
> you gave yourself the trouble of appearing there, that I might not only
> have justified the truth of my not saying what it is reported I did, but that
> I might have told you that I wrote not that letter to avoid fighting you. I
> am ready and desirous to meet you when and where you please to assign.
> If otherwise, I expect your Author's name in return to this, that I may
> take my satisfaction there; or else conclude the Imputation sprung from
> Blickling, and send you a time and place; for the matter shall not rest as it
> is though it cost the life of Your Servant, Oliver Neve Aug ye 20th, 1698.[3]

On the very same day the two men rode to Cawston Heath, midway between their estates. A gambler would have been wise to back Sir Henry to win this duel as he was taller, stronger and an accomplished swordsman to boot. Le Neve was unsuited to this adventure and ill-fitted for combat as, although he had once been head of the local militia, his more recent occupations were breeding his beagle pack and writing ribald poetry.

It may be that Sir Henry was unaware that Le Neve was left handed. It is said that the only witness was a servant girl, hiding in a hedge for reasons best known to herself, who reported later that Sir Henry took first blood by passing his sword through Le Neve's arm; presumably his right. Le Neve, in defence, retaliation, and probably sheer blind panic, ran his sword through Sir Henry's body. Realising a little too late that he had not only inflicted what appeared to be a fatal wound but also remembering that duelling without Seconds in attendance was illegal, Le Neve jumped on his horse, made for the coast and fled to Holland.[4] Sir Henry,

The Dueling Stone, marking where the fateful duel took place.

although mortally wounded, somehow made the four mile journey back to Blickling Hall. It may be that the story of the servant girl is folklore and that the duellists had grooms attending to their horses whilst they fought. In which case Sir Henry's servant would have helped him home and Le Neve does not appear quite so callous in simply leaving him alone to die. But whomever was there, it is known that after an anguished night spent screaming in agony, Sir Henry died in his West Turret bedroom at Blickling Hall on the morning of 21 August 1698.[5]

In the midst of her grief the newly widowed Lady Elizabeth Hobart arranged an opulent funeral for her husband. She was said to have offered £500 for Le Neve's apprehension and later commissioned a monument to mark where the duel took place at Cawston. But as the realisation dawned upon her of the dire financial position in which Sir Henry had left the estate, she frantically sought assistance from her wider family. To her considerable relief an invitation arrived from her distant relative Mary, Countess of Suffolk, and she and her eight children spent the next few summers at Gunnersbury House near Kew in Surrey. Although the journey was onerous, taking about a week to travel the one hundred and fifty miles, Elizabeth at least had the burden of running the Blickling Estate removed from her shoulders for those periods. There were rumours of more than one prospective bridegroom, which she may have considered as a way out of her financial difficulties, but in the summer of 1701 she was stricken with what turned out to be the last stages of consumption and three years to the very day of Sir

Henry's demise, she succumbed.

The orphaned children, with the sixteen year old twins Mary and Anne now in charge, returned to Blickling, but less than a year later Anne died. Death, no respecter of age or class, then took her twin Mary, and sisters Philippa, ten, and Elizabeth, eighteen, to the graveyard at Blickling in the space of the next three years. John Hobart, who was four at the time of his father's death, inherited Blickling, but trustees would run the estate on his behalf until he came of age at eighteen. After the death of their mother and sisters it was Henrietta, now the eldest at sixteen, who took on the care of her younger siblings. She reasoned that if she could marry well she would be in a position to help her family prosper.

Notes

1. Ketton-Cremer, R.W., *Oliver Le Neve and his duel with Sir Henry Hobart*, 1941, privately printed.
2. Ibid.
3. Ibid.
4. After living for two years in Holland under several aliases, Le Neve returned to England and was tried for manslaughter in 1700. His neighbours, with whom he had always been far more popular than Sir Henry, spoke up for him and he was triumphantly acquitted of any blame in Sir Henry Hobart's death; and the "honest gentlemen in two counties drained repeated bumpers to his health for many nights to come". Oliver Le Neve died (of natural causes) in 1711.
5. It has been reported by some National Trust Volunteers that they occasionally hear Sir Henry's ghostly screams echoing through the house.

Henrietta: Wife, Mistress, Aunt, Mother?

Following her mother's example, Henrietta appealed to the Suffolks for help and as a result was invited to live at Gunnersbury. During her stay their third and youngest son, a captain in the Dragoon's, came home on leave. To outward appearances the handsome and dashing Charles Howard was charming and attentive but this concealed a very much darker side of his character. Known to be "wrong-headed, ill tempered, drunken, extravagant and brutal"[1] by others, Charles had learned of the large dowry which would accompany Henrietta on her marriage (her father had lawfully protected this money from his debtors) and artfully hid his true nature until his proposal was accepted and their wedding arranged. Fortunately for Henrietta her uncle, Brigadier-General John Hobart, was aware of Charles' dubious character traits and he drew up a marriage settlement which again protected her money but this time from her own husband. Nevertheless married life became intolerable very quickly for Henrietta as Charles renewed his habits of drinking, whoring and gambling and he frequently took out his violent rages upon her. The arrival of their son Henry, nine months after the wedding, changed nothing except that Charles would leave Henrietta and the infant alone for months on end whilst he pursued his nefarious habits.

After enduring several years of humiliation at his hands, the intelligent and resourceful Henrietta eventually found a way out of her predicament. Reduced to living in penury with Charles and the now six year old Henry in the poorest back streets of London, by spring 1714 she had somehow scrimped together enough money for them to travel to Hanover, to the court of the Elector George Louis at Herrenhausen. Her plan was to find employment for both herself and her husband at this court and in this her hopes were fulfilled. The Electress Sophia immediately took to Henrietta who became a favourite and to all intents and purposes a lady-in-waiting to the eighty-four year old lady, who was next in line to the British crown. Henrietta also found favour with the Electoral Princess Caroline and only a few months later, following the death of not only Sophia but also the English Queen Anne, the Hanoverian Court moved to London. Henrietta's qualities of modesty, tact and intelligence had made her such a popular figure that Caroline, now the Princess of Wales, appointed her a Woman of the Bedchamber. Charles Howard, who had surprisingly managed not to disgrace himself at Hanover, in public at least, was made a Groom of the Bedchamber to George Louis, now King George I of England. Henrietta's career at Court then took an unexpected trajectory when the Prince of Wales, George Augustus, turned his amorous attentions towards her. George was much given to expounding upon long and intricate explanations about obscure events in historical Hanoverian militia, not a subject that would necessarily enthral a young English lady from Norfolk, but her presumably feigned interest in his interests, together with her physical allure, proved irresistible and before long he made her his mistress. This can only have been an intensely awkward scenario for Henrietta as she was also a servant in his wife's household, but it was one she navigated with skill and diplomacy, calling upon her considerable depths of resilience, diplomacy and charm. A combination of natural serenity coupled with a sense of humour stood her in good stead and she quickly earned the sobriquet 'The Swiss' because she invariably took a neutral stance in the many scandals and tangles of Court life. Charles Howard, so enraged and humiliated was he by her position as the Prince's mistress, once attempted to abduct his wife but she escaped his clutches, ironically with the help of the Princess Caroline. As a cruel punishment Charles forbade Henrietta any contact whatsoever with their young son Henry knowing this would cause her the most grievous hurt. It is said that the Prince of Wales came to a financial arrangement with Charles Howard, giving him an annuity of £1,200.

At Blickling Henrietta's brother John and their two other surviving sisters, Catherine and Dorothy, had in the meantime been cared for by guardians and educated as befitted their status. Executors had ensured the careful management of the Estate in his minority, and on coming of age John succeeded his father as 5th Baronet Hobart. He studied at Clare College, Cambridge, and "afterwards travelled beyond the seas."[2] On his return he was elected a member of Parliament for the borough of St Ives in Cornwall and later to the borough of Beer-Alston in Devonshire. In 1717 he married Judith, daughter of Robert Britiffe of Hunworth Hall, a local lawyer and Norwich Whig MP who acted as legal adviser to the powerful Townshend and Walpole families. The couple were married in Thorpe Market and as the bride brought a substantial dowry of £15,000 the Hobart family fortunes took a welcome turn for the better.

Judith swiftly produced a son named Henry but no sooner was he christened than he died at just six weeks old. Then came Dorothea, always known as Dorothy, in 1719. She is of particular interest because of speculation that she was in fact the daughter of Henrietta Howard and George Augustus, the Prince of Wales (the future King George II). Not only was there a vast gap in Mrs Howard's attendance at Court in 1719, which was almost unheard of during her time as his mistress, but there was also a strong resemblance between Dorothy and the King, especially in their large and somewhat bulbous eyes. Henrietta would have gone to considerable lengths to keep any such baby a secret, in part for the sake of her privacy and her reputation, but also to avoid provoking her husband's ever vengeful nature. Dorothy's baptism was recorded at Hampden House, the family seat of the Hobart's cousin Robert Hampden, with whom Henrietta frequently corresponded. It is significant that Judith Hobart bore a daughter in the same year and that her baby Mary died before reaching her first birthday and plausible that Henrietta's adoring and protective younger brother John would have been willing to take his sister's child into his household at Blickling. Furthermore, five of John and Judith's seven children's baptisms are recorded at Blickling Church and the name Dorothea is not amongst them (another son Robert died soon after birth and was not recorded). It is therefore within the bounds of possibility that the Hobart family arranged the matter amongst themselves and replaced Mary with Dorothy without exciting undue curiosity in either London or Norfolk.

Henrietta Howard, Countess of Suffolk, c1724 by Charles Jervas.

Whatever her true provenance, and it cannot be known for certain, the wider world and Dorothy herself believed she was a Hobart.

Within the next two years Judith produced two more daughters, but Judith died at eight months and Henrietta at six months. Finally their desire for a new son and heir was fulfilled with the arrival of John, the hero of this history, on 17 August 1723 at Greenwich.

Sir John Hobart had followed in his father Henry's footsteps into politics, firstly as a Whig MP for St Ives and then as Vice Admiral of Norfolk. At Blickling Hall he commissioned William Aikman to paint portraits of the most influential gentlemen of his acquaintance to hang in the Long Gallery: Charles, Viscount 'Turnip' Townshend, (so called because he helped to popularise the rotation of crops in fertile Norfolk farmlands); William Morden, a Baronet married to Judith's sister Elizabeth Britiffe; Henry Kelsall of Colkirk; Sir Thomas Sebright, 4th Bt of Herts; Sir John Cope; a Mr Crawley; Sir William Leman; Sir Robert Rich of Roos Hall, Suffolk; Edmund Prideaux, a Cornish artist and architect; Col. Harbord Harbord, a cousin; and two of the most distinguished names of the day, Thomas Coke, 1st Earl of Leicester of Holkham Hall, and the powerful Sir Robert Walpole, Britain's first Prime Minister, of Houghton Hall.

John's sister Dorothy died, unmarried, at Bath in 1723 and Catherine, who had married General Charles Churchill, died in 1726. In August of that year, Mrs Ann Bedingfield, an impoverished family friend and sometime servant of the Hobarts, wrote to Henrietta Howard:

> We staid four days at Norwich—were at two assemblies; there was a prodigious crowd in the hall, the rooms, and the gallery. Sir John Hobart and Lady M Coke began the ball. Sir T Coke and Lady Hobart, Mrs Harbord and Mr Kelsey made a party at quadrille, as did Sir J Woodhouse,

Mr Harbord, Mrs Baily and Mrs Ann Bedingfield (two old maids, one a great fortune, the other so in imagination). The game being new, drew many spectators, which made it hot and disagreeable. The next day, the company met at the Raffling Shop; from thence they went to the Play. The house was too small for the company, and the stage too full for the actors; but a trap door opened, and four of the company fell in—one a particular tall man, who was high sheriff last year, fell upon a pretty woman, and liked his situation so well that they could not get him out. This occasioned great mirth; the man received no hurt, but the woman was bruised. We returned to charming Blickling....a wasp fixed on her ladyship's neck. Sir John would not let it be touched—it staid some minutes—all that time she suffered so much by fear that it has made bleeding necessary. The operation is over, and she upon the bed. The children were both ill with coughs. Master's (John) was the most violent, but Miss Dolly's (Dorothy) lasts the longest; his is quiet again, and hers is better. If you have time to read, I hope you'll have time to write; for every word of yours is a vast pleasure and a real satisfaction—when you tell me stocks go on prosperously. I have hopes that fortune will turn the wheel in my favour when they do begin to draw the lottery. Your most obedient for ever, A.B.[3]

Judith had been in early pregnancy at the time of the wasp sting and six months later gave birth to the short lived Robert, and, probably as a result of complications in childbirth, she died shortly afterwards on 7 February 1727. Mrs Bedingfield became a beloved companion to the motherless children and just a year later, on 10 February 1728, John married Elizabeth, the daughter of Robert Bristow MP. In May he was made Baron Hobart of Blickling and had been returned as Whig MP for both Bere Alston in Devon, and Norfolk, and chose to sit for his county. Both on his own merit and perhaps aided by his sister's influence at Court he was made a Knight of the Bath in 1725, Treasurer of the Chamber in 1727 and Baron Hobart of Blickling in 1728.

In September 1731 a half-brother for Dorothy, John and Robert arrived with the birth of George. Three years later their aunt Henrietta's circumstances altered significantly and the lives of the two elder Hobart siblings soon followed suit.

Notes

1. Sedgwick, R. (ed.),"*Some materials towards memoirs of the reign of King George II*" by John, Lord Hervey, Vol I, Chapter II, King's Printers, 1931, p.54.
2. Collins, A., '*The Peerage of England*' Vol III, H. Woodfall, 1768, p.745.
3. *Letters to and from Henrietta* ..., Vol. I, p.256.

I Dreamt I Dwelt in Marble Hill

Henrietta Howard's fortunes at Court rose with her lover's accession to the English throne in 1727. Although she was now the mistress of a King, her position as Queen Caroline's Woman of the Bedchamber mightily oppressed her; tasks such as holding the wash bowl during the ceremony of dressing became humiliating when the jealous Queen insisted that she perform this duty on bended knee. The rigid, boring repetitions of Court life wore Henrietta down and took a toll on her health. She often took to her bed with debilitating headaches and she suffered from rheumatism, no doubt exacerbated by living in damp quarters in Kensington Palace, and gradually her hearing began to deteriorate. In one sense this may have been a blessing in disguise, as it was the King's routine to visit her between the hours of 7 and 10 o'clock in the evenings (if he arrived early he would pace up and down the corridor until the exact hour before entering her apartment) and his topic of conversation still often focused on the minutiae of long gone Hanoverian militia. More helpfully, George was instrumental in obtaining a financial Settlement for Henrietta after a formal Deed of Separation from Charles Howard was granted on 11 March 1728 and this thoughtful action on the part of the King served to greatly alleviate, if not completely remove, her anxiety about Howard's future interference.

Bright intervals during these tedious years arrived in the shape of her young niece (possibly daughter) Dorothy Hobart who made frequent visits to Henrietta at Court. Their close and loving relationship gave them both a great deal of comfort. Then in 1731 Henrietta's fortunes changed dramatically when Charles Howard's elder brother Edward died suddenly, elevating Charles quite unexpectedly to the title 9th Earl of Suffolk.[1] This meant that Henrietta was now not only titled Countess of Suffolk, but because her brother-in-law had generously chosen to bequeath his money to her rather than to his despicable brother, she was also considerably better off financially. Furthermore, her resultant higher status meant she was immediately promoted to be Mistress of the Queen's Robes, a role that commanded greater respect and involved duties which were considerably less onerous than those of a Woman of the Bedchamber. However, she did not have to endure even these duties for long as just two years later Charles Howard himself died, most likely as a result of his years of depravity and dissipation. It was this event that propelled Henrietta into making a determined bid for freedom as she was no longer in fear of his spiteful and vindictive retribution and could realistically envisage living away from Court and retiring in peace. She had endured trials and crushing ennui as the King's mistress and the Queen's servant for twenty long years. Furthermore, in the last of

Her Most Excellent Majesty, Queen Caroline, 1739, by John Faber the Younger, YCBA B1974.12.413.

those years George had begun to tire of her company and became increasingly irascible towards her. When his cutting remarks about her age and cruel jibes about her loss of hearing became more frequent it was abundantly clear to everyone at Court that his affection for her had diminished. Fortunately for Henrietta, when their relationship had been more amicable he had been generous. In 1724 he presented her with £11,500 in stocks and shares together with jewellery and furniture, stipulating in writing that it should be used by her "as if she was sole and unmarryed."[2] This condition was considerately and deliberately designed to prevent Charles Howard from getting his grasping hands on any of it. Henrietta used the funds to

George II.

quietly build Marble Hill House, a charming Palladian villa at Twickenham and it was at this Thames-side idyll that she longed to set up her permanent home.

Two developments coincided to further intensify her desire to escape from Court. Whilst Henrietta was away on her first real holiday in twenty years, taking the waters at Bath, the King's daughter Princess Amelia, who harboured a long held deep aversion towards her father's mistress, started a false rumour. She put the word out that Henrietta and Lord Bolingbroke were conspiring together to turn the King against his chief minister Robert Walpole and maliciously hinted that the conspirators were romantically involved.

Returning to Kensington Palace seven weeks later Henrietta discovered that the King had heard the poisonous rumours, that he was incensed, and that he refused point blank to see her. She requested a private talk with Caroline, and these words are from Henrietta's dictated recollection of an extraordinary exchange between a Queen of England and her husband's mistress:

> Lady Suffolk:
> Madam, I beg that if in talking to your Majesty I use any word that does not mark the greatest respect to the King, you will be pleased to tell me, for I come fully determined to take my leave with the same respect, submission and duty, with which I have behaved for twenty years. Your Majesty has often told me that I have never failed in anything for your service in either of those places you have honoured me with, and indeed, Madam, I don't know how far your Majesty may think it respectfull to

make this declaration but I beg it may be permitted me for a moment to speak of the King as of a man only who was my friend. He has been dearer to me than my own brother, so, Madam, as a friend I feel resentment at being ill-treated and sorrow to have lost his friendship, but as my King and master, I have the greatest submission to his pleasure, yet I wish I knew of what I am accused, tho' I know my innocence, as it must be some horrid crime.

Queen:
Oh, fie ! You commit a crime! Don't talk so.

Lady Suffolk:
Madam, as I know his Majesty's justice and his warmth of friendship, I know he could not for anything less punish me so severely. Consider, Madam, I have been absent seven weeks, returned sooner than was proper for my health to do my duty in my place to your Majesty, and to show my respect to him upon his Birthday.

Queen:
Well, Child, you know the King leaves it to me. I will answer for it, that all will be as well with you as with any of the Lady's, and I am sure you cannot leave my service then.

Lady Suffolk:
No ! Madam ! I never will be forgiven an offence I have not committed. I beg your permission to retire; indeed Madam, I have not slept since I came into your house, and believe I never shall under this suspicion of guilt.

Queen:
I will not give you leave to go. I tell you plainly if you go today you go without my consent.

The ladies had reached an impasse but eventually the Queen persuaded Henrietta to stay for another week, although she maintained that "as I am under his Majesty's Displeasure you will not expect my attendance, or that I come again to receive your commands."

Queen:
Yes, I do, and I will see you again. Be sure you come again.

Lady Suffolk:
I will obey your Majesty.

Queen:
Harkye, Lady Suffolk. You will come up as you used to do.[3]

The irony of a wife arguing strenuously to keep her husband's mistress near him can be explained by the Queen's instinctive determination to prevent Lady Suffolk from vacating a role which might be filled by a younger, less discreet and perhaps more ambitious woman.[4] Henrietta's plaintive appeals to the King brought nothing but resounding silence so a week later she summoned up the courage to talk privately once more with the Queen after which, and contrary to Caroline's express wish, Henrietta left Court for the last time. Despite the King's recent unchivalrous behaviour he found it in his heart to continue her allowance of £2,000 a year as a pension, paid out of his own pocket.

The second major catalyst had appeared some time earlier in the form of George Berkeley, youngest son of the 2nd Earl of Berkeley. As well as being the MP for Hedon, Yorkshire, he was also the Master Keeper and Governor of St Katherine's Hospital in London. Amiable, good humoured and well-read, he became acquainted with Henrietta through her relationship with his sister and over time their friendship developed into a greater intimacy. Unsurprisingly, a ripple of scandal accompanied Henrietta's sudden retirement from Court. Lord Bathurst mistrusted the press, "I did not give credit to what I saw in the newspapers until I had it confirmed under the hand of a friend of ours" and went on to console her,

> Now, to comfort you madam there must be some satisfaction in
> discovering who were friends to one's person, and who to one's fortune,
> which you could never have found out without this change. Perhaps you
> will not believe it, but it is literally true, that the sun shines, even where
> I am, above one hundred miles from London; and that there are men
> and women walking about on two legs, just as they do about St James's,
> only they seem to stand steadier upon them: they can talk too, only it is
> in a different dialect, and for my part I like it better. A great king, who
> happened to be a philosopher, could find out nothing more to be desired
> in human life, than these four things— old wood to burn, old wine to
> drink, old friends to converse with, and old books to read; you may be sure
> of enjoying all these, and the third of them (which I suppose he thought
> the most valuable) in a more perfect degree than *his majesty or his queen*.[5]

The diarist Horace Walpole represented the Queen as unwilling to part with Lady Suffolk for the reason that "however jealous of her, she dreaded the king's forming a new attachment with a younger rival" and Lord Hervey reported that "the king complained very warmly of this: 'What the devil did you mean,' said his Majesty, 'by trying to make an old, dull, deaf and peevish beast stay and plague me when I had so good an opportunity of getting rid of her?'"[6]

In spite of the King's spectacularly ungallant attitude, Henrietta was ecstatic and revelled in her new found freedom. Marble Hill, in its idyllic rural position on the river Thames, was a relaxed and peaceful antidote to the constant hubbub and stultifying strictures of life at the Palace and only a few months later she was declared to look healthier and more beautiful than ever. Doubtless this rejuvenation was caused in no small part by her deepening relationship with the Hon George Berkeley. George was not considered particularly handsome, neither was he

Marble Hill House, 2010.

particularly rich; and although he was four years younger than Henrietta, he did not enjoy particularly good health, suffering, as did she, from debilitating bouts of gout. Nevertheless the couple were temperamentally well matched and deeply in love. When George declared his devotion and proposed marriage, Henrietta was overjoyed and their wedding took place on 26 June 1735. The Earl of Strafford waited until August to send his congratulations and explained the delay, "That I always wished you happy I hope you believe, and I now conclude you are entirely so, in your marriage with the most agreeable lady in Europe; on which give me leave to sincerely wish you joy, which I had done sooner, but I always doubt printed news, especially in this lying age."[7]

Married life agreed with the couple as their affectionate, teasing letters when parted attest, "The moment your ladyship was gone, I went to bed—lay half an hour—disliked it extremely—got up again; never found Marble Hill so disagreeable"[8] to which Henrietta replied "Baron Sparre affirms I look better than I did seventeen years ago, and Lord Cobham says I am the best looking woman of thirty that he ever saw. These compliments have entirely cured my headache. God bless you. I do with all my heart and soul, nor do I yet repent that I am, H.Berkeley."[9] Henrietta was at this time aged forty seven. Although she signed herself Berkeley in this letter, she reverted to Lady Suffolk in all her subsequent correspondence and everyone, including George Berkeley, always addressed her thus.

෨෬

Marble Hill was for Henrietta a labour of love and with the constant help of her near neighbour the poet and satirist Alexander Pope, who had helped to oversee the building works and the decoration of the house, it became a graceful adornment atop wide sweeping lawns which gently sloped to the riverbank. A three storey Palladian villa sporting a fine mahogany staircase and light, pleasingly proportioned rooms it was both elegant and welcoming, an accurate reflection of its gentle owner's qualities. Delicately painted Chinese wallpaper featured in a first floor entertaining room, chinoiserie lacquer furniture and blue and white porcelain were in everyday use, and an intricate Chinese screen confirmed that oriental fashion was at its zenith. Henrietta and George's bedroom displayed two Italianate pillars, and throughout the house and garden Henrietta's refined good taste was in evidence. Semi circles of trees swept from the corners of the house down to the river and flower gardens and enticing serpentine walks were created. Charles Bridgeman, later a gardener to George II, designed these delights with Henrietta's enthusiastic encouragement. One walk led to a nine-pin bowling alley, at least whilst that sport was in vogue.

The roads from London to Twickenham (or Twittenham as it was then known) were unfinished and haphazardly routed which made journeys by coach and horses long and extremely uncomfortable. To add to a traveller's dismay there was also the likelihood of being held up by highwaymen who lurked along the way, camouflaged by the lonely, unpopulated heaths and woodlands. Hyde Park, so much closer to the centre of London than Twickenham, was also plagued by these robbers and even Horace Walpole was counted amongst their victims obliged by cries of "Stand and deliver!" to hand over his money and valuables. A considerably safer and more pleasant method of travel was by boat. As the Thames between Westminster and Hampton Court had been in use for centuries it was generally more populated than the roads. Visitors arriving at Marble Hill in this fashion entered through a grander entrance door than that on the opposite side of the house and found themselves in a delightful pastoral refuge from London life.

Further enhancing Henrietta's happiness was the almost constant presence of Dorothy and John Hobart who had been sent to live with her, leaving behind them

Two songs from John Gay's 'The Beggar's Opera' :'Over the Hills and Far Away' and 'Virgins are Like the Fair Flower'. Buckingham would have known these songs from his time growing up at Marble Hill House.

at Blickling Hall their father, step-mother, little brother Robert and baby half-brother George. Henrietta had by now adopted Dorothy (another indication of their true relationship perhaps) who was a bright and entertaining addition to the household. However, as she grew older, her wilful character caused concern. Henrietta to George, "Miss Hobart and I are upon very ill terms; Master Hobart, for whom, I know, you have the greatest tenderness, we suspect has quarrelled with his musical playfellow; and Mrs Bedingfield, who used to command her passion, was very much ruffled this morning."[10] In her effort to keep the young girl happy Henrietta over indulged her, as George mentioned when writing from his constituency in Yorkshire, "I have long thought that you should, for Miss Hobart's sake, begin your office of rebuker with her. I was always apprehensive she might learn ill tricks from Mrs Bedingfield and that keeping such constant company with that paralytic woman might in time make her shake herself, if you did not prevent that bad habit. As for my school fellow Jack, quarrel with whom he will, I know he is in the right, and uses them as they deserve."[11] It appears that Mrs Bedingfield had accompanied her charges to Marble Hill but had acquired some questionable habits along the way. George Berkeley's "school fellow Jack" refers of course to the young John Hobart, the future 2nd Earl of Buckinghamshire, who returns now to take up his leading role in this history.

Notes

1. Charles Howard's eldest brother Henry had died in 1718 and the title passed to his son Charles; but this Charles died childless, so the title then passed to his Uncle Edward, who became the 8th Earl of Suffolk.
2. NRO 22955 Z76.
3. *Report on the Manuscripts of the Marquess of Lothian*, p.169.
4. It was not until seven months after Caroline's death in 1737 that George II took up with Amelia Sophia de Walmoden, later Lady Yarmouth.
5. *Letters to and from Henrietta ...*, Vol. 2 p.121,122.
6. Sedgwick, *Some Materials*, Vol. II, p. 601 (cited in Borman, T.).
7. *Letters to and from Henrietta ...*, Vol. 2 p.130.
8. Ibid. p.138.
9. Ibid. p.140.
10. Ibid. p.178.
11. Ibid. p.182.

Education from Books and 'ladies'

Reverend John Nicoll, Headmaster of Westminster School, 1756. PMA acc no: 1985-52-22523.

Some three years after Sir John Hobart's marriage to Elizabeth Bristow, their son George was born on 8 September 1731 and six months later his eight year old half-brother John found himself enrolled as a Scholar at Westminster School. His arrival coincided with that of a new Head Master, John Nicoll, who was long remembered for the mildness of his rule. This was John's great good fortune, as in that age it was something of a phenomenon to find a Head Master who believed that an offence might be "liquidated by sincere repentance instead of a thrashing."[1] Those before and after this enlightened man were believers in plentiful use of the Rods for the slightest misdemeanour. It is possible that John lodged in one of the boarding houses around Dean's Yard, next to the school. These were usually run "by elderly ladies, who could not be expected to control a mob of thirty or forty unruly boys, so one of the masters would be engaged as resident or non-resident usher to keep order."[2] Nevertheless, high spirits and practical joking could not be suppressed. One small boy, on his very first night at school, wrote plaintively:

My Dear Dear Mother,

If you don't let me come home, I die—I am all over ink, and my fine clothes have been spoilt—I have been tost in a blanket and seen a ghost.

I remain, my dear dear Mother,

Your dutiful and most unhappy son, Freddy.

P.S. Remember me to my Father. [3]

Quite how eight year old John Hobart managed to get through those first days in this chaotic environment is not recorded, but it can be assumed that as with most other boys, he settled in, made life long attachments and like most English

27

public school boys then and now, just 'got on with it'. 'It' included learning how to fist fight and taking part in escapades both within the school walls and without. Then, as now, those who wished to learn learnt, and for those who did not there was the river Thames and the wide expanse of Tuttle Fields to explore. Academically Greek and Latin were the order of the day, every day, and each year there was the institution of the Westminster Play which was performed in Latin at the end of the Michaelmas Term. Edward Gibbon, best known for his *Decline and Fall of the Roman Empire*, later maintained that "a finished scholar may emerge from Westminster or Eton in total ignorance of the business and conversation of English gentlemen"[4] but he was willing to allow that they "might assume the merit of teaching all that they pretend to teach, the Latin and the Greek languages."[5] Young John also became fluent in French which would stand him in good stead in adulthood. During school holidays John occasionally visited his father and stepmother at their house in Pall Mall and joined his sister Dorothy at Marble Hill House. Later, he spent time at his aunt's fine London residence at 15 Savile Row, an acquisition she made in 1735. Henrietta and George Berkeley acted in loco parentis and the easy banter that existed between John and George, and the faux combative nature of the quarrels between the male and female contingent were the cause of much merriment and both homes frequently resounded to gales of laughter. Charles Hotham, a young friend who often visited Marble Hill with his father Sir Beaumont, became a popular playmate of both John and Dorothy and "under the guardianship of their aunt, enjoyed a liberty of which they occasionally took undue advantage. John Hobart especially had occasionally wrung from his long-suffering relative the epithet of 'saucy whelp!'"[6] Sir Beaumont Hotham fondly remembered "that gay and hospitable house, all came joyously and left with regret. An assemblage of all the talents, wit and satire flourished there, badinage became a fine art, laughter crystallised into verse, and every jest served for the outpourings of genius." Henrietta's wide circle of friends included many of the great and good of the day including the politicians William Pulteney, William Pitt, Lord Pembroke, Lord Chesterfield and Sir Richard Temple; and her regular correspondence with Lord and Lady Bolingbroke, the Duchess of Queensbury, Lady Hervey, the Earl of Strafford, Lord Peterborough, Lord Lovell, Lord Bathurst, and the Duke of Argyll to mention but a few, meant she still had a finger on the pulse of society without the dull necessity of embroiling herself in it daily. Her literary and artistic acquaintance were many, numbering amongst them an incomparable trio of the writer Jonathan Swift, the poet Alexander Pope and the satirical librettist John Gay of 'The Beggar's Opera' fame. The Right Hon Horace Walpole, diarist and youngest son of the Prime Minister Robert Walpole, was also a regular visitor. Young Dorothy and John, often in the company of these illustrious and influential people and more importantly of those who loved them best, blossomed. It was clear that their presence brought Henrietta great joy and although she had been cruelly deprived of her son Henry's presence she was at last able to give free rein to her maternal instincts. With seasons spent at Marble Hill and at Savile Row, she felt that "my family" as she referred to the quartet, was complete. The children journeyed occasionally to Blickling to see their father and stepmother Elizabeth, small half brother George, whose Godfather was King George II, and their beloved maternal Britiffe grandparents at Hunworth Hall. Now sadly absent was their little brother Robert who had died at the age of six, just a year after John left for school.[7] In 1736 Dorothy accompanied Henrietta and George Berkeley to France whilst John was at School, and Henrietta occasionally took the waters at Bath for the sake of her health, but otherwise the quartet preferred each other's company.

1738 brought the birth of Henry Hobart, a second half-brother for Dorothy and John.

After Westminster John went up to Christ's College, Cambridge where he was "admitted as nobleman under Mr Rooke on 30th October 1739"[8] and it seems likely he read Classics, judging from the easy references made in his correspondence. When visiting Blickling around this time John would have found the The Long Gallery, hitherto graced by the noble countenances of local grandees, being prepared at great expence for the arrival of a magnificent twelve thousand five hundred book collection bequeathed to Blickling by his father's first cousin Sir Richard Ellys of Nocton Hall, Lincolnshire.[9]

There is little evidence of what the Cambridge scholar John got up to when not studying, although there are several letters from ladies which strongly suggest that it was by no means a case of all work and no play. One of his companions, Diane, who met John surreptitiously in both Cambridge and London, coyly wrote:

Christ's College, Cambridge: second court. Line engraving by J. Le Keux after J.A. Bell.

The unexpected favour I received from your Lordship last Post, gave me two very different sensations; Pleasure at being remembered by you at so great a distance & distress at feeling myself incapable of answering as I could wish & as it deserves; our disappointment at meeting was equal. I was at your House the day you went, to ask you to be of a party; we went to Vauxhall that evening. I was told by way of comfort you was by that time many miles off, which when I heard, I accused you of the levity generally imputed to your sex for flying without leaving me one Sigh, or tender Adieu. Your letter has quite reinstated you in the Opinion I had of you, all my rancour is vanisht, & every thought of you is an advantageous one. I am with great sincerity your Lordship's much oblig'd and faithful, Diane - Much obliged to Mr Rooke for his remembrances. I leave it to yr discretion to return the Compliments.[10]

New Spring Gardens in Vauxhall was London's leading venue for public entertainment. The Gardens were made up of several acres of trees and shrubs with attractively designed walks perfectly suited to romantic assignations. It was effectively a playground for members of society, and those of lower birth but lofty ambitions and ulterior motives, to promenade and generally enjoy themselves. It was in this setting that a rendezvous with Diane was planned,

It is so long since I have received any Billet Doux from fine Men that by the Vermillion which o'erspread my Countenance, any body of experiences would have thought it came from a tender Engagement. How tender I keep discreetly to myself. With thanks I accept the invitation & will not fail ordering the Watch man to wake me time enough to be with you at the Hour appointed. I fear on reflection it's a little Bourgoise to own one can Sleep with such a Rendevous on one's hands, but I hope you'll Pardon this Sincerity in favour of that with which I profess & own myself yr Oblig'd & Affect friend, Diane[11]

Whatever transpired at this tryst John left Cambridge having matriculated after the Michaelmas term of 1743 and the mysterious Diane is not mentioned again.

In early 1744 Dorothy and John visited their grandparents at Hunworth Hall. Whilst there John wrote to his aunt in a teasing, provocative manner intended to amuse her:

Since we have been at Norwich, I have seen almost every letter my sister has sent you; and, as it is evident, by your writing twice to her and not once to me, that you prefer her style to mine, I shall try for the future, if possible, to flatter you as much as she does, and will constantly tell you that I like every thing I ought to dislike. The poor girl has lately fallen into a very odd way: for about two days ago she took a gardener in a black waistcoat for a rat, and immediately after, fancied she was turned into a pine-apple. This was really vapours and not affectation: for there was nobody present at the time but your humble servant. In your letter to her, by way of making my amends for not writing, you bestowed the gentle epithet of "saucy whelp" upon me. I am sorry to say, that your behaviour has convinced me, that when people have once got the character of being well-bred (by eating with their fingers, never drinking to any body, never taking leave when they go out of an assembly, never being out of countenance, even when they ought to be so, calling modesty *mauvaise honte*˙ and impudence a good address) they think they have a patent for being impertinent with impunity, and that every thing they do is polite, because they are esteemed so by that insignificant sect of people who style themselves fashionable. I must indeed own, that I hope soon to be one of that insignificant sect: but until they will take me into their number, I will enjoy the noble privilege which every free-born Englishman claims, of abusing those I envy. But, my dear Lady Suffolk, let me entreat you not to indulge in that scurrilous way of writing. You may get a habit of it, which in the end may be disagreeable, even to yourself. For my part, as you have already frequently experienced my good-nature, I do not care if I give one more proof of it, by excusing this: but do not offend any more in the same way; or at least, if your resolution is too weak to get over this style, date your letter for the future from the Gun, at Billingsgate.˙˙ Thine, as though usest him, J.H.

P.s. I pity Mr Berkeley[12]

Another impudent letter to his aunt demonstrates that John had been "one of the boys who wishes to learn" to judge by his rather flowery prose and allusions to Greek Mythology. John had tentatively raised the possibility of his taking the Grand Tour but his father thoroughly disapproved of the idea even though he had himself travelled abroad following University. Perhaps he had found the destination disappointing or had been made to travel with a dull tutor who obliged him to study to excess, or he deemed the venture had become too frivolous since his day and was not worth the expense. It is also possible that his wife objected to lavishing money on a child not her own. Young John pleaded for help in persuading his father to let him venture abroad,

> Tuesday 22 May, 1744—I am going to undertake a task not altogether so difficult as those which Eurystheus (who must have been a Berkeley) imposed upon Hercules, but full as disagreeable as any of them; viz. to write to you. I must stuff a letter full of praises, of which every sensible creature knows you do not merit the least part, and must try to persuade you upon paper that I love you prodigiously, when I have full as contemptible an opinion of you as you deserve. However, your husband will chastise you for your errors sufficiently in this world; and a Supreme

---

 ˙   bad taste.

˙˙   An east London pub, infamous for being frequented by smugglers.

Being will in all probability take care of you in the next. Your faults are obvious and palpable to every one: your virtues it would be very difficult to count, as each day discovers new. After this, it would be vain to assure you that I love you; as my honesty has thrown off the mask of flattery, and compelled me to disclose the real opinion I have of you. You will certainly conclude from my manner of writing that I am mad; indeed, my head is a little turned: but you have already overlooked so many of my failings, that this may very easily be passed over with the rest. Methinks it would be a very proper employment for those few happy mortals who have no faults of their own to excuse, to study excuses for those of others. Mr Britiffe sent for us yesterday into his study and assured me that he would make what addition to my allowance you should think necessary, and told me I should never want money whilst I was prudent. Lord Hobart came over here this morning, and stayed about two hours. He has invited us to dine with him at Blickling on Thursday. He mentioned nothing of carrying us back to London; so that in all probability we shall return as we came. Mr Britiffe talked to him of my going abroad, which he treated as a ridiculous scheme; but Mr Britiffe seems determined to follow your advice absolutely in relation to both my sister and me. Upon my telling him that I was sorry to be burthensome to him, he said that it was the same thing to him; that he should only have the less to leave me at his death.[13] He does not seem to disapprove of me going abroad; but hinted that he expected to hear from you on these heads. He is excessively fond of us both; and Mrs Britiffe expresses great regard; they dote upon my sister, who takes great pains to be agreeable to them. Let me hear from you soon, if possible. I will write again the next post. Pray make my compliments to Mr Berkeley.[14]

When no answer arrived soon enough for the impatient youth he wrote to George Berkeley, knowing that he would share it with his wife:

As Lady Suffolk, by neglecting writing to me, has convinced me how cheap she holds my correspondence, and consequently how unworthy she is of it, I shall for the future favour only those with it who know how to value it, and duly acknowledge the pleasure they receive from my writings. You have sense, you have taste; you had the advantage of being educated first at Westminster, and afterwards at Cambridge; you have a high opinion of my understanding, which is a sufficient proof to me that you have a good one. I once thought that silly woman who has the honour to call you husband had been free from at least the more glaring foibles of her sex: I almost loved the woman for her sake, and thought the bitter apple began to digest, and that, in time, they might attain to a sagacity equal to that of the lords of the creation. But, alas! How is she fallen! There was a time when she would have been thankful even for a line from me; but she shall gormandize no more on my golden apples. No: she shall feed on garbage, and chew the scraps that the Grenvilles, and Pitts, and such like, send her; the cold viands of politics; the half picked bones of a debate. If I was to stay in Norwich long enough, I dare swear you would convince me by writing every post of your gratitude; but as you will now have no opportunity of doing it, I shall charitably conclude you would if you had. I shall for the future confound Lady Suffolk with the rest of her illiterate sex, and conclude, from her at last undeceived me, and discovered her bad taste, that no woman can have a real one. When they are handsome, they have just enough sense to make men ridiculous; when they are ugly, they have sufficient eloquence to expose one another. Lest you should think I only rail because I am piqued, and that these are the pangs of despised love, I shall say no more upon this subject, which, though in general I despise, in some particulars I must confess I love to dwell upon. Sir, I honour YOU'[15]

By early 1745 John's wish was granted and plans were formulated for his Grand Tour. His grandfather Britiffe's fond blessing and the approval of his loving aunt, who had made concerted efforts to persuade her brother of the merits of such an undertaking resulted in Sir John caving in to the combined coercion. He reluctantly gave permission for young John "to goe abroad" but flatly refused to allow him more than £400 a year.

In late April news reached the family that Henrietta's long estranged son Henry Howard had died at twenty-eight. This was a severe blow to Henrietta as it rendered extinct any chance of any reconciliation between them but she was consoled by the care, attention and company of John, Dorothy, and her beloved husband George. John however would soon depart for the Continent.

Notes

1. Carleton, J. D., *Westminster School: A History*, Blackie, 1938.
2. Ibid.
3. Ibid.
4. Ibid.
5. Ibid.
6. *The Hothams ...*, Vol II.
7. The burial record at Blicking says: 'The Honourable Robert Hobart the Second Son of the Right Honourable Lord Hobart by Dame Judith his Former Wife, was brought down from London to this Place and was Buried upon the Twenty Sixth day of May 1733, but no affidavit was made of his being buried in Woollen.' This last refers to the Act of 1678 which intended to make compulsory the use of English sheep's wool for burial clothing, rather than anything more exotic such as imported linen, and an affidavit had to be sworn to prove it. However, those with the means to do so merely paid the £5 fine and dressed their dear departed loved ones in linens, lace and whatever other luxurious materials they preferred.
8. *Christ's College Biographical Register*, Vol II, 1666-1905 p.238.
9. This transformation came at no small cost, at the equivalent of £100,000 today, and in 1742 on the death of Sir Richard Ellys the collection was installed.

10. NRO NRS 14623, 29D1.
11. Ibid.
12. *Letters to and from Henrietta ...*, Vol. 2, p.202/203.
13. Robert Britiffe died on the 22nd September, 1749.
14. *Letters to and from Henrietta ...*, Vol. 2, p.204-207.
15. Ibid. p.207/208.

Venturing Abroad

Careful navigation was required to travel safely to Italy, one of the most favoured destinations for young gentlemen wishing to undertake the Grand Tour at this time. The War of the Austrian Succession had been rumbling along for five years and would not conclude until the Treaty of Aix-la-Chapelle in 1748. Triggered by a dispute over Maria Theresa's entitlement to the Habsburg Monarchy, ostensibly on the grounds that she was a woman, it pitted the forces of Britain, Holland, Sardinia and Saxony in support of her claim versus Spain and France who did not. These alliances would reverse and alter constantly over the coming years; these shifts were dubbed the 'Stately quadrille' whose purpose was to maintain the balance of power in Europe and to prevent any one alliance or country becoming too strong. In the long run Maria Theresa was confirmed as Archduchess of Austria and Queen of Hungary.

It was into this scenario that John prepared to set out from Harwich for Holland, prudently avoiding France, to begin his European adventures. Having left England with a burgeoning interest in opera, upon reaching Italy his enjoyment developed into a life-long passion. During his sojourn in Venice, in the autumn of 1745, the premiere of the opera 'Ariodante' at the Teatro Grimani S. Gio Gristostorno was dedicated to *Sig. Giovanni d'Hobart, Nobile Inglese* (*Noble Englishman*) in the presence of its young composer George Christoph Wagenseil.[1] From Venice John journeyed on to Rome whose art and history would have entranced even the most cynical of Englishmen, in whose number John was most assuredly not included. His youth, curiosity and enthusiasm led to many discoveries, one of which was the ancient tomb of Cestius[2] which so impressed him he bought a print of the unusual pyramidical structure.

In preparation for embarking on the Grand Tour it was the habit of young gentlemen to furnish themselves with letters of introduction to influential Englishmen living in Europe. One of these was Sir Horace Mann who had been appointed by Sir Robert Walpole as the English representative in Tuscany, a post he held for forty eight years, never returning home. Mann was renowned for throwing sumptuous parties for the Florentine gentry and it was rumoured that he supplemented his income by taking commission on objets d'art which he sold

Whilst on his Grand Tour, the premiere of Wagenseil's opera 'Ariodante' in Venice was dedicated to Buckingham (or Lord John Hobart as he was in 1745.) This track is 'Ombra Cara'.

The Pyramid of Gaius Cestius, from Vedute di Roma c.1756 by Giovanni Battista Piranesi.

to visitors and collectors. He and Horace Walpole exchanged over 1,800 letters during over fifty years of friendship. Either John, or his aunt Henrietta on his behalf, asked Walpole for an introductory letter to Mann which was reluctantly written:

> I have the pleasure of recommending you a new acquaintance, for which
> I am sure you will thank me. Mr Hobart proposes passing a little time at
> Florence, which I am sure you will endeavour to make as agreeable to him
> as possible. I beg you will introduce him to all my friends, who I don't
> doubt will show him the same civilities that I received. Dear Sir, this will
> be a particular obligation to me, who am Your sincere friend and humble
> servant, Hor. Walpole.[3]

This seems a pleasant enough introduction but unbeknownst to John, Walpole wrote separately to Mann, "I have just been giving a recommendation letter for you to Mr Hobart; he is no particular friend of mine, but is Norfolk, and in the world; so you will be civil to him. He is of the Damon kind and not one of whom you will make a Chute. Madame Suares may make something of him."[4] The "Damon kind" refers to a character in Virgil who was a swain, a wooer of women, and Chute refers to Lord William Wildman Shute Barrington who Walpole much admired. (Lord Barrington later became Secretary at War during the American War of Independence and, no doubt to Walpole's chagrin, one of John Hobart's closest friends.) Walpole infers that John will amuse Mme Suares because she is a woman and he a womaniser, and insinuates that he will not be intelligent enough company for Mann. However, Mann formed his own, quite different opinion,

> Florence 24 May 1746 Your reccomande Mr Hobart is come at last, and is so unlike all the English that I adore him. His regard and esteem for you is motive enough, but besides he is extremely well bred, introduces himself vastly well to all your acquaintance, and is by them as well received. He is indeed the only Englishman for a long time that has thought it necessary to speak to a 'dama'*. They go about with their jemmy frocks and frightful staring hats and exhibit themselves for brutes everywhere, whilst they despise all the best company. Mr Hobart seeks it, and is contented to be laughed at by the rest. When he met Lady Orford in Holland she pressed him to accept of her house, which he did, but expects to soon be turned out by her arrival. I cannot think her Ladyship will be sorry to have so pretty a young man in the house with her. I told him t'other day that on my lady's return he would hear such strange stories of me that, as fond as he now seemed, he would then hate me. He promised he would not, and I really believe him. However it be, it shall not be my fault if any coolness happens.[5]

Mann's remark "strange stories of me" might be explained by the diarist and social commentator Mrs Hester Lynch Thrale Piozzi who, with startling frankness, labelled Mann a "finger-twirler." Homosexuality then was illegal and sodomy a capital offence; nonetheless, whilst virile 'masculine' men were content to take lovers of both sexes, effeminate behaviour was damned by the English as being "a French style" heterosexual affectation. Mrs Piozzi wrote,"I call those Fellows Finger-twirlers;—meaning a decent word for Sodomites: old Sir Horace Mann & Mr James the Painter had such an odd way of twirling their Fingers in Discourse."[6] Despite his friend's approbation of John, Walpole resolutely maintained his low opinion, "Sure you must have had flights of strange awkward animals, if you be so taken with him! I shall begin to look about me, to see the merits of England: he was no curiosity here." He then delivered the epithet that blighted John Hobart's reputation for over two and a half centuries: "I used to call him Clear cake**: fat, fair and seen through in a moment."[7]

This remark and the relationship between the two men requires inspection. As the fifth child and youngest son of Britain's first Prime Minister Robert Walpole, a Norfolk neighbour of the Hobarts at Houghton Hall, it is safe to say that Horace was not his illustrious father's favoured child. Effete and physically feeble he bore little resemblance to his robust parent and Sir Robert was content to keep him at arm's length. Sir Robert provided financially for his son but that was as far as things went, and when his parents became estranged the young Horace was brought up by his

---

*   Dama in jemmy frocks - spruced, dandified ladies.

**   'A kind of confection, partly transparent' (OED)

wealthy, beautiful mother Catherine in Arlington Street, Piccadilly. It is thought the relationship with his mother was the most important of his life and that he never quite recovered from her death when he was twenty. He pursued a desultory career in Parliament but as his father arranged sinecures for him from which he earned a very considerable income he was not obliged to exert himself unduly. He cultivated an army of acquaintance, but whilst he was a well educated and witty writer and many of his waspish observations could be devilishly accurate, they often seemed born out of spite or jealousy. Walpole repeated his barbed comment about John Hobart more than once as he

Horace Walpole, YCBA B1977.14.15130.

evidently thought it, and himself, amusing. It must be said that the word "fat" was relative, coming as it did from a man described by the contemporary writer Letitia Hawkins as "a pallid aesthete tripping everywhere on his toes. His figure was not merely tall, but more properly long and slender to excess: his complexion and particularly his hands of a most unhealthy paleness—he always entered a room in that style of affected delicacy—knees bent and feet on tip toes as if afraid of a wet floor."[8] "Fair" might be considered a complimentary word but from Walpole's pen it appears condescending. "Seen thro' in a moment" disparages a young man whose innocence, exuberance and good humour endeared him to many others. If he seemed transparent to Walpole, it may be that he was simply young and naive. It is feasible that Walpole was simply jealous of the time and attention lavished upon the exuberant young man by his doting aunt Henrietta, a lady Walpole thought of so highly and whose time he probably believed would have been much better spent gossiping with him. John, unaware of Horace's true opinion of him, thanked him for the introduction to Mann:

> Tuesday 21 June, Florence—You cannot conceive how much I am ashamed at having so long deferred acknowledging the infinite obligation I have to Mr Walpole for his letter to Mr Mann. Had I wrote when it was my duty my thanks might then perhaps have borne a little more proportion to it, but his goodness has increased so much upon me every day, that all I can now say will express very faintly how excessively I feel myself obliged to you. We are very glad to send news to our friends in England, that of the victory at Piacenza, the Spanish are said to have lost in all about twelve thousand men.[9] I shall not trouble you with the detail as you will see so

many better than I can possibly send you. Mr Whitehead and Mr Chute left us three weeks ago, you are acquainted with them; guess, therefore, how cruel it was for me only to know them, that I too might so soon feel their loss. I like Florence extremely, and am happy in many agreeable acquaintance that Mr Mann has procured for me. The people in general seem very amiable; at least their appearing so very sensible of the merit of Mr Walpole has prepossessed me infinitely in their favour[10].

Mann continued to think well of John, reporting that he was a great favourite with the ladies,

14 June 1746 - Mr Hobart is frequently witness to my epuisements, and to my embaras.[11] He supplies the place of the Chutes by coming to me after he has set all the 'dame' in a twitter. You can't think how they admire him, and how he admires them. How he will resist I can't tell, but he has much business upon his hands. Hitherto he supports it very well. He often asks for Cypress wine[12], which he says is the best restorative in the world. He contents himself to eat gooseberry tarts every night with me, after having been so long used to the elegant suppers with you at White's—what a change![13]

But later vacillated and dissembled,

Tuesday 19 July 1746

How can you be surprised that I take so much to those whom you recommend me? It is natural for them to affect to have been vastly intimate with you, and then I must esteem them. I even, with that idea, doubt of the faults and queerities I sometimes think I observe in them. I told you the Chutes and I were vastly fond of the clear cake, not on the first visit, but after he seemed to court us and talk vastly of you. He is a very good creature, however, and an angel amongst the strange bears we have; and then consider how long I have been used to seamen. Their ignorance and roughness make me think everything perfect that does not resemble them. I own to you my present acquaintance is rather too heavy upon my shoulders, but I treat him with no ceremony. I think I don't like him half so well since I received your letter.[14]

In September news reached John via Horace Mann that his father had been elevated by King George II and created 1st Earl of Buckinghamshire. It has been surmised that Sir John Hobart's appointments were awarded to him because of his sister's relationship with the King but there is evidence against this assumption in the case of Earldom. Henrietta, even when at Court, had very little influence on political matters and she almost never asked for favours of any kind, preferring to keep the status quo. Indeed "the only reproach which we find her friends making against her, is the extreme reluctance which she always manifested to ask favours for those who thought they had claims upon her interference."[15] Furthermore Sir John's skilful political ability made him a valuable asset to both the King and to Parliament. Whilst being the brother of the King's mistress certainly did not hinder his career it was also on merit that he was appointed Treasurer of the Chamber in 1727, made Baron in 1728 and Lord Lt of Norfolk in 1739. But as his Earldom was bestowed a full twelve years after Lady Suffolk had retired from Court, when every shadow of her influence had evaporated, his elevation can legitimately be viewed as a reward for his loyal service.

John Hobart senior did not escape Horace Walpole's sarcasm in a letter to George Montagu, "Do command me; in what can I serve you? Shall I get you an Earldom? Don't think it will be any trouble; there is nothing easier or cheaper. Lord Hobart and Lord Fitzwilliam are both to be Earls tomorrow: the former of Buckingham, the latter by his already title."[16] On hearing from Walpole, Mann replied, "I thank you for your news; Mr Hobart was glad of that I gave him of being a Lord, which he had not heard from anybody else, and with difficulty permitted me to call him so till he received a letter from his father signed Buckingham, but I would not allow his delicacy, as my authority was so good."[17] It was and is the reigning monarch's prerogative to choose the geographical name for newly created Dukes, Marquesses, Earls and Barons. In the case of John Hobart, his preference may have been for 'Buckinghamshire' as he owned an estate there, was descended from John Hampden, a member of one of the great families of that shire (albeit Parliamentarian) and his maternal grandfather was Sir Joseph Maynard of Clifton Reynes in that county. It may be that the King took all this into account, although it is just as likely that he did not. When young John received confirmation in writing from his father that he was now heir to an Earldom it made him an even more desirable catch for ladies of marriageable age. But young Lord Hobart was in no hurry whatsoever to be caught.

The next month brought him grievous news of the death of George Berkeley. Having for many years suffered from gout Henrietta had taken him to Bath hoping the waters would sooth his increasing and agonising pain. They stayed there through the autumn but on 29 October George fatally weakened and died. John was grief stricken on his own behalf and for Dorothy, for they had lost their dear friend and surrogate father, and even more so for his Aunt. He knew she must be heart-broken but he, far from home, was unable to comfort her except with the consolation of letters.

There follows a dearth of surviving correspondence until one from Mann to Walpole in January 1747, which places Lord Hobart still, or back, in Florence,

> Twenty English that are now here—they embarrass me much. It is vastly the mode to entertain; they have separate lodgings and French cooks, and one it tormented to death. Some indeed, entertain vastly well, and have their hors d'oeuvres in great order. Others, who won't give ten zecchins a

month to the cook, do not succeed quite so well, but yet will imitate the fine way. Lord Hobart and I were ready to burst with laughter t'other day at a noble table, when ten people were set down to a first course of soup and two hors d'oeuvres, literally consisting of a mustard pot in a small dish, and opposite to it a plate of the vile white radishes.[18]

There follows another six month absence of correspondence until this letter from Rome. As he prepared for his to return to England, John found time to send a thoughtful gift to Horace Walpole. This was a printed copy of Benedict XIV's speech on creating Henry Stuart, brother of 'The Young Pretender' Bonnie Prince Charlie, Cardinal of York on 5 July 1747. The 'Old Pretender' was their father James Stuart who had failed to take the British throne and whose Jacobite Court was frequented by Englishmen of all political affiliations when visiting Rome.

> July the 8th, 1747—Though I have an infinite pleasure in putting you in mind of me, I should not have troubled you with this, if I did not flatter myself that you would receive some pleasure from the enclosed. I have had a great deal of trouble in getting it and have but just time enough to read it once over before I send it. It is certainly a most original piece, and I fancy a translation of it would not make a bad figure in the Evening Post. The young gentleman was half cardinalised a week ago, and this morning I saw him receive the hat by which the finishing stroke was put to that great work; the Pretender was present at the ceremony and seemed most extremely pleased. I have not the time to say anything of myself, nor if I had would I venture to tire your patience with it. I shall leave this place in a few days to go to Florence in my way to England, where I hope to have the pleasure of assuring you that I am, With great regard, Your most obedient humble servant, John Hobart.[19]

The imperative for John's recall to England was that in his absence he had been elected as a Whig MP for Norwich on 19 June, as Mann explained to Walpole on 11 July:

> At the time of writing I may suppose you are in the height of elections. I hastened to send this sudden resolution to Lord Hobart, who ought long ago to have obeyed his father's summons to return home, but as he did not explain himself sufficiently (perhaps then he did not know it) and Lord Hobart thinking he had time enough, was unwilling to leave his loves at Rome. He is however arrived here today, and is become my guest till next Thursday sennight (fortnight). Lord Hobart tell me he has sent you the Pope's famous speech on the creating the youngest Pretender cardinal. It is, to be sure, very ridiculous, but I don't see what the Pope could say on the occasion. They were so difficult to get that I have been forced to keep a copy only for myself.

The English General Election of 1747 was held between June and August and local elections had taken place at different dates in every constituency. As young Lord Hobart was abroad his father had appointed an agent to represent him. Extremely reluctant to "leave his loves at Rome" and it seems there was no shortage of them, it was not until 22 July that John made his final farewells and tore himself away to journey homeward after two years abroad.

Notes

1. The theatre still stands and is now known as the Teatro Malibran. Not to be confused with Handel's 'Ariodante', Wagenseil's version starred Filipa Elisi as 'Ariodante', Giacinto Cestini 'Dalinda', Ottavio Albuzio 'Donaldo' and Catterina Scheri 'Ginerva'.

2. Built close to Porta San Paolo in 12 BC for Gaius Cestius, in the reign of the Emperor Octavian Augustus, the Pyramid took its inspiration from the pointier shaped pyramids in Nubia, rather than those at Giza. It is thought that Gaius was in the Roman army and fought in the Nubian campaign. It may represent the travels of its occupant, rather as John Hobart's does in his case. Later, between 270–274 AD, the tomb became incorporated into the Aurelian walls. When it was opened in 1660 it revealed a beautifully preserved barrel vaulted chamber decorated with frescoes. In 1716 Pope Clement XI created a Protestant or non-Catholic graveyard at the front of the pyramid, originally for members of the Stuart Court in exile, followed by many young people on their Grand Tours, including the oldest rediscovered grave, that of Oxford student George Lewis Langton who died in Rome aged twenty-two in 1738. In 1821 and 1822 the remains of the poets John Keats and Percy Bysshe Shelley were interred there.

3. *Horace Walpole's Correspondence*, Yale Edition, Vol. 19, p.60.

4. Ibid. p.63.

5. Ibid. p.252.

6. Brian Fothergill, *The Strawberry Hill Set: Horace Walpole and his Circle* (London: Faber, 1983), p.50.

7. *Horace Walpole's Correspondence*, Vol. 19, p.263.

8. Hawkins, L. M. (col.) *Anecdotes, Biographical Sketches and Memoirs, 1822*, Vol I, F.C. & J.Rivington, 1822.

9. On the 16th June Austrian forces led by Prince Josef Wenzel claimed victory over the Franco-Spanish at The Battle of Piacenza in Northern Italy.

10. *Horace Walpole's Correspondence* Vol. 40, p.56.

11. exhaustion and awkward situations.

12. a sweet, strong wine made of half dried grapes known as commanderia.

13. *Horace Walpole's Correspondence*, Vol. 19, p.261.

14. Ibid. Vol. 19, p.275.

15. *Letters to and from Henrietta ...*, Vol 1 p. xxii.

16. *Horace Walpole's Correspondence*, Vol. 9, p.45.

17. Ibid., Vol. 19, p.307.

18. Ibid. p.356/357.

19. Ibid., Vol. 40, p.57/58.

Politics and Affairs of the Heart

On his return to England politics necessarily became the focus of John's endeavours and given the choice to become MP for either Norwich or St Ives[1] in Cornwall he chose to sit for Norwich.

Never neglectful of his artistic leanings he was delighted to be inducted as a member of *The Society of Dilettanti*. This London dining club was established in 1732 initially for the purpose of convivial meetings between those who had returned from their Grand Tours; journeys to foreign courts and capitals were, in their opinion, considered an indispensable qualification for wealthy young men of high birth. Its detractors considered it an excuse for hard drinking, gambling and quarrelling but eventually the love of art and the ambition to encourage the same sentiment in others became its ruling principle. They may well have wished to be regarded as arbiters of good taste and culture but it is also a plain truth that all their meetings were held in drinking establishments. Situated around Covent Garden they included the Bedford Head Tavern, the Fountain in the Strand, the Star & Garter in Pall Mall, The King's Arms, Westminster and the famously fashionable Almack's in King Street. At these inns the members were given to toasting each other frequently and, as it was an offence paid for with a guinea fine to decline, many ended these evenings much the worse for wear. It comes as no surprise to find a disparaging remark from Horace Walpole who described the Society as

The Society of Dilettanti in Rome by Augusto Daini.

"a club, for which the nominal qualification is having been in Italy, and the real one, being drunk."[2] The Dilettanti met on the first Sunday of every month from December to May. Their attention to detail was scrupulous, if frivolous, as when it was solemnly declared that "a Roman dress is thought necessary for the President of the Society" and later decided "the Society agreed with the Committee as to the model of the Roman dress, disagreed with them as to the Colour being Crimson. Resolved that it should be of Scarlet."[3] Sir James Gray's position as Secretary to the Venetian Embassy had afforded him special opportunities within the rules for annually enlisting two young English travellers in Italy. For the 1747 intake he proposed Lord Hobart and Sir Thomas Sebright and these young gentlemen were seconded and received into the Society.

At Twickenham John was welcomed home with open arms at Marble Hill by his now twice widowed aunt Henrietta and his sister Dorothy. He also found that Horace Walpole was now a close neighbour at his eccentric gothic villa, Strawberry Hill. Walpole had a well known penchant for the company of old ladies and unmarriageable or disgraced noblewomen and was especially attracted by the "peculiar glamour" of one who had been the mistress of a King. "Becoming neighbours and both, after her second husband's death, living single and alone, our acquaintance turned to intimacy. She was extremely deaf, and consequently had some satisfaction in narrating than in listening, each of us knew different parts of many court-stories; and each was eager to learn what either could relate more. Those evenings, and I had many of them on autumnal nights, were extremely agreeable."[4] Although he was fawning and deferential towards Henrietta in person and positively revelled in boasting of their friendship, Horace elsewhere condescendingly observed that "her mental qualifications were by no means shining" and regarding her relationship with George II she was "agreeable, but had neither sense nor art enough to make him think her so agreeable as his wife."

Charles Hotham, who had taken part in the Battle of Lauffeld[5] as aide-de-camp to the Earl of Albemarle, was by now a dashing Colonel. He reappeared at Marble Hill to renew his acquaintance with the family and in particular with Lady Dorothy, who quickly became enamoured of her erstwhile childhood playmate. This caused great consternation for Henrietta who was perhaps reminded by both his name and his uniform of her own courtship by the dreadful Charles Howard and she was horrified when she learned of what she considered to be Dorothy's infatuation with an extremely handsome young man ten years her junior. But Dorothy's lively spirits would not be thwarted however much she was entreated to seek another suitor. Although she adored her aunt, she and Charles were madly in love and in their determination to marry they eloped. Henrietta succeeded in having them tracked down to Tunbridge Wells before they had the opportunity to fulfil this aim, but if she hoped that Dorothy's return would bring her to heel she was sadly mistaken as nothing she said made a scrap of difference. Thoroughly exasperated and in desperation Henrietta turned to her brother for advice, and he instructed her to send Dorothy to Blickling where both he and her brother John would talk sense into her. Always a remote parent, it is not surprising that the 1st Earl was unaware of the closeness of the childhood friendship between his eldest son and Charles Hotham. Dorothy arrived in Norfolk resolutely defiant and showing no remorse whatsoever for her actions. In fact she dramatically declared her love for Charles to be deeper than ever and resolved that she would never on any account give him up. Her father protested vehemently and demanded that she break off the match immediately, but Dorothy dropped the bombshell that she was pregnant. Whilst shame and horror transfixed the Earl it also altered his outlook on the instant. The imperative now was to avoid any further scandal and so the lovers were married at Duke Street Chapel in Westminster on 21 October 1752 and their baby was born in the spring of 1753, a daughter they named after Henrietta. As it soon became apparent to Lady Suffolk that the couple's union was genuine and seemed likely to last, her heart softened. That she would have desperately wanted to know her new great niece (perhaps grand daughter) undoubtedly influenced her decision to invite the trio back into the fold. Unfortunately the 1st Earl could not bring himself to forgive his unrepentant, wilful daughter and he and Dorothy were never reconciled. The newly weds lived at Richmond, not far from Marble Hill, and it was at this time that the relationship between Charles and John, now his brother-in-law, developed into deeper, profound

Sir Charles Hotham painted by Gilbert Stuart.

Lady Dorothy Hotham as 'Diana'.

friendship. The Hothams often visited Blickling and when in 1754 John was re-elected as MP for Norwich he told Charles the glad tidings,

> Dear Brother, I have had the satisfaction of being toss'd about in a chair for three hours, but am at length happily landed. You can hardly conceive the Number of People of different sorts that have appeared upon this occasion: many handsome women did not a little contribute to give the whole an agreeable appearance. My head is a little confused at present with hurry, but not with drink, for I have tasted but one glass of wine today. We are now going to dinner, & in the evening there is to be an Assembly where, in all probability, the women of the first rank & the least beauty will fall to my lot.

As shown in letters from the mysterious 'Diane' amongst others and from Walpole's remark likening him to 'a swain', John Hobart had shown a keen interest in women well before and during his two years away on the Grand Tour. Other letters in French and Italian from ladies he met on the Continent are undated, unsigned and barely legible, and remain tantalising. One remarkable letter from a distressed anonymous English woman tells a sorry tale which reflects very badly on John,

> I don't doubt My Lord but upon seeing this you will expect an Abusive letter as it is a thing you've been Lately used to from a Woman who thinks you've used her ill. I being in the Same Situation, you must Consequently Expect the Same behaviour but in that you'll be mistaken, for I'll never abuse you. I pity you, for I'm sure you don't know the pleasure of true love & I believe it Contrary to your Nature to be Constant to a Woman for any number of years as I believe it impossible for me to be otherwise than uneasy at your behaviour, but I shall use my own reason in getting the better of myself, the worst that can happen upon this Occasion is Miscarrying, which I expect but I diserve so much greater punishments from providence than that, I shall be quite resigned & I've only one comfort, which is never more to offend—I was told by Lady L at the beginning of my Acquaintance with you, that you never did otherways than tire of every woman you had known & was sufficiently warned against loving you. Beleave me I never had vanity Enough to think I had Charm's sufficient to keep you, after your acknowledging your having left a Woman upon my Account Every way I beleave My Superior, but I allways for your own sake recommended you to marry & get into Publick life, being Well assured that a Man of Sense must find mour real satisfaction in that way of spending his time than in any other & I've so good an Opinion of you as to think no Man more fit for that life than your Self—to my great Concern I find you still continue to have the same inclinations of the life you've so long lived in. So that Marrying now is now out of the quishon for no woman that's her own Mistress will marry a Man she sees so fickle nor no

father will ever give his Consent for his Daughter to be so soon tired of. Which I conclude you've long since done of this letter but I shall trouble you very little more. I shall endeavour to keep out of your sights as much as I can without being particular. I shall go into the Country as soon as I can & I hope perswaid my Self every thing is for the best; in the meantime I from my Soul with you every Blessing & most Heartyly forgive you making me uneasy. This is the last trouble I'll ever give you.

This ill-used lady was clearly not a suitable candidate for marriage with a future Earl and was obviously to him a mere dalliance, and her letter gives the impression of John as a young buck who was extremely cavalier in his youthful dealings with the fair sex, especially if the allusion to a pregnancy was true.

A lighter, flirtatious letter, whose skittish author is unknown because the signature has been deliberately torn off, gives a glimpse of John's flair for theatrics, "You ask me about the Masquerade, how could you imagine it could succeed when you had deserted the management, but supposing even you had been there as Director, I don't think the scheme would have been pursued; I am much obliged to you for the Characters, you dressed them admirably."

John enquired of his aunt, "Don't you think it impossible for me with so many bad examples before my eyes, ever to make a tolerable Husband? I pity her beforehand, poor woman, tho' who what & where she is, is at present a secret to me." Whatever the state of his love life, and it does appear to have been very lively, John's main focus was ostensibly his political career. He continued as MP for Norwich until 1756 with Horatio Walpole as his number two. Not to be confused with his cousin at Strawberry Hill, Horatio[6] was Sir Robert Walpole nephew, and Blickling's close neighbour at the elegant Thomas Ripley designed Wolterton Hall.

In 1749, to celebrate the end of the War of Austrian Succession and the signing of the Treaty of Aix-la-Chapelle, Handel's 'Music for the Royal Fireworks' debuted in Green Park. The event was spoiled somewhat firstly by rain then by one of the pavilions catching fire in the middle of the recital, by a lady's clothing being set alight by a stray rocket and several other gruesome accidents involving the 101 canons employed to serve the score. For the next two years Parliament was relatively stable and so pacific that Henry Fox remarked during 1751 that "a bird might build her nest in the Speaker's chair, or in his peruke, and never be disturbed."[7] Several reforming legislations were passed; the 1751 Calendar Act brought the British

Handel's 'Music for the Royal Fireworks'

This was played in Green Park in 1749. Background/scene setting information.

Calendar into line with general European practice by eliminating the days between 2 and 14 September 1752. "Give us back our eleven days!" became a common cry of protest and was the cause of several riots. The Gin Act helped to reduce public drunkenness and the Marriage Act declared illegal the scandal of clandestine or secret marriages carried out either without parental consent, or bigamously. And in 1755 Lord John Hobart was appointed Comptroller of the Royal Household, an important role that meant he was also the Keeper of the Privy Seal.

But everything was about to change.

Notes

1. The Hobart family had previous interests in the constituency of St Ives in 1588 when the first Baronet Sir Henry Hobart sat as MP. Later, from 1715–22, John's father, Sir John Hobart, 1st Earl of Buckinghamshire also sat as MP for St Ives.
2. Horace Walpole, quoted in Black, J., *The British and the Grand Tour*, Routledge, 1985, p.120.
3. Cust, L. & Colvin, S. (ed.), *The History of the Society of Dilettanti*, Macmillian, 1914.
4. Walpole, H., *Horace Walpole's 'Reminiscences' Written in 1788*, John Sharp, 1819, pp.64-5.
5. The Battle of Lauffeld, 2 July 1747 during the War of the Austrian Succession. A French army of 80,000 faced the combined force of British, Dutch, Hanoverian and Austrian soldiers led by the Duke of Cumberland.
6. Horatio Walpole was Admiral Horatio Nelson's Godfather.
7. The History of Parliament, The 10th Parliament of Great Britain, 1751 session.

Life Changing Events

On 22 September 1756, sixty-one year old John Hobart, 1st Earl of Buckinghamshire died and was buried vertically in the Hobart family brick built vault in St Andrew's Church, Blickling. Thirty-two year old John inherited his father's title, lands and messuages in Buckinghamshire, Lincolnshire and in Norfolk, including Stodey, Hunworth, Salle, Heydon, Oulton, Baconsthorpe, Maylask, Gresham and most importantly Blickling Hall and its Estate. As the 2nd Earl of Buckinghamshire, John relinquished his seat as MP for Norwich and took his place in the House of Lords. The King appointed him firstly as a Privy Counsellor (a position which lasted the lifetime of the holder) and then as a Lord of the Bedchamber. Soon after succeeding to the title, he met the King's 'favourite' Amalie von Wallmoden, Duchess of Yarmouth, who had taken Henrietta Howard, Lady Suffolk's place as his mistress in 1735.[1] He told his aunt,"My behaviour at Kensington the other day was I believe very exactly what you advised. I was at the Levee yesterday & the King was pleased to notice me. Lady Yarmouth received me with the greatest politeness. Yr affectionate Nephew, Buckingham."[2] Dating from his succession John Hobart was universally addressed as and signed his letters as 'Buckingham' and this history shall from hereon follow his example.

Buckingham's widowed stepmother Elizabeth moved to Hobart Hall, a handsome house on the banks of the River Thames at Richmond, in part because she desired to live near her sister-in-law Lady Suffolk at Marble Hill. His youngest half-brother Henry, newly matriculated from Christ Church College, Oxford, was sent on his Grand Tour, funded by both Buckingham and his mother, which kept him abroad for two and a half years.

Buckingham's replacement as Norwich MP was his cousin Sir Harbord Harbord, the son of Sir William Harbord and Elizabeth, his mother Judith's half sister. Buckingham supported Harbord not only by giving him considerable financial backing but also by using his influence to help him win the seat in the belief that their political ideologies and allegiances were aligned.

With ambitious plans for alterations to the structure and decoration at Blickling Hall, Buckingham often invited his aunt to visit her childhood home. As always he took great pleasure in Henrietta's company and listened carefully to her advice because he considered her style and taste to be second to none. In September 1757, after one of her visits, he wrote, "If the partridge-pie gives you as much pleasure as your letter did to me, it will be the best pie that ever was tasted. You do not indeed mention any thing of your health; but there is a cheerfulness in your style which induces me to flatter myself that you are very well." He then departed on what may have been a flight of fancy designed to amuse his aunt since there is no record of any such structure as the Madman's Tower,

> The Torre del Pazzo (for such we now find by authentic records to be
> the ancient name of the building lately discovered at Blickling) was
> erected by William I of the Norman line, as a residence for an Italian
> of remarkable wit and humour, who used by his sallies to enliven the
> dull, gloomy disposition of his barbarous court. He gave him also divers
> manors in the pleasant vale that leads from Aylsham to Yarmouth. The
> king then married him to a maid of honor, a young lady of great spirit
> and factiousness—(maids of honor are still the same)—who brought him
> numerous issue, sold all his manors, and broke his heart. His indigent
> children were squandered in various parts of Europe, and from them are
> descended all the Harlequins, Pierrots, Columbines, & co who so much
> contribute to the diversion and improvement of the present age. Torre del
> Pazzo, which was the name he gave his habitation, signifies, in Italian, the
> Fool's or Madman's Tower. I need not tell your ladyship, that, after passing
> through various families, some of the manors, and the whole tower, are
> in my possession. It gives me great concern that it is not in my power to
> follow exactly the footsteps of the illustrious first proprietor. I may indeed,
> by singular good fortune, find a maid of honor who will condescend to
> sell my manors and break my heart; but I have too just an opinion of the
> measure of my own understanding not to be sensible, that if she produces
> Harlequins or Pierrots, it must be by another father.[3]

Buckingham was content in his single state, unlike his valet-de-chambre Monsieur
Pauquet[4] (the inventive spellings of the object of Pauquet's desire are the lady's
own) as he related to his aunt,

> Your ladyship must be fully sensible, from what you heard during your
> short stay at Blickling, of the disorderly inclinations of poor Pauquet. His
> passions increased as the fruit ripened; nor did they subside, as I flattered
> myself they would, upon the approach of winter. The frequent complaints
> of insulted modesty and terrified virgins made it necessary for me, about
> a week ago, to represent to him in the strongest possible manner the
> impropriety, immorality, and danger of such proceedings. It hurt me to
> see that the latter affected him most. Upon my return last Friday from
> Norwich, I received a letter from a lady in the neighbourhood, with one
> inclosed, which had been addressed by M Pauquet to her. In this, after the
> due encomiums upon the beauties of her person, the elegance of her mind,
> and the strongest assurances of the most violent passion, disinterested
> tenderness, &c. &c. &c. he lays himself and talents at her feet; offering to
> pass his days with her in that holy state in which he assures her it is only
> possible for man and woman to be truly happy. The lady is by no means
> his superior in birth, but happens unfortunately to be possessed of near
> three thousand pounds; and therefore, looking down upon Pauquet from

the height of her riches, complains to me of his 'intolerible insulance, prisumshon, and unpairallil cunfitence' and insists upon a 'ripermand.' I have answered in a most respectful manner, allow his error, but approve his flame; in short, make that kind of excuse for him which a good natured woman will receive as an apology for almost anything. The future progress of this affair shall be laid before you. In the meantime, we are all alone, very well, and most truly and affectionately, Yours'[5]

Buckingham continued to be, if not always alone, certainly far from the married state. His elevated status should have spurred him towards matrimony with the aim of producing heirs and ensuring the Hobart line, but for a further two years he made no effort whatsoever to find a suitable bride. If asked he may have claimed that his concentration was wholly focused on political matters at Westminster, in Norfolk and on his duties at Court, but his lack of interest in matrimony was because he had fallen deeply in love with an unattainable woman. Her identity is shrouded in mystery but eventually, though it caused considerable anguish, he realised that their clandestine relationship must come to an end. Having broken many hearts himself he was now compelled to break not only the lady's but also his own. In a heart rending letter to a mutual, unidentified, friend of the lady he implored him, or her, to take care of his lover,

If the portion of misery which I feel could be taken from that of our poor friend, there would be but very little left for her, my heart bleeds at every vein & nothing would have made me admit the thought of that which gives her so much uneasiness, but a conviction that ultimately it will tend to her peace & happiness as well as mine. It but ill becomes the Man who has for some years not only acted in opposition to the dictats of religion & morality himself but combated nay even ridiculed them in others, to say that from thence arises his present scheme of life. But long experience & frequent reflections have taught me, that <u>to be good, is to be happy</u>. This for the future shall be my object in every situation, & when you see me at a different part Esteem me, that every bad thing, in one, a Hippocrite. I will ever love her with the most affectionate tenderness, ever regard what bears in relation to her, & it shall be the study of my life by every justifiable method to make some atonement for that distress which I have been the most unfortunate occasion of. Let her consider, that in the nature of things it is impossible that this or something worse must not have happened very soon, that being the case is there any way so eligible, so little mortifying as this? If I had not thought it right to break it early to her, she could not have heard anything of the transaction in many months. For charity's, for humanity's sake watch over her, Cherish her & assist her reason. Be with her as much as you can; it is laying me under an obligation which whilst I live shall never be forgotten, & assure her how much she wrongs me if she thinks I do not feel every sentiment for her as friend or lover can.[6]

Perhaps his beloved was married, lived at some distance from Buckingham or even in another country, but whoever she was, she was clearly not eligible or free to become his wife.

One Miss Harriott Pitt however was free and the transaction referred to in the letter was nothing less than her engagement to Lord Buckingham. Miss Pitt was at this time fourteen years old and the only daughter of George Martin Pitt and Sophia Bugden. Her parents had both lived in Madras where her father was Governor for five years. Sophia, daughter of Charles Bugden of Fort St George, Madras, had previously been married to George Drake, also of Fort St George, with whom she had one son and three daughters. After their marriage in 1743 the Pitts lived at Orleans House, not far from Marble Hill House and Horace Walpole's Strawberry Hill. George Pitt had amassed a great fortune through his extremely lucrative positions in the East India Company but died when Harriott was ten years old. Her mother Sophia encouraged her daughter to aim high in her marriage expectations because although Harriott was not of an elevated rank she would bring an immense dowry to a successful suitor. She was described by Count Frederick Keilmansegge as "a very pleasant young lady, who possesses at least £100,000 and who dances remarkably well into the bargain."[7] A young lady with a very great fortune who could also dance well presented an irresistible combination. The Lothian papers refer to "A draught letter from the 2nd Earl of Buckinghamshire to Miss H. Pitt, with her answer relating to a Proposal of Marriage" and Miss Pitt's answer must have been in the affirmative because the couple's engagement was announced in November 1759. Horace Walpole felt obliged to spread the happy news and wrote to George Montagu on 23 December 1759, "Lord Buckingham is going to be married to our Miss Pitt of Twickenham" adding enigmatically, "the daughter of that strange woman, who had a mind to be my wife."[8] But six months later Miss Pitt quite suddenly broke off the engagement. Buckingham's good friend the Rt Hon Charles Townshend, second son of Charles, 3rd Viscount Townshend and brother to George, roundly congratulated Buckingham on what he perceived as his very lucky escape, "My brother tells me nothing is so magnificent as Brickling (sic), nobody so popular as the master of it. Also let me take this opportunity of saying that I rejoice in your own late escape; the person would have disappointed you; the fortune would to you have been no recompense; the manner in which it went off proves you have no reason to lament it; and you have acted throughout with sense and temper. I beg you will present my best affections to all our friends at Brickling, my heart is wherever they are."[9] Even Horace Walpole felt Buckingham would do better to marry elsewhere and wrote to his cousin General Henry Seymour Conway, "Have you heard that Miss Pitt has dismissed Lord Buckingham? Tant mieux pour lui.* She damns her eyes that she will marry some captain—tant mieux pour elle***. I think the forlorn Earl should match with Miss Ariadne Drury."[10]

---

*   Much better for him.

**   Much better for her.

The capricious Miss Pitt had determined to raise her sights higher than an Earl for a husband, and it appeared that Buckingham had broke his lover's heart, and his own, for nothing.

In early November a diversion from these romantic tribulations was reported by Horace Walpole to George Montagu:

> An extraordinary event happened today: George Townshend sent a challenge to Lord Albemarle, desiring him to be with a 2nd in the fields. Lord Albemarle took Col Crawford, and went to Mary-le-bone; George bespoke Lord Buckingham, who loves a secret too well not to tell it: he communicated it to Stanley, who went to St. J's, and acquainted Mr Caswall, the captain on guard. The latter took a hackney-coach, drove to Mary-le-bone, and saw one pair. After waiting ten minutes, the others came; Townshend made an apology to Lord Albemarle for making him wait. 'Oh' said he 'men of spirit don't want apologies: come, let us begin what we came for.' At that instant, out steps Caswall from his coach, and begs their pardon, as his superior officers, but told them they were his prisoners. He desired Mr Townshend and Lord Buckingham to return to their coach; he would carry back Lord Albemarle and Crawford in his. He did, and went to acquaint the King, who had commissioned some of the matrons of the army to examine the affair, and make it up. All this while, I don't know what the quarrel was, but they hated one another so much on the Duke's account, that a slight word would easily make their aversions boil over.[11]

It may be that Buckingham's action prevented a catastrophe, confident as he was that Hans Stanley would take measures to stop the reckless duel.

୫୦୯୨

In a bizarre coincidence the daughters of the participants in the duel between Sir Henry Hobart and Oliver Le Neve in 1698 became good friends. Isabella, one of Oliver Le Neve's three daughters, had acted as a companion to Lady Mary, one of Robert Walpole's daughters, until her charge married in 1723. From then on Isabella spent most of her time with Horace Walpole and she and Lady Henrietta met often over the tea and card tables at Strawberry Hill and Marble Hill House. Whether the two now elderly ladies ever broached the delicate subject of the infamous duel in which the father of one killed the father of the other is unknown and what rules of etiquette would have applied in such a circumstance must remain a subject for conjecture.

୫୦୯୨

Some while after his peremptory dismissal by Miss Pitt, Buckingham gathered up his courage and turned his attention back to the minefield of courtship. Horace Walpole's comment on a match with "Ariadne" now seems prescient because the Earl's eye fell upon the young woman Walpole alluded to, Lady Mary Anne Drury. But much to his chagrin he found a rival 2nd Earl blocking his path.

Notes

1. The Duchess of Yarmouth remained the King's mistress until his death in 1760.
2. *Reports on the Manuscripts of the Marquess of Lothian*, p.170.
3. *Letters to and from Henrietta ...*, Vol. 2, p.239-240.
4. "*the great luxury is to have a Frenchman but very few people can go to that expense. In each grand house there is one who has the responsibility for the expenses, combining the duties of steward, butler and valet. Very often, he is a Frenchman.*"
5. Scarfe, N.
6. *Letters to and from Henrietta ...*, Vol. 2, p.241-242.
7. NRO NRS 14623, 29D1.
8. Keilmansegge, F., Count, *Diary of a Journey to England' (1761-1762)* p.224.
9. *Horace Walpole's Correspondence*, Vol. 9, p.263.
10. *Report on the Manuscripts of the Marquess of Lothian*, p.241.
11. *Horace Walpole's Correspondence*, Vol. 38, p.57.
12. *Horace Walpole's Correspondence*, Vol. 9, p.319.

Three Weddings and a Coronation

In 1737 a young Oxford educated scholar by the name of Thomas Drury was making a respectable living as a Barrister at the Courts of Chancery when he unexpectedly inherited £230,000 from his maternal uncle Thomas Beacon's estate. This resourceful unmarried man had made such an immense fortune as a brewer in Shoreditch that he bequeathed the same amount to another nephew, coincidentally also named Thomas. Later that same year, that most unlucky nephew also died and left his share to his cousin, turning the twenty-five year old Thomas Drury into an exceptionally wealthy man and a highly desirable catch. Marriage didn't evade him for long however, as in October he wed Martha Tyrell, daughter of John Tyrell, 3rd Baronet of Heron, Essex. On 4 September 1738 Thomas James Joseph was born, followed two years later by a daughter they named Mary Anne. Yet more good fortune fell upon Thomas when he inherited another estate near Maldon in Essex, was created a Baronet in 1739 and returned as a Whig MP for Maldon in 1741.

All was pacific in the Drury family until the untimely death in 1746 of their son and heir Thomas James. A sister for Mary Anne, Jocosa Katherina, was born three years later and Sir Thomas and Lady Martha lavished all their care and attention upon their daughters, but in January 1759 Sir Thomas died, leaving Lady Martha alone to educate her two pretty daughters in music, dancing, etiquette, French and Italian; all the necessary accomplishments of refined young ladies. It did not hamper their cause to be offering considerable dowries to successful suitors but Lady Martha was in no hurry to part with either daughter, even though Mary Anne had now reached her majority at twenty one. Lady Martha desired only those who could elevate the family to a higher rank.

The first to meet this requirement was the notoriously licentious forty-five year old George Montagu-Dunk, 2nd Earl of Halifax. Known as 'the Father of the Colonies' and after whom Halifax, Nova Scotia was named in 1749, he had lost his first wife seven years earlier. Famously extravagant, he had occupied himself since then by building Hampton Court House for his mistress, the famously tempestuous Irish singer Anna Maria Faulkner, for whose cuckolded husband he had conveniently found occupation in the Caribbean. Despite this attachment, Mary Anne and her dowry proved irresistible to the Earl and the couple became engaged just as he was appointed Lord Lieutenant of Ireland. Anna Maria was outraged and scuppered his plans by making known her vociferous objections in public, loudly and in no uncertain terms. Halifax broke off his engagement to Mary Anne, and it was the redoubtable Miss Faulkner who accompanied him to Dublin Castle.

Following this scandalous episode it must have been a welcome relief to both Lady Martha and Mary Anne when the handsome thirty-seven year old Buckingham, without a noticeable encumbrance of mistresses, came to pay court. The match appeared attractive and beneficial to both parties, as Buckingham would gain a pretty, vivacious young wife with an enormous dowry of £50,000 and she would become Countess of Buckinghamshire and mistress of Blickling Hall. George Montagu[1], a cousin of the 2nd Earl of Halifax, told Horace Walpole, "I hear Lord Buckingham is to be married to the Ariadne Drury; it will whitewash my cousin who has been so blackened for gaining her tender young heart."[2] In Greek mythology Ariadne translates as

Miniature of Mary Anne, Countess of Buckinghamshire by Samuel Cotes.

'holy and pure' and it appears to have been common knowledge that Lady Drury was keen to keep her daughters in a similar state for as long as possible. This time the engagement held and Buckingham and Mary Anne were married at Lady Drury's house, St Anne's in Soho on 14 July 1761. Another wedding followed on 22 July, that of Buckingham's younger half brother Henry Hobart to Anne Bristow of Quidenham, Norfolk. And just a few weeks later a third, very much grander wedding took place.

King George II had died on 25 October 1760 and a suitable bride had since been sought for his twenty two year old grandson and heir George. After a thorough search through the eligible princesses of Europe the chosen bride, seventeen year old Princess Charlotte of Mecklenburg, journeyed to England. Newspapers reported that "after three different storms, and being often in sight of the English coast, and often in danger of being driven on that of Norway, the fleet, with her most serene highness, during her tedious passage, continued in very good health and spirits, often diverting herself with playing on the harpsichord, practising English tunes, and endearing herself to those who were honoured with the care of her person." Arriving in London on 8 September 1761 the Princess was welcomed by His Majesty, the royal family and several dozen noblemen including Buckingham, and just six hours after they first met George and Charlotte were married in the Chapel Royal, St James's Palace. Since Earls and Peeresses were amongst the wedding guests it is likely that Buckingham (whom King George had retained as a Lord of the Bedchamber) and his new Countess were in attendance at both the wedding and the Grand Ball held the following evening.

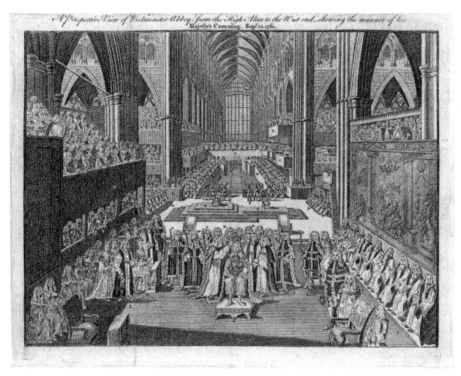

A Perspective View of Westminster Abbey from the High Altar to the West end, showing the manner of His Majesty's Crowning, Sept. 2nd 1761.

Two weeks later, the Coronation took place at Westminster Cathedral and it is recorded that the procession included "Earls and Countesses in their robes of estate with their coronets in their hands." All participants endured a longer day than they expected. King George and Princess Charlotte were carried in sedan chairs from St James's Palace to Westminster Hall from whence they walked to the Abbey, setting out at 11am, but unfortunately the Sword of State, which was an essential part of the ceremony and was no small item, had somehow been misplaced and the Bishop and clergy were kept waiting outside for an hour and a half whilst it was located. The procession took so long that many spectators sent for food and drink to be brought in which meant that at solemn moments during the ceremony the inappropriate sounds of glasses clinking and cutlery clanging could be clearly heard. The royal couple were at last crowned at 3.30pm and a lavish but rather disorganised supper followed. Although Horace Walpole damned the occasion as

Buckingham and Mary Anne were present at King George III's Coronation and would have heard 'The King Shall Rejoice' by William Boyce, 1761.

"a wretched banquet, and a foolish puppet-show"[3] young Mary Anne must have been thrilled to have married Buckingham during such a whirl of high society activity, when the balls, feasts and firework displays carried on for days.

After these excitements Norfolk beckoned and Buckingham introduced his Countess to her new home at Blickling Hall. The county was far removed from Mary Anne's life in London both geographically and socially and it took considerable time for the young woman to acclimatise and adapt to country living. The journeys to and from were not pleasurable as the roads were far from the standard of those around the capital and to begin with Mary Anne keenly felt the remoteness of her new home. To keep his young bride content, and it is very likely that she made her discontent known, the couple spent a great deal of time at their house in Bond Street, from which base the new Countess continued to play her part in the social milieu at parties, balls, and the gatherings at the Georgian Pleasure-grounds of Vauxhall and Ranelagh Gardens. Naturally the couple were frequent visitors to Lady Suffolk at 18 Savile Row and at Marble Hill House.

Early in the following year Mary Anne's relationship with her mother Martha was put under considerable strain. Her father Sir Thomas, quite inexplicably for an extremely wealthy lawyer and barrister, had died intestate and in the absence of a Will the court had awarded his widow an annuity of only six hundred pounds a year. Lady Martha took what she deemed to be a paltry offer as a personal affront and brought her case to the House of Lords claiming that because she had been an infant at the time of her marriage, that is, under twenty one, she must therefore be entitled to a third of the entire estate and to the ongoing revenues from it. The case had dragged on for two years with the eventual judgement that the estate should be split three ways between Lady Martha and her daughters Mary Anne and Jocosa. But the judges also recommended that there should be further investigation into the law regarding circumstances such as these, which originated with a ruling under King Henry VIII, and the result was held in limbo. Significantly, now opposing her in the case were Mary Anne and Jocosa, led by Buckingham, whose aim was to sensibly manage the finances of his unpredictable and rather scatty mother-in-law. The case was adjourned many times because Counsel was 'indisposed' and whose illness must have been fairly serious as the case dragged on for weeks without being heard. Finally, in May 1762, the previous decree was reversed leaving Lady

Karl Friedrich Abel dedicated Six Sonatas to Buckingham in 1762, and this is one of them.

Martha with her original legacy of six hundred pounds a year and Mary Anne and Jocosa with an equal Moiety, sharing the entire estate between them. Lady Martha was permitted to live in her large house in Soho but as she would lose financially if Jocosa married before reaching her majority she became adept at keeping any potential suitors at bay.

Buckingham's love of music was rewarded in this year when Karl Friedrich Abel, a renowned German composer and Chamber Musician to Queen Charlotte, dedicated to him 'Six Sonatas for the Harpsichord with accompaniments for a Violin or German Flute & Violoncello.' Abel shared a house in London with Johann Christian Bach, with whom he performed legendary concerts at Mrs Cornely's high society establishments, and was once described as "A tall, big, portly person, with a waistcoat, under which might easily have been buttoned twin brothers."[4]

Nine months after their marriage Mary Anne gave birth to a daughter in London and John was instantly smitten by his first born child. Baptised Henrietta after his beloved aunt she would always be known as Harriet. That she was a daughter made no matter to him as there was plenty of time to have more children, which would surely include sons, in the future. Two months later, in good spirits, he wrote to Mary Anne from Blickling. Letters to his wife always began 'Dear Madam'

> They kept me at Norwich till yesterday not a little contrary to my inclination, and oblig'd me on Tuesday evening to be present at the Ball which would not have been a very bad one if the Musick had not got very drunk at the Mayor's Feast. I was told it would be extremely proper for me to dance with the Mayor's daughter in Law, a beauteous maiden of fifty, but declined the honor and content'd myself with gazing upon her at a distance with that veneration which the dignity of her appearance inspired. The dog and birds are in the most perfect health, the dog is falling in love with the Under Butler and is absolutely deaf to all my tender advances. The Bottom of my water is almost covered and the surface increases not quite so fast as the motion of the hour hand of a watch. My Bowling Green looks like an Ant Hill through a Microscope, all in motion. I flatter myself with the hopes of hearing soon that you are well, and am with the greatest affection, Your most obedient servant, Buckingham'

"The Bottom of my water" refers to the serpentine lake he had instructed his men to dig out by hand, a gargantuan task which took rather a long time to do, and then rather a long time to fill. His father had outlined a plan for this project as far back as 1729 and now Buckingham brought it to fruition. Although not particularly deep the lake ran a mile in length covering twenty-two acres and was artfully designed to give the illusion of a river when viewed from either end, echoing the view from Marble Hill House towards the River Thames. But soon the myriad other ideas he had in mind for improving Blickling would have to be postponed, because King George III had other plans for his Lordship.

Blickling Hall showing the serpentine lake, November 2021.

Notes

1. A longtime correspondent of Horace Walpole's, Montagu was also an indefatigable gossip. In 1761 he was Gentleman Usher of the Black Rod in Ireland in the vice-royalty of his cousin but *'he was so fortunately placed in life with powerful friends and relations, but was palaryzed by laziness. George Hardynge called him one of Walpole's witty and effeminate friends. He drank port and nursed his gout, dozing in front of the fire.'*

2. *Horace Walpole Correspondence,* Vol. 9, p.357.

3. Ibid. Vol. 21, p.535.

4. *Reminiscences of Henry Angelo, with memoirs of his late father and friends, including numerous original anecdotes and curious traits of the most celebrated characters that have flourished during the past eighty years,* Vol. 1, Colburn, H & Bentley, R., p.65, 1830, (archive.org)

At the King's Request

As Harriet reached eight months of age Buckingham accepted the King's invitation to take up the significant role of Ambassador Extraordinary and Plenipotentiary to the Court of Peter III in Russia, which gave the holder full powers to sign treaties on behalf of the Monarch. That the position was offered to him was due in no small part to the recommendation of his long standing friend George Grenville who was at this time Secretary of State under the Ministry of Lord Bute. Buckingham decided to undertake the prestigious commission alone and to leave Mary Anne and Harriet safely at home in England under the care of his aunt. Mary Anne would also have her mother and sister Jocosa for company and she had many friends in London society with whom to distract herself during his absence; there was no length of time stipulated for his term in office but it was not likely to be any less than a year. As preparations were made for his departure to St Petersburg, a journey calculated to take above two months, Buckingham received useful practical advice from a previous Ambassador. John Carmichael, 3rd Earl of Hyndford had been in post during the reign of the Empress Elizabeth,

I must acquaint you in friendship that during five years of my Embassy I was out of pocket, for 'tis a very expensive Court, and, contrary to common sense, an ambassador must give great entertainments and make a vast show in equipage to be respected. As to your coaches I would advise you to send them by sea from England, except what you want for the journey for yourself and servants which you may provide in Utrecht. But take care there to avoid a great rogue called Prichard, who takes upon himself the character of the King's Commissary, who has cheated many an English traveller and me in particular. You can't do without a German secretary and if he understands the French language, it will save you a third, for I make no doubt you carry an English secretary with you. The next thing is servants, and I must begin with good cooks and a Maitre d'Hotel, all of which you may get at Hanover, and I would advise you to carry as few English servants as possible, except those about your own person, for they are sooner debauched at Petersburg than at London (c'est beaucoup dire˚). Your Lordship may buy horses there of all kinds without the risk of sending them thither. Mr Keith, the King's Minister, will put you in the way of providing your family with all kind of wines and necessarys. I need not give you any caution as to wine or women, for I know your delicacy as to both, but you will be tempted. I dare not desire to be remembered to Peter the 3rd, altho' I fancy he has not forgot me, at least he assured me he never would etc.. He is a great lover of musick, and if you carry some good

---

˚ and that's saying a lot

fiddles, he's very fond of them.[1]

In Europe the *stately quadrille* was causing alliances to shift once again. In Russia the wildly eccentric Emperor Peter III had made peace with his hero the Prussian King Frederic, a powerful ruler bitterly hostile towards England. This move was seen as an outrage and a downright betrayal by the Russian people. Frederic accused the English of concluding a separate peace with France without due regard to the interests of Prussia and of attempting to deter Peter III from making his alliance with Frederic. King George discovered that Frederic had instructed his ambassadors to foment sedition against his Prime Minister Lord Bute and a few days before Buckingham's appointment he refused to hold any communication with the Prussian Ministers in London "until they should decease to interfere in the internal affairs of the kingdom."[2] Sir Robert Keith, the incumbent Ambassador to Russia, was known to be an admirer of Prussia and as a result was in favour with Peter III, but "his flattery of Peter's extravagant admiration for the King of Prussia was contrary to his British Majesty's pacific view"[3] and put Keith in a difficult position at home. Buckingham's views on Prussia were very much in line with those of his King and his "young and strikingly handsome presence"[4] and good humoured nature were deemed a better fit than Keith's for a Court known for "its gaiety and dissipation which had well-nigh worn out more than one sober and middle-aged ambassador."[5] (In 1755, Guy Dickens, a previous Ambassador, had begged to be recalled, complaining that he was too old to go to EVERY ball.)

Suddenly, just as Buckingham's preparations for departure were almost complete, startling and momentous news arrived from St Petersburg. The principal character in the unfolding drama there was Peter III's wife, the Grand Duchess Catherine.

₧₧

Catherine's rise to power was as unpredictable as it was extraordinary. As the daughter of an inconsequential minor Prince, the Princess Sophia Augusta Frederica, as she was named at birth, lived in the tiny German principality of Anhalt-Zerbst-Bernburg. Her family might have hoped that she would marry reasonably well, perhaps even a little above her station, but when the Empress Elizabeth summoned her to Petersburg as a potential bride for her nephew Peter, Sophia's ambitious and supremely selfish mother Princess Johanna Elizabeth of Holstein-Gottorp saw scope for her own advancement. The highly intelligent and spirited fourteen year old Sophia vastly impressed the Empress, who persuaded her to disavow her Lutheran faith and be admitted into the Orthodox Church under her new name of Catherine, after the Empress's own mother. Peter treated his future bride as a playmate, confessed that he was in love with another but was resigned to marrying her only because his aunt wished it. This did not bode well and after their marriage in August 1745 Peter proved to be a spectacularly useless husband.

Ten years later Charles Hanbury Williams (following the Earl of Hyndford's tenure) was appointed English Ambassador and his mission was to arrange a British alliance with Russia against France and Prussia. A famous wit and satirist, this sophisticated man befriended the beleaguered and lonely Duchess Catherine. By this time Peter was routinely either ignoring or insulting her, not least by flaunting his mistress Elizabeth Vorontsova in full view of the Court, and Catherine's foolish mother had been uncovered as a spy in the pay of Frederic of Prussia and sent home in the utmost disgrace. Catherine wrote in her memoirs, "The Chevalier Williams sat near me at supper, and we kept up a conversation as agreeable as it was gay. As he was lively, well informed and extremely witty it was not difficult to

Peter III and Catherine II by Georg Cristoph Grooth.

carry on a conversation with him."[6] Quite the young buck in his youth Sir Charles had initially toyed with the idea of taking a romantic approach to the attractive Duchess but as he had reached middle age he ruefully acknowledged to a minister in London who suggested the same route that, "A man at my age would make a poor lover; alas my sceptre governs no more."[7] It is just as well he decided against this avenue since in the unlikely event he had been successful, he may have transmitted the syphilis he had contracted some years earlier, to Catherine. He had been serially unfaithful and it was common knowledge that he had "pox'd his wife", Lady Frances, who unsurprisingly left him, taking their two daughters with her. Sir Charles therefore chose to become an avuncular, even paternal figure on whom Catherine could rely not only for good counsel but also for financial aid at a time when she was sorely in need of both. In time the deep trust between the Grand Duchess and the English Minister led Catherine to aver that, "You will see, if one day I wear the crown, that I shall partly owe it to your counsel" and when Sir Charles took his final leave of her in 1757[8] she told him, "I love you as my father. I count myself happy to have been enabled to acquire your affection."[9]

In the summer of 1755 Sir Charles heard from England that his second born daughter, seventeen year old Charlotte, had "thrown herself at an impecunious son of the Earl of Buckinghamshire."[10] This was probably Buckingham's exuberant brother George Hobart, then twenty four, as Henry was at Cambridge and only seventeen himself. Sir Charles withheld his consent to marriage between the couple unless her suitor could provide £1,000 per year for their upkeep. Lady Frances initially said she would contribute but then withdrew her offer and the relationship was considered to be over. Charlotte ostensibly agreed but clandestinely continued a covert correspondence with her admirer for many months afterwards. When their deception was uncovered Sir Charles was incandescent with rage and demanded that the affair be terminated and, by the end of 1756, it was.

To remark that the Grand Duchess Catherine's marriage to Peter was difficult would be grossly understating the many and varied traumas he inflicted upon her, but he was also the architect of his own downfall through the actions taken after succeeding to the throne on the death of the Empress Elizabeth in January 1762. His initial intentions seemed calculated to win over his people but whilst in some instances he bowed to their interests, in many more he shocked them by his complete and total disregard for their beliefs. His blind allegiance to, and boundless admiration of Frederic of Prussia, with whom Russia had been so long in a state of violent hostility, was to the Russian people both mystifying and repugnant. It was one matter, and considered disgraceful enough, to dress himself in the Prussian uniform but he outraged the proud Holstein Guards by forcing them to don Prussian uniforms too, and to burn their old ones. His interference in matters of religion was just as grave, as when he seized upon the revenues of the clergy, whether monks or seculars, bishops or inferiors, and for compensation allowed them some mean pension in such a proportion as his fancy suggested. His capricious order that the clergy should no longer be distinguished by beards was in itself of less moment but it was nevertheless deeply offensive to them and he also created petty regulations concerning the images and pictures in their churches. Added to this, everyone was uncomfortably aware that he constantly humiliated Catherine by flaunting his vulgar mistress to the Court. Having affronted his army, irritated his clergy, offended the nobility and alienated his own family, Peter carried on regardless, blindly unaware that a storm of revolution was fomenting.

In July 1762, upon discovering that her husband intended to have her permanently incarcerated, Catherine feared for her life. She took swift and drastic action, escaped under cover of night to the barracks of the Guards regiment and won them to her side. Peter, on hearing that she rode at the head of fourteen thousand troops dressed in the uniform of the famously loyal Preobrazhensky Guards, "Allowed himself to be dethroned like a child who had been sent to bed" related Frederic of Prussia on learning of Peter's pathetic and immediate abdication to his wife.

John Carmichael had been accurate in his assessment of Peter's partiality to fiddles as, together with begging Catherine to allow Elizabeth Vorontsova to be exiled with him, his most urgent requests were for "his own bed from Oranienbaum, his poodle, his German doctor, his black servant, and his violin."[11] The Empress generously granted all of these requests with the entirely understandable exception of the company of his mistress. Just a few days later Peter was declared dead, but the rumour that Catherine ordered him to be despatched has never been proved.

Although poison was posited as the cause of Peter's death it is widely believed that Catherine's devoted admirers and protectors, led by the brothers Alexis and Gregory Orlov, went too far in their restraint of a drunk and panicking prince, and inadvertently strangled him. The official Palace line was that the Prince had died of "haemorrhoidal colic" an imaginary complaint that swiftly turned into a satirical euphemism for assassination. The French philosopher Jean le Rond d'Alembert, who was later invited by Catherine to "transplant himself to Petersburg"[12] to educate her son, declared facetiously that "I dare not go, since I am prone to piles; a very dangerous condition in Russia."[13]

One of Catherine's first acts on taking power was to set 22 September for her coronation at the Kremlin. She also decreed that fines and taxes would be lifted, pardons given for lesser offences, and proclaimed a three day holiday for the occasion. The Muscovites erected four triumphal arches along the four mile passage from the city gate to the Palace and decorated the route with silk sheets and evergreens. Feasting and celebrations abounded throughout the country; Moscow was illuminated every night for weeks and balls and banquets continued without pause for several weeks after the Coronation Day. On the day itself cannon thundered from five in the morning and the crowds cheered wildly wherever Catherine appeared.

Having accepted the role as Ambassador to the Court of Peter III, Buckingham instead found himself on his way to the Court of the remarkable woman who would later be known as Catherine the Great. Horace Walpole wrote witheringly, "my Lord Buckingham, who is going Ambassador to Petersburg, may try the remainder of his charms upon the heart of an empress."[14] Walpole was obviously unaware of the situation at Catherine's Court because firmly ensconced as her lover was Gregory Orlov, soon to be the father of her third child[15], and who would be by her side for the next thirteen years.

Notes

1. *Report on the Manuscripts of the Marquis of Lothian.*
2. *Grenville Papers ...*, Vol. I, p.467.
3. *Despatches and Correspondence ...*, Vol. 1, p.207.
4. *Despatches and Correspondence ...*, Vol. 1, p.57.
5. Ibid.
6. Massie,R.K., p.174.
7. Ibid. p.177.
8. After a particularly stormy journey through the Baltics, this once agile and erudite diplomat's health swiftly declined, apparently hastened by his having suffered tertiary syphilis for some time. A year later, whilst the balance of his mind was violently disturbed, he cut his own throat whilst staying at the house of Lord Bolingbroke in Chelsea.
9. Massie,R.K., p.198.
10. Fox Strangeways, G.S.H., *Life of Sir Charles Hanbury Williams*, (1928), p.306.
11. Massie,R.K., p.270.

12. Translation of a letter from the Empress of Russia to M. D'Alembert, at Paris:
    Moscow, November 13, 1762 M. d'Alembert, *I have just received the answer you wrote to*
    Mr Odar, in which you refuse to transplant yourself to assist in the education of my son. I easily
    conceive that it costs a philosopher, like you, nothing to despise what the world calls grandeur
    and honour: these, in your eyes, are very little; and I can readily agree with you that they are so.
    ... to be born and called to contribute to the happiness and even the instruction of a whole nation,
    and yet decline it, is, in my opinion, refusing to do that good which you wish to do.

13. Massie,R.K., p.465.

14. *Horace Walpole Correspondence*, Walpole to Sir Horace Mann, 31 July 1762.

15. Catherine's first child was Paul I of Russia, who may have been fathered by either her
    husband Peter III or by her lover Sergei Saltykov. Her second child, Anna Petrovna, who
    died aged 15 months, was fathered by another lover, introduced to her by Sir Charles
    Hanbury Williams, Count Stanislaus Poniatowski. Her third child, Alexei Bobrinsky, born
    in April 1762, was the son of her lover Gregory Orlov.

From Russia with News

Buckingham took the news of revolution in his stride and pressed onwards together with his half-brother George who accompanied him as his Secretary. Reaching Copenhagen, despite being warned that it would be safer for them to remain there incognito until matters in Russia became more settled, he insisted they journey onwards. Even so, frustrating delays on the roads meant that he missed the coronation. Arriving too late, and not yet even in Moscow but in Petersburg, he wrote several times to George Grenville.

24 September[1], It will be impossible for me to get there in time enough to be present at that ceremony, as my equipages, baggage, and servants are not yet on shore, nor is there any house ready for me at Moscow. I am also informed that the roads are very bad, and the horses too much fatigued with the concourse of people who have lately travelled that way, as to make any degree of expedition impracticable.

1 October, Mr Keith on his return will be so good as to explain the many difficulties which have attended me...as this country has none of the conveniences which are found elsewhere.

5 October, Sunday, being the day appointed for the Coronation of the Empress, was celebrated as a high festival. The illuminations and other rejoicings were repeated last night. I propose to set out for Moscow on Saturday morning.

6 October, I shall use my utmost endeavours to be able, in a little time after my arrival at Moscow, to send you an authentic account of the state of this country. At present it appears to me that the people are uneasy and fluctuating; the Court sensible of it, and alarmed.[2]

A few days later his servants and equipages (horses, carriages, grooms and so forth) having at last caught up with him, Buckingham set out for Moscow. Once arrived there he grumbled to his aunt, Lady Suffolk,

A great deal of fasting, some praying, nine days and as many nights through the most detestable roads in the universe, covered with snow just enough froze to let us through, brought us yesterday to Moscow, where we found ourselves in a most wretched, ruinous house, furnished with no fixtures nor any movables but rats and bugs, detestable animals in themselves; and yet I pity even them when I consider what they hourly suffer from the inclemency of the weather. I will however, try to laugh at what I cannot remedy, and attempt at least to acquit myself with credit of the commission that is entrusted to me. My brother is a good deal out of spirits; he has been used to a cheerfuller life for some time past, but I hope use and reflection will make it easier to him. I ought not to have wrote to you until I had seen the Empress and her Court, but my vanity told me you would be glad to hear this journey was accomplished.[3]

From the outset George discovered he was not a good traveller and, moreover, was almost immediately homesick. On reaching Russia he struggled to acclimatise himself with the country, its people and cuisine and his unhappiness was not improved by the severe winter weather. In an unwelcome addition to his woes he almost always felt ill, and to compound his misery, soon after they arrived in Petersburg, the news caught up with them that his mother Elizabeth had died suddenly. After completing the arduous four hundred and sixty mile journey from Petersburg to Moscow, Buckingham wrote to Grenville,

I arrived at this place yesterday. The journey was a very disagreeable one, and with all the expedition that could be made, took up nine days. The news of Lady Buckinghamshire's death, and my brother not being well, detained me at Petersburg a day and a half longer than I intended. The Master of Ceremonies is to let me know when I am to have an audience, which is to be private. The Court is certainly in great confusion, the troops are turbulent and riotous, yet, as they have no head to resort to, it is consequently natural to suppose that the disturbance must soon subside.[4]

He surmised correctly as four days later the troops were calmed and his first meeting with Catherine was arranged,

I had the honour yesterday of my first private audience of the Empress, to which I was conducted in one of her Majesty's coaches; the whole ceremony was according to a form which they showed me, and assured me was what they never deviated from with regard to any ambassador. I made my compliments in English, of which I have enclosed a copy, and hope it will meet with his Majesty's approbation. The Empress answered me in Russian; I have asked for a translation. In the evening there was a drawing room and a concert of music. I had the honour of playing at picket with her Majesty. She asked me a great many questions about England; and upon the whole her behaviour to me, both then and at my audience, was extremely gracious.[5]

Their employment of different languages conformed to diplomatic etiquette but once the initial formalities were over the Empress and the Earl conversed fluently in French over games of picket (piquet). This is a card game for two and from their first introduction it seems they were easy in each other's company. Perhaps Catherine heard and saw in him echoes of the kindnesses shown to her by the Chevalier Hanbury Williams and was therefore predisposed to look favourably upon him. No doubt she also responded to his genuine appreciation of a handsome woman. Both flirtatious by nature, they spent a great deal of time together, dancing, horse-riding and conversing on the many topics that interested her so much about British and European culture. Perhaps this closeness might have been the cause of more gossip and Court speculation than there was, had Catherine's attachment to Gregory Orlov been less obvious.

Buckingham's principal mission was to renew the Treaty of Alliance of 1742 but, realising quickly this was an unrealistic ambition, he perceived that a new Treaty would have to be formulated. As he navigated his way solo through the diplomatic world he was uncomfortably aware of his inexperience. He asked Grenville to ensure he was kept informed of activities in London and the other European Courts as often as possible, but the distances involved meant that he was often behind the times with letters taking three weeks or more to arrive.

Encouragingly, Vice-Chancellor Prince Galitzen, who had initially been extremely frosty towards Buckingham, sent a messenger in November to inform him that England had taken the Havannah, saying he had "more pleasure in giving this

A Plan of the siege of the Havana. Drawn by an officer.15th August 1762 LOC G4924.H3 1762 .P5.

piece of intelligence as such an event must forward the conclusion of that peace which is so wished for here."[6] Another dance step in the Seven Years' War had played out in Cuba where the siege of Havana ended in August with British forces seizing the port. This had been an important naval base for the Spanish and it was to be returned to them in yet another reversal in the following year's Treaty of Paris, which would formally end the war. Buckingham reported to Grenville that he was cultivating acquaintance with the Prussian and Danish ministers despite their reserved manners and was attempting to form relationships with the Russian hierarchy. At the top of his list was Nikita Panin, Catherine's most powerful advisor and tutor to the eight year old Grand Duke Paul.[7] Buckingham wrote of Panin, "He is esteemed a man of honor and integrity, in a country where, for the first, the language has no name."[8]

At home Lady Suffolk was suffering from migraines, vision disturbance and debilitating attacks of gout but wrote to Buckingham as often as her health allowed, eager to know how he was faring. He sent his first impressions,

> The Empress's appearance would prejudice you greatly in her favour, but her address much more so. Affability and dignity are blended in her manner, which inspires you at once with ease and respect. When the hurry, the unavoidable consequence of a revolution is over, she has every talent to make this a great and powerful country. The Russians, as they themselves complain, have very little society amongst them; the men and women mix scarcely even in public places with one another, and are attentive and polite but extremely reserved to strangers, particularly to those who have a public character. I have been long used to other customs, and do not greatly approve these. I shall labour, as far as relates to myself, to break through them, but rather by complaisance and insinuation than by appearing to set the usage of England in opposition to that of Russia. A foreigner, to pass his time agreeably, must suit himself to the country, and not attempt to suit the country to him.[9]

This last sentence could be employed as a maxim for diplomats and travellers of all stripes throughout history and marks Buckingham out as a natural Ambassador. The letter ends with the revelation that he harboured a secret admiration for Lady Anne, the wife of the 2nd Earl of Strafford (Horace Walpole declared her 'a vast beauty') who had recently fallen ill. "You have known, or guessed at many of my partialities, but that is one which I have ever most religiously kept to myself. Your sex in general find out these affections at least as soon as they happen, but I am firmly persuaded that she never guessed at mine. When you favour me with a line, let me know how she is, for I am by no means satisfy'd with the accounts sent me from England."[10] (Lady Anne recovered and lived another twenty-one years.)

There are myriad documents which describe the machinations of the Russian and British political participants at this time, their allegiances and fallings out; the intricacies and self interests of those involved and the tangled mesh of intrigues and deceptions that develop when countries attempt to make treaties with each other. At the Russian Court, Buckingham was vying for attention with diplomats from all over Europe clamouring for one favour or another. Simmering beneath the polite protocols, etiquette and formality, it was a bear pit.

Buckingham witnessed first hand the passionate relationship between Catherine and Gregory Orlov, her less than faithful lover, observing in his private notes,

> There are five brothers of the Orlovs, but the eldest declines taking a distinguished part, and the youngest, not more than nineteen years of age, is abroad. Gregory, the eldest of the remaining three, is the favourite of the Sovereign, and, as far as her distinction can make him, the first man in the Russian Empire. The wish of her heart is to see him great, that the approbation of the public may justify her partiality. He had no advantages of education, but, allowing for that, does not make a bad appearance in conversation upon common topics. He has lately awkwardly affected an air of stiffness and surliness, qualities by no means of his natural character. He neglects his person, smokes, hunts frequently, and is not so unobservant of the beauties he meets with as policy makes necessary and gratitude should enforce. It is asserted, but falsely, that the object to whom his whole attention should be dedicated is unmindful of transitory infidelities. One of those women who, without being handsome, are liked for their youth and we know not what, had for some time been distinguished by the Count. As she called herself my friend I joked with her upon the subject, she answered me I could not be ignorant of her passion for another man and her prudence must incline her to discourage Orlov; that lately, in the country, upon the Empress entering into the room where he was attempting to romp with her, she was a little confused, upon which the Empress came behind her and leaning upon her shoulder whispered, 'don't be embarrassed; I am convinced of your discretion and your regard for me. You need not fear of making me uneasy; on the contrary, I think myself obliged to you for your conduct.'

> Alexis, the next brother, is a giant in strength and figure (the least of these three brothers is six feet high). He speaks German, but no French, and, perhaps from feeling himself of less importance, is more sociable and of easier access than the elder.

> Feodor, the youngest, is the pride and ornament of the family. If a travelled lady was to describe his figure she would tell you that he had the features of the Apollo in the Belvedere with the strength and muscles of the Hercules Farnese. His address is easy and his manner engaging.[11]

As negotiations began in earnest Vice Chancellor Prince Galitzen brought up a treaty of commerce which had been delivered to Robert Keith but Buckingham objected in no uncertain terms to its content, telling Grenville that "it appeared to me merely calculated to take from the English every privilege and every advantage which the equity and policy of Russia had formerly allowed them, and at the same time, to overturn the most essential laws of our own commerce and navigation; that it was in effect driving a nation out of Russia who had every pretension to better usage, at a time too when they had the least reason to expect such a mortification."[12] Prince Galitzen asked for a statement in writing and Buckingham agreed to send extracts from the Board of Trade Report to further explain his concerns.

Whilst Buckingham had been travelling to Russia, George Montagu-Dunk, the 2nd Earl of Halifax who had been so briefly affianced to Mary Anne Drury, had been appointed Secretary of State for the Northern Department. This meant he was responsible for relations with the Netherlands, Scandinavia, Poland, the Holy Roman Empire and Russia. Buckingham told him, "I cannot omit this first opportunity of congratulating you on this fresh mark of his Majesty's favour and confidence."[13] Unfortunately another appointment had not worked out at all well. George Hobart was "extremely out of spirits and determined to ask leave to return to England. He has in every instance behaved as well to me as possible & would not now think of it without my approbation."[14] Buckingham asked his aunt to sound out Charles Hotham if he would replace George as his Secretary, as to have the company of his dear brother-in-law would be a great boon and solace.

Buckingham spent the remainder of the year attempting to keep talks of the Treaty of Commerce alive but as Bestuzhev,[15] Catherine's first appointed member of the Imperial Council was old and ailing, he occupied himself by keeping channels open via the Vice-Chancellor Prince Galitzin and by cultivating links with the Swedish Ambassador. He received instructions from King George to try to keep up a measure of civility with the Austrian Minister, and to live upon an easy and amicable footing with him. Mr Wroughton, the British Resident at Warsaw, but who was then visiting England apprised him that, "We have here daily reports of the little probability there is of the Empress of Russia keeping the reins for long. These reports are spread with so much industry that it must be by people very ill-intentioned to her prosperity."[16] Those at the Russian Court had no such doubts, as they firmly believed that Catherine's strength of character, the loyalty of the army and her growing political acumen would keep her in power.

Buckingham's natural charm and affability led him to please and befriend many at Court. The myriad desires and requests of so many Ambassadors from so many nations inevitably caused a degree of chaos but Buckingham swiftly learned to navigate his way skilfully through the diplomatic minefields. In Petersburg he and his entourage settled into a grand house on the banks of the Neva, large enough to host one hundred and fifty guests at dinner. This was a necessary extravagance which demonstrated the importance of the British Ambassador's position and was impressive enough for the purpose of throwing the many diplomatic soirees, balls and the like which he was obliged, and it must be also be said very happy, to host. Social life in general was lively, "There was a ball at Court on Saturday, and last night an Opera, which was extremely magnificent in every respect. It was given at the Empress's expense, and I should imagine there were not less than two thousand persons present. It is to be continued as soon as the mourning for the late Empress is over. It is Her Imperial Majesty's intention to make her Court as gay and as splendid as possible."[17]

In January 1763 Buckingham had his first encounter with Paul, Catherine's eight year old son and heir, "I had this morning my audience of the Grand Duke. I made my compliment to him in French which he answered in the same language. His address and manner are agreeable and engaging and his deportment is very extraordinary, considering how very young he is."[18] Initially somewhat bemused by the Empress's lack of affection for Paul, Buckingham subsequently learned that any normal relationship between mother and son had been thwarted literally from the day he was born. The Empress Elizabeth had whisked baby Paul away from the birthing chamber and taken the role of mother, molly-coddling the boy dreadfully, and she deliberately ensured that there was little or no contact with Catherine throughout his crucial formative years. Buckingham noted that Paul was said to have a great deal of the air and something of the disposition of the late Emperor, particularly in that he was remarkably fearful. That the boy did indeed resemble the Empress's late husband unfortunately served as a strong disincentive for her to care for him at all.

New Year's Day celebrations were opened by the Empress and the Great Duke and "at night there was a ball, the Empress afterwards danced with me and the evening concluded with a firework."[19] This event and many further extravagant balls and parties were held in Petersburg's sumptuous palaces, adorned as they were with the most beautiful, opulent decoration and exquisite treasures.

Relations with the Prussian minister were somewhat strained, as Buckingham related to Halifax,

> As I was carrying him in my coach from dinner at the Great Chancellor's to Court, he attacked me, without the least introduction, upon the conduct of the Court of England to his Master. He was pleased to say that the English were not contented with forsaking him, but were trying to prejudice his interests there. His manner of expressing himself is never very agreeable, and upon this occasion was less so than usual, so that to avoid improper warmth I cut the conversation short by telling him that England had no reason to be pleased with the King of Prussia's behaviour, but that it was a subject we had better not enter upon. I was sorry to decline a discussion in which the advantage of the argument is so clearly on the side of England, but from the style in which it began it would have been impossible to have carried it on with temper.[20]

Buckingham confessed irritably that his aquiline nose had been put out of joint by the Empress paying close attention to the French minister, Monsieur de Breteuil. The exceedingly handsome Frenchman was a rival diplomat who had the temerity to be seven years younger than Buckingham, who observed scathingly, "HIM (Her Imperial Majesty) has for some time past very greatly distinguished M. Breteuil upon which he seems to presume a great deal. He is lively and speaks his own language well, and I should hope it is rather that his conversation is entertaining than from any political reasons that she takes so much notice of him."[21] He took comfort from "a very good authority that the Empress and those she most confides in are determined to cultivate the friendship of England in preference to that of every other country, that our Treaty of Commerce will be entered upon as soon as the Carnival is over, and that the French propositions will not be in the least attended to."[22] He told of the ongoing disputes between Prussia and Austria and of his desire that the English Ambassador to King Frederick's Court be directed to give him intelligence to guide his conduct in Moscow.

Lady Suffolk was not forgotten and received this, dated 3 February 1763, written in the midst of an increasingly hectic social whirl. He had found that John Carmichael's warnings about great expenditure had been entirely accurate.

> The Carnival is now nearly at an end but as yet the hurry of pleasures increases daily. I had the honour of seeing the Empress at my house on Monday last. It was a bal masque for about one hundred and fifty persons and one hundred and six persons sat down to supper. I believe this is without exception the most expensive place in Europe, and at the same time where, to be on a tolerable footing, the greatest show is necessary. The Russians themselves have all their attendants and all their provisions, except wine, for nothing and nobody who has not been here can have any idea of the profusion of meat and game which appears upon their tables; they expect to see the same at the houses of foreigners, without considering the difference of the situation. We have now masquerades at Court or at some private house every night; a hot supper of three courses and a dessert at ten o'clock, and then minuets, country dances, and Polish dances till everybody stops from being no longer able to proceed. All the ladies about the Court are jaded to death, and out of fourteen maids of honour thirteen are lame. In a fortnight a great deal of bigotry will succeed this gay scene. In the Greek Church if you keep the appointed fasts rigidly, and cross yourself twenty times a day, you are a good Christian.[23]

Buckingham described to Halifax a Russian tragedy performed before the Empress in a magnificent hall fitted up with a stage, scenes, and all proper decorations. He deemed the French translation inaccurate but thought the sentiments and the dialogue would "do honour to any author in any country."[24] The principal role was taken by Countess Bruce, Catherine's long time companion and lady-in-waiting, who "acted the part with spirit, ease, and propriety which is seldom met with even amongst those who are bred to the stage."[25] He wrote of the Countess that "though more than thirty years of age, she is the first ornament of the circle at St Petersburg. She dresses well, dances tolerably, speaks French with fluency and elegance, has read a dozen plays … is not averse to gallantry, but discreet in her choice of those she favours."[26] After the play maids of honour and several of the first nobility performed dances, "I believe so many fine women were never seen upon any stage, and must add that few countries could produce them."[27] Buckingham professed himself amazed at the sheer elegance and magnificence of the evening and asserted that his written description could not do it justice, and added condescendingly "When we consider how very few years have elapsed since the politer acts were first introduced into this country, and how considerable a part of that time they have been but little cultivated, it will appear very extraordinary that a performance of this kind could have been planned and executed in a few weeks"[28] and noted that Voltaire's *Tragedy of Zara* was acted upon the same theatre two days before. The Bacchanalian festivities continued for another ten days until the beginning of Lent, a period the Greek Orthodox church took much more seriously than the Catholic. All entertainments ceased and restrictions were placed on all day to day activities. He painted a picture for Lady Suffolk,

> The Carnival is over. The virgins, wives and widows mourn. Mushrooms, pickled cucumbers, prayers, and priests, succeed to the active dance, the becoming dress, the genial banquet, and the gallant officers. Your good true Greek abstains for the first week of Lent from every earthly thing which innate sensuality disposes human frailty to delight in. The females suffer most. No ornament, not the faintest shade of red is allowed them; their roses all must fade. Nothing is left them to subsist on but faith, hope, and meditation upon pleasures past. I have not suffered myself to be absolutely carried away by the torrent, but have glided down the edge of the stream for company.[29]

Catherine's aim was to teach her subjects how to enjoy themselves in European fashion and Buckingham poetically observed "They are a little awkward at first, and tread the paths of refined pleasure with the same caution that the forest deer first enter an inexperienced pasture but they will graze in time."[30] His own efforts to assimilate into Russian life bore fruit when he and George were invited to balls and suppers attended by no other foreigners, "I only work to convince them that the English have at least as good ideas of society as the French, to acquire some knowledge of their manners and opinions, and to pass my own time here agreeably. In Lent I shall see little of them, and in the first week nothing at all, for they literally are obliged to shut themselves up with their priests, and to eat nothing but vegetables. Pleasure first, and now mortification has put an absolute stop to business, but I flatter myself that another week will set our negotiations in motion."[31]

Buckingham, who had been hopeful that Charles Hotham might join him in

Petersburg, was sorely disappointed when Lady Suffolk explained that, "his health, from the severity of the service he has undergone, obliges him to decline an offer he is at present unequal to undertake."[32] The Colonel's onerous war duties during the eight years he had been out of England had taken their toll.

The King of Poland's health at this time was also variable and rumours regularly circulated that he was at death's door. This occasioned much speculation as to whom his successor should, or would, be. King George sent instructions to Buckingham that "his Majesty must content himself by assuring the Empress, as your Lordship will accordingly do, of his very sincere inclination to promote, so far as may depend upon his influence, what may be most agreeable to the princess in the affairs of the Polish succession, and acting therein, when the case shall exist, in perfect concert with her."[33]

With treaty negotiations faltering in the face of obfuscations and delays Buckingham was reluctantly forced to the conclusion that he must resort to low methods to obtain the King's desired result, "It is, therefore, no small disappointment to find that perhaps it will be necessary for me to try by intrigue and underhand application to obtain that which in fact it is the interest of this country to grant."[34] His earlier high regard for Panin had dissipated and he now thought him to be "entirely in the French interest" and further noted that the Empress had enjoyed the carnival so much that she had taken her mind off business altogether and seemed far more interested in cavorting with Count Orlov. To add to the confusion, conflicting instructions arrived in cypher from London. Halifax advised him that "if a pure and simple renewal of the expired Treaty be all that can possibly be obtained, it ought not to be finally rejected. You will at the same time understand that this instruction is meant only for the last extremity, you must employ all the means in your power to pursue this commercial negotiation with all possible zeal and diligence."[35] This was swiftly followed by instructions to open negotiations for a Treaty of Alliance.

Buckingham reported that "Count Bestuzhev is better; he sent me word yesterday that it was not as yet time to think of the Treaty of Alliance, but that the Treaty of Commerce was in a very good way. He also desired me to be cautious of what I sent by post, as there was a man at their office who could decypher any cypher."[36] There followed extensive correspondence between Buckingham and Halifax which consistently repeated the frustrations inherent in not only attempting to negotiate with a country so haphazard in its dealings with foreign powers but also pointed up the inevitable time delay between their posts. Letters between the two men strayed in their journeys for weeks on end when even the usual length between posts was four weeks at best during winter. This in itself led to cross overs and misunderstandings which then necessarily took months to resolve. To compound matters Buckingham noted, "Uninformed nations, like ignorant men, are ever the most suspicious. The Russians imagine all foreigners, and more particularly the

English, have some hidden designs in all the propositions they offer."[37] By March the undignified but requisite foray into the practice of giving "presents" a euphemism for "inducements" or to put it more bluntly "bribes" had begun. Buckingham's first request was for permission to "make a compliment to Count Orlov" in the shape of a watch set with diamonds to the value of about five hundred pounds, which he "fancied would not make a bad effect." The second was for Alsufiow, a private secretary of the Empress,[38] who Buckingham believed had more information than any other person he had met in Russia, "I should wish to be empowered to offer him 1,000l."[39] The King approved both requests. Buckingham's problem thenceforth was knowing to whom and when it was best to offer these 'presents' as "I may not very possibly know who those persons are till a few days before the negotiation is entered upon, and such is the course of correspondence that it would be three months before I could know if I could make any offer to them or not."[40]

In April the French Ambassador M. Breteuil received his recall papers. Buckingham suspected that it was partly owing to the intrigues of the French Court that his own Treaty of Commerce had not yet been concluded, but this did not alter the fact that Breteuil's own mission to conclude a similar treaty between Russia and France had failed despite France paying "a very high price" to influence Gregory Orlov. Buckingham's jealousy of the French minister proved unfounded as Catherine's attitude of benevolence and courtesy towards Breteuil had been coloured by her knowledge of many dubious actions of other French agents in Constantinople, Warsaw and Stockholm. As the Frenchman left for his next appointment as Ambassador to Sweden her parting words to him were unequivocal, "Vous serez mon ennemi a Stockholm. Si votre ministere est tel que vous me le depeignez sa franchise est une fausette de plus."[41] (You will be my enemy in Stockholm. The ministry there will be just another fake.)

Buckingham always found time to compose letters home, writing as often to Mary Anne as to his aunt (but only a handful to his wife have come to light). To Lady Suffolk he mentioned his aquiline nose, which he was always first to make fun of,

> Some Men pique themselves upon the Qualitys of their Mind, Upon their Wit, their Sound Judgement, a general knowledge of Polite Learning, or a profound penetration into abstract Sciences. Some, upon those of the body that they are Strong, active, or Indefatigable. Some upon their talents, Musick, Dancing, Oratory & c. Some upon their Personal appearances, that General elegant disposition of all the parts which constitutes a beautiful whole. Some upon their Limbs, a well turn'd Leg, a foot without a fault, a delicate Hand. Others upon particular features, amongst which your affectionate Nephew prided himself, in his nose. I had a Nose, but Alas the Biting Frost has nip't it & his Glory's are now no more. Lest this makes you too unhappy, let me add, that there is a possibility of recovering it in the Spring. You had better not mention this

to Lady Buckingham, but if you must I am sure your good nature will break it to her by degrees.[42]

Buckingham's continued efforts to befriend those in his host country began to be rewarded, "My situation here grows every day more agreeable as the Russians begin to treat me less upon the footing of a Stranger than they treat the other Foreigners."[43] He often rode out with the Empress and sent to England for some grey horses, which were then en vogue, to present to her. "HIM permitted me to attend her at the Court Menage, & I had the honor of seeing her Ride; she was dressed in Men's Cloaths & it really is not flattering to say that few Men ride better." After complaining that his letters were now being sent via Sweden and therefore taking two weeks longer than they should, he mentioned that "George is better in both health and spirits than he was but it principally arises from his living in hourly expectation of His Majesty's permission to return to England" adding that "the River has the appearance of a Broad street & on Sunday is cover'd with thousands of people who resort there to see Sledge Races & Boxing Matches" and declared himself amazed that Mary Anne had been "pleased to depreciate the valuable presents I sent you & quotes Mr Vorontsov's Authority. I shall not soon be guilty of such another act of Extravagance."[44] Count Vorontsov had been sent by Peter III as Plenipotentiary Minister to London and the remarks alluded to were only the seeds of his mischief making. His interference in more important matters would be amplified a hundredfold in the not too distant future.

Notes

1. Britain changed from the Julian to the Gregorian calendar in 1752, but Russia did not follow suit until 1918; the dates Buckingham uses are Gregorian 'N.S.' (New Style), eleven days ahead of the Julian.
2. *Despatches and Correspondence ...*, Vol.1, p.73-75.
3. Ibid. p.75-76.
4. Ibid. p.77.
5. Ibid. p.80.
6. Ibid. p.84-85.
7. Paul was her son by either her late husband Peter III or her first lover Sergei Saltykov. It is often claimed that Saltykov was the more likely father since Peter had shown next no interest in his wife, but the boy grew up to have Peter's looks, eccentric mannerisms and shared his extreme passion for soldiering.
8. *Despatches and Correspondence ...*, Vol.1, p.98.
9. Ibid. p.88.
10. Ibid.
11. Ibid. p.204 From 'Russian Memoranda'.
12. Ibid. p.89.
13. Ibid. p.89.
14. *Reports of the manuscripts of the Marquess of Lothian* p.171.
15. Of Count Bestuzhev Buckingham wrote, *'He was originally a man of lively parts, and long experience has given him a general knowledge of the affairs of Europe. Though debauched,*

profligate, deceitful, and interested to excess, the vanity of transmitting his name to posterity is his ruling passion. This induced him to risk a fresh disgrace in his last moments and to waste the dregs of his life in feebly struggling for a situation which his mind and body are too much enervated to fill. Ever a creature of the House of Austria, his professed system has been to check the power of France. Yet, blind to the late political revolution and to those variations in the connections of the European Powers which entirely change their views and make the history of the last hundred years as little instructive to the negotiations of (today) as Livy or Tacitus, he perseveres in the same notion with that obstinacy and that aversion to conviction which has too often characterised the latter days of abler heads than his. He has been esteemed and always professes himself a friend of England, but when he found our views were no longer subservient to the House of Austria, the moment that union of interests ceased, all former professions were forgot, and every obligation that our liberality showered upon him was cancelled.'

16. *Despatches and Correspondence ...*, Vol 1, p.196.
17. Ibid. p.111.
18. Ibid. p.196-197.
19. Ibid. p.198.
20. Ibid.
21. Ibid. p.214.
22. Ibid. p.202.
23. Ibid. p.214-215.
24. Ibid. p.218.
25. Ibid.
26. Ibid. p.224 from 'Russian Memoranda'.
27. Ibid. p.221.
28. Ibid. p.221.
29. Ibid. P.223.
30. Ibid. p.223.
31. Ibid. p.233.
32. *Letters to and from Henrietta ...*, Vol. 2, p. 271.
33. *Despatches and Correspondence ...*, Vol 1, p.221.
34. Ibid. p.226.
35. Ibid. p.232.
36. *Despatches and Correspondence ...*, Vol 2, p.11.
37. Ibid. p.13.
38. Buckingham later revised his opinion of Alsufiow in his 'Russian Memoranda'—'a man of an easy address and a polite scholar. Latin and most of the modern languages are familiar to him; a happy memory and a judicious taste place his conversation in the strongest light and make it appear more extensive that perhaps it might be found upon a nice examination. The table is his first passion, women the second, affluence sufficient lavishly to indulge them, his third. Ambition brings up the rear. When pressed his application is infinite, but, as his rage for pleasures is too decided for him not to force his constitution to the last possibility of enjoyment, already gouty, corpulent, and unwieldy, it is not to be expected that he can long maintain any degree of activity of consequence.'
39. *Despatches and Correspondence ...*, Vol 2, p.15.
40. Ibid. p.22.
41. Ibid. p.32.

42. NRO MC3/285 Letter 52.
43. NRO MC 3/284 Letter 53.
44. NRO MC 3/284 Letter 53.

Dances and Disappointments

After the long and to him tortuous winter George Hobart's longing for England had grown into quiet desperation but he did not have to wait much longer to return to the arms of Albinia, his wife of five years. Doubtless he would omit confessing to her the many infidelities he had consoled himself with in Russia but Buckingham let the cat out of the bag to Lady Suffolk in what he jocularly termed one of "his Rhapsodys" from Moscow,

> Before this letter is finished George will be set out, his Carriages & Horses are nearly ready, at this moment he embraces his Wife in thought & Gallops an imaginary Horse upon a visionary England. My Uxorious Chaplain returns with my Uxorious Brother. I hope Erskine (the Chaplain) has not as much to confess to his Wife, as George, ever with an indifferent memory, could tell to his. Many of his sins have been lodged at my door, but now they are removed I shall have at least the Comfort to think that my virtue will be vindicated.[1] I hear every moment of the disasters which attend George in his hasty journey to Petersburg, by all accounts his person has never been in any danger but his Apparel & so forth have been considerably injured.[2]

He apologised to Lady Suffolk that as his letters to her must be matched with a letter to Mary Anne, "This makes me a worse Correspondent to both than if I wrote alternately, for the same materials which might compose one tolerable letter will make but an Indifferent figure when drawn out into two."[3] He enclosed a Silver Medal of the Empress which was "very like her & finely executed, the air of the face is, in my opinion, rather older than hers."[4] (The medal was later delivered to King George via Lord Halifax.) At Court Lent continued so Buckingham had very little to report, "I have no letters to acknowledge, nothing to rejoice in, nothing to be sorry for, no event to Communicate, No Comet, No Monster, No Earthquake."[5]

Sir Charles Hotham, who had been obliged to decline the post of Buckingham's Secretary on account of ill health, was appointed instead as a Groom of the Bedchamber in the Royal Household, an altogether less onerous position. He was also, with Buckingham's assistance, elected as MP for St Ives in a by-election. This cost Buckingham £1,175 even though his candidate was returned unopposed and the expenditure ironically included payments ('presents') of 7 guineas each to 124 people. Buckingham decided that if he couldn't have Charles Hotham as his secretary then he would "insinuate & desire that nobody may be sent at all."[6] In Parliament, Lord Bute resigned as Prime Minister and on 16 April Buckingham's old friend George Grenville took his place.

In London Buckingham's erstwhile fiancee the redoubtable and determined

Miss Harriott Pitt succeeded in her ambition to marry into a higher echelon when in November 1962 she married Brownlow Bertie, the future 5th Duke of Ancaster and Kesteven. But, having been married for only five months, she ultimately failed in her ambition to become a Duchess when she died just a month short of her eighteenth birthday on 23 April 1763. Buckingham's reaction to this news is unrecorded but presumably it gave him pause for thought.

On 6 May 1763 his friend Lady Mary Molesworth died in a London house fire together with her brother Commander Arthur Ussher and two of her six children. This caused Buckingham to ruminate mournfully, "Life in general is a trifle, half of those who covet it, who grasp it most, can scarcely tell you why, but an amiable mother, with beautiful, engaging children, whose merit promised them many agreeable days, cut off at once— the idea is shocking, even to me, who do not think existence of very great importance."[7]

John Wilkes Esq.

Drawn from the Life and Etch'd in Aquaforth by W.R.ᵐ Hogarth.

"John Wilkes Esq.", a satirical engraving by William Hogarth, who shows him with a demonic-looking wig, crossed eyes, and two editions of his The North Briton: Numbers 17 and the famous 45 where he attacked George III's speech endorsing the Paris Peace Treaty.

Buckingham was concerned for King George who had been placed in a difficult position over the scandalous libel case of John Wilkes. A notorious libertine with a skewed lantern jaw and squinty eyes, Wilkes was an MP who anonymously published a newspaper called 'North Briton' that had lampooned Prime Minister Lord Bute as an enemy of English liberty. 'North Briton' was how Scotland was termed by the English, and Lord Bute was a Scot who had written the King's Speech in which he endorsed the Paris Peace Treaty (the Seven Years' War had ended with the French ceding Canada to Britain). Wilkes was highly critical of the speech and George III, personally insulted by the article, ordered his arrest. Lady Suffolk, realising how keenly her nephew felt the remoteness of his posting, gently chided him,

> What answer can Lady Suffolk make to those constant complaints of Lord Buckingham, *that he knows nothing of what passes in England* ? She is not

conscious that any thing *has*, in which he had a personal concern, that she has not given him a hint of it, before it was publicly known: and how to write at once prudently and minutely on those great events, and what has been consequent upon them, is much beyond her capacity."[8]

Sad and worrying news followed, "Lord Buckingham's former passions go off very quickly: poor Lady Northampton[9] is dead at Naples, and it is much feared Lord Northampton is by this time dead at Venice; and they are now carrying Lord Brownlow Bertie[10] to see what the air of France will do for him. Lady Buckingham has given Lady Suffolk great uneasiness: she did not think her well; and Lord Buckingham knows she is not apt to take care of herself; but by a little art she has been brought to drink asses milk, and to follow some other directions, by the use of which she is now much better." Henrietta reassured Buckingham that Mary Anne would be safe under her care, adding,

> Lady Harriet Hobart is a very fine child, very healthy, forward on her feet, and takes great pains to be so with her tongue. Miss Hotham is vastly pleased with Lord Buckingham's taking constant notice of her; and really seems grateful for, as well as vain of it. Mr Hobart is now expected every day; by accounts from Berlin his illness was no trifling affair. All Lord Buckingham's public and private friends, not mentioned, are well. God bless and preserve him is most sincerely wished by his affectionate old aunt.[11]

Lords Halifax and Buckingham exchanged dozens of letters almost solely concerned with the increasingly tortuous and convoluted negotiations. Halifax stressed,

> The business is of too great consequence to bear any longer delay, and I must therefore in his Majesty's name insist with your Lordship that not one moment that can be employed in so material a negotiation may be lost, and that you send me constant accounts from post to post, for the King's information, of every step which you shall take in it, and of all that shall pass between the Imperial Court and yourself upon the subject of both these capital transactions."[12]

To which Buckingham replied, "Your Lordship must already have traced in several of my letters the disagreeable, distracted situation of the affairs of this country. The foreign ministers supped with me last night. We were all questioning one another, each man doubtful of his own information, yet every one agreeing that we ought to be prepared for any event."[13] In July Buckingham related a maddening conversation, "The Prussian minister wished me joy, as he said he had been informed I was to sign very soon. I answered him that it was very true that high hopes had been given me that this Court would very soon enter into the consideration of the renewal of the Treaty of Commence. He explained to me he meant the conclusion of the Treaty of Alliance, to which I replied that I knew nothing of it."[14]

He described the Russian weather to his aunt,

> The Empress made her Public entry on Saturday last, Fireworks were play'd off upon the River in consequence, they were very fine, but as it is now light here during the whole twenty four hours, it greatly took off their effect. The weather has been so sultry for this past Fortnight as to produce that state of relaxation which puts everybody out of humor & indeed disqualify them for every sort of enjoyment but that of drinking cool liquors & swallowing quantity's of Ice. One might imagine now that it would ne'er be cold again, but probably within six weeks we shall have convincing proof of the contrary.

George Grenville by William Hoare (Prime Minister from May to October 1762).

He continued mysteriously, "I am concerned with three worthy gentlemen whose names all begin with an H: who are all Hectick, all Happy in the approbation of fine Women & all Handsome, except George, who tho' he is in possession of an agreeable little figure, does not quite arrive at the beautiful" and ended in philosophical vein, "Here I am & must now expect to remain till another Summer. What is to be next I know not, let it come in its own good day."[15]

George Grenville had not forgotten his friend and wrote from Downing Street, "Tho' the constant scenes of busyness which I have been engaged in for some time passed have scarcely allowed me to perform the common offices of civility to my friends, yet I trust they know me too well to believe that I can be wanting in those of friendship. Many changes have happened in my own situation and that of the public since we parted, but none can happen in my sincere regard for you or in my desire to express it more effectually than by the assurances contained in a letter." Grenville assured him that his brother George had at last arrived home and had quickly recovered from his illness, and that, "As you seem not to wish to have any body appointed Secretary in the room of Mr Hobart, I may assure you that no body will, at least for the present."[16] George Hobart's future included a desultory attempt at being Whig MP for St Ives and Bere Alston, but his true passion lay in operatic theatre. His wife Albinia's main occupation however was gambling

The Lofs of the FARO·BANK ; or The Rook's Pigeon'd — When Greek meets Greek, then comes the tug of war!

George Hobart enters from a strongroom on the left and tells his wife Albinia, who is playing the card game faro with her cronies, that her gambling bank has been stolen. James Gillray.

and the cartoonists had a field day portraying her as a jewel encrusted, vastly overweight profligate. Horace Walpole observed that, "Mrs Hobart, clad in gauze and spangles so that she looked like a spangled pudding, performed admirably"[17] and when she grew even larger one observer was so astonished at her agility he said that "he was sure she must be hollow." Albinia was magnificently unrepentant of her behaviour, and their long marriage, in spite of George allegedly keeping many mistresses over the years, produced four sons and four daughters.

In August 1763 Buckingham made a request to Halifax for his recall, "I must entreat the favour of your Lordship to lay me at his Majesty's feet, and to express my earnest request that he would be graciously pleased to recall me the next spring (if it should be his pleasure that I should remain here until that time) as my family affairs were left greatly unsettled at my departure from England. I flatter myself that before that time both the treaties will be concluded in some degree to his Majesty's satisfaction."[18] The expression "family affairs were left greatly unsettled" was a diplomatic euphemism employed to cover other reasons for wishing to return home, in this case perhaps a dawning realisation of the futility of the task assigned him. The negotiations he had optimistically hoped would be concluded by spring ground slowly on. The Empress frequently indicated that the Treaty was at the top of her list, "HIM mentioned to me on Sunday evening that I had no reason to be uneasy about the conclusion of the Treaty of Alliance, as it was a point she was absolutely determined upon, and that the draught was at that time upon her table, and she would give it an immediate consideration."[19] These and many other reassurances from Ministers transpired to be false hopes as copious amendments and yet more unreasonable demands were made. Buckingham wrote despondently,

> (Most secret.) The plan for a Treaty of Alliance was at length delivered to me this afternoon. It is a very sensible mortification to me to observe that every alteration is made in favour of this country, without the least reciprocity for England. The separate Article is the most extraordinary of all, as it puts off the entering into the consideration of the Treaty of Commerce till the conclusion of the Treaty of Alliance, notwithstanding their repeated assurances that they would give it an immediate consideration. I have so often complained of their delays that I could say nothing new upon the subject.[20]

On the same day he wrote another missive to Halifax marked "separately and most secret" expressing deeper concern, "There is at present no minister, nor is there any prospect of any persons being placed in that situation. Every little department has a nominal head, but little is done in any of them."[21] Although there were tantalising glimmers of hope, "I was a few days ago with M Panin, who unexpectedly entered into conversation with me upon the Treaty of Alliance. He said he was glad it was under consideration, assured me that her Imperial Majesty set the highest value upon the friendship of the King of Great Britain, and that no one was more fully convinced of the common utility of the connection between England and Russia than himself"[22] Buckingham offered an explanation for the constant postponements, "Many disagreeable delays I have experienced, but some allowance must be made for the first year of a new reign, a distracted empire, and the particular situation of the Sovereign. There is no minister; Count Orlov is an all-powerful favourite, and Bestuzhev and Panin are principally consulted by her Imperial Majesty upon foreign affairs. Bestuzhev is very infirm, and his abilities visibly fail him."[23] The beautiful Countess Bruce was considered to be in the first rank, "She was in the Empress's confidence when she was Grand Duchess at the time Count Poniatovski was here and she is now connected with Major-General Orlov."[24] Buckingham observed that the Empress's life was a widely contrasting "mixture of trifling amusement and intense application to business."[25]

To write to his aunt was a welcome distraction from the unremitting frustrations of politics and his tone veered from the introspective, "I sometimes am a little deficient in faith upon matters of Religion, and more frequently of patience (or endurance, shall I call it?) in the affairs of this world; we must correct ourselves, we must try to amend even constitutional errors—I was born with a disposition to doubt and to fret —original punishment for any sins I could probably commit"[26] to the light hearted, "Lady Buckingham informs me that Lady Dorothy has repatriated, and has retired into the North, loaded with recipes for to make marmalade, White Pot, Tandy, Wet-your-whistles, Merry Downs, Firmity and Almanzanis."[27]

The gift of handsome greys Buckingham had sent to England for arrived,

> The Empress has most graciously received two English horses which she had permitted me to send for; when she bestrides one of these English horses with a French feather in her hat she carries the feather, but the Horse carries her. Which will have the greatest influence, horse or feather, the carrier or the carried? Answer, for you know your sex. Perhaps you may wish to know my opinion and to prevent your wishes, tho' it is treating a political point, I will say that in general I should give it for the feather, but in this instance I hope and believe the horse will win.[28]

The merry-go-round of balls, dinners and dances continued at a relentless pace and although his was a robust constitution, even he occasionally found it exhausting,

> I find myself so much fatigued this morning with dancing last night with the maids of Honour, that it is with difficulty I can undergo the fatigue of writing. Is not this very much the stile an Ambassador should write in? But you must know that here the most venerable personages dance, that in Russia it would not appear extraordinary if Lord Ligonier led up a Polish dance, and Lord Henley and Lord Hardwicke quivered in their fantastic toe to the tune of 'Buttered Pease'. The youth Buckingham however did not dance yesterday to fatigue him, but as amusements are rare, he seizes all that offer, and perhaps it might be better for his friends and for himself if he danced more and wrote less.[29]

In 1763 Lord Ligonier was eighty-three, Lord Henley was in his sixties, Lord Hardwicke seventy-two and "the youth Buckingham" a mere stripling of forty.

Notes

1. NRO MC 3/284 Buckinghamshire papers Letter 54.
2. NRO MC 3/284 Letter 55.
3. Ibid.
4. Ibid.
5. Ibid.
6. NRO MC 3/284 Letter 54.
7. NRO MC 3/284 Letter 56.
8. *Letters to and from Henrietta ...*, Vol. 2, p. 274.
9. Another of Buckingham's 'former passions', Lady Northampton was born Lady Anne Somerset, daughter of the 4th Duke of Beaufort. She died in May 1763 about the time that her husband made his public entry as Ambassador at Venice. Lord Northampton did indeed die on his return homeward in October, 1763.
10. Brownlow Bertie married again seven years later.
11. *Letters to and from Henrietta ...*, Vol. 2, p. 274.
12. *Despatches and Correspondence ...*, Vol. 2, p.41.

13. Ibid.
14. Ibid. p.50.
15. NRO MC 3/284 Letter 57.
16. *Report on the Manuscripts of the Marquess of Lothian*, p.246.
17. *Horace Walpole's Correspondence*, Vol. 32, p.111.
18. *Despatches and Correspondence ...*, Vol. 2, p.52.
19. Ibid. p.56.
20. Ibid. p.59.
21. Ibid. p.56.
22. Ibid. p.63.
23. Ibid. p.64.
24. Ibid. p.57.
25. Ibid. p.57.
26. *Report on the Manuscripts of the Marquess of Lothian*, p.175.
27. Ibid. p.176.
28. *Report on the Manuscripts of the Marquess of Lothian*, p.176.
29. Ibid. P. 176-177.

Deep Water

"Nothing new here, but bad accounts from Russia. I think our friend the Earl of Bucks has spoiled our affairs at that Court, as Sir Charles Williams did some years ago; with less excuse, as the other could at least plead a very good one for acting like a madman."[1] Thus wrote Lord Charles Egremont, a former Secretary of State for the Southern Department[2] to his brother-in-law George Grenville in August 1763. Buckingham had fallen foul of the unwritten rule that whereas it was widely expected that 'favours' should be offered and accepted, it was absolutely not done to record such transactions.

In January the Great Chancellor Michael Vorontsov had told Buckingham that the capture by English privateers of the 'Christine Elizabeth', a Russian ship which contained valuable items en route to him from France, had caused him to suffer great losses. These privateers owned armed ships which held government commissions authorised for use in war. Hinting that he was greatly in debt as a result, Vorontsov left papers with Buckingham in which he claimed losses that amounted to a value of £2,000. Buckingham calculated the items totalled no more than £1,500 but recommended to Halifax that it would be looked upon as a very great obligation if His Majesty would order him to honour the payment. At the same time he expressed the Chancellor's gratitude to the King for the kind reception given to his nephew Alexander at the English Court.[3] In April Halifax ordered Buckingham to award the Chancellor £2,000 on the understanding that he would work towards a successful outcome for the Treaty negotiations, and on the condition that "his Majesty will expect to be no more troubled with these applications for redress of losses pretended to have been suffered from English privateers during the war." In May the Great Chancellor brought up the subject of privateers once again, this time lamenting his loss of some fine tapestries, leading Buckingham to believe that the anticipation of hard cash had "greatly cured him of his partiality to the French interest."[4] However, hopes that the Great Chancellor would accelerate a conclusion to the Treaty negotiations faded when the Empress promoted Panin and gave Vorontsov permission to resign and leave Court in August. Buckingham asked Halifax for new instructions regarding the £2,000 payment as Vorontsov was not now likely

Count Mikhail Illarionovich Vorontsov.

to be directly involved. In July Buckingham, in an uncharacteristic fit of pique, wrote a private letter to the Great Chancellor, complaining freely about the lack of progress of the Treaty, to which Vorontsov professed himself highly offended at the condition attached to the payment of his demand, going so far as to state that he would refuse the money. Halifax told Buckingham, "it is his Majesty's pleasure that you should still give him the £2,000 though upon the same condition, that the King should be no more troubled with applications relative to captures supposed to have been made during the war"[5] adding that credit would be given to Vorontsov for his good intentions and favourable assistance upon future occasions, even though he would not be involved at the conclusion of the Treaty. In August the repercussions of Buckingham's rash letter to Vorontsov came home to roost with a remonstrance from Halifax,

> I must not be silent to your Lordship of the surprise his Majesty expressed at the unguarded and indelicate manner in which you had proposed terms to the Chancellor, which it was not possible for him to accept or even to keep secret without putting his honour and safety into your Lordship's custody. The favour his Majesty declared himself willing to show him with regard to the losses he has suffered by English privateers should have been delicately managed in private confidence. The Empress has complained in the strongest terms of the insult put on her servant, and the Chancellor has as strongly expressed his resentment at an attack made on his honour.

Buckingham was both embarrassed and contrite,

> the concern I have felt at my own imprudence and the very disagreeable consequences of it could not have easily received any addition; during the whole of that time I have been exposed to the reproaches of self-conviction, the worst of all reproaches of a feeling mind. Caution of what is trusted to paper is so known and necessary a rule in private, and greatly more in public, transactions that it were vain to attempt to excuse any indiscretion; let me, however, be permitted to offer some little (defence) in mitigation of it. I had heard so many reports circulated tending to prejudice this Government against the English traders that I wished in some degree to prevent their effect, to use every means which could contribute to hasten the conclusion of the Treaty of Commerce. I had called upon the Chancellor eight times in ten days and had never seen him; hurried and mortified, I wrote that unfortunate letter which I cannot help thinking he has made a most ungenerous use of.[6]

Buckingham, having been assured by the Chancellor that all their transactions were confidential, felt betrayed and had rather naively believed he "seemed to wish to make me, and indeed to consider me, as his friend." Halifax's tone softened, reporting that the King was "well pleased that you had since dined with the Chancellor who had acquainted your Lordship by the Empress's command that she had ordered the old Treaty of Alliance to be drawn out for her consideration, and that she would appoint the Chancellor and Vice-Chancellor to go through it with you article by article till clear." He stressed that any alterations be sent to England rather than be authorised solely by Buckingham and assured him "it is with great satisfaction I end my letter by acquainting your Lordship that Count Vorontsov, who was with me at Mr Grenville's in Buckinghamshire when he received his letter the day before yesterday from the Chancellor, expressed himself wholly satisfied and declared to me the Chancellor's wishes that no further notice should be taken of what had passed between you."[7] The Count Vorontsov referred to was the Chancellor's young and ambitious nephew Alexander. Lord Egremont's comparison of Buckingham with Hanbury Williams, whose syphilitic madness had driven him to suicide, was rather an over reaction to what was, after all, a rare misstep.

Buckingham sympathised with Halifax who was following the negotiations from a great distance, "you will certainly make some allowance for the many anxious moments of the minister who is the channel of such correspondence, and who can have no wish but to merit his Majesty's approbation, though at present he has a most melancholy prospect of success."[8] Meanwhile, a suspicion was growing in Buckingham's mind of the reason for the increased delays to the post, which he confided to Mr Mitchell, "I am informed that there is a person at Berlin who makes a constant practice of entertaining, and consequently delaying, all the English couriers who pass that way."

By the end of August Buckingham's dogged persistence succeeded at last in prising a draft Treaty of Alliance from the Russian ministers but reading it caused him the utmost dismay. One new and crucial condition insisted upon by Russia was that war with Turkey would not be specifically excluded. This meant that if the Ottoman Empire were to attack the Empress, Britain would be obligated to come to Russia's aid. This stipulation was a major stumbling block and two other new and secret articles also caused serious concern. Firstly, that in any future vacancy for the Crown of Poland, Britain would work with Russia to secure the election of "a candidate most favourable to their mutual interests." This was diplomatic code meaning that Britain would be obliged to fund any such campaign. Furthermore, if military action became necessary in order to win such an election Britain would be contracted to pay 500,000 roubles towards Empress Catherine's costs. Secondly, an article asking for cooperation between Britain and Russia in Stockholm implied that similar demands would be made with respect to Sweden. In addition, the Turkish Clause was closely connected to the Polish situation. The central government of the Ottoman Empire, the Sublime Porte in Constantinople, viewed with suspicion the growth of Russian power in Poland, and French diplomats with their constant insinuations further enflamed their concerns. Catherine was fearful of the Ottoman Empire and the prospect of being forced to fight on two fronts simultaneously was a nightmare to contemplate. All in all, Buckingham declared he "hardly knew how to send such a proposition to His Majesty"[9] and when he did London agreed that the demands were utterly inadmissible. Just as matters reached this impasse Halifax left to take charge of the Southern Department of Foreign Affairs, in the place of Egremont who had died nine days after sending his letter to Grenville. Halifax's replacement was John Montagu, 4th Earl of Sandwich who wrote at once to Buckingham in the most friendly terms. He stipulated in intricate detail what was acceptable to the British Crown within the revised treaty, reassuring him that,

> I am extremely happy to open my correspondence with your Lordship by acquainting you with the high approbation his Majesty expressed of your dispatch. The King is particularly pleased with your great zeal and attention in procuring so many satisfactory informations upon points so important and essential. I am likewise to inform you that Count Vorontsov has been with me and mentioned in the strongest manner the Empress his Mistress's desire that everything upon the subject of your letter to the Chancellor might be totally forgot, and that her Imperial Majesty would be extremely concerned if that affair should make any impression here to your Lordship's disadvantage.[10]

In early October news of the death of the King of Poland spread rapidly throughout Europe. Lord Stormont immediately wrote to Buckingham from Vienna,

> I take the opportunity of sending your Lordship the earliest account of his Polish Majesty's sudden death. Nothing ever was more unexpected. He had been indisposed for a few days with a slight cold, but was well enough to go to Mass yesterday morning, and had appointed an opera for tomorrow. He had a fainting fit yesterday when he came from chapel, and died at five in the afternoon of a suffocation. I thought your Lordship would be glad to have the earliest intelligence of an event of such importance and so interesting for your Court.[11]

This event distracted the Empress's attention from almost every other matter, including the proposed Treaties with England and France. Catherine communicated to Frederic of Prussia that her former lover Count Poniatowski was her favoured candidate for the Polish Crown and he approved her choice. The French naturally enough angled for someone who would favour France. King George initially declined to engage with the Empress on the appointment of a successor to the Polish Crown and as a consequence of his stance, Buckingham found himself on the back foot with Catherine, "When I spoke to her of the Treaties she cut me short by saying it would now be her turn to press the conclusion of them (I suppose she meant upon her own terms). She then changed the conversation."[12]

Matters took a sinister turn when Panin requested funds from Britain that Buckingham, following the King's instructions, was unable to provide. Although the Russians had not withdrawn the alarming Turkish Clause they instead now offered

Buckingham the Alliance in return for British support in Poland and 500,000 roubles. Put bluntly, the Treaty was up for sale, but an insurmountable barrier was the inviolable principle entrenched in Britain's foreign policy that categorically no subsidies whatsoever in any circumstances could be paid during peacetime. Sandwich told Buckingham, "It is neither consistent with His Majesty's dignity, nor does the situation if his Kingdom requires that the King should purchase, or solicit, an Alliance in which the interests of Russia are at least as much connected as those of Great Britain" to which Buckingham replied flatly, "it seems evident that a refusal will prevent the Treaty of Alliance from being concluded upon the terms prescribed to me by your Lordship's instructions."[13]

Mr Mitchell's reply from Berlin eventually arrived in late October, assuring Buckingham that there "was not the least truth in the information you have had of a person here making a constant practice of entertaining and delaying all the couriers who pass this way."[14] Nevertheless, Buckingham's post continued to arrive much later than he would have wished.

Buckingham enquired of his aunt whom she favoured in the election of the King of Poland, "The liberties of that antient state cannot be in danger, as all the constables in the neighbourhood are hurrying together to preserve them. There is no surer way to prevent a Riot than by knocking those down first who might otherwise make it. The voters in Poland are rather more numerous than at St Ives, otherwise I am convinced that the Election is as like the other tho' in miniature as a Sprat is to a Herring."[15] Homesick for news from England he protested once again about "that chaos of truth and falsehood, which composes the English newspapers"[16] which so often misled their readers. Reminiscing about dramas on stage, rather than in Politics, he mused, "I shall always, were it only in gratitude for former amusements, interest myself with the Theatres Royal" continuing enigmatically, "But there is another theatre, other actors and other scenes nearly opening, an accurate description of which I am still more solicitous to receive. Is the season to begin with a Tragedy or a Comedy? If the former I hope the fifth act will be over before my return to England, and that I shall find all my friends laughing at the farce."[17] By "other theatre" he meant the Parliamentary session in November at which Lord Sandwich read out John Wilkes'[18] obscene parody of Pope's Essay on Man, entitled Essay on Woman. This was voted libellous together with edition No 45 of North Briton in which he had insulted the King's speech written by Lord Bute. After fighting a duel in Hyde Park with the MP Samuel Martin, who severely wounded him in the stomach, Wilkes fled to France accompanied by his beloved daughter Polly. In his absence he was found guilty of obscene and impious libel and when he failed to return was pronounced an outlaw for impeding royal justice.

Lady Suffolk heard a rumour that Buckingham's close friend Hans Stanley was to go to Holland as British Envoy. Stanley was a highly respected MP and a fellow member of the most convivial London Clubs. His outlook on occasion seemed jaded; he said if he had a son he would advise him to "Get into Parliament, make tiresome speeches; you will have great offers; do not accept them at first, then do: then make great provision for yourself and your family, and then call yourself an independent country gentleman"[19] but Lady Hervey, who knew him well, considered him "a very ingenious, sensible, knowing, conversable and, what is still better, a worthy, honest, valuable man. He has books which you will like to read; he has acquaintance with whom you will like to converse; and he himself you will like the best of all."[20] William Pitt agreed, saying Stanley was filled with spirit, sense, and cleverness, but others thought him humourless and excessively vain. The rumour that Lady Suffolk heard about Holland proved false because Grenville instead persuaded Stanley to take a position in London. In March, at a time when Stanley was occupied in negotiating the peace with France, Buckingham fondly wrote,

> I may regret my not hearing from you, lament your silence and expect a letter from you with an anxious degree of impatience. But believe me no delay of that sort can ever alter my feelings for my friend, or make me doubt of his partiality for me. Were you at Moscow you would prefer the Empress to every woman in the country, take her for all in all, tho' many of them are handsome and some very agreeable. In some of the Russian houses I am received not quite upon the footing of a stranger, but in every country it is a misfortune not to speak the language. You mention nothing of the Club, yet let me hope that it flourishes and that the Evergreens vegetate around the genial Board. Remind them of their old Servant, whose next wish to that primary consideration of renewing the sacramental engagements on Friday night is to find himself with them on Saturday.[21]

Another envoy however, the young Russian Count Alexander Vorontsov, could not be counted amongst Buckingham's friends. The younger brother of Elizabeth, the mistress of Peter III, and of Princess Dashkova, he was also the Great Chancellor's nephew. He began his career at fifteen years old in the Izmailovsky Guards after which his uncle sent him to Strasburg, Paris and Madrid to "learn diplomacy." A precocious young man, by nineteen he had been appointed Russia's Charge d'Affaires in Vienna and in 1761 when he was just twenty one the Emperor sent him as his Minister Plenipotentiary to London.

Count Alexander Vorontsov by Johann Schmidt.

Why Vorontsov had made disparaging

remarks about the gifts Buckingham sent to Mary Anne is not clear but he soon became a more sinister and disruptive presence, manipulating a strategically important Court whilst in thrall to the Prussian Court of Frederic II. While Buckingham was consistently reassured by the Great Chancellor, by Panin and indeed by the Empress herself that she was teetering on the verge of signature, Vorontsov was busily sending negative messages back to the Russian Court which sabotaged such an outcome. The talks dragged on inconclusively with Buckingham unaware that his dogged attempts to conclude the Treaties were being routinely scuppered in London. The knotty question of who would succeed to the Polish Crown rumbled on in tandem with the negotiations and as King George forebore to weigh in until Catherine publicly named her choice this, together with the King's refusal to furnish her with the requested 500,000 roubles, was an insurmountable obstacle to Buckingham fulfilling his mission. By the autumn nothing had changed but at least the embarrassment of the indiscreet letter had been forgiven and forgotten. The Count correctly predicted that as a consequence of his understanding and forgiving stance Buckingham would be grateful to him but behind the scenes the Count's dispatches violently opposed any alliance between England and Russia. Vorontsov covertly reported back to Russia that "England never made a political alliance but in accordance with the interests of her trade" that "the English Ministry were much more occupied in supporting an election of an MP for Essex than in any events upon the Continent" and further fuelled matters by saying "the instability of the Government made an alliance unadvisable—they could not be depended upon to keep faith; it was too much against their interests."[22]

To make matters worse Frederic II himself was actively encouraging Vorontsov's dissent. This was proved beyond doubt in a letter from Frederic to the Prussian Ambassador Michell in London, "When you have occasion you will adroitly feed the Count Vorontsov's dissatisfaction and even embitter him against the (English) ministries. You must not neglect to do so."[23] But Vorontsov's behaviour in London directly opposed his own Court's wishes and winter brought the announcement of his imminent removal from London. Yet even now Buckingham was reluctant to condemn him. In December he defended the Count to Sandwich,

> I told him (Panin) that in the course of my correspondence I had never
> met with any complaint of M Vorontsov's behaviour; and that all my
> private letters mentioned him as a very amiable young man who had acted
> with too much vivacity without instructions from his Court. Panin said he
> hoped the English ministry would not mortify him so far as to discover
> that they were acquainted with the cause of his recall, and that they would
> make his disgrace as light to him as possible.[24]

But Lord Sandwich informed Buckingham that the Count's duplicity was beyond doubt "for he not only enters in the cabals and factions of this country, but communicates in his capacity as minister with those who are most opposed to measures and are most active in endeavouring to obstruct the King's servants in the execution of their respective duties."[25] Maintaining that Vorontsov's actions worked against any kind of union between England and Russia he sternly warned Buckingham to be on his guard. The Count was now mired in conspiracy with undesirable people,

> It appears that the Russian minister in London, from too much zeal to serve his Court, has embarked himself in an improper affair, and it is probable that he will be the dupe of it himself, as the people he had engaged are of too volatile a disposition and of too bad characters in general to be worth receiving in any country having neither trade nor art to set up, and being mostly common adventurers, without even an industrious inclination, whom the late circumstances of Europe had sent a-travelling, and who, not finding nor deserving employment in England, embraced any scheme or proposal which could give them an immediate and momentary subsistence.[26]

Buckingham finally joined with the wider belief that Vorontsov had been undermining his mission and Sandwich, relieved that he had at last seen the light, wrote in January 1764, "how little Count Vorontsov deserves the kind and generous offers you used in his favour" and ventured that it would mean releasing the particulars "in order to undeceive the Russian ministers and to set objects before them in their true light, which is impossible for them to have seen through the false colouring which I take for granted Count Vorontsov has thrown upon them."[27]

In the meantime, Vorontsov remained in London diligently feeding untruths back to Russia, constantly repeating that Britain was so desperate for a Treaty of Alliance it would accept any terms offered. Buckingham still seemed disinclined to place all of the blame on Vorontsov whom he thought had been led astray by unidentified nefarious persons, but it must also be taken into account that he was treading a very fine diplomatic line and understandably reluctant to declare as an enemy a nephew of the former Great Chancellor.

On 14 February Buckingham and Sandwich wrote letters which crossed each other. Buckingham's said he was convinced that it was the Vice-Chancellor who wished to misinform his Court that England would accept almost any terms and that Count Vorontsov had played a lesser role. Sandwich however was absolutely certain of Vorontsov's wrongdoing and told Buckingham unequivocally that, "there is too much reason to believe that he has been extremely deficient in his duty. Your Lordship will have no need of instructions to overthrow the weakness of such insinuations" and was pained because Russia should have been aware of King George's friendly disposition towards his ally instead of being misled by "the groundless jealousies and ill-founded surmises" put forward by Vorontsov. If Buckingham feared disapproval from London his concerns were allayed when the King expressed confidence in him via Lord Sandwich "the King is thoroughly convinced of your Lordship's zeal and ability…and should you at last leave that Court without effectuating the ultimate end of your ministry there, it will not be imputed to any deficiency on your part, but…principally owing to the bad intentions of Count Voronstov."[28]

Notes

1. *Grenville Papers …*, p. 92.
2. The Southern Department covered Ireland, the Channel Islands, France, Spain, Portugal, Switzerland, the states of Italy and the Ottoman Empire. Until 1768 it also covered the American colonies.
3. *Despatches and Correspondence …*, Vol. 1, p.203.
4. *Despatches and Correspondence …*, Vol. 2, p.30.
5. Ibid. p.48.
6. Ibid. p.67.
7. Ibid. p.55.
8. Ibid. p. 68.
9. Ibid.
10. Ibid. p.85.
11. Ibid. p.79.
12. Ibid. p.85.
13. Ibid. p.108.
14. Ibid. p. 81.
15. Ibid. p.179.
16. Ibid. p.179.
17. Ibid. p.179.
18. Wilkes is now seen by some historians as an advocate for free speech.
19. Namier, L. & J. Brooke, J. (eds.),*The History of Parliament: the House of Commons 1754-1790*, 1964. (historyofparliamentonline.org)
20. *Letters of Mary Lepel, Lady Hervey*, John Murray, 1821, p. 204.
21. *Report on the Manuscripts of the Marquess of Lothian*, p.172.
22. *Despatches and Correspondence …*, Vol.2, p.119.
23. Ibid. p.143.
24. Ibid. p.116.
25. Ibid. p.116.
26. Ibid. p.122.
27. Ibid. p.132.
28. Ibid. p.146.

Should I Stay or Should I Go Now?

George Grenville recommended a new secretary to Buckingham, but neither actually met the gentleman before his appointment and the result was not a match made in heaven. Buckingham grumbled to his aunt,

> The only person here with whom I can possibly converse with any degree of confidence, that is to say, my secretary, is the most disagreeable, illiterate, underbred wretch in the Universe. I am forced to do almost everything myself, tho' I pay him two hundred pounds per an. which is full double the usual stipend. Two obligations I must confess I have to him, the one that he gives me a good deal of employment, the other that he properly humbles me with regard to my own performances, for that author musts be very conceited indeed who could be vain of his works after having heard them read by him.'[1]

At Court, Buckingham was thoroughly exasperated by constantly hearing about Russian partiality towards the French. He concluded that Russian ministers in all the foreign courts were "prejudiced in favour of a nation whose fashions, manners, and language their education has taught them to admire," hinted darkly that the naval preparations of France and Spain might "ultimately be ruinous to England" and enquired of Panin, "if he did not imagine that in the late war we had sufficiently corrected the French vivacity to keep them quiet for at least ten years. He answered that he believed indeed that it would be five before they would choose to stir."

Political matters reached a total stalemate. This gave Buckingham more leisure time and he occupied some of it by writing to his aunt. He had received unwelcome news of an untimely death at Blickling,

2 December 1763,

> Shall I tell you that I am out of spirits & out of humour, not quite liking my situation here, nor quite wishing myself anywhere else? There is a vast deal of truth in that short sentence. My Steward's death, which Lady Buckingham will have mentioned, is a real and most serious calamity to me. I would not hesitate at the giving of a thousand pounds for such another. I never indeed knew anyone in that situation who, in my opinion, was so valuable a servant. I began to see myself as a Country Gentleman & thought him a usefull Man who would have lasted my time.[2]

By January 1764 his spirits had revived somewhat,

Since my last I have received a letter from Mr Hobart & another from Col
Hotham which have a little restored my sweetness of disposition. I keep
up in general to that resolution which I formed early upon my arrival
in the Country to be cheerfull & to live as much a life of amusement &
dissipation of my acquaintance & the Duty's my situation would admit
of. Amongst all the attempts I have hitherto made to render my little
Gazettes not totally uninteresting to you, I do not recollect having said
anything of Count Orlov, tho' a person who acts no inconsiderable part
in the scene which is now before me. His appearance is noble and full as
handsome as is consistent with a manly and rather athletic figure. His
manner is surprisingly affable and easy, allowing for his most sudden
rise to greatness and that excess of most obsequious adulation which is
necessarily paid to his situation. He has not forgot his former state, and
said to me lately, "Autrefois je me promenais beaucoup par necessite; a
cette heure, je me trouve Grand Seigneur et je roule en carosse."*[3]

Buckingham knew the Empress trusted that Orlov would die for her if called
upon and she returned his devotion "in shewing him new marks of her favor. Her
delight is to see him great."

He sent his compliments to his niece Henrietta Hotham ('Mrs Harriet') who was
now almost ten years old, asking his aunt to "desire her to attend to her French and
her Dancing, as I probably before we meet shall have forgot my English and am
determined upon my return to dance the first minuet with her."

In February he was a guest at a Russian wedding, which differed from an English
wedding in most respects, as described to Lady Suffolk,

> I was present at all the ceremonys of the day and some of those of the
> night, but the whole was conducted with so much dignity and solemnity
> that it were in vain to attempt making the description of it entertaining
> without deviating from the truth. I was admitted to the bride's toilet
> whilst she was dressing, she was in her stays, and several of her relations,
> women of the first distinction, were employed in adjusting her different
> ornaments. The toilet finished, the Company in about twenty coaches
> and six attended her to Court. Just before we set out the mother of the
> bride ordered us all to be seated and the doors of the room to be shut, as
> a prognostick of the future tranquillity of the newly marry'd couple, but
> unfortunately a child of the family who was offended at the prospects being
> intercepted, burst out into a most violent fit of roaring, which seemed to
> me a much apter emblem of what might hereafter insue. Arrived at the
> Palace the bride was introduced to the Empress, who with her own hands
> ornamented her with the Crown jewels and pinned them on her tresses.
> The bride then proceeded to the Chappel, where the impatient bridegroom

---

* I used to walk by necessity; now, as a great man, I ride in my carriage.

waited. He was crowned and she was crowned, he walked around the altar and she walked around the altar, he laughed and she cried. In the course of the ceremony the bride dropped her wedding ring, which, as a bad omen, gave great uneasiness to her mother. We then went home with them, sat down to a supper of sixty covers, undressed the bride, who kissed every jewel of the Empress separately. We then kissed her and retir'd.'[4]

Thankfully there were many other distractions to be encountered within the opulent mansions and gilded palaces in and around Petersburg and Buckingham took pleasure in accepting invitations to a great number of them. At Court itself there were frequent entertainments often involving over a hundred of the highest calibre actors, singers, dancers and musicians. Buckingham's irrepressible friend Barrington in turn kept him in touch with news from the London scene,

> Dull Politicks, my dear Lord, are a very poor inadequate return for the charming letters you send me from Petersburg. I have communicated parts of the two last where it was proper, and they were much admired. The club is at your devotion and goes as well as it can without you. Strange and Stanley have had your messages, love you very much, and talk of writing to you. There is an antiministerial club set up in Albemarle Street, but I hear of no amusement or vice going on there, so I conclude it will soon be abandoned.[5]

Letters for the next few months reveal Buckingham's indecision as he vacillated wildly between a strong desire to be recalled to England and the polar opposite

View of the Palace Embankment from the Peter and Paul Fortress by Fedor Yakovlevich Alekseev.

wish to remain in Russia. From Petersburg, to his aunt,

> The Russian spring is begun, that is to say, it freezes all night and thaws all
> day. Early in the morning you travel upon ice, but all the rest of the day the
> streets are canals. I know not what to make of my country by the accounts I
> receive of it, perhaps when I return my country will not know what to make
> of me, the Individual and the General in some respects resemble, they are
> both passionate, both capricious, and both unhappy. It is ridiculous what
> a trifling circumstance will sometimes influence my temper for a whole
> day. You will tell me it ought not, which is just what I tell myself, but our
> united remonstrances will have no effect. Don't you find by the disjointed
> sentences which compose these pages, the attempts at an idea which with
> difficulty stumble to the end of the period, that I am at this moment most
> delightfully dull? Indeed I cannot help it. Nature wants a fillip, but knows
> not when it may be had. I often think of what Fontenelle, dying at the age
> of a hundred, said to his physician, who asked him if he felt any pain, 'je
> sens le mal d'etre.'* A fair lady was telling me my fortune last night, and
> informed me that I should live to be very old, mais que cela ne'n vandroit
> pas la peine, comme je deviendrois hypocindre et goutteax. Voila un bel
> horoscope!**[6]

Lady Suffolk informed Grenville of her nephew's desire to return home but he
replied from Downing Street "nothing further will be done with regard to the
appointment of any other person, or to his recall at the present. Lady Suffolk will
always prefer Lord Buckinghamshire's credit and reputation even to the joy and
comfort of seeing him."[7] Mary Anne sorely missed her husband and longed for his
return, "Lady Buckingham feels this delay, but behaves very properly: I will do my
utmost to keep up her spirits: she dotes on you."[8] Mary Anne had expressed her
fear of variolating[9] little Harriet and Buckingham scolded his aunt, "Why don't
you govern her better? But I flatter myself it will all be over before you receive
this."[10] He encouraged Mary Anne to proceed, "I think of you and yours very often
but have so little idea of the danger of inoculation to a healthy child, that tho' I
both approve and pity your anxiety I cannot say that I have any doubt myself of
Lady Harriet's going through the trial, and producing herself afterwards in new
beauty, health and spirits."[11] Mary Anne was further emboldened by the example
set by George III and Queen Charlotte who led the way in combatting the scourge
of smallpox by inoculating all their children. A measured dose of infected material
was introduced to the patient via two points in the arm made with the point of a
lancet through which a thread was dragged several times under the skin and on
both arms. The child would then be kept in bed, mostly in the dark, until such
time as the disease showed itself in a fever and rash which would then, if all went

---

*   I feel the pain of being.

**   But that it would not be worth the trouble, as I would be a hypochondriac and gouty. What
       a lovely horoscope!

to plan, swiftly disappear. In the same letter Buckingham referred to his Norfolk neighbours who were evidently behaving in an unneighbourly fashion, "It gives me pleasure to hear of the great affectionate regard which Lady Suffolk shews you, tho I never doubted of her acting the most becoming part in the absence of her unworthy Nephew. I was also rejoiced to hear that no unavailing efforts were made upon my account in Norfolk, and that the opportunity was not given to the Walpoles and Townshends of parading their proscription on my family. So much for serious matters."

The satisfaction he felt upon hearing that the Townshend and Walpole contingent had failed to stop his half-brother George's attempt to become one of the two elected Members for Norfolk in the April election proved premature because George and the third candidate Sir Edward Astley were obliged to yield in face of concerted opposition. The vacancy had been created at this time because the sitting Member, George Townshend, succeeded to the title of Viscount; he then threw his considerable weight behind his preferred candidate Thomas de Grey who easily won the seat. The letter continued, "Here are two sheets left for Gaiety without one Gay thought to fill them. It is unpleasant to me upon her account and extremely inconvenient upon my own that Lady Suffolk for so long together be unable to write to me. But I will hope when next we meet to find her with eyes as good as mine are not, tho, as one indication of age amongst many more, I have been dignified with a bloodshot eye for three weeks past." Perhaps he was feeling his age, particularly in relation to his young wife where the sixteen year age gap was apparent, at least in their social tastes, "I flattered myself that Ranelagh[12], ere this, would have been no more, and that at my return to England some of the old regained" but vowed in future to keep up with her. "To convince you that my connubial affections are not impaired by time, I will attend you there as after that last year of my life that I am able to walk, as I did the first of our acquaintance" and sweetly told her, "Tho' you are incapable of writing such Idle Nonsense as this, yet you will endure it as a welcome proof of my present cheerfulness. Take it as such, yet I sincerely hope that you are much happier than your affect. Buckingham."

By Easter Buckingham was impatient to know if he would be recalled and if so, when. In the meantime he entertained as much as ever and told his aunt,

> I feel every day more and more that the Russians are sensible of the pains I have taken to contribute to their amusement and grateful for the desire I have shown to oblige them. It is at present my intention to have only two balls more, as though now we freeze with only sixteen hours sun, the weather will soon be too hot for such sorts of amusements. The Assemblies on Tuesdays and Saturdays I shall continue as long as I stay here. The river has got loose from the ice and so far my prospect is improved, but bleak and most ungenial are the gales which waft the snow across it. The very concise summer of Petersburg will begin in about a

month. What we call three seasons are in great measure united here—
Spring, Summer and Autumn when the weather is particularly favourable
will together make nearly four months.[13]

Unlike his brother George, Buckingham thoroughly enjoyed the extremities of
Russian weather and marvelled at the swift growing season. "The vegetation of such
things as will vegetate in such a soil and such a climate is performed almost with
magic celerity, and reminds me of what in my early days I have seen exhibited by
the dexterity of an ingenious artist, who produced a tree which budded, blossomed,
bore ripe fruit, and withered in less than ten minutes. The depth of winter to those
who can endure cold is the finest season, excellent roads, and a clear air which
sharpens the appetite and enlivens the animal spirits."[14] Eternally indebted to
his aunt for the care of his young family he told her, "Lady Buckingham's letters
overflow with her sensibility of your goodness to her and her child; not being able
to say enough upon the occasion, I shall desire you only to put a candid conjecture
upon my feelings."

Panin casually mentioned to Buckingham that the Empress, on going through
her papers, had discovered she still owed 44,000 roubles (£10,000) to the English
Court. He said the loan had been arranged by Sir Charles Hanbury Williams
when Catherine was Grand Duchess and that she now wished to repay her debt.
Buckingham thought this was an uncomfortable time to raise this delicate matter
and said that he "was persuaded that my Court had forgot"[15] to which Panin
replied, "the Empress would be particularly concerned if this was understood in
an improper light." Buckingham assured him that he "could take no steps in an
affair of that nature without his Majesty's particular instructions." Lord Sandwich
instructed Buckingham to avoid accepting the £10,000 and to assure the Empress
of the King's earnest and sincere friendship and also carefully imply that although
his Majesty was unable to take an active public role in the affairs of Poland "without
being the first to kindle a new war, just as he has restored peace to Europe after such
an expense of blood and treasure"[16] he would most certainly support her decisions
in private. The Seven Years' War which had affected Europe, the Americas, West
Africa, India, and the Philippines had at last ended.

Another pact was reached when Panin's long desired Russo-Prussian Treaty of
Alliance was signed on 11 April (31 March in the English calendar) in which each
nation agreed, for an eight year period, to commit 10,000 soldiers and 2,000
horses to the defence of the other in the event of an attack. Buckingham still
ventured to hope that if he stayed just a little longer he might fulfil his mission,
"my own inclinations and private objects may induce me to wish to leave this
country as soon as possible, yet I would a little delay my departure in the hope that
some fortunate change of circumstances might prevent that coolness" but added
"I strongly expressed concern to find that there was now scarcely any probability
of our negotiations being brought to a present conclusion" and that he "desired
to have continuance of his (Panin's) friendship and esteem during the little time I

might as yet have to remain at Petersburg."[17] The Empress's mind was focused on other matters, foremost of which was the still unresolved question of who would take control in Poland. European countries vied strenuously for consideration of their candidates and Turkey kept a beady eye on developments because Poland had strategic significance for them all. The Court of Vienna constantly undermined Catherine's position, as Buckingham told Sandwich, "I am assured that Count Mercy, the late Austrian Ambassador at Petersburg, insinuates at Warsaw almost in direct terms that to his knowledge it is impossible she should long continue upon the throne of Russia."[18] (Count Mercy's predication rather underestimated the Empress because Catherine reigned for a further thirty two years.)

In May Barrington heard rumours of his friend's return but concluded, "you were soon to begin your journey hither, but I have since found reason to believe I was not so near the comfort of seeing you as I hoped and expected."[19] He gossiped that Halifax had been awarded the Order of the Garter[20] and that he hoped "my dear Lord to see it round your leg, while that leg is able to perform all the offices a true knight can require from it. Mr Pitt is almost worn out from gout. The Earl of Pomfret has at last taken that deep laden rich aquapulca Miss Draycott—you see what middle aged Lords of the Bedchamber can do!" but also reported the sad fate of a mutual friend,

> I must conclude this letter by informing you of poor Jack's death at Paris the 2nd of last month, the heaviest affliction I ever knew. He was seized with a sort of palsey, which ended in an apoplexy. Water and matter were found in his head caused I believe by a shot when he was unfortunately hit by David Hamilton in Norfolk. I cannot make a new friend at the Coffee House when I have lost an old one. Come therefore my dear Lord and comfort your ever affectionate Barrington.

In Petersburg three Maids of Honour were married on the same day, one of whom George Hobart had previously befriended. Buckingham told his aunt,

> As two of the brides are my particular favourites and one of my relation, I am tolerably well acquainted even with the most secret transactions which passed upon the occasion—it is a usage established from old times in Russia that the nearest relations of the bride and bridegroom after they are put to bed remain in the next room, and after a certain time—the length of which occasionally differs—the newly married couple pay them a visit and eat and drink with them. You think this idle stuff, but you like I should write often and I like to write to you, and the unavoidable consequences of our two likings must be just such stuff as this. I have a great deal to do, am in a hurry and very hungry.[21]

In late May he thought "at present there appears to me a great probability of my being detained here another winter. I am offered a little place in the country about a Marble Hill distance from Petersburg, where probably I may wander for a few days, but my Town House will be my chief residence as more agreeable than any country situation in this neighbourhood."[22]

The Russian ministers frequently gave him every assurance that the Treaty of Commerce would soon be concluded on equitable terms, but also stated that the Treaty of Alliance, although deemed the more important, had stalled. This was because the Russians flatly refused to remove England's principal obstacle, that of England's obligation to finance any future military action against the Ottoman Empire in the event of its attack on Russia. However there were always pleasant diversions to be found, as described to his aunt,

> I told Lady Buckingham in my last letter but one that I intended to give some prizes to be rowed for upon the King's birthday, and now I will tell you that they absolutely were rowed for. There were nine barges, seven of twelve and two of ten oars. Count Orlov's barge won the first heat, but lost the second and third, which were won by a boat belonging to the Corps de Cadets, a sort of Academy where all the young people of distinction are prepared for the Army and Navy. Count Orlov's barge won the second prize and the Hetman's the third. The day was fine and upon the whole everything went off to my satisfaction.[23]

A little hypocritically he then told Sandwich "this Princess would greatly distinguish herself by promoting the honour, happiness and advantage of her subjects, were it not for that fatal, that most unfortunate inclination which occasionally leads her into dissipation and trivial amusements."[24] In conversation, Buckingham remonstrated with Panin about the "assurances given me so often, that deceived my Court with the expectations of an immediate conclusion, which, though in effect no fault of mine, might still bring reflections upon me, and entering into some explanation of my own private situation entreated him to let me know what I might really depend upon. He solemnly protested that the Treaty of Commerce should be settled in a few weeks, and that he hoped that the other would be adjusted."[25] What Buckingham meant by his "private situation" is unclear, but it is likely that he informed Panin that he had requested his recall papers and wished to conclude negotiations before he left Russia, or perhaps he had resorted to concocting some more dramatic reason in a desperate attempt to push the negotiations forward. Either way it was of no consequence because Panin's solemn protestations were made out of hot air. Certainly nothing whatsoever would be resolved in June because the Empress was preparing to travel. In a counter to his earlier criticism he praised the Empress in glowing terms to Lady Suffolk,

> The Empress is preparing to leave Petersburg for a month; she intends to visit the conquered provinces of Livonia and Esthonia, to see her fleet and a port which she is making under the direction of the venerable Marshal Munnich upon the Baltic. Great is the glare of her situation, and I hope her heart is happy from self-approbation. She reigns over almost a third of

the known world. She gives her attention to the comfort and improvement of the numerous nations submitted to her sway. She has fixed a sovereign in Courland, and is at the moment gratifying the ambition of a man she esteems with the Crown of Poland. She has showed mercy to many of her avowed enemies, and treats the secret machinations of others with contempt, and if she is not totally free from that passion to which the greatest minds are most exposed, she enjoys the superior pleasure of raising to the highest honours the subject of it.[26]

Rumours swirled about Petersburg that nefarious deeds were planned in the Empress's absence and Buckingham was so alarmed that he arranged via Count Orlov a private talk with Catherine. In his personal notes he wrote candidly of his feelings towards the Empress,

> What I said to her was in substance what follows: That what fell from me was the effect of a sudden emotion, arising from the real interest I took in everything that regarded her welfare. That had I known any fact of real importance I would have sought an opportunity of immediately communicating it myself. That I feared they might imagine the little information I had to give of too trivial and vague a nature, which I hoped M Cherkasov had already mentioned. That indeed reports were brought me every day from different quarters, which, though trifling when considered separately, might together be deserving of attention. That though not extremely timid in my nature where I was myself personally concerned, yet I was very much so, where the interest and safety of those might be effected whom I sincerely respected and revered. She answered that she was informed of the indiscreet and seditious conversations which were held, that it had been found necessary to inflict punishment, and that punishment had been inflicted. That such precautions had been taken that if two persons had formed an agreement they could not communicate with a third without almost a certainty of being discovered. That she was fully acquainted with the dispositions of —, that she knew they were lazy and discontented in their natures, and that occasionally they could talk, but were incapable of acting with spirit. [27]

The Empress told Buckingham she was fully sensible of his attachment to her and deeply grateful for his concern, but stated categorically that she refused to be intimidated by those with malicious intent. She told him that nobody should learn the subject of their conversation, not even Orlov.

Buckingham's fears for the Empress and the uncertainty of his own situation took its toll and caused him to fall into an unusually introspective frame of mind. He confided in the person who understood him most, Lady Suffolk,

> I cannot help thinking myself of that stock of men who will ever be most respected by their friends when in absence. Some of mine I will believe

frequently recollect my desire to act in every instance with honour and humanity, my anxiety to please and oblige, my wish to contribute to their ease and amusement, without recollecting that absence of mind, that captiousness, that gloom contracted by an unfortunate disposition ever to ruminate on the dark side of my own story, which make me often a melancholy and sometimes a disagreeable companion. It seems to me that I have lived long and that most of my days have passed as tediously as unprofitably. Necessity might have made your nephew good for something, but indolence and dissipation have ever prevented me from any useful application except when immediately called upon. In reviewing my past life and judging my actions by the loose rules of world morality I have neither done anything very wrong or very right. One unfortunate disposition, which I believe I picked up from my nurse, has principally shaded my conduct; guess it if you can, I am tired of my own reflections and undoubtedly so are you.[28]

What the "unfortunate disposition" of his nurse was is open to conjecture but if he was referring to Mrs Bedingfield perhaps he shared her predilection for drinking a little too much.

Mr Mitchell, the British Ambassador to the Prussian Court, was "alarmed to read in the newspapers a few days ago that your Excellency was immediately to return to England"[29] but, as was so often the case, the newspapers were wrong. He informed Buckingham that Michell, the Prussian Minister at London had been recalled and that "his behaviour since he knew exceeds all descriptions for weakness, malice, and absurdity." In Europe wild rumours abounded that not only did the Empress plan to wed Count Poniatowski after he was placed on the throne of Poland but also that she would resign the Government of Russia in favour of her son Paul. In truth the Empress had no intention whatsoever of marrying her former lover, but she was determined that he should wear the Polish crown and single minded in that endeavour. Riga, which had been within the Russian Empire since Czar Peter the Great had successfully besieged the city, was the logical place from which to rally support for her candidate.

In Petersburg Buckingham discovered his successor would be George Macartney and responded that he had been encouraged by "such marks of her Imperial Majesty's confidence as must induce me to think that her goodness to me though it would not bias her opinion in a matter of negotiation, might determine her to accelerate a conclusion which would otherwise be deferred" and resolved on her return to use his "best endeavours to obtain at least a positive answer." If none was forthcoming he would "make it my most humble request to his Majesty that Mr Macartney may set out."[30]

At the beginning of July 1764 Buckingham travelled fifteen miles from Petersburg to Cronstadt, an island in the Gulf of Finland, where the Empress was viewing her fleet. He told Lady Suffolk,

> During her stay she made every one happy who had the honour of
> attending her and you will be flattered to hear she was particularly
> gracious to Your Nephew. When she went to dine on board the Admiral
> she took me with only three other Persons in her Barge, when she return'd
> to Petersburgh I was the only Foreigner who was admitted into her Yacht.
> The wind failing, she got into her Barge & permitted me to attend her,
> when she arrived over against my House, she told me that as she knew I
> had no Coach at the Palace she would set me down at my own door.[31]

The next day, although it was not a Court day, he went to the Palace to thank the
Empress for her thoughtfulness, and the Vice-Chancellor brought him a message,
"Que sa Majeste etoit extremement contente de mes attentions, & que comme
Ma conduite etoit telle qu'elle m'envisageoit plutot comme un Compatriote que
comme un Etranger, Elle me prioit de diner avec elle."[*][32]

Hoping not to appear immodest about this extraordinarily flattering statement
he advised his aunt, "You will show this only to those who love me well enough not
to laugh at any little vanity which may appear in the relation." From London Mary
Anne told Buckingham that George Grenville would write to him very soon and
that she dearly wished her beloved husband might return before Christmas. When
no letter arrived from Downing Street he perceived a lack of support and began to
fret about his reception on his return to England. He unburdened himself to Lady
Suffolk,

> Your Ladiship knows full well that Mr Grenville is the only Friend I can
> in the least depend upon in the present Administration: Lord Halifax has
> no longer any regard for me & tho Lord Sandwich ever since he came into
> office has behav'd to me with the greatest civility & attention, I have no
> right to expect any particular support from His Lordship. Your Ladiship
> & Ly Bm will be glad to see me, I cannot answer for any more. My Norfolk
> History weighs heaviest upon me & the thought that I must never expect
> to pass a cheerful day at Blickling. Lord Walpole who, tho a worthy Man,
> must from his Connections ever sit in Opposition to me on the one side,
> & Mr Harbord who has taken the opportunity of absence to desert the
> Man who essentially hurt himself to serve him on the other; I will however
> leave a door open for reconciliation as long as possible. I always doubted
> of General Townshend's real regard for me, he has been upon many
> occasions lavish in his professions of Friendship but ever avoided entering
> into any engagements relative to the affairs of Norfolk.[33]

As usual, articulating his concerns to his aunt lifted Buckingham's spirits, "Now

---

[*]   "That her Majesty was extremely content with my attentions, and that, as my conduct was
such as she considered me rather as a countryman than as a stranger, she invited me to
dine with her."

I have said this much my heart is lighter, & upon reviewing my History bad as it is & drawn with a discontented pencil, it do's not absolutely amount to Tragedy. Notwithstanding any peevish aversion I may have taken to England & the inordinate affection I have conceiv'd for Russia, yet, were it not for the hope that from a little delay I may return with more credit, I should humbly intreat that Mr Macartney might set out immediately." Lady Suffolk sought to reassure him that he had completely misread the situation both in London and in Norfolk,

> Oh my dear Lord Buckingham, must I employ my pen, which is so precious, only to scold you? Indeed you are much to blame; for I do most sincerely believe Mr G is your friend, and has not failed you in any point. As for Norfolk, you seem to have had some false accounts. Mr H in politics may have differed from you; but if you think that father and son are not in Norfolk warmly your friends, and will be so there on all occasions, you are cruelly deceived, and take care that those wretches intelligence make no impression on your mind, till you hear with your own ears, and see with your own eyes. Farewell: love your old aunt; be easy; I think you have reason.[34]

Buckingham was heartily relieved and took solace, "Many, many thanks for your kind letter. I will on the whole in obedience to your commands make myself as easy as I can and confide in the good intentions of my friends. I have no other dissatisfaction in relation to Mr Harbord but his having taken the opportunity of my absence to change his political conduct."

In fact Harbord Harbord's father, Sir William Harbord of Gunton Hall, had questioned George Townshend's loyalty when he spoke against Buckingham's preference. "I can't indeed wonder that your Lordship should be a little mortified at his deserting you upon a late occasion. However, tho' he carried his point, he gained no credit by it, nor has your Lordship lost any. His breach of friendship to you, which is the light in which it is generally looked upon, is condemned even by those who have no particular regard for your Lordship." Sir William followed this with details on work he had had carried out for him on the Blickling Estate and "expressed regret that Buckingham might stay another winter away from England in so severe a climate and so uncomfortable a situation."[35]

Notes

1. NRO MC 3/285, Letter 66.
2. NRO MC 3/285, Letter 68.
3. NRO MC 3/285, Letter 69.
4. NRO MC 3/285, Letter 71.
5. *Report on the Manuscripts of the Marquess of Lothian*, p.249.
6. NRO MC 3/285 Letter 73.
7. *Report on the Manuscripts of the Marquess of Lothian*, p.249.
8. *Letters to and from Henrietta ...*, Vol. 2, p.288.

9.   Variolation preceded vaccination, which began in 1796.
10. Ibid. p.182.
11. NRO MC 3/284 Letter 2.
12. Ranelagh was considered more fashionable than its older sibling Vauxhall Gardens and charged two shillings and sixpence, compared to a shilling at Vauxhall. Soon after opening in 1741 Horace Walpole noted, 'It has totally beat Vauxhall.....you can't set foot in it without treading on a Prince, or the Duke of Cumberland.'
13. NRO MC 3/285 Letter 75.
14. *Report on the Manuscripts of the Marquess of Lothian*, p.182.
15. *Despatches and Correspondence ...*, Vol. 2, p.165.
16. Ibid. p.180.
17. Ibid. p.177.
18. Ibid. p.178.
19. *Report on the Manuscripts of the Marquess of Lothian*, p.249.
20. Lord Halifax had been awarded the prestigious Order of the Garter, an item worn about the left calf on ceremonial occasions and which indicated the high regard the King placed in the recipient.
21. NRO MC 3/285 Letter 76.
22. NRO MC 3/285 Letter 77.
23. NRO MC 3/285 Letter 78.
24. *Despatches and Correspondence ...*, Vol. 2, p.193.
25. Ibid. p.195.
26. Ibid. p.195-196.
27. *Despatches and Correspondence ...*, Vol. 2, p.198.
28. NRO MC 3/285 Letter 79.
29. *Despatches and Correspondence ...*, Vol. 2, p. 196.
30. Ibid. p.197.
31. NRO MC 3/285, Letter 80.
32. *Despatches and Correspondence ...*, Vol. 2 p. 185.
33. NRO MC 3/285 Letter 81.
34. *Letters to and from Henrietta ...*, Vol. 2, p.289.
35. *Report on the Manuscripts of the Marquess of Lothian*, p.251.

Tragedy at Fortress Schlisselberg

As the Empress set out for Riga a tragedy was unfolding twenty-two miles east of Petersburg. Situated on a tiny island on the edge of Lake Ladog at the head of the River Neva, the fortress of Schlisselberg held captive within its forbidding walls the pitiful figure of Prince Ivan VI. Proclaimed Emperor when only a babe in arms, Ivan's reign ended when his second cousin Elizabeth staged her coup before he was fifteen months old. As the Prince was a viable contender for her throne, and therefore a threat, Empress Elizabeth kept him imprisoned from the age of two along with his parents and siblings in several remote and inaccessible locations. It was said that from then onwards Elizabeth hardly slept at night for fear that his supporters would stage a coup d'etat, just as she had staged her own to seize the Crown from him. When Ivan was four she ordered the infant to be separated from his family and the poor boy spent the next eighteen years of his life in solitary confinement.

On her accession the Empress Catherine felt equally threatened by Ivan's existence because as long as he lived it remained a temptation for forces hostile to her to engineer his release and place him on the throne. At one point she hoped the young man would be persuaded to choose a cloistered life as a monk, as this would automatically disqualify him from taking the throne, but it was not to be. Another solution hoped for was that Ivan should die of natural causes and Panin instructed the guards that should the Prince happen to fall gravely ill, to allow a priest to enter, but not a doctor. Elizabeth's instructions were renewed, that if anyone attempted to take the prisoner away "without an express order personally signed in the Empress's handwriting, he shall not be allowed to fall alive into the hands of any rescuers"[1] and reinforced; Catherine commanded the guards to be even more rigorous than before. On 20 July 1764 Buckingham communicated what he had heard about the events to Sandwich,

Ivan VI.

In the night between the 15th and 19th[2] Lieutenant Mirowitz, of the regiment of Smolensko, who was upon guard in the citadel of Schlisselberg where Prince Ivan was confined, having first seduced the soldiers under his command, went to the commandant and insisted upon his immediately releasing the Prince, which the commandant declining, he caused him to be bound. He next obliged the keeper of the magazine to deliver powder to his soldiers. The noise which these proceedings occasioned alarmed a captain in the ante-room. The lieutenant having afresh encouraged his men advanced to the Prince's apartment, and demanded with the most violent threats in case of refusal that his Emperor (as he called him) should be produced. After some resistance the captain and lieutenant, finding themselves in danger of being overpowered, told Mirowitz that if he persisted it would endanger the Prince's life, as their instructions were in case they found their efforts to guard him ineffectual, immediately to put him to death. Mirowitz, deaf to all remonstrances, forced the door, which put them under the most unhappy necessity of executing their orders. The first stab waked the unfortunate youth, who was asleep in bed. He made so stout a resistance as to break one of their swords, and received eight wounds before he expired. The officer then produced the body to the lieutenant and his soldiers, and told them they might now do with their Emperor what they thought proper. Mirowitz carried the corpse to the front of the guard and covered it with the colours, and then with all his soldiers prostrated himself before it and kissed the hand. He next, taking off his own gorget, sash, and sword, laid them by the body and addressed himself to Korsakov, colonel of the regiment of Smolensko, who was then arrived, and pointing to the body told him, 'There is your Emperor; you may do by me as you please. Adverse fortune has blasted my design; I mourn not only my own fate but the misery of my poor fellow soldiers, the innocent victims of my undertaking.' He then embraced the under-officers and surrendered himself and his soldiers. The body, it is said, has been carried to a Russian church.[3]

It was widely assumed that Mirowitz's audacious attempt to release the prince was incited by the notion that the Empress was about to abandon Russia for Poland. But Mirowitz was a bitter, proud young man, heavily in debt and given to excessive drinking. His attempts to win back his family lands had failed and created an unreasonable yet deep resentment of Catherine. He convinced himself that God would welcome the overthrow of the "usurping woman" and the means of fulfilling this aim appeared obvious when he discovered the identity of the solitary prisoner guarded within the Citadel at Schlisselberg. The completely innocent, unfortunate Ivan, imprisoned in solitude for almost his entire life, died because a man he had never seen nor heard of wished to place him on the Russian throne.

Believing this terrible event would deflect the Russian ministers from any treaty

Vasily Mirovich Standing over the Body of Ivan VI at Schlusselburg Fortress by Ivan Tvorozhnikov, 1884.

negotiations Buckingham told Sandwich "I have not neglected his Majesty's instructions. It is unnecessary to add that great allowance must be made for the times. The Empress is expected tomorrow or next day."[4] Then unexpectedly, just a few days later, he reported, "a new plan of the Treaty of Alliance has been promised me but the present situation of the interior of this country must unavoidably delay foreign business. This would certainly throw me into a winter's journey, and, as the two treaties are in agitation I hope his Majesty will permit me to remain here till the spring, that a further chance may be given me of accomplishing the objects committed to my case, lest I should return with the mortifying appearance of not having merited that confidence which my sovereign was graciously pleased to place in me."[5]

News of the murder of Ivan VI travelled far and wide. Sir Joseph Yorke was horrified and wrote from the Hague, "My blood still runs cold at the tragical fate of the ill-starred Prince Ivan, and I fancy I am reading history from three hundred years ago. M. Panin sent a circular letter—and mentioned the prisoner as an unknown person out of his senses—not one word of the mortal wounds. This story will adorn the stage in future ages, but it makes one blush for this."[6]

Buckingham soon informed Sandwich, "'The late disturbance seems almost forgot, and there is now an appearance of the most perfect tranquility"[7] although Count Orlov's manner was a cause for concern,

> His increasing favour occasions a secret discontent, which it pains me to
> think may have in the end very fatal consequences. At present he interferes
> not with foreign affairs, but with regard to the whole of the domestick

his decisions are absolute. He has lately taken upon him a haughtiness of behaviour which those who remember his beginning cannot brook without an indignation, not the less violent for being smothered. At times he seems to forget that respect and deference which is due to his sovereign, and addresses her with the air of a man who feels and means to exert the full of his influence. Some of those who are near her Imperial Majesty have hinted to me that they believe she retains still some ideas of marrying him; if she should in the instance yield to her inclinations she inevitably seals her ruin.

During her long reign marriage rumours continually swirled around her but Catherine never married. Gregory Orlov remained loyally at Catherine's side for another eight years, after which he was replaced in her affections by the next of her dozen lovers. Now though, her ambition to place Count Poniatowski on the Polish throne had been evident to all and made obvious not least by the expenditure laid out in support of his election campaign which ran to almost two and a half million roubles. Catherine's industry in the matter was misinterpreted in Constantinople, mainly as a result of rumour-mongers in France and Austria, who frequently announced that the Count was about to marry the Czarina. The Turks were moved to announce that they would consider such a match a declaration of war from Russia. Plans were consequently afoot to safely marry off Poniatowski to a lady unconnected to any other foreign power and he was obliged to swear to wed a Polish noblewoman. Over the course of time he took several mistresses and sired seven children by two of them, but like Catherine, he never married.

ဆဩ

Count Alexis Razumovsky had been the Empress Elizabeth's loyal subject, devoted lover and companion for the last thirty years of her life. His passionate interest in her, combined with a total disinterest in politics, served to keep him out of harm's way and he had retired safely to his country estate. Buckingham travelled the forty miles from Petersburg where he found him,

> in the midst of twenty young people, who made it their employment, as it was their pleasure, to fulfil his wishes, which he repaid by an increasing attention to render their situation agreeable. His reception of me was most flattering; his words I could not understand, but the gestures which accompanied them assured me of a most cordial welcome. My ignorance of the Russian language was never so irksome to me as upon this occasion, but there was no remedy. I passed the day as pleasantly as any I ever knew, and returned the next morning most reluctantly to my secretaries, my desk, and my duty.'[8]

Buckingham's natural flirtatiousness temporarily deserted him, as he told his aunt,

The Empress' particular goodness had almost tempted me at her departure for Riga to desire leave to attend her, but that abominable bashfulness which has so often essentially hurt me kept me silent. However, in a letter which I wrote to one of the chambellans who is with her I mentioned my envy of his situation. He showed her the letter, though wrote in my flippant vein, and she directed him to send me such an answer as makes me more out of humour with my bashfulness than ever I was before.

Buckingham enjoyed his time so much at Razumovsky's that he visited often and, "return'd, as before, with contrition, to Ministerial conference & the consequences." He took great pleasure and comfort from simple things, as described to Lady Suffolk,

It is in the garden of the Summer Palace, a most pleasant & cheerfull retirement, in which I pass three or four hours every morning, when my leisure will admit of it, that this letter is wrote. It is the third or fourth which might have been dated from thence, but at the other times it did not occur to me to mention the Scene which stood before me. The Garden is laid out in English, or rather in the Italian stile, Shady Walks, Marble Statues & Fountains innumerable, the Palace is at one end, & a Terras which commands a very fine view of the River on the other. Distant Thunder, Dark Clouds & screaming Pea Cocks prepare me to expect a Storm, but I shall write on in perfect tranquillity till the first drops reach me. Whether it is a change of temper, or the effect of advancing further in life, I know not, but I every day find that I contemplate every kind of Storm with increasing tranquility, or if any emotion arises it is more from general humanity, or particular regard to Individuals, than from my own fears or feelings.

Empress Catherine visited Count Razumovsky's estate on her way back to Petersburg and Buckingham rejoiced at the news of her imminent return "both in my Publick & private capacity, as I have sensibly felt in both the difference of her absence."[9]

He then performed a complete *volte face* and declared that he was now exceedingly unwilling to leave Russia. Perhaps the dramatic turnabout was because his hopes for the Treaty negotiations had unexpectedly risen, but in view of the countless previous occasions when these hopes had been dashed, this seems unlikely. Although it was natural that he was loathe to return with his mission unfulfilled and that he feared an unpleasant reception on his return to London, it is also not beyond the realms of fantasy to suspect that he had formed a romantic attachment. Whatever his motive was the Earl of Sandwich reacted to this sudden change of heart with extreme irritation, not least because George Macartney, having accepted the position of Ambassador, had entirely reasonably enquired when he might set out for Petersburg. Sandwich told Grenville,

> Lord Buckingham in his last letter avoids naming any particular period
> for his leaving Petersburg, and as he expresses himself to be much pleased
> with the Empress's present behaviour to him, and to be flattered by the
> marks of distinction she now shows him, I am much inclined to think that
> he liked his situation so much better than he did that he will endeavour to
> spin out his stay in Russia as long as he possibly can. I have directed Lord
> Buckingham, immediately after (the Empress's) arrival, to fix the time of
> his coming away, and not to suffer himself to be any longer amused about
> the Treaties in agitation, which if that Court was in high earnest, might be
> finished at any time in a very few days."[10]

Only four days later Sandwich again expressed his frustration "as what relates to
Lord Buckingham's return, I cannot help thinking that he now wishes to protract
it as much as possible; it will be two months before I shall have an answer to my
last letter, and Mr Macartney cannot be allowed less than two months from the day
of his appointment to prepare for his journey."[11] He expressed his concern that in
view of the uncertainty Macartney might take offence and decide not to take the
position after all.

In mid-August Buckingham wrote to Lady Suffolk, "I am not pleas'd at this
moment with myself or indeed with any body else, not even with you, for either you
are Idle & will not write to me, or you are ill & cannot. I am sorry to think that the
latter by much the worst of the two reasons may unhappily be the true one."[12] He
again felt alienated from England and fretted that "except for Deaths & Marriages
I know nothing of my own Country, & am never able to contradict any Idle report
which the Flippancy of a Gazette Writer, nor the real or wilfull misinformation of
a Foreign Minister prompts him to propagate" and confessed that he had been
putting on a brave face, "When you hear of my Balls, Assembly's & entertainments
you must imagine my hours not only pass cheerfully but riotously Gay, yet some
day or other you shall learn how flimsy are my pleasures & how real my anxiety's."
He considered not sending the letter for fear of upsetting his beloved aunt, but
admitted "you are the only person to whom I fully open my heart & the only one
who loves me in the manner I most wish to be lov'd. Of this sort however you shall
never receive any more letters from me, & if facts must be mention'd they shall be
mention'd without comments." He then made a point of ending on his habitual
lighter note ,

> My writing & Stile are both affected by the quantity of Flies with which
> Petersburg is pester'd at this season. There are at this moment three of
> those animals (the purpose of whose existence I can as little account for
> as of my own) taking their venting walk upon my forehead, two upon my
> hand, seven upon this Paper, besides a Regiment who are grazing upon
> the green-sward of my writing table. Tell Mrs Harriet that I am somewhat

offended at her not having answered my last Letter. I believe to desire you to make my Compts to all those who trouble themselves about me, will be giving you no trouble at all.

There was no hint of an illicit romantic liaison but he would not have burdened his aunt with information of that nature, at least not in writing. The Panin affair had taught him the danger of committing secrets to paper.

Buckingham formally stated that it was his greatest desire to remain in Russia and again requested Lord Sandwich to beg the King's permission to stay until the following spring. Sandwich responded in a conciliatory manner quite different to the complaining one employed when writing on the same matter to George Grenville, "It will give me real concern if the answer you will receive to your request to remain where you now are till the next spring should give you any uneasiness. If I had had the least idea that you wished to continue in your embassy I would on no account have proposed anything to his Majesty that could have hastened your return"[13] and very reasonably pointed out that because Buckingham had repeatedly asked for his recall, that is precisely what he had taken him to mean. As for the Treaty, "Russia exacts a condition which we are as determined to refuse as they are to insist on, therefore it is time to show that we will not suffer ourselves to be longer amused upon this subject." Maintaining that whilst he wanted what would please Buckingham most, and had no wish to upset him, it would be awkward to change the arrangement because "it was fixed for Mr Macartney (to relieve you) before your Lordship showed the least inclination to stay; he gave up his pretensions to a seat in Parliament upon the promise of this appointment, and expected to be dispatched some months ago. Should his appointment be now postponed till the winter is over, he would have great reason to complain, and to think that he was led on with the hopes of this commission because we wished to choose another person into Parliament instead of him."[14] In quiet desperation, Buckingham resorted to employing the severity of the winter weather as a reason for staying on until the spring and pleaded again that the extra time could make all the difference to the negotiations. On reading this Lord Sandwich told George Grenville, "This, I own, I have long expected, as it has been plain to me that something or other has happened that makes him like his situation more than he did; however, I can see no reason for indulging him in this request, and His Majesty is of the same opinion."[15] Whilst there is no evidence that what made him like his situation more than he did was a romantic interlude, it is difficult to imagine what other alteration to his circumstance could have caused such a dramatic and badly timed change of heart. But whatever the real reason Lord Sandwich was having none of it and insisted that Buckingham return home. Then, just as unexpectedly as before, Buckingham changed his mind again et voila! made it known that of course, naturally, he would be equally happy to stay or to leave, whatever was the King's pleasure. He airily claimed that he truly did not mind either way and requested that "George Macartney should set out immediately, unless my request of remaining here the winter should have been granted. I am prepared in either case most chearfully to obey his Majesty's instructions." If Buckingham had indeed been conducting a love affair, it had now come to an end.

Treaty negotiations continued to grind on in their distressingly familiar repetitive pattern. At the end of August Panin assured Buckingham that "they have been busy revising it these two days"[16] and the latest excuse was that "they were fully employed in preparing for the trial of Mirowitz." The Prussian minister sided with England and urged Buckingham to press for the conclusion of the Treaty of Alliance and also sought an agreement between England, Russia and Prussia to act in concert with regard to the unsettled country of Sweden. Buckingham expressed his wish that the French would not take advantage of their indecision, raising the spectre of another war.

In Poland Count Poniatowski was unanimously elected King.

In Petersburg Mirowitz told the judge "he considered himself as no longer a citizen of this world, that he was sensible he had nothing to expect but an ignominious death, which he was prepared to meet with a degree of magnanimity which he hoped would expiate for the offence he had committed."[17] Following the guilty verdict Buckingham reported, "Mirowitz was publicly beheaded on Wednesday last. Six of the soldiers and under officers who were engaged with him ran the gantlope[18] the same day; they were so severely whipped that it is said three are dead since." Later, when in the Empress's party at Czarskoselo[19], she brought up the subject with him and with tears in her eyes asserted her innocence, maintaining that nothing had ever "given her so much uneasiness as the suspicion that she had directly or indirectly contributed to the unfortunate catastrophe at Schlisselberg."[20]

From England, Barrington wrote sadly that "Lady Barrington has long been in a declining way. I left her in no sort of immediate danger a week ago, and came hither for a few days, but last Friday she was rather worse and dyed in an hour after her danger had been perceived. However it was known by every body but herself that she could not last long. I return to Beckett after her funeral." Beckett Hall was the Viscount's family home in Shrivenham, Berkshire (now Oxfordshire).

Awaiting further instructions from London and metaphorically twiddling his thumbs, Buckingham eloquently explained a bout of writer's block to his aunt,

> I think you will have found my letters always running into extremes, either the deep Tragedy, or the whimsical Farce. It seems to me that according to regular Rotation this ought to be the Cheerful Post and tho' a cloud has intercepted the sunshine of the morning and in consequence Cats, Flys & most Englishmen mourn, still the Doleful Fit has not seized me & if not Gay I am however at the moment calm in the possession of that artificial tranquility, resignation. Well, what is this introduction to lead to? Why I

really cannot tell. After having taken some turns about my room in order to put the animal spirits in motion & arouse my imagination, I return yawning to my paper & am reluctantly obliged to acknowledge that my calmness savours not a little of stupidity. The evidence singly of this paper would condemn me in any Court in Europe. After all don't you think the extremes preferable to the boasted Golden Mean, nothing really can be worse than this. I am looking out at the Window in hopes the Street or River might furnish something, but Alas! they are each as dully uniform as my Mind. A Storm, a Boat overset, a Coach over turn'd, an Elegant or an awkward Figure, a Quarrel, Nay even a Dog with a Canister ty'd to his tail might be of use to me. Providence, deaf to my applications will not operate the least incident in my favour. I do not indeed deserve greatly at her hands, but why should you be punish'd for my faults?[21]

He had observed a fissure in the relationship between the Empress and her lover Orlov, cynically noting that "for some months past (she) has frequently had little differences with her favourite, who sometimes even in public is wanting in due respect and even in common attention to her. There are of those who reason from thence that they are certainly married." Buckingham thought "perhaps the best description of her is that she is a woman as well as an empress" and that Orlov was not the only one with a roving eye, "her Imperial Majesty has at times eyes for others, particularly for an amiable and accomplished man who is not undeserving of her affection." To whom he referred is open to conjecture.

Notes

1. Massie,R.K., p. 324.
2. Buckingham's dates are New Style; Russia records the events as taking place between 3 and 5 July.
3. *Despatches and Correspondence ...*, Vol. 2, p.203.
4. Ibid. p. 204.
5. Ibid. p. 207.
6. *Despatches and Correspondence ...*, Vol. 2, p.217.
7. Ibid. p. 218.
8. NRO MC 3/285 Letter 82.
9. NRO MC 3/285, Letter 83.
10. *Grenville Papers ...*, p. 415.
11. Ibid. p. 417.
12. NRO MC3/285 Letter 84.
13. *Despatches and Correspondence ...*, Vol. 2, p.219.
14. Ibid. p. 220.
15. *Grenville Papers ...*, Vol. 2, p. 415.)
16. *Despatches and Correspondence ...*, Vol. 2, p. 222.
17. Ibid. p. 230.
18. 'gantlope' meant 'running the gauntlet' i.e. running between two rows of soldiers who struck out and attacked the guilty parties. The Russian soldiers in this particular case

obviously did not hold back.
19. Tsarskoe Selo (Tsar'sVillage), now known as Pushkin.
20. *Despatches and Correspondence ...*, Vol. 2, p.236.
21. NRO MC3/285 Letter 85.

Packing Up

As 1764 drew to its close and negotiations lumbered on with no realistic prospect of an end to the impasse, Buckingham resigned himself to leaving Russia with his mission unfulfilled. "As soon as ever that gentleman (Mr Macartney) comes to Petersburg I shall ask for my audience of leave so that in all probability it will not now be many months before I embrace my Good Aunt in Savile Row."[1] In the meantime he found himself in a new role, that of matchmaker,

I grow old very fast, it is a melancholy truth which if I had not penetration enough to find out & resolution sufficient to whisper to myself, the good nature of some & the conduct of others would unintentionally acquaint me with it. The Women treat me as a Man of no sort of consequence. I am already the Confidant of many & fear very soon that some will propose to make still a more mortifying use of me. A Grown Gentleman much about my own age has, since my Residence here, honor'd three different Lady's by his addresses. The First refus'd him with a most mortifying perseverance, the second he Coqueted with for about six Months & then left abruptly with that unembarrassed Countenance which would have done Honor to a better cause; the third he is half in love with, except, when he recollects the superior Fortune & greatly superior merit of the First & his vanity whispers him that he still has a chance of succeeding with her; to do her justice she spares no pains to humble that Vanity, but still from time to time it rears its head tho' faintly. All three speak their sentiments freely to me upon this subject. The First expresses her aversion in the strongest terms & seems surprised at his presumption in expecting to please her, the Second arraign in General the Perfidy of Man, hints at her own disgrace & with a downcast eye decently appeals to my Judgement whether she deserv'd it; the Third, who set out upon that Plan of parading her passion & exposing herself to the censure of the world for the sake of the Man she loves, which frequently captivates a vain Gallant, artfully try's to sift the others secrets from me, & asks me if the Gentleman does not defer too long the much desired conclusion of the Novel. I answer, that he has at least as much Indecision as Vanity & more of each than of that affection of the true bent which makes Mole Hills out of Mountains. These Ladys and this Gentleman were all under my roof last Night, where some contrivance, a happy concurrence of circumstances, & a gleam of good humour which beam'd upon almost every Individual, produc'd one of the prettiest Balls & cheerfullest evenings I was ever a Party to. Amongst twenty Women there were literally fifteen whom most of my Sex would have thought interesting, tho' most of Yours would probably have judg'd otherwise.[2]

Magnificent celebrations of the anniversary of her Imperial Majesty and the birthday of the Grand Duke took place which he enjoyed enormously, but Buckingham was growing increasingly weary of politics. Sandwich sympathised and offered some consolation,

> I will own to you, my Lord, that the whole face of things within the place of your residence wears so lowering a cast that I may congratulate your Excellency upon having obtained your recall, and being ready to retire from so unpromising a scene. Mr Macartney will set out in eight or ten days, and will lose no time in repairing to his place of destination. In the meantime, if these clouds should disperse and business should be carried on with vigour, your Excellency may still have the satisfaction of concluding the Treaty of Commerce, though you may be assured that the want of success in this or any other charge, his Majesty being too just, as well as too well acquainted with the real state of affairs, ever to impute that to a neglect in his servants which is really owing to particular circumstances of the place and persons which render ineffectual all that the best ability, actuated by the warmest zeal, can propose and undertake.[3]

Unsurprisingly the clouds did not disperse and Buckingham unburdened himself to Lady Suffolk,

> In about six weeks I am to leave a Country where I have now past more than two years, & whatever pleasure a Man may promise himself in breathing the air of his native soil & renewing his Antient connection yet the approach of a moment when you are to take an eternal leave of those with whom you have liv'd in an agreeable familiarity and a state of mutual benevolence cannot but be painful to a feeling mind. The unwearied pains I have taken, the difficulty's I have submitted to, & the unpleasant moments I have past in order to attain my purpose makes the assertion, that no Foreigner ever liv'd upon that footing which I now do in Russia, scarcely liable to the censure of Vanity. My situation has improved by degrees, but it is only within these few Months that I have been quite satisfy'd with it, to which the Gracious distinctions which the Sovereign has condescended to shew me have not a little contributed. What welcome I shall meet with in England except from my own family seems to me rather uncertain, as from the extreme Negligence with which my Friends have corresponded with me, I almost suspect that I shall find myself a little upon the footing of a Stranger. In a few Months the experiment will be made & till then I will hope for the best, but so many alterations have happen'd in the interior of England that even at the best a New Man cannot avoid some disagreeable embarrassments.[4]

Buckingham heard that George Macartney was ready to embark on his journey to Petersburg. Sandwich expressed the hope that by the time Buckingham left Russia "the frosts will be so well set in and the weather so favourable that you will meet with no difficulties in your way, and that your journey will be as safe and pleasant as your friends can desire it."[5] Lady Suffolk received several of Buckingham's 'rhapsodies' as he awaited Macartney's arrival,

> This will not be the first letter I have begun by saying truly that I write because of the two I had rather you should find me dull than think me inattentive to the good regard I owe you. It is certainly a very great misfortune to me & many other ingenious Men of Modern times not to have existed some twenty century's ago, how many discovery's have been since made of which we might probably have had all the merit, how many inventions which we should have invented, how many facetious things should we have said, how many agreeable sentiments should we have wrote ! but Alas our wit & wisdom has been forestall'd by those who, greatly otherwise our inferiors, have avail'd themselves of the fortuitous advantage of being born our elder Brother in the Universe! Men of Genius who never read any books but Grammar, Dictionary's, & Almanack Lists of successions of Kings & Queens, illustrated with most succinct relations of Battles, Fires, Revolutions, Plagues & Hard Frosts, by which means the whole field of Human wit, wisdom, & invention would lay open to their ability's. My Education, for which you are in some sort answerable, was unfortunately in a different stile, this puts me in the disagreeable situation of hardly ever being able to say or write a good thing but what my memory tells me some elder puppy has had the impertinence to say or write before.[6]

The next 'rhapsody' began with a quote from 'The Beggar's Opera' with which Lady Suffolk was so familiar,

> 'Not with a Highwayman you sorry Slut!' says Mrs Peachum to Miss Polly when after the discovery of her marriage with the seducing Captain she sweetly sings. Can love be controlled by advice? Extraordinary as my letters usually are the beginning of this will still surprise you till you know that I am just inform'd that the Sister of the M of D & the Niece of the E of N has thrown herself into the arms of her Irish Footman. As the Lady has a full grown child the Footman is the proper object of compassion. It is most amazing to me that the numberless instances of ruinous & disgraceful Matches should not suggest some serious reflections to parents & Guardians & introduce a different Mode of education. Yet what expedients can avail? How can you preserve & protect your Child, when the Physician who feels her Pulse, the Surgeon who breathes the Vein, every Person whose Profession or talents are essential to improve her, the Footman who carry's the Flambeau & even the Spritely Ostler, who expeditiously Harnesses two miserable Hack's to a Post Chaise, are equally dangerous? It may be said, why should not Young Women have opportunity's of looking

round the world, of seeing a variety of Men, of sifting their characters and chusing him whom their inclination favors & their Judgement approves? Ans: because for obvious, & indeed, very excusable reasons, nineteen times in twenty they will chuse wrong.[7]

He wrote that the Empress had lately given Count Orlov a very fine village near Petersburg, that he felt the Prussian Minister was jealous of the distinctions Catherine gave to her nephew, and that he anticipated mild weather might make the roads impassable for George Macartney.

In December the Empress invited Buckingham to stay at Sarskoe Selo where,"Sir George Macartney arrived yesterday with a very bad cold and sore throat, and found me much in the same situation."[8] In January he had his formal audience of leave but to his disappointment it was not with the Empress, "I was greatly surprised that the Vice-Chancellor spoke for her."[9] Although this was traditional court protocol no-one had thought to forewarn Buckingham and he complained of the "most unfriendly inattention not to acquaint me previously." His hurt feelings were soothed when the Empress "was pleased to signify a desire that I would come to Court during the short time I had still to remain here, and I had the honour of supping with her last night at Count Orlov's." This intimate dinner was Buckingham's last private encounter with Catherine. He planned to leave soon afterwards but there had been a fortnight's thaw and he hoped to be "excused remaining here a few days more in hopes of a frost, as the roads are excessively bad, which is evident from the post's coming in later than ever I have known it since my residence in Russia." Eventually, when in mid-January the weather conditions were judged conducive for travel, Buckingham left Petersburg laden with gifts from the Empress and with mixed emotions.

Treaty—the Post Script

Following Russia's insistence on a financial transaction, Britain and Russia stuck rigidly to their opposing viewpoints and monotonously reiterated their positions. In 1766 Buckingham's successor George Macartney concluded the Commercial Treaty but unlike Buckingham he found his tenure in Russia for the most part extremely arduous and unpleasant. On his arrival, the twenty-seven year old newly knighted Macartney endured ten weeks of an unspecified crippling illness and by May he grumbled that the treaty of commerce went on with uncommon slowness and that he had given up entirely on the Treaty of Alliance. Although a Treaty of Commerce was signed in August there was a clause within it which he ought to have sent to London for clearance and he was very severely rebuked for not doing so. It took another period of intense wrangling before both sides reached agreement on the wording. As soon as the treaty was ratified Macartney was immediately recalled but not told when his successor Hans Stanley would arrive and a further nine months went by before he left Russia. During this time he found a diversion from his unhappiness in a liaison with Mademoiselle Khitrov, one of the Empress's Ladies in Waiting who was also, unfortunately for Macartney, a cousin of Panin. When the lady fell pregnant and was packed off home threatened with banishment to the cloister, Macartney's name and reputation was for a time severely damaged at Court. When the scandal abated he was accepted back into society and felt moved to thank the Russian Court for their "great consideration in a very private affair".[10] Despondent during his last months in Petersburg he believed that "a treaty of alliance (to be) as distant and unlikely to be brought about as a league with Prester John or the King of Bantam."[11] (Prester John was a legendary Christian patriarch from the 12th century, said to be the

George, Earl of Macartney.

descendant of one of the Three Magi and King of India. The East India Company had a trading post at Bantam at the western end of Java in Indonesia, but had lost it to the Dutch.)

Despite all his efforts no Treaty of Alliance was made and Macartney left, deeply critical of Russia, "vain of past success, giddy with present prospects, blind and incredulous to the possibility of a reverse, this Court becomes every day more intoxicated with pride, more contemptuous towards other powers, more elated with her own."[12] Longing for home, depressed, and feeling extremely unwell he said he would "drag on a miserable existence until I am relieved either by the arrival of my successor or by a natural dissolution."[13]

Most galling from Buckingham's point of view was that Panin later made no secret of the fact that 500,000 roubles would most certainly have resulted in an Anglo-Russian alliance in the critical months that followed the death of Augustus III in Poland. Sixteen years later the matter still rankled when he wrote to Lord George Germain, "The idea of Russia never offers itself without my lamenting the economy of the English Treasury during the year 1764; as it rendered ineffectual a negotiation, which, most honourable to me, would have proved materially usefull to my country. It could not indeed but have given a different cast to every political transaction in which England has since that time been engag'd."[14] It was a small comfort to know that although it was Macartney who was present when the Treaty of Commerce was signed, King George appreciated and fully recognised Buckingham's years of endeavour.

When Buckingham left Russia the Empress Catherine, who considered him her friend and "compatriote", presented him with many gifts including a brilliant diamond ring and a truly magnificent tapestry of Peter the Great.

When Macartney left Russia, she gave him a snuff-box.

Notes

1. NRO MC 3/285 Letter 88.
2. NRO MC 3/285 Letter 89.
3. *Despatches and Correspondence ...*, Vol. 2, p.241.
4. NRO MC 3/285 Letter 90.
5. *Despatches and Correspondence ...* Vol. 2, p.245.
6. NRO MC 3/285 Letter 92.
7. NRO MC 3/285 Letter 93.
8. *Despatches and Correspondence ...*, Vol. 2, p.269.
9. Ibid. p.272.
10. Roberts M., *Macartney in Russia*, (archive.org), 1908. p.74.
11. Barrow, J., *Some Account of the public life of the Earl of Macartney*, Vol. 1, Appendix No IV, p.424.
12. Ibid. p.29.
13. Ibid. p.63.
14. *Report on the Manuscripts of the Marquess of Lothian*, p.371.

Homeward to Life with the Wife

O n the long journey home Buckingham had time to ruminate upon his sojourn in Russia, recording his impressions in his *'Russian Memoranda'*.[1] His long acquaintance with the Empress caused him to see her in a new light compared to his initial rather rose-tinted view, and although his comments were less favourable than earlier, he reiterated his profound admiration for Catherine's considerable political acumen and credited her with the no small achievement of keeping the peace. He also admired the consistent efforts she made to elevate Russia and her people to higher standards.

En route to England he wrote to Lady Suffolk:

Feb ye 21st 1765. Koningsberg, in Brandenburg

P.s. Feb the 23rd. We are at Berlin. I addressed Lady Buckingham yesterday & now it is my disposition to address you. If I delighted in repetitions or was lazily dispos'd the copy of my letter to her with only a change of the date would be an exact account of the transactions of the day & of my situation in the evening, two little circumstances excepted that I have traveled without a tilt & am not within hearing of a crying Child.

It cannot help but affect every one who has a feeling heart to trace the cruel effects of the war upon these unfortunate Country's through which I am passing. Ruined Villages, large & well built towns absolutely depopulated are objects which continually meet the eye. I have suffered greatly all this day from cold & warm winds, the first came from the South the most piercing I ever experienced from that quarter the latter was a sort of subscription Gale for which I was oblig'd to the Footmen & the Man who drove my cart.* I am refreshing myself at an Old Burgomaster, & whilst a Room is warming for me I have taken possession of his private Apartment; he has very much the air of the old Dutch soldiers that came over with King William & he interrupts me every moment to talk of the events of the succession, & of other Antient story's in most Abominable Latin, to which I answer in rather worse as for example—Excellentissme Domine si been memini Serenissimus Orangia Princess Anglian invasit anno Salutis 1689. Ego e contra—88—but I forget that you don't understand Latin, it is ten thousand pity's, you may however intreat Lady Betty Germaine to explain the meaning of those few words to you. My poor landlord is afflicted with

---

* i.e. they passed wind!

the Gravel & the Colick & retires every five minutes into the next room, leaving prudentially the door open that I may distinguish which of his complaints occasions his absence.

A joyful letter arrived from Lord Barrington who welcomed news of his dear friend's imminent return to England, "In obedience to your commands I write to you, and direct my letter to Berlin with great pleasure, because your instruction to do so is a proof that you are soon to return home. I have thought you too long absent for some time, on your account and on my own; I hope I shall never more have another uneasy thought about you." He briefly outlined news from Parliament, "a dull subject" and brought him up to date on events at the Opera House "Our tenor is much admired and Gardini conducts the orchestra. We hissed one set of dancers off the stage the first night; it is said a better set is coming." He passed on scandalous gossip about the Duke and Duchess of Grafton, "she has £4,000 a year for herself and the children. The Duke has declared he has no objection to her conduct, but chuses to live alone, having found they could not live happily together. His Grace passes his time with Nancy Parsons, and her Grace lives in retreat. No court, no spectacles, no assemblies." He pointed out an astounding similarity between the looks of the Duchess and Buckingham's own Mary Anne and mischievously suggested that "an infidelity must be excused. Perhaps when you arrive your ANTICHE PENE may revive also."[2] The resemblance between portraits of the two ladies is indeed so remarkable they might have been mistaken for twins. Buckingham's appetite for London was further whetted by his friend's comment, "Mrs Cornelys has made Carlisle House the most elegant place of Public entertainment that ever was in this, or perhaps any country and the opera club is very impatient for its dear president. Adieu my dear Lord, make haste hither."

After an arduous ten week journey Buckingham arrived in London on 28 March 1765. On 6 April *The Norwich Mercury* was pleased to report that "His Excellency the Earl of Buckinghamshire arrived on Wednesday se-enight at Harwich, from his Embassy at the Court of Russia; and the next day about Noon, at his house in Charles Street, Berkeley Square, London. On Sunday his Lordship was introduced to the Queen at St James's and was graciously received."

Buckingham's fears of having been forgotten were immediately and gratifyingly dispelled when he was welcomed home by his family and friends with open arms. With open arms and tears of joy in the case of aunt Henrietta and of Mary Anne, who had sorely missed her husband. It was no doubt with a mixture of relief, excitement and apprehension that she greeted him after two years and nine months apart, including the two long journeys there and back. For his part, Buckingham was happily reacquainted with his wife and delighted to discover that Harriet had grown into an enchanting and precocious three year old. Soon the The *Norwich Mercury* reported that "On Wednesday, the Right Hon the Earl of Buckinghamshire, late Ambassador to the Court of Russia, arrived here in perfect health, and passed through the City to his seat at Blickling, Norfolk." On arrival

Peter the Great tapestry at Blickling Hall.

at Blickling he was quickly made aware that Mary Anne had discovered that the house, in her estimation, was sorely lacking in both style and comfort. She made many appeals for improvements and Buckingham, with the twin aims of pleasing his wife whilst enhancing the house, took notice. Lady Suffolk, with her impeccable good taste, was an enormous influence on them both and between the trio plans were drawn up which over the next decade dramatically altered the scope of the house and transformed the estate.

The Empress Catherine's most generous parting gift to Buckingham was a magnificent wool and silk tapestry depicting Peter the Great on horseback at the Battle of Poltava in 1709. It measured 14 feet 4 inches by 16 feet 7 inches but there was no room large enough at Blickling in which to hang it. Because the tapestry was priceless not only in monetary terms but because it was a visible statement of the high esteem in which the Empress held the Earl, a dramatic, if expensive solution was found in the shape of Norwich architects Thomas and William Ivory who were charged with demolishing and rebuilding the north and west ranges of the Hall. Within these they created the magnificent Peter the Great Room with its striking illusionist ceiling by local artist William Wilkins the Elder, and impressive grand State Rooms. At Mary Anne's behest Buckingham also had sections of the south wall demolished and a new wall constructed further south in order to enlarge the entrance hall, which she had condemned as too old fashioned and dark. To further enlighten the hall, a central doorway was created and a grand staircase installed and painted white. In recesses to either side of new stained glass windows stood carved wooden statues of Elizabeth I and Anne Boleyn, acting as a reminder of Anne Boleyn's birth within a previous house on the site.

For his wife's further comfort and pleasure the bedrooms were redecorated; his became the Blue Room and Mary Anne's, separated from his by her new dressing room, was beautifully embellished with en vogue chinoiserie. The State Bedroom, designed by Samuel Wyatt, contained a white marble fireplace and a suite of Adam white and gilt furniture and the bed hangings were fashioned from the canopy of state Buckingham had taken to Russia. With its impressive Palladian pillars, this room replicated on a larger scale that of Lady Suffolk's bedroom at Marble Hill. In the wider estate, gardens with pretty walkways were created for Mary Anne's enjoyment and 'Lady Buckingham's Garden' was hidden in a new part of the wilderness to the north of the Hall. A great transformation in the grounds was made by damming the nearby Silvergate stream which helped to fill the serpentine lake dug out before Buckingham's departure for Russia. His loyal and astute Estate Manager Robert Copeman had kept his master regularly informed during his long absence, reporting the condition of crops and livestock, and no doubt the two men thoroughly inspected the grounds together on the Earl's return.

Buckingham's by now well honed diplomatic skills were put to good use locally. His neighbours' petty disputes were swiftly resolved through his good natured willingness to listen, discuss and thereafter reach solutions to the satisfaction of everyone concerned. However, the more serious issue of Sir Harbord Harbord's perceived disloyalty in Parliament took longer to repair. Harbord had continued to speak against the Government and Buckingham took this as a betrayal of not only the party but of George Grenville in particular. This disloyalty, on top of what he saw as deep ingratitude to himself, having been instrumental in obtaining the Norwich seat for Harbord, upset him greatly. Sharing his concern with Grenville brought a reply from Downing Street dated 9 July 1765,

> I am extremely sorry, my dear Lord, for the uneasiness which you express at your political situation and at the many disagreeable circumstances which have occurred to you in the course of it. I have felt them for you very sincerely and I hope I need not say that my best wishes and utmost endeavours have at all times been employed to remove or diminish them. The change which the King has been making for these two months in his administration and which I understand will be declared tomorrow, you will easily see it makes it quite impossible for me to be any use at present to any of my friends.[3]

His prediction proved correct as Grenville was removed from office the very next day and replaced by Lord Rockingham.

Locally Buckingham continued his attempts to find common ground with his stubborn Gunton cousin but Harbord persisted in opposing his wishes at every turn. The following is taken from Secretary Mr Thomlinson's draft of 'Minutes for a Letter to Mr Harbord' in which Buckingham suggests the expedient of pulling rank,[4]

It may further be necessary to observe how unnatural it is for two persons who take different parts at Westminster to make a common political interest in the country. That if Mr Harbord proposes in opposition to Mr Grenville to support the present administration, in justice to Lord B he ought to decline standing for Norwich at the next general election. That the idea of a probable coolness with his neighbours at Gunton has given Lord B more uneasiness than any misfortune he as yet has experienced. That it is mutually for their honour and interest to give each other every public and private support. That no two persons can always be exactly of the same opinion and therefore for the sake of consistency it is indispensably necessary that upon such occasions one must give way to the other, upon which supposition it is submitted to Mr Harbord, which of the two may best expect such a deference.

Buckingham conceded that Lady Suffolk's accusation that he found it harder to write interesting letters to her from home than from Russia was accurate. In September, en route "to take my week's waiting" at Court as a Lord of the Bedchamber, he explained, "The reasons are obvious; things are always the more esteemed the further they come from; and the relation of events will always be more entertaining when the writer is at such a distance as leaves some scope for his imagination to play, without any danger of the little ornamental fictions with which he dresses his pictures being discovered."[5] Later in the month he dined in Norwich with a new sheriff "upon turbot, venison, swan, and turkey, which it was strongly enjoined me to wash down with copious drafts of Lusitanian wine. In spite of the cordial entreaties of my landlord, I remained sober, and reached Blickling time enough to see the chit you so kindly enquire after, before her hour of sleep."[6] Back at Blickling with 'the chit' Harriet, he and Mary Anne entertained his younger half brother Henry and his wife Anne whom he had married in July 1761. Henry was a bright and amiable young man who had travelled extensively through Europe after attending Oxford. He loved France and often visited Paris with Anne by his side and shared with his brothers their passion for opera. Glimpses of the Buckingham's own marriage were revealed in a candid note to his aunt,

> Lady Buckingham is tolerably well, and most intolerably lazy: she will have her own way; and I am so very fond of mine, that I dare not press her too far, for fear of retaliation; a manner of vindicating their rights, to which in all times, and upon every occasion, offended ladies have been eager to recur. As yet she will not determine whether she will come to London in December or January, insinuating that it depends upon a circumstance. What that circumstance may be, I do not exactly comprehend. An ill-bred philosophic friend of mine was pleased to say, that he never gave himself the trouble to unravel the flimsy thread of feminine mysteries. I neither approved his idea nor his expressions, as I can well remember the pleasure I took in penetrating through the silken web with which even the most

innocent delight to veil their meaning. Pray does your little silkworm, Harriet, begin to spin? I am persuaded she will very soon.[7]

The little silkworm referred to was his lively niece Harriet Hotham who was approaching thirteen. As her relationship with her mother Dorothy was extremely volatile she had lived relatively peacefully with her aunt (perhaps grandmother) at Marble Hill since she was eight. Mary Anne's secret 'circumstance' had been that she was in early pregnancy, but she suffered a miscarriage soon after this.

In October, as Parliament squabbled over its leadership, Buckingham wrote to the MP Robert Nugent, a favoured family friend,[8] "Whatever face of triumph the second-rate politicians who have embarked in the frail green vessel* may display to the public, I am well assured the leaders are fully conscious how little they are equal to their situation, and that they can never wear those new robes, which hang by a cobweb to their shoulders, with honour to themselves or utility to their country."[9]

He lamented Grenville's departure from office, "When avarice or extravagance makes nineteen in twenty deaf to every other consideration but their own monetary advantage, surely the Treasury ought to be directed by a minister who acting from experience, knowledge and integrity, despises popular clamour, resists it with temper and firmness and whose measure, founded on true principles will best be justified by their consequences."[10]

In November Buckingham candidly told his aunt,

> I feel myself at this instant in the most indolent, good-for-nothing humour possible; and though there is no person in the universe to whom I more willingly communicate my ideas and no-ideas than to your ladyship, yet much languid deliberation had preceded my taking the pen in hand, and great resolution is necessary to keep it in motion. There is also a strange kind of merit in laying down a book full of superior sense, to fill a sheet of paper with flat nonsense; but it is a merit which arises from duty rightly placed, and a desire to testify affection: and so much for my introduction.[11]

The book he had laid aside was the Memoir of the famous French Frondeur** Cardinal de Retz, which he favoured over those of contemporary politicians, "I should prefer his parts, his presence of mind, and his comprehension, to those of any man whom reading or conversation has made known to me."

He reported on the building works at Blickling which were well underway,

> The alterations in the eating-room go on: Gothic it was, and more Gothic it will be, in spite of all the remonstrances of modern improvers and lovers of Grecian architecture. The ceiling is to be painted with the loves of

---

*   The House of Commons

**   a political rebel

Cupid and Psyche. Cupid is to hover exactly over the centre of the table, to indicate to the maitre d'hotel the exact position of the venison pasty. I have determined what is to be done with the hall, which you ought to approve, and indeed must approve. Some tributary sorrow should however be paid to the nine worthies; but Hector has lost his spear and his nose, David his harp, Godfrey of Boulogne his ears, Alexander the Great his highest shoulder, and part of Joshua's belly is fallen in. As the ceiling is to be raised, eight of them must have gone, and Hector is at all events determined to leave his niche. You will forgive my replacing them with eight worthies of my own times, whose figures are not as yet essentially mutilated, viz. Dr Shebbeare, Mr Wilkes, Dr Hill, Mr Glover, Mr Dep. Hodges, Mr Whitfield, Justice Fielding, and Mr Foote; and as Anna Boleyn was born at Blickling, it will not be improper to purchase her father Henry the Eighth's figure (which by order is no longer to be exhibited at the Tower), who will fill with credit the space occupied by the falling Hector.

This last was a slip of the pen of course as he meant Anna Boleyn's husband, and in fact the two statues eventually ensconced in the niches represented Elizabeth I and Anna Boleyn. The eight worthies he jested about included Dr Shebbeare, a political satirist; Mr Wilkes, of the famous trial; Justice Fielding, a Magistrate and social reformer known as Blind Beak; and Samuel Foote, the famous one-legged comic actor-manager. He continued, "Nothing is more amusing than to see numbers of workmen within and without doors: it is not exactly the same thing to pay their bills. I have numbers of workmen employed around me, and in consequence am amused and ruined." Mary Anne and his sister Dorothy Hotham had colluded against him,

by entering into a conspiracy against the old chimney-piece in the eating-room. Their little intrigues can never shake my settled purpose, but they tease me, and your authority is necessary to silence them, (they) are as well as may be, and are laughing a great deal at something very little in the next room. They have but one young man with them at present, whom they meritoriously cherish; nor do they quarrel about the single sheep, as I have promised them at least two more on Tuesday next. The countess, not choosing to have a whole horse to herself, has signified her intention of airing upon a pillion, and we are now in quest of a horse who will take up the odds. Lady Dorothy has borrowed the ale-wife's gray nag, which she prefers, as his complexion is best suited to winter roads.[12]

In December he informed Lady Suffolk he would soon return to London and that,

Lady B and Lady Dorothy propose to burn the old chimney-piece in my absence. Let them at their peril; for you will resent it as well as I. The joiner had put an earl's coronet over the door; but it is ordered to be changed into a bull. Lady B and my sister's decency proposed a cow; but to compromise the matter, directions are given to the carver to make it as like an ox as heraldry will admit.[13] [14]

Upon arrival in London on 12 December 1765 Buckingham told Mary Anne that he hoped to be back at Blickling before long. Finding "politicks indefinable beyond expression"[15] he made time for pleasurable pursuits to offset them. "The Opera, Tuesday, very thin, ten pounds and four shillings in The Pitt and Front Boxes, Drury Lane Wednesday. The Duchess of Bolton acknowledged me from the Balcony, Mrs Pitt from a Stage Box. The Countess of Northumberland did not notice me, but Mrs Grenville did, as well as her charming daughter." A week later he was still detained in London and apologetic,

> I hope you will not be angry at my being obliged by business of serious consequences to stay in town until Thursday, as I believe it will be in my power to remain at Blickling till the 13th of next month. We had a division in the House of Lords on Tuesday, the Minority's of which I was one consisted of only 24, but I never remember any set of Gentlemen make so miserable a figure in debate as the present prime Minister.* His majesty continues to receive me most graciously. Lady Suffolk is well, Mrs Grenville, better; all are returning into the country and the town will soon be thinner than ever. The two Nugents are to come with me into Norfolk, which they flatter themselves will be agreeable to you. The poor Prince Frederick lingers on from day to day, but cannot last much longer, he has suffered greatly from scarrifications tapping & etc.[16]

Fears about the health of the King's youngest brother were sadly warranted because the fifteen year old Prince died on 29 December.

Buckingham made a speech about which he was self deprecating, "I tried on Tuesday in the House of Lords if I had not lost my voice as well as my nose in Russia, but I had no opportunity of speaking till the House was tired of hearing much better speakers than myself. The King has been most gracious to me ever since I was in town." He was keen to make his way home to Blicking and Mary Anne,

> I have had a bad cold these three days, and was really a good deal out of order in the Night, but recovered myself so far as to be able to dine with the Duke of York today, and all now as well as a man can be, who has a sore throat, a pain in his lower stomach and finds the softest cushion much too hard for the part he sits upon. All these miseries should not have determined one to put off my journey one day, if that wretch Nugent had not sworn he would not leave Gosfield till Thursday; if he stays longer, it shall not stop me, when you see us punish the Guilty as they deserve, but censure not the innocent.[17]

---

*   Rockingham

At last, having successfully prised the Nugents out of their family seat at Gosfield Hall near Braintree in Essex, Buckingham's party arrived in Norfolk to see in the new year at Blickling.

Notes

1. *Despatches and Correspondence ...*, Vol. 2, pp.273-276.
2. *Report on the Manuscripts of the Marquess of Lothian*, p.253.
3. *Report on the Manuscripts of the Marquess of Lothian*, p.255.
4. Ibid. p.284.
5. *Letters to and from Henrietta ...*, Vol. 2, p.296.
6. Ibid. p.298.
7. Ibid. p.298.
8. Afterwards Lord Nugent, Lord Clare and Earl Nugent, known as 'a jovial and voluptuous Irishman'.
9. *Report on the Manuscripts of the Marquess of Lothian*, p.258.
10. Ibid.
11. *Letters to and from Henrietta ...*, Vol. 2, p.30.
12. Ibid. p.307.
13. Ibid. p.310.
14. The Hobart family crest is a bull passant (striding) which represents valour and magnanimity,"*party per pale sable and gules, all bezanty, and a ring in his nose.*" The fact that the Boleyn, or Bullen, family is represented by bull's heads on their crest is coincidental.
15. NRO MC 3/285 Letter 5.
16. NRO MC 3/285 Letter 7.
17. NRO MC 3/285 Letter 6.

The 'Tea Room' at the Assembly Rooms, Bath photographed in 2012.

1766—Domesticity & Riotous Assemblies

The close and fond relationship between Buckingham and his Countess is discernible in the consistent tenderness in his letters to her. They also show that his diplomatic skills were occasionally put to good use as Mary Anne was a capricious young woman used to getting her own way. He indulged what he condescended to see as her feminine traits, allowed her moods and tantrums to express themselves, then diffused her complaints with tender admonishments and apparent acquiescence. It came naturally to employ his sense of humour when scolding, placating, reassuring or comforting her, and undoubtedly his considerable experience with women and the large age gap between them, in tandem with his affable nature and innate kindness, made him a considerate husband. In this first of a series of letters written during travels in the West Country on a rare visit to his properties there, he related the awkward experience of wandering alone around Bath, in a tale designed to entertain her.

19 June 1766. Tho you heard from me on the 19th in the evening from Reading, yet as your Norfolk journey will make it some days before you receive this, and as some little complaisance should occasionally be shewn to that impatience in your temper which makes so strong a contrast with the bearing and forebearing of mine, it may be as well for me to indulge myself in the pleasure of writing to you. After having travelled some nine hours through wind and rain, I arrived yesterday between five and six; the dinner was my first care, a Turbot, Peas, and a Tart were immediately ordered and almost as immediately produced. Mr Phillot (the Landlord) attended dinner, I talked to him of former times, which his memory had forgot, but his complaisance recollected. Dinner over, I walked forth in the rain in search of Adventures, finding nobody in the streets (indeed not even in my way, for I lost it three times to my no small humiliation). I entered the Coffee House trying to look insolent because I felt myself out of countenance. In an instant every eye was upon me, and not one eye I knew. As it has since been insinuated to me the Company were divided in their opinions; I was taken for a Gambler, a Lieutenant of a Man of War, exalted into a Captain of a Merchant Ship, a Bristol Bankrupt, and a Surgeon who has turned all his attention to a particular Malady. From thence, I proceeded to the Assembly Room. It is ninety foot in length, seventy of which I was obliged to advance before I came near any part of the Company, which consisted of two miserable card tables. At one of these sat Lady Arundel, a Hampshire friend, to whom I bow'd obsequious,

but she would not own me, and I navigated back the seventy feet with great precipitation. I stopped to read a printed paper which catch'd my eye, it informed me of the Landlords' humble hope that Gentlemen would not come often without subscribing. I left the room just after, and I read in the waiters faces that they thought the purport of that paper had hasten'd my departure. Then I met Mr Gore in a chair, he stopped and first I called him Mr Morris and then I called him Mr Gore. Next I met Mr Kind and Mr B Kind. Lastly I discovered—you have been told that when Ld Grosvenor labor'd himself to make himself agreeable to the now Lady C Spencer, she said he resembled a Figure pendant from a Gibbet. Lastly I say I discovered Lord Grosvenor who at that moment fully justified her Ladyship's simile. We accosted each other in rather an awkward stile, and in three words he informed me that I had little chance of seeing him, and none of feasting my eyes upon the charms of Lady Grosvenor. He never goes to the Rooms and the poor woman is confined with a swell'd face, upon the whole it appears to me that she is doing penance for having deviated from the kind of conduct prescribed to her by her arbitrary Lord. Since that Mr Charnock had appeared to me and we walked and talked and talked and walked. I am just now returned from the Square, from where the Circus is, from where the Crescent is to be, and from a little Hill which commands a most pleasant prospect of the City, all the New part is very fine indeed. Send me a particular account of your Dairy, Cows, Pigs and Chickens, if you breed any of the latter let me advise you to prefer the Barking sort. I mean to leave this place tomorrow.[1]

As was his habit he ended with a message to his daughter, "Comps to Ly Harriet" and travelled onwards to visit George Edgcumbe, a fellow Privy Counseller.

Mount Edgcumbe 29 June, 1766 (Near Plymouth)

I received two days ago your Letter of the 21st which, as it seems wrote in the complaining stile, obliges me to take notice that this is the fifth letter I have wrote to your Ladiship since the 19th of this month. My Journey would not have hitherto been disagreeable if constant pain had not prevented me from enjoying anything. Lord and Lady Edgcumbe are extremely polite and good humoured; he is most amiable in that part of his character which leads him to do justice to his Brother*, one of the Frankest, cleverest and honestest beings that ever put a thinking (person) in good-humour with his Kind.

Canon Snow's[2] Wife threw me almost into a fever with her unceasing attentions and repeated questions; she is without exception, the most indefatigable Querist my experience ever met with, as for example

---

* George's late elder brother Richard Edgcumbe had been a frequenter of White's Club where he gambled heavily. He died childless in 1761.

Bm.	I stopped at Berlin in my way from Petersburgh.
Mrs Snow.	Pray My Lord were you ever at Berlin?
Bm.	I thought the Winters in Petersbugh agreeable.
Mrs S.	Pray My Lord were the Winters in Petersburgh agreeable?
Be.	This coat was embroidered in Russia.
Mrs S.	Pray My Lord is that Russian embroidery?
Bm.	I had a pleasant walk this morning.
Mrs S.	Pray My Lord had you a pleasant walk this morning?

Guess how I must be delighted with that sort of discourse for three days together; and yet when a peevish word broke out as in spite of my teeth it sometimes did, I detested my own ingratitude which would not suffer me to be pleased with one whose whole intention was to please me. You will take care not to live too much alone as Mrs Laton and Miss Gay will be pleased to see you.[3]

From Exeter, Buckingham described an encounter with tenants in the village of Beer, over whom he played lord and master, "Mary Marshal was the daughter of a Farmer at Tavistoke, a far more elegant and finished piece of work than ever before was hammered out of an anvil" whereas, "Mr John Stapleton was the eldest born of an industrious farmer at Beer, who left him possessed of an ample fortune. John, tho' prudent in the management of his fortune, was dissolute and indiscreet in his pleasures, and in none so much as in that most justifiable of all excesses, an indefatigable pursuit of the fair sex." The richest bachelor in the Parish had seduced many "unwary Maidens and some frail Matrons" several of whom "could not prevent the same of being notorious" (pregnant). Stapleton fell in love, or lust, with Mary Marshal who refused his advances and "in the weakness of a tender moment he offered her Marriage" and she accepted his proposal. On reflection Stapleton "recollected that he was sixty, and that forty years spent in revelry might make him a little unequal to the expectations and pretensious of twenty five" and that she might later succumb to a younger man, reasoning that "a cautious Virgin might prove a frail Wife." He tried to extricate himself from the engagement but Buckingham, on hearing the circumstances "sent for John, insisted upon being present at the Wedding, gave the Bride away this morning, made the happy pair dine with me afterwards, and have just order'd them to bed."[4]

He then confessed to Mary Anne his longing for Blickling,

Lady Suffolk has wrote a few lines to me and seems in such good spirits that there is great probability of her being persuaded to accompany me to Blickling. It is a great satisfaction to me to find you are so well pleased with every thing, but it concerns me to think that as we should want at least thirty chairs for the New Eating Room, it will be impossible to have them made in time this summer. You may however consult: the seats must be either Black Hair or Black Leather and the frames Mahogany but less than those in the Study. I most heartily wish myself at Blickling.

P.S. Tell Bailey I am not in the least angry with him, but as to your complaining Postscript —I will say nothing, as it pains me to distress you even when you most deserve it.

After a few days spent in London "to consult lawyers how to secure a seat in Parliament" he made his way to Blickling and spent the remainder of the summer with Mary Anne, planning further improvements and additions to the Hall and the wider Estate. The couple's happiness was increased in late July by the knowledge that Mary Anne was pregnant and they looked forward to the arrival of a brother or sister for four year old Harriet.

Autumn brought civil unrest, a direct result of the draconian taxes levied on the sale of wheat. Ordinary people throughout England suffered greatly as the price of bread rose wildly beyond their means to buy it, and local businessmen were accused of profiteering. The *Norwich Mercury* predicted in January that, "We are informed the Exportation of Corn will soon be prohibited for six months; and it is thought the Embargo will be general throughout the Kingdom" but this prediction proved wildly inaccurate. The wheat crop in most parts of Europe had failed and in Great Britain it had fallen well below average. In consequence the price of wheat and flour shot up on the continent and English producers, millers and dealers were, perhaps understandably, tempted to ship the bulk of their supplies to these profitable foreign markets. This in turn caused the domestic price to increase even further and in a knock-on effect the prices of other foodstuffs also rose. Instead of the predicted Embargo the opposite happened when the Act on the statute books allowed the exportation of wheat after 16 August. A swift repeal of this act would have saved the situation, but following the advice of his ministers, the King prorogued Parliament until November, thereby making further legislation impossible. The *Norwich Mercury*, 20 September 1766: "On Saturday last a Petition signed by the Magistrates and principal Inhabitants of this City, was sent up by Express to the Privy Council, praying them to take into their Consideration, how to prevent the farther Exportation of Wheat, on Account of the high Price it is now at, as well as every other Kind of Provision."

When a Norfolk butter woman raised her price from 8d. to 9d. per pint a crowd gathered and angrily started to throw butter and vegetables around the market and when the magistrates attempted to intervene, they were driven off. Violence swiftly escalated as the mobs sought to intimidate the purveyors and destroy property, including houses and mills. News spread that riots were breaking out all over England and that there were nowhere near enough troops to quell them. In Norfolk, Buckingham's authority was called upon a significantly more serious matter than the trifling matrimonial affair in Devon. John Patteson, the Mayor of Norwich, had "the honour of transmitting to Lord Buckinghamshire three petitions, relative to the dreaded scarcity of wheat, which we are persuaded you will not, my Lord, think it a trouble to cause to be delivered, one to the Rt Honble the Earl of Northington, one to his Grace the Duke of Grafton, and one to the Rt Honble Ch Townshend, Esq.. I cannot but esteem it is a most fortunate circumstance that these petitions will thus under your Lordships's countenance go with so much weight as I make no doubt will obtain such relief as may be in the power of government to make."[5] Buckingham duly sent the petitions and the Mayor thanked him on 24 September, "I have had a letter from the Treasury requiring the prices of wheat for three market days last past, which have accordingly been transmitted and this gives us hopes that the matter will again be brought under the consideration of the privy council."[6] But a few days later councillor John Gay urgently requested the Earl's intervention,

> We have perpetual alarms and informations of threats, thank God no further mischief has happened in the city. But some has been done in the neighbourhood in Trowse by almost demolishing the house of one Mr Money there, and speeches given out with threats against Mr Bacon's at Earleham. Under our present circumstances it would have been happy for us if your Lordship was with us to advise and assist us and I do believe the knowledge of your presence amongst us would awe and restrain the mob, the apprehensions of many are great for this night. We do and will endeavour to do all we can to prevent further mischief. But we really want help, assistance and advice and the sooner we had your Lordship's the happier I think it would be for us all and might prevent further outrages.[7]

A hastily scribbled post-script said that the Malthouse by Conisford Gates had been set ablaze. Buckingham immediately sought military aid from his old friend Lord Barrington but before his reply could arrive John Gay delivered more distressing news,

> The insurrection here began yesterday in the afternoon between 1 and 2 in our Market Place by a tumultuous assembly of disorderly persons driving the country people away and overturning the provisions they brought. One of our sheriffs, who happened to be there, went immediately amongst them to appease them and prevent further mischief, but in vain. We sent to others to come there to us, and immediately drew up, printed and dispersed the enclosed (paper). This had not the effect we wished; mob increased; great threats. We had the proclamation read in seven different places. The New Mills which supply us with flour were soon after attacked by the mob. Bags and sacks of flour were cut and thrown into the river, the buildings unroofed and greatly damaged. Most of the bakers in town visited by the mob, their windows broke and persons threatened. We have no military assistance. About 5 an express sent to Lord Barrington,

The King agt. Robt. Boardman —
now in Gaol.

Edward Jenkins. Says that at about 5 o'clock in the afternoon of Sunday the 28th. day of September last he was told that the rioters were gone to the house of Richard Lubbock of St. George of Tombland Baker, upon which he determined immediately to go and give all the assistance in his power to the said Mr. Lubbock and accordingly went that upon his coming near the said house he found a great number of riotous persons armed wth. clubs, staves &c. tumultuously assembled at and near the said house which they had then begun to demolish That some of the rioters who stood in the street near the said house were then breaking in pieces and destroying the furniture and goods AND that he saw Robert Boardman near the door of the said house and amongst the rioters there, that he seemed to be one of the most active amongst them in committing acts of violence and outrage and that he there saw the said Robt Boardman with the door of a closet or cupboard in his hands which he endeavoured to break against his knees, but not being able to effect that he threw it upon some other broken furniture which then laid near the place where he then stood, and getting upon the said door he stamped upon the same with great violence until it was broken — That in a very short time after he heard the said Robert Boardman in a loud voice utter the following dreadful expression — viz: God damn my soul, if I don't pull up all the stones in the street and drink blood —

NB. In May next Edward Jenkins intends going to settle at Bath, of which City he is a Native and therefore could not appear against him the aforesaid, should it be thought proper to defer Boardman's Trial till then

Witness statement of Edward Jenkins giving evidence against Robert Boardman, regarding damage to the house of Richard Lubbock and the destruction by fire of John Clover's malthouse at Carrow. Jenkins states that Boardman cried aloud, "God damn my soul, if I don't pull up all the stones in the street and drink blood!" NRO NCR 6h/2/8/5.

Secretary at War, requesting immediate assistance, as we know not where this will end, or how it may cause disorderly people from the country to join the mob here, who threaten the neighbourhood in the country. I remained in the Hall with the Mayor etc., till near 1 this morning, where we planted a guard to preserve the Militia fire-arms lodged there. All our constables charged and a double watch in the night. Could wish your Lordship might come which may have a good effect.[8]

Barrington's response to Buckingham arrived with a measure of good news,

I am this moment sending by express orders for two troops of dragoons to march from Colchester to Norwich to assist the civil magistrates there. It may be useful to acquaint you that let the call be ever so urgent I can send no further military aid into Norfolk, for the troops of the whole kingdom are employ'd and we have not enough by one quarter. I know your weight, authority and spirit; I also know your discretion, my dear friend, and I am certain if this hint does not good, it can do no harm. Adieu, in great haste, but great affection, Barrington.[9]

The *Norwich Mercury* reported, "With army dragoons about to ride from Colchester, Mayor John Patteson took his life in his hands to read the Riot Act, and called out the more respectable citizens who, armed with clubs, broke up the trouble without military assistance."

The Riot Act

Our sovereign lord the King chargeth and commandeth all persons, being assembled, immediately to disperse themselves, and peaceably depart to their habitations, or to their lawful business, upon the pains contained in the act made in the first year of King George, for preventing tumults and riotous assemblies.

God save the King.

If a group of people failed to disperse within one hour of the proclamation, the Act provided that the authorities could use force to disperse them. Barrington regretfully informed Buckingham there were no additional troops available,

All we have are disposed of, and we have occasion for 30,000 more at least to keep the mob of this country in order. I am happy to hear that you are going to Norwich, for I know how much a good man of your quality, spirit and discretion may do. PS The troops have all had orders to obey the civil magistrate, so what there is may be disposed of where most wanted. I know how inadequate the force is to the need, and lament to the last degree that I can send no more. I need not desire you to keep our poverty unknown as much as possible consistent with the circumstances of your situation. The mob is up in my own neighbourhood. I have no troops to send, but I am going myself to see whether an English gentleman who has never injured his neighbours cannot influence them now in their madness.[10]

William Wildman Barrington, 2nd Viscount Barrington, Secretary at War. LC-USZ62-107368.

Barrington's intention to confront the mob which threatened his London neighbourhood was reflected in a simultaneous act of courage on Buckingham's part in addressing the vast unruly mob which had assembled in the centre of Norwich. He had been their respected local representative for approaching twenty years and his convivial personality had endeared him to many. That he was known to be a good landlord and a fair Magistrate also gave him a fair chance of being heard. He was of philanthropic bent too, often giving out largesse to the needy, such as his order for One Hundred Pounds to be disposed of by the Corporation for the further endowment of Doughty's Hospital, "for the more comfortable subsistence of the poor people there." Nonetheless it must have been daunting to make his way through the crowds and summon up the nerve to address a furious, hungry mob, but Buckingham knew the people of Norfolk well. Employing tact, understanding, sympathy, and probably a well judged smattering of humour, he managed to soothe and console the unhappy crowd. He assured them that the King would make a Royal Proclamation "that an Embargo be forthwith laid upon all Ships and Vessels laden or to be laden, in the Ports of Great Britain, with Wheat or Wheat Flour, to be exported to Foreign Parts"[11] and calm was restored. A letter to Lord Barrington, signed by "forty magistrates and principle inhabitants" gave thanks for Buckingham's intervention "it would be extremely ungrateful in us to omit mentioning in the most respectful manner the assistance we have received from the gentlemen of Norfolk, and particularly from the Earl of Buckinghamshire, who on the first notice of this unhappy affair instantly came hither and did us the honour personally to assist us in putting a stop to the insolence and madness of the daring multitude, and by his appearance and counsel greatly contributed to peace and quiet amongst us."[12] Mayor John Patteson also gave thanks for "the eminent part which the Earl of Buckinghamshire has taken in the suppressing of the late riots."[13] Barrington was both impressed and grateful, "I return you a thousand thanks for the early and good news you send me. Norwich has the singular honour of reducing a mob without military aid, an example which I hope other places will endeavour to imitate. Though you ascribe all to the Mayor, forgive me if I suspect your spirit and good sense to have contributed the most to this event."[14] Two days later he congratulated him again "most sincerely on the compleat victory obtained under fair auspices against the mob without military assistance. I carry'd the Mayor's letter to Court and shewed it to the King, who was much pleased with it and commended you. The hanging committee, as it is called, were in the ante-chamber, where I communicated the same letter to them all. They unanimously applauded what has been done. Lord Mansfield was particularly your panegyrist." The post-script this time read "Pray hang as many of your prisoners as possible."[15] The *Norwich Mercury* reported on 4 October, "The Embargo on all Corn Ships may justly be deemed a very timely and fortunate Circumstance to the People of this Kingdom for by the last letters from Italy all agree that their Corn has failed this Year almost everywhere; particularly in Russia, Turkey, France, Spain, Portugal and all over Italy except in the Sicilies, and there the corn runs thin as in England, and that the Turks have felt the scarcity so much as to order their Gallies to seize on all the Corn Ships wherever they can find them." The editor felt it incumbent upon himself to comment on the recent behaviour of the mob and to issue threats against those who might consider repeating such calumnies,

> It is thought sufficient to acquaint our Readers, that from specious
> Pretences a great Number of the lowest People wantonly destroyed
> Provisions in the last Saturday's Market, and committed many other
> Outrages. The real purpose of this licentious Rabble, though covered with
> pretences of redressing Grievances, being manifested by their Robbing,
> plundering and destroying the Houses of Inhabitants, demolishing the
> Corn Mills and Granaries, setting Fire to a very large malthouse, which
> was entirely consumed, and practicing every Kind of Villainy which the
> most wicked Malice could invent. We are authorised to say that on the
> first future attempts to raise fresh commotions in this City the Alarm Bells
> will be rung, the Inhabitants instantly assembled and the whole Force
> of the City will be employed in crushing the Delinquents on their first
> appearance.

A snippet in the same edition announced "On Friday last the Russian Ambassador and his lady arrived at Blickling-Hall, the Seat of the Right Hon the Earl of Buckinghamshire and on Monday last returned from thence to London." Fedor Ivanovitch Gross and his wife had certainly chosen an interesting time to visit Norfolk. The following week Buckingham was summoned to London to a meeting with Lord Shelburne. This was not entirely unexpected as the rumour mill had been working well and Buckingham surmised correctly that he would be invited to go as Ambassador to Madrid. The latest incumbent, Buckingham's friend William Nassau de Zuylestein, 4th Earl of Rochford, had been instructed to leave Spain immediately for Paris to replace the Duke of Richmond and it was this move that created the vacancy at Madrid. Following his talk with Shelburne,

Buckingham told George Grenville,

> After the first compliments, he entered into a dissertation upon the
> critical state of affairs in Spain, which I interrupted before he had well
> concluded his first period, by telling him it would not be candid in me
> to bear his Lordship to enlarge upon the subject, as I had no thoughts
> of accepting the mission. But not unnecessarily to trouble you with the
> detail of a conversation of nearly two hours, it will be sufficient to inform
> you that the proposition was flatteringly stated, strongly pressed, and
> decently declined. The world in general guess the occasion for which I was
> summoned, but I would avoid, as it appears to me illiberal, parading a
> refusal, and therefore let these particulars sleep with you.[16]

By turning down this offer from the Rockingham administration, Buckingham
reaffirmed that his loyalties lay with Grenville, without making an undue fuss
about the matter. Madrid was a prestigious posting and the offer must have been
both flattering and tempting but he stuck to his principles. It is also probable
that he did not wish to be separated from Mary Anne whilst she was with child.
The next day he presented the Address from Norwich to the Levee expressing
"thankfulness for his Majesty's gracious and paternal goodness, in attending to
the humble Representation laid before him by his faithful Subjects concerning
the Exportation of Wheat and Flour. That nothing could so strongly support
their Confidence in his majesty, or more firmly assure to him the Happiness they
enjoy under his auspicious Government, that Goodness and Condescension with
which his majesty had, so instantly and effectually, relieved the fears of his people."
Afterwards he attended an audience of His Majesty to, as he told Grenville,
"acquaint him with my having received a letter from the Vice-Chancellor of Russia,
informing me that the Czarina had sent me her picture for their Majesties, and a
compliment to them upon the occasion." Adding that nothing had been mentioned
of Spain, he enquired as to Mrs Grenville's health, "I return to Blickling tomorrow,
where a line from you, informing me of her better health, would give particular
satisfaction to your faithful and affectionate Buckingham."[17] George Grenville was
grateful for his friend's unfailing loyalty,

> I do not wonder at all that the present Ministry should desire your
> concurrence and assistance, or that they should offer you the Embassy
> at Madrid in the critical state of affairs in Spain; but I am surprised,
> considering the great importance of the object, after they had given the
> option of it to Mr Stanley, as he informed me, so long as July, that they
> should delay the making that offer to you till now. Your honourable
> conduct has convinced them of the falsehood of that opinion which has
> been so industriously propagated of late, that everyone is willing to treat
> with them, which is but a copy of Sir Robert Walpole's, that 'he knew every
> man's price.' Your behaviour in stopping Lord Shelburne when he was
> entering into a dissertation upon the situation of the affairs in Spain is at

once a proof of your own firmness and determination and of your candour and fairness towards them.

He in turn enquired about Mary Anne's health, whose pregnancy had caused concern, "I flatter myself that Lady Buckinghamshire continues perfectly well, and that you are now free from alarms of all sorts."[18]

In November Buckingham visited Kimberley Hall near Wymondham, where four years earlier its occupant Sir Armine Wodehouse had commissioned Lancelot 'Capability' Brown to remodel his estate by developing a lake and creating sweeping parkland. Also visiting were Lord and Lady Huntingtower[19] from Helmingham Hall in Suffolk. Buckingham sent a gossipy letter to Mary Anne, "Sir Armine's Park is in High Beauty, the Lake & River put your Puddle out of Countenance" a reference to their own slowly expanding lake at Blickling.

> Sir Armine rejoiced at my arrival, Mr Wodehouse smiled, Miss Bacon unclouded her Virgin forehead. The Mayor gave me an excellent dinner, admirable Turbot, exquisite tongue & Udder, & as no Longing Women were present, I tasted Woodcock for once. Supper at Mr Woods, Cadrille, smelts hot & hot, eat six at the Lady's entreaty. His Lordship has not forgot Lady Dorothy, & Lady Huntingtower speaks of her with a regard that is seasoned with the veiled pique of a Wife Jealous of her honor, or rather of her property. You none of you like any body should eat mutton but yourselves, yet the scabby sheep will wander.[20]

In his speech on the opening of the Sixth Session of the Twelfth Parliament of Great Britain on 11 November 1766, King George announced to Parliament, "I have the satisfaction to inform you that since I last met you, I have concluded a Treaty of Commerce with my good sister the Empress of Russia whereby that considerable Branch of Trade is fixed on a just and satisfactory Footing."[21] Buckingham's reaction to this news is unrecorded.

Notes

1. NRO MC 3/285 Letter 9.
2. John Snow, Precentor and Canon of Exeter.
3. NRO MC 3/285 Letter 10.
4. NRO MC 3/285 Letter 11.
5. *Report on the Manuscripts of the Marquess of Lothian*, p.266.
6. Ibid.
7. Ibid. p.267.
8. Ibid. p.270-271.
9. Ibid. p.267.
10. Ibid. p.268.
11. The increasing and alarming reports of violence from around the country had convinced the ministry that they must impose the embargo on foreign exports of wheat or flour from

all British ports. In addition, local authorities took steps to regulate prices and some public spirited citizens made bread available to the poor. When Parliament reassembled the Commons began action at once on a bill forbidding export of wheat and flour or the extraction of low wines and spirits from these commodities. The bill became law on December 16, 1766.

12. *Report on the Manuscripts of the Marquess of Lothian*, p.270.

13. Ibid.

14. Ibid. p.271.

15. Ibid.

16. *Grenville Papers ...*, Vol. 3, p.328.

17. Ibid.

18. *Report on the Manuscripts of the Marquess of Lothian*, p.272.

19. Lady Huntingtower was none other than Charlotte Walpole, one of three illegitimate daughters of Edward, brother of Horace Walpole.

20. NRO MC 3/285 Letter 12.

21. *Cobbett's Parliamentary History of England*, Vol. 16, p. 236.

"Ensign, or Maid of Honor?"

Buckingham was proud of Mary Anne and often mentioned her many admirers. Always solicitous of her welfare and comfort he was extremely worried when eight months into her pregnancy she suffered serious complications. In January 1767 George Grenville sympathised,

> I rejoice extremely to find that you and Lady Buckinghamshire are got back safe and well to Blickling. Lady Buckinghamshire's safety and your future happyness is of too much consequence to all those who love you for you to risk them upon any account, much less for an object so uncertain and contemptible as the political state has been. You are not bound to obey any decisions of my lady to send you to London one moment before she is perfectly safe and you perfectly easy and happy. You will I think, find nothing here worth your coming for, except the affection of your friends, who at this moment can only wish to be without you.[1]

By the end of the month her doctors were satisfied that Mary Anne was returned to good health and assured Buckingham he could safely attend to his duties in London confident that she was in no danger. Whilst there he wrote to Mary Anne assiduously almost every other day throughout February and into March. His primary concern was that his dear young wife would be safely delivered of a healthy child and whether it should be a boy or girl was of the least import. He left her at Blickling in the care of their good and faithful friends Admiral and Mrs Laton, certain that she was in the best possible hands.

Naturally quick witted and lively Mary Anne was prone to sudden and dramatic mood swings. These occasionally irritated Buckingham as he considered that her "dolefull" periods were a waste of time. Generally optimistic himself, his wife's depressions and tantrums perplexed him, although she was enduring a difficult and uncomfortable pregnancy at this time. On this occasion she had prompted him to leave Blickling early and he teased her by pointing out that Mrs Laton's present figure was permanent,

> If I had not been fearful of hurting the Ensign who is not old enough to be whipped, you would certainly have received a little wholesome correction on Saturday Night & Sunday morning, nothing is certainly so boring as the indulging of those dolefull fits when the occasion does not in the least call for them. Consider how very cheerful Mrs Laton is yet her abdomen is twice as big as yours, hers she must carry to her grave, & yours will probably be disposed of in less than ten days. We were all very comfortable at Blickling, & if circumstances had suited & you would have permitted me I should have been very glad to have remained there.[2]

He updated her with cheerful news of the health and welfare of their friends in London, ending "My Post Chariot waits at the door to convey me to the Catch Club."

Catch Club silver medallion.

The Catch Club[3] was Buckingham's latest musical passion. Founded six years earlier by, amongst others, Lord Sandwich and the Duke of Queensbury, its principal motive was to arrange regular meetings in order to practise a favourite pursuit, namely singing. Limited to "twenty one pleasure-loving men of the world" the club had many rules and regulations and gave out annual medals for the best compositions. Perhaps predictably the weekly meetings took place at an inn, the Thatched House in St. James's Street, from the opening date of the autumn session of Parliament until 4 June, George III's birthday. Shortly after joining this elite company Buckingham was mentioned in the Minutes, "The Committee having tasted several sorts of Claret were of the opinion that a sort sent in by Lord Buckingham's order was the properest to be laid in for the use of the Society."

The Club brought into their exclusive circle 'Privileged Members' who were professional singers and musicians of the highest calibre such as Thomas Arne of 'Rule Britannia' fame and Signor Felice Giardini, Orchestra Leader and Director of Italian Opera in London. These two luminaries, knowing the rules of composition and counterpoint, acted as examiners of the competition pieces. A Club rule was that, "If any person who takes part in any piece of music during the first round, is found deficient in his part, and actually sings out of time or tune, or stops before the piece is finished, he is to drink a glass of wine of any sort at that time upon the table, at the requisition of any member, and by order of the President." One nobleman, celebrated for his conviviality, fined Signor Giardini for his foreign accent so often that the he seldom returned home sober. Rules about toasts were both stringent and comical,

> When the dinner is ended, the President is not to permit any Catch, Glee or other song to be sung, till besides the usual glass to His Majesty's health and two others shall have been likewise circulated. The toast and Catch must be circulated alternatively, and any order may be observed, provided every person at the table is called upon, and No Person twice, till everyone at the table has been called upon Once. Any person may decline his song when called upon, provided he drinks a glass of wine as an acknowledgement of his inability to sing. All freedom of conversation

is permitted as becomes a Society filled with men of rank and of liberal Education, except upon Political topics which are not to be introduced, upon any pretence whatsoever, nor Religious subjects. No coffee tea or any other heterogeneous beverage is to be brought upon, or drank near the table where the Club is seated upon any account.[4]

The insistence on excluding political and religious discussion was in common with that of the Masonic Lodges and many members belonged to both societies.

A Catch song was written out at length as one continuous melody to which each singer had to take up or catch his part in time and "words were selected so constructed that it was possible by mispronunciation or by the interweaving of the words and phrases given to different voices to produce the most ludicrous and comical effects." Buckingham indulged his love for music by singing with this merry company which included his friends Hans Stanley, Lord Rochford and, in the following year, his half-brother George Hobart. Some songs were serious, with mournful titles such as 'The Dirge', and 'Round the Hapless Andre's Urn' but more often they concerned romance, as 'Why so pale and wan, fond Lover?' 'Dear Jenny' and, appropriately, wine, as in 'Fill the Bowl':

> 'Bacchus great Bacchus place me near the bowl
> That I may quench my thirsty soul
> In floods of wine; Bring me, Boy
> The largest goblet, fill it high
> Sparkling like fair Hebe's eye.
> Who does not drink and fill again
> Endures a life of care and pain.
> Quaff the rich and purple stream,
> Joy in every eye shall beam,
> And in transport of delight
> Let Wine and Music crown the night'

Buckingham did his best to amuse Mary Anne via letters and kept her abreast of juicy London gossip, and although parts are obtuse, viz., "The Red Cow has not been milked yet & I hear such an abominable account of all the Dairy Maids that it would be highly indiscreet to trust her in any of their hands," in the main they speak for themselves as on 7 Feb 1767,

An example of a Catch Club song (although the music in this version was composed later by Hubert Parry).

This Post will bring you a letter from the Countess of Rochford which is so voluminous as to oblige me to send out for some large paper in order to make a cover to it. This letter was brought by the Earl of Fife together with a most gorgeous Muff which unless you direct to be sent into Country shall be kept safe in town till your arrival. Nothing extraordinary has happened since my last, Lady Huntingtower is just come to town, she was at Almack's & her Lord told me yesterday that tho she went away before supper, she had catched cold & was ill. Madam Kepple is greater & larger than ever; she told me, in her mildest manner, that she despised me & thought me a Brute for not remaining with you in the Country. My recollection tells me that you had heard before my leaving Norfolk of a Russian Maid of Honor's having so far yielded to the importunitys of a Foreign Minister as to suffer herself to be with child by him. Fresher advice assumes that England & Sweden were equally concerned in the Negotiation, but that Sweden had prudently withdrawn before the secret Article was made Publick. The Lady in question was very well known to me, she is about forty, short & thick, her face greatly resembling the Pictures of good Queen Ann, she pique's herself upon literature and dancing, yet it is not quite judicious in her to indulge the latter inclination, for when she dance she sweat, and when she sweat, she stinks. Some eight years ago she fell in love with Count Butterlin who is envoy in Spain, & as he did not meet her ardour with equal warmth, by the advice of a Gypsy, she gave him a love Letter which nearly cost him his Life.

Lady E Stanhope is not yet marry'd, it seems Lord Barrimore is troubled with a violent Scorbutick* disorder which has hitherto always broke out upon the day fixed for the Nuptials, & his delicacy would not suffer him to receive so elegant a creature into his bed when his own person was not as free from blemish as hers.

Lady Dorothy is much better, poor Lady Fortrose is dying.

Mr Howard & Lord M have both got the measles.

Mrs Grenville tho she has been a little out of order lately is surprisingly mended.

Tho I went into the supper Room at Almack's, none of the exquisite viands tempted me to eat, but I returned to my Roasted Apples.

Lady Bolingbroke is come to town & seems particularly happy in her new admirer.

A Favourite of yours seems to have a sort of attachment for Mrs Pitt, which however your coming to town will probably put an end to.

No Letter from yr Ladyship, surely this evening's Post must bring me one.[5]

---

*   scurvy.

The voluminous letter from Lady Rochford was most probably crammed with salacious gossip for Mary Anne's edification. Lucy Rochford's husband William, the talented new ambassador to Paris, was a contemporary of Horace Walpole, who had hated Rochford since their Eton schooldays and never missed an opportunity to belittle him. Unsurprisingly Buckingham took the contrary view of Rochford and the two men had been fast friends since both were made Gentlemen of the Bedchamber and Privy Counsellors. Rochford married Lucy, who brought no dowry, for her great beauty and because their appetites and desires were well matched. Lucy was described as "a lady of free manners who said and did

Lucy, Countess of Rochford, Maid of Honour to Queen Caroline.

whatever she pleased; she was clever and entertaining"[6] and the notorious rake Casanova recorded in his Memoirs that "this lady's gallantries were innumerable, and furnished a fresh topic of conversation every day."[7] Lucy took many lovers including at one time the Duke of Cumberland and his brother-in-law the Prince of Hesse.

Rochford was well aware of his wife's affairs and had plenty of his own. In 1758 Lucy had insisted her husband break off an affair with an extremely expensive mistress, known as "the Banti" but Rochford countered that she should instead give up Lord Thanet, her lover at that time. Lucy retaliated that this was unreasonable since Lord Thanet "creates no expense to the family, but rather the contrary."[8] Rochford agreed there might be some weight to this argument and tried pleading sentiment, to which Lucy replied unromantically, "a fiddlestick for sentiment, having been married so long." The solution was neat: Rochford left the Banti and Lord Thanet took up with her. Rochford's next mistress gave him a daughter named Maria and by the time the girl was five years old he and Lucy had adopted her (they had no children of their own). The Rochfords lived in Madrid when Rochford was Ambassador to Spain, but as his current posting was now France, Lucy's letter to Mary Anne came from Paris. Mary Anne was thrilled and impressed by Lady Rochford's cavalier attitude to life and whilst not behaving in quite the same fashion, Mary Anne tried hard to emulate her older friend's style of witty badinage.

On 10 February Mary Anne's friend Harriet Bladen became engaged to William,

4th Earl of Essex. Buckingham wrote, "In all humility I throw myself at your Ladiships feet to ask your pardon for having thrown the Ink all over the Newspaper and more particularly as part of it has fallen upon the article which announces to the Publick the auspicious Nuptials of Essex and Bladen."[9] He enjoyed teasing Mary Anne about his admiration for a dancer who performed at Covent Garden, the enigmatic Miss Charlotte Twist, "I dined at home yesterday in order to treat myself with the new Play and Farce. My dinner and the Farce were very bad indeed; as to the play which is called 'The Perplexitys', nothing ever more deserved its name. But Miss Wilford made it interesting and Miss Twist danced round it, so I came away in love with both and not caring greatly for either." He noticed the portrait artist Mr Cotes was seated in the Front Box and this reminded him "of a certain piece of canvas which is almost covered by my Nose, you did not tell me if it was to be framed and sent for home. Upon the whole perhaps it had better remain with him till you visit London that this important decoration may be entirely settled to your own good liking."[10] He had visited his aunt Henrietta, who was "tolerably well" but thoughtfully avoided contact with his sister Dorothy because she had recently had the measles, "but they tell me neither her figure nor complexion are affected by it. The Town does not furnish any Political News which I lament as it is the sort of intelligence which most interests you. We hear from France that Monsieur de Hainville a Man notorious for his Gallantrys has sent his wife into Lorraine by a Lettre de Cachet for some slight indiscretions. The Paris Lady's are in a rage, and some English Lady's fret, not totally indifferent to so shocking an example." Lettres de cachet were a form of French law signed by the monarch, but heads of families also employed them as a means of correction. Wives took advantage of them to curb the profligacy of husbands or, as in this case, vice versa.

Their small daughter had evidently made an impression at Court because Buckingham discovered "that the King and Queen talk in private about Lady Harriet." On 12 February he teased Mary Anne over a supposed encounter with Miss Twist,

> Miss Twist was so obliging as to call in upon me to take a cup of chocolate in her way to St James's Park. You know the warmth of my feelings for that delicate creature too well not to figure to yourself in some degree the ecstacys which her presence gave me. Yet those ecstacys had an interval, and to amuse that interval I invited her to look over your Ladiship's finery; she accepted my offer with all the eagerness of female curiosity, she turned over, and admired, and gazed, and sighed, and gazed again. At last, she said in a low voice (a most becoming blush overspreading her elegant features) 'I wish I could have one of those delightful Gowns to dance my Minuet in the evening of my benefit.' You must think it was impossible for me to refuse her; had she asked for my own Buckskin breeches and New Calico Waistcoat they must have gone. In short it was settled that she should have (but only for the Night) your last New White & Gold. How

flattering that preference! & how fortunate the circumstance of my having prevented you from turning it into a Niggle-d-g! I also propose to trespass so far upon Miss Drury's good nature as to borrow your Earrings & Feather for the occasion. It is to be hoped that yr Ladyship will be in town early enough to see the Idol of my heart draped to the best advantage.[11]

Of her mother he remarked "Lady Drury is very much fallen away" and that he usually found alternative company with whom to dine. "Tho I am far from being fashionable the rest of the day, about dinner time somebody or other always thinks of me." Finances were not as fluid as he could have wished. "There is a possibility but not a probability of my regaling you with a new Post-chaise this year. I looked into my Bankers book this morning & did not quite like it. The New Chariot is however already paid for as well as the broad wheel Waggon, tho I have used it now above a week no creature has as yet been in it but myself."

He was impatient for the arrival of the baby and longed to be reunited with his wife. On 14 February he wrote, "I am at this time expecting to hear every moment of your being happily delivered, & in truth if you delay the business much longer it will seriously vex me. You are destined to stay far too long in the Country already, & every addition to it will be more and more provoking"[12] and said of his own health that "A very bad cold kept me at home all Thursday, but it is now better and I now trundle about as usual. There are those who attribute my indisposition to the wearing of Callico Wastcoats in cold weather, but they must be mistaken." His brother George had been unusually successful at the gaming tables, "he is come to town in most immense spirits and quite rejoiced me with the account of the affluence in which he finds himself." British politics were once again in disarray. "The Ministers, or rather the several Deputies which Earl Chatham has thought proper to place in the several departments of Government are in the greatest confusion. But their Opposers have no regular Plan and are divided into seven or eight different Connections who have no concert with each other" and on Mary Anne's other great interest he informed her that "The Opera's are excessively crowded, many persons were turned away on Tuesday; this evening we are to have a new serious Opera of Bach's from which there are very great expectations, but in my opinion the bon ton has determined to prefer the Burlettas for at least this year."

J.C. Bach's opera 'Carattaco' premiered that night at the King's Theatre, Haymarket, and was in fact received extremely warmly by the public. Burlettas were rather more low brow, short comic operas performed in English which also went down well with their audiences. The King's Theatre was the home of Opera where a diverse audience from all walks of life appeared over the course of an evening. Early arrivals were the occupants of the boxes and the most expensive seats, where the main objective was to see and be seen. Those in the cheap seats, known as "the footman's gallery," occasionally erupted into fisticuffs, and towards the end of the evening others could come in for half price to watch the dances and a short play or farce put on for their delectation after the main event. Each evening, under blazing chandeliers, audiences would chatter, stroll about, and some even set up card games, tables and all. In the pit the aisles were known as "Fops Alley" where young men would wander hither and thither madly flirting with the ladies. Only the arias in the main opera caused the audience to pay attention and listen quietly, but as soon as they ended the clamour broke out once more.

The King's Theatre, Haymarket.

At home, Buckingham had been studying Hobart family history, "I have amused myself these two days with looking over very old family papers, and it would astonish you to know what an immense property, ill fortune, and the inattention, mismanagement and injustice of others has deprived me of"[13] and with his mind still on monetary matters told Mary Anne, "Men I meet with are increasing their expenses and great as the extravagance of the age has been it does not seem as yet to have reached its height. I dine upon a Neck of Mutton and Sallad."

It was accepted that ladies of rank were considered too fragile after childbirth even to read letters for themselves, let alone write any. "For a week I suppose it will not be permitted you to read any letters; how will poor Mrs Laton be able to decipher mine? This thought comes across me too late but my next shall be wrote more legibly and I will try to keep up the custom for at least two or three Posts." The measles epidemic had continued apace and some ladies in London had been affected, "Lady Bolingbroke has been very ill but is rather better, good nature and ingenuity have found many different names for her disorder, but in truth if a child had had it, one might without peril of contradiction have called it the measles. The Lady Stanhopes were pleased to ornament Kensington Gardens this morning, they looked very handsome and becomingly afflicted."[14] Whimsically ruling that "it is impossible to mention too many Colonel's in a Letter to a Lady" he wrote about Col Johnston, Col Leland, Col Nugent and Col Clinton, and informed her that "Col Ligonier continues to love his amiable Bride with unabating ardour." Lord Jean Louis Ligonier was eighty-seven in 1767, and although he never married he had a long relationship with Penelope Miller who gave him a daughter. Buckingham

Buckingham was present at the London premiere of JC Bach's opera 'Carattaco', conveyed distressing news about Mary Anne's friend Maria, the twenty-four year old wife of the 12th Earl of Suffolk, who had died giving birth to their first child on 7 February. Buckingham had initially kept this from Mary Anne, even going so far as to forbid Mr Chase, the editor of the Norwich papers, from publishing an account of her death, but his sister urged him to to alert Mary Anne to the supposed cause of Maria's demise "Lady Dorothy however thought better of it as she tells me, and has, so far properly, warned you not to change your Linnen too hastily, as the poor woman fatally did." Another friend, Lady Caroline, wife of Lord Fortrose, had also died, at only nineteen, "I did not choose to give you melancholy news in your retirement—Lord Fortrose and Lord Suffolk are the most inconsolable of Husbands—Romeo, Othello or Postumus never lamented more." His French valet had evidently been forgiven his clumsy attempts at wooing Norfolk's rich spinsters and retained his position, "This is a Letter of great intelligence, great hurry made it necessary for me to write whilst my hair was dressing. Paulin's meritorious curiosity has read it all, and blushes at this moment as I turn back to look at him."

As Mary Anne awaited the now overdue arrival of her baby she was comforted by her husband's assiduous and determinedly lighthearted letter writing, as on 19 February, "It rejoices me that you write with a tolerable degree of cheerfulness notwithstanding your situation which in effect cannot be but very teazing; but fretting cannot make it better and therefore fret if you dare. The Queen was pleased a few minutes past, to enquire with her accustomed graciousness after the latest intelligence which had been received of you, my answer was concise expressive and clear, Viz: that you had put IT off for a week."[15] He was in danger of being late for dinner with Lady Martha, "and to judge from the time of the day and the slowness with which I write, either her Ladiship must wait dinner for me, or Your Ladiship content yourself with a side of scrawl less than usual." It is likely that Lady Martha was kept waiting because he added risqué anecdotes,

> And now to narration. As His Majesty the Duke of York and company were riding this morning up Constitution Hill they met a young Damsel— the Duke of York examined her figure and observed to his Brother that she had a good Leg. 'Yes (by ___!)' say'd the Damsel, 'and a good —— too,' at the same time, with an easy negligence, she lifted up the Drapery, and gave them the fullest opportunity of judging how far her assertion was just. A Gentleman Spectator of this Scene asked the Lady how she could so far forget the delicacy due to her sex, and the respect she owed her Sovereign as to present him with such an exhibition. She calmly answered, 'What, must he never see but one?'

Buckingham had another encounter of his own, with the ubiquitous Miss Twist,

> As I was walking yesterday morning in New Bond Street, I overtook an agreeable figure, tall, strait, in short in Miss Twist's best manner, she was reading a letter, and I was villain enough to study the contents of it over

her shoulder. It began "My Dearest Charlotte (the Queen's namesake you see) how can you doubt of the tenderest affections of my devoted heart, devoted to the imperial charms of your heavenly person. Let me talk a little my Angel, strong are my feelings, eager my desires, but meanly inadequate my power of expressing them. I waited and languished for you at Mrs Sophia, all the evening in vain, meet me there this evening, or would you make me more divinely happy, come into the Park tomorrow before Your Lady wakes, we may drink a Mug of Milk, white as your snowy bosom, and take a walk in the Bird Cage." When I had got so far I whispered in her ear "Many pretty birds have been caught in that Cage." She started and fell into the prettiest confusion imaginable. I took her by the hand but her confusion increased so fast that in compassion to her and for fear my malicious passenger should insinuate that my virtue was in danger, I withdrew.

A mild flirtation took place at Almack's, "there was a Miss Miller there who gave me a kick of the heart; but a little Arquebasade Water externally and a bottle of Claret in my Thorax radically cured me." (Arquebasade Water was a herbal potion normally prescribed to heal gunshot wounds.) Buckingham's friend had clearly gone much further than flirtation with an unnamed lady, "It is said that Lord Barrimore has at last owned his distemper to be something worse than the scurvy and that Mr Adair cannot undertake to make him a proper subject for the marriage bed in less than a Month."

Paulin was arranging Buckingham's suspiciously lively coiffure when he composed this letter,

Many circumstances have contributed to hurry me this morning and therefore my letter must either be submitted to Mr Paulin's curiosity, his head being at this moment hanging over my shoulder, or the Post would not bring you your usual's on Monday. One fortunate circumstance however may happen from my present attitude that something may probably fall from my head which will render this an animated paper. If Mr Paulin reads he shall read the account of his own faults, particularly his having suffered me to go out every morning this last week into the very best of Company with a ragged Neckcloth.[16]

He finished with a rumour, "There are of those who think Lord Ossulston will take the other Miss Bladen. Matrimony is shockingly infectious when once it gets into a family." (In fact Harriet Bladen's sister Barbara married the Hon Henry St John, brother of 2nd Viscount Bolingbroke.) On 24 February Buckingham sought to console Mary Anne by convincing her that she was missing nothing of consequence. "Believe me however you do not lose much, except in Idea, by your absence from London, the Times as suspicious, dull and dissatisfied, and the marks of it may be tried even in the youngest countenance" and he wondered if the baby would ever arrive,

> Will the maid of honor or the ensign or both or whatever it is to be
> never come? I should think it an asset to be a Girl for a female would
> undoubtedly present herself for the opening of Ranelagh, whereas the
> male in this time of Peace will think himself in time if he is here for the
> Shooting Season! Let me now recollect if anything very interesting has
> happened to me since my last Letter. Yesterday in the evening, I was at
> the New English Opera, it appears to me one of the most abominable
> performances that ever disgraced our Theatre. No more shall you know
> from me upon the subject, except that the entertainment was rendered less
> disagreeable by the politeness with which Mrs Tom Hervey made Room
> for me and suffered me to sit close, as close as possible, with decency to
> her. In my way to that Opera from Lord Hillsborough, I saw a coach in
> distress, I immediately stopped with the ridiculous politeness of the last
> age, and found it was the happy vehicle of Lady Portsmouth. I immediately
> offered with all the eagerness of twenty to convey her to any given spot in
> the Universe. She civilly declined it, saying she only wanted a Lynch Pin
> and could not think of taking mine.[17]

Despite the jocular tone he was exceedingly anxious and confessed that, "My
Letters which are calculated as much as depends upon me to make you laugh,
would lead you to think I divert myself. In truth it is otherwise and I am so very
unfashionable that I begin to think of returning no more either to Almack's or
Cornely's."

The radical notion of a lady breast-feeding her own baby was an anathema on
health grounds alone,

> Mr Iernegan's anniversary is published, it is called Il Latte, which is
> Italian for Milk. In your present situation you had a right to expect to be
> distinguished by the Dedication, as the purport of it is to persuade young
> Women to let their infants get drunk with the Milk of their own breasts.
> Perhaps it may be better for you not to read the Poem, lest the doctrine
> it is meant to inculcate should persuade you to a measure which would
> scarcely contribute either to your own health or that of your Child.

At Blickling Hall Mary Anne was unappreciative of the efforts her husband was
making to enhance their surroundings and strongly objected to the work carrying
on around her, especially the alterations in the gardens. As the baby was almost two
weeks overdue she certainly had grounds for feeling irritable but on 26 February
he gently admonished her,

> You go out to take the air every day, not from inclination, but by order.
> A very becoming declaration indeed, & very flattering to a Man who is
> puzzling his head & draining his pocket day after day in order to make

his place & the roundabout, or, as the French more elegantly stile, the environs of it agreeable & interesting to the eye. Write me such another word & I will turn every tree within a Mile of Blickling into ready Money. By the by the Lady's of Petersburgh used to call my late Secretary, 'Ready Money'.[18]

This last was a reference to his incompetent and overpaid Secretary in Russia. Appraising Mary Anne of a very bad play he had seen he noted, "The Month ends on Saturday & with it in my opinion the best of the London Season, which best has this year proved very indifferent" adding sweetly that "The Parliament will certainly sit late, a lucky circumstance for you Ranelagh Romps who seek your round of pleasure in that frowsy dissipated Ring. And yet with all this I have charity enough to wish you could be in town at the opening of your Paradise." Whilst writing this missive the news he was so anxious to hear at long last arrived, "My Letter is interrupted by receiving one from Mrs Laton with an account of your being brought to bed. It concerns me to hear you have suffer'd so much pain, as to the child's being a female don't let that make you uneasy for it does not me."

Notes

1. *Reports on the Manuscripts of the Marquess of Lothian*, p.274-275.
2. NRO MC 3/285 Letter 13.
3. *Nobleman & Gentleman's Catch Club: Three Essays towards its History*, Gladstone, Boas and Christopherson, Cypher Press 1996.
4. Ibid.
5. NRO MC 3/285 Letter 14.
6. Lewis, W. S.(ed.), *Lady Louise Stuart, Notes on Jesse's Selwyn*, 1928, p.10.
7. Machen, A. (tr.), *Memoirs of Casanova*, ix., 1922, p.172.
8. *The Works of Lord Chesterfield*, Harper & Brothers, Publ. Franklin Square 1860, p. 555.
9. NRO MC 3/285 Letter 15.
10. The portrait by Francis Cotes RA now hangs in the main hallway at Blickling.
11. NRO MC 3/285 Letter 16.
12. NRO MC 3/285 Letter 17.
13. Ibid.
14. Ibid. Letter 18.
15. Ibid. Letter 19.
16. Ibid. Letter 20.
17. Ibid. Letter 21.
18. Ibid. Letter 22.

Naming the Baby

Whilst relieved that the new baby was healthy, Mary Anne was disappointed she was not the hoped for son and heir. On 28 February 1767 Buckingham sought once again to reassure her, "I hope you are in some degree reconciled to the little female, the only uneasiness I have as yet felt for her being of that sort, was that the word daughter took so much longer writing than the monosyllable Son in all the notes I was Obliged to circulate upon the occasion."[1]

Mary Anne's lying-in period meant Buckingham was obliged to continue writing letters for a further five weeks. Casting around for material with which to cover the pages he shared the information that an unwelcome financial imposition was threatened, with the Chancellor suggesting in the House of Commons that "we miserable Country gentlemen should pay four shillings in the pound Land Tax in the coming year." This news, which affected only the wealthy, "reached an immense Assembly at Lady Grey's last night about ten o'clock, disordered the tranquility of many fine women, & faded the Roses on their Cheek." He dined again with Lady Drury and sympathised with the predicament in which Mary Anne's sister Jocosa found herself, "her patience is a little try'd by a course of life so ungenial to the natural & justifiable best of Maidens of her age, seems always in good-humor, & hoping hereafter for better days, bears her present Lot with temper." Jocosa was still under age and unable to marry without Lady Martha's permission and was obliged to care for her increasingly irascible mother.

Another clash of personalities made for amusing gossip, "Mrs Albinia Hobart & the friends of her earlier days the beauteous Bladens were by accident cast into the same party at Mrs Cornelys; Lady Bridgman, who unacquainted with their state of warfare, brought them together, assured me last Night that they neither bit nor scratched, but contented themselves with letting sullen reserve express their natural detestation." In Norfolk Buckingham's loyal friends Mr and Mrs Laton were assiduous in their attendance to his wife and Buckingham often asked Mary Anne to give his "compts to the Latons & thank them in my name for their care of you."

It is perfectly understandable that Mary Anne, recovering from childbirth as she was, was not best pleased with the disruption at Blickling Hall during March. According to accounts furnished by Wm Bailey to the Earl, ten workmen, under the direction of Mr Ivory, were employed for at least a fortnight to pull down the 'old Hall'. (Bailey also made it known that he was selling sheep at a guinea a head, and that the butcher was supplying the house with meat at 4s a stone.) Buckingham attempted to pacify Mary Anne with a present, "Mr Thomlinson will be at Blickling as soon as this Letter, the Ring inclosing Lady Harriet's hair most gorgeously decorated with Brilliants is committed to his care, if he betrays his trust there is no faith in Man."[2] Meanwhile Harriet's sister remained nameless, "Upon mature deliberation it does not seem to me expedient to trouble her Majesty about the Christening business, so that you may call the young Lady Sophia Charlotte or Julia which so ever you please." He passed a risqué comment about her friend's nuptials, "Yesterday & not before, the charms of Harriet Bladen were surrendered to the impatient desire of the Gallant Essex. We must hope she will survive it, & so far she has some chance as we all know that he was not in the least accessory to the Death of his first Wife." Their dear friend Hans Stanley had been proposed by Pitt to be the next British Ambassador to Russia despite his declaration that "Nothing can be further from the plan of life I had proposed to myself (but as I am) tired and disgusted with all the late scenes of domestic politics I have accepted the embassy to Petersburg as a temporary retreat from the present confusion."[3] (Pitt neglected to inform the Leader of the House or George Macartney in Petersburg or Sir Andrew Mitchell, the British representative in Berlin, and nine months later, without ever having set foot in Russia, Stanley waived his right to the appointment.)

Buckingham judiciously flattered Mary Anne, reassuring her that society most certainly noticed her absence and sorely missed her, "His Excellency as well as General Vernon, inquire daily after you, & upon every occasion speak of you with the highest regard. You may be proud of this circumstance for they never lavish their praises but upon the best grounds."[4] The Government was still in a parlous state and his private life was "in a seeming state of activity, but is in fact stupidly employed in nothing's, unentertaining, & intertwined." As an example of this he wrote on 7 March,

> Last Night everybody was invited to Lady Gage's, Lady Melbournes, & Lady Aylesburys, & as every body made a point of attending all three, the hurry & circulation in the streets & upon the Stair-Cases is scarcely conceivable. As the Court Yard at Lady Gage's is too small to admit more than one Carriage, a covered scaffold matted as at the Coronation was erected from Arlington Street, Numbers of Footmen were ranged at proper distances, & I think I heard Mrs Brampston & Lord Buckingham repeated by more than twenty voices before we reached her Ladiships presence. You know that part of Arlington Street is no thoroughfare, Warwick Street the same, so that the bustle in each was inconceivable, at the first I left my Chariot in Piccadilly, at the second at Charing Cross.[5]

A lady with an unpronounceable name provoked a flurry of gossip,

> The conversation & observation of London are a good deal taken up with a Lithuanian Princess who is lately arrived, her Figure is comparatively more elegant than her name, you may pronounce it as you please, that circumstance being by no means settled, but upon her visiting cards she writes herself Thexgeewhuskny. She has been rather unfortunate in her

Journey with regard to her baggage, for two of her trunks fell into the sea at Calais, & two others were burnt with the Canterbury Stage at Dartford. I knew her husband who is lately dead; inconsolable for his loss, she travels to mend a broken heart.

Buckingham was struggling to find newsworthy topics but he made valiant efforts: 10 March, "These last two or three days have been absolutely Barren, yet I hold myself as much in honor obliged to fill up the paper as if the times were more prolofick."[6] He told of their friend Col. Nathan who had "fallen desperately in Love with a little dancing Girl at Drury Lane, he has not as yet declared his passion, nor do I think, notwithstanding all you have heard about his inordinate proceedings & his regular Appetite for the Old Cheese after dinner, that he will propose to draw her Curtains in the year 1767" and expressed his increasing concern about her mother's treatment of Jocosa, "I have not seen Lady Drury or your Sister this week, indeed her situation & course of Life gives me very serious uneasiness, lest from never seeing or being seen by those who might be proper Matches for her, she should fix or imagine she has fix'd her inclinations upon one whom she too late may find a very improper one. She has however great appearance of prudence which may preserve her."

Mary Anne recovered sufficiently to be permitted to pen her own letters and requested that Hans Stanley be Godfather to their still unnamed daughter. Buckingham replied on 12 March, "I was much rejoiced to receive a letter from you in your own hand writing tho you seem rather poorer in spirit than mite be wished. Mr Stanley most readily accepted the Fatherly office you destined him" adding "Lord Clare was present when Stanley talked of his Godfathership, & look'd as if he thought you ought to have preferr'd him." Buckingham asked Jocosa to stand as Godmother.

> I called upon your Sister who blushingly assented to the proposition, upon the whole she looks as if she was tolerably well prepared to be a mother in good earnest. I talked to her more than half an hour in my best manner upon the care a young Lady should take, however great her situation, not to fall a prey to Indiscreet designing Men. My reasonings upon the subject were worthy of being engraved on Gingerbread for the use of Infant Heiresses, but your Ladyship has eat your Gingerbread & therefore shall not be troubled with them. You will inform me if any Cake must be sent to your London Gossips & what name her as yet anonimous Ladyship is to be called by. I shall also be glad to hear how Madam Harriet behaves herself upon the occasion. She is expected in town with great impatience & great things are expected of her.[7]

He warned Mary Anne that Lady Martha had "a disorder in her breast which there is but too much reason to fear may in time be attended with bad consequences, but you must not say anything to her upon the subject unless she begins with you."

To celebrate Mary Anne's return to London he arranged a visit to see Miss Twist's great rival,

> By advancing a considerable sum of Money, by great assiduity & address, & by promising Miss Macklin to withdraw my illplac'd affection from Miss Twist, & transfer it to her superior merit, I have procur'd a Side Box for her Benefit, the 6th of April. As you seem latterly to have behaved tolerably well, you may if you please have a place in it & bring a female friend with you. Not Ly Dorothy or Mrs Hobart, but any body else you please.[8]

This last plea was made because he had lately seen more than enough of his unpredictable sister Dorothy and his embarrassing sister-in-law Albinia, with the result that he had fallen out with both of them.

Mary Anne's friend Harriet Bladen, now Countess of Essex, "was presented on Thursday & look'd surprisingly well, Poor Young Woman, considering what she must have gone through." This was a sarcastic remark as the Earl of Essex was universally acknowledged to be exceedingly charming and handsome. Another of Mary Anne's friends was the beautiful Lady Maria Waldegrave, one of Edward Walpole's illegitimate daughters (and therefore Horace Walpole's niece). Widowed in 1763 she secretly married[9] Prince William, 1st Duke of Gloucester, the younger brother of George III. Buckingham commented "Lady Waldegrave looks in very good spirits, her Lover rather grave, the whole world agree in the idea of consummation, but differ'd widely upon the Mode, to the shame of my penetration I must own that I have no fixed opinion upon the subject, except that ultimately it must make your old friend miserable." The political scene continued in disarray, "Divided as the leading Men are, alienated so much from each other, so many contending for first situations, so few equal to them, there is reason to expect a change every hour, but that change would very probably be soon follow'd by another."[10] Domestic arrangements were in a better state, "Attentive to your taste I have purchased more Grey Horses, they are become exceeding scarce as all the Stage Coachmen & Butler Carriers are as partial to that particular color as myself. When the new Post Chaise comes home, what three Splendid Equipages you will have: that is to say, when in consequence of your behaving well, & my feeling myself in superlative good humor, you are induldg'd in the use of them." Members of the Catch Club had raised their glasses in a toast to her, "You should be vain of the praises of those who do not indiscriminately or lightly lavish them." Buckingham had been warned about little Harriet's temperament, "You say Lady Harriet is become too cunning for you & Mrs Laton, by which you mean tacitly to insinuate that upon her coming to town she is to have a trial of skill with me; very possibly; I am tolerably well vers'd in the ways of the sex from thirteen to thirty, but I never yet attempt'd to fathom any young Lady of her time of life." He shared gossip about Lady Sarah Bunbury, nee Lennox, who was a great beauty notorious for her scandalous affairs, "You must have heard how she came home one Night with her Coach and Coach Box cover'd with Dukes and Marquises." On a more prosaic note he ended, "P.S. Tell Bailey to send up ten pounds of Turnip seed with your Baggage & to let me know the price."

The difficult childbirth had left Mary Anne fragile and Buckingham was determined to make their London abode as comfortable as possible for her,

> March ye 19th. Dear Madam. Dear Madam - that repetition arrives from haste, as indeed I do write in very great haste. If you don't like mine you may call your Baby what name you please. Your Old Apartment has been very agreeable to me during my last Residence in town & as you do not like traveling up & down stairs I shall order our Beds to be remov'd into my Old Dressing Room & put you in possession of the whole floor below, this will be attended with some little inconvenience to me, but is a sort of sacrifice I shall always be ready to make to your satisfaction. You will have one essential comfort to your retired disposition, more especially as the trees are considerably grown, in not being over look'd.[11]

He sent his new valet Charles to Blickling (what became of Paulin is unknown) with instructions to pack up Mary Anne's things and ordered Mr Gay to bring back his Broad Wheel Wagon from Norwich to their house in Spring Gardens.[12] He asked Mary Anne to "convey it back loaded with Wine for me, & Porter & Drams for Your Ladyship" adding that "The King & Queen were acquainted last Night with Lady Harriet's most gracious & generous behaviour to her Anonimous Sister who in Compts to Stanley you ought to Christen Hans." Tense relationships with the women in his family spread to his ill-tempered mother-in-law when Buckingham insisted that Jocosa should visit the House of Lords with him in order to be seen with the best company,

> Your Lady Mother is a little peevish with me for something which it appear'd necessary for me to say upon the occasion, but I call'd there and weathered three quarters of the Storm last Night, & I am thoroughly persuaded that it will be all blown over before you reach London. The particulars of this business are not important enough to be laid upon Paper, so your Curiosity must be hung upon a Peg or pinn'd to the back of your Traveling Equipage for the present.[13]

He had crossed paths with Albinia Hobart at Almack's where she "seemed mortify'd the last evening, nobody was dispos'd to roll her in that dancing attitude which so much flesh however fine that flesh but ill becomes. I have been there most Nights but have never yet been tempted to sup." He had also decided that Jocosa should share the theatre box with Mary Anne and that "unless you are particularly sollicitous the rest of the box shall be fill'd with He Creatures." Increasingly impatient for their reunion in London he ordered her "to set out the Minute whenever that Minute falls out, which finishes your five weeks." On 24 March he announced, "This is the last of twenty four Letters which you probably received from me during your tedious exile, making in all eighty eight pages of the most uninteresting nonsense that ever disgrac'd or wasted paper, if it has appeared to you otherwise so much the better for me, & indeed for Your Ladyship."[14] He then regaled her with an astonishing tale of mistaken identity. A "worthy Gentleman" of his acquaintance had informed Buckingham that he knew of his "secret,"

> It is now ten years since I took under my protection the Orphan Daughter of a French Refugee at that time only fifteen years of age, but form'd in her Person, elegant in her manners & accomplished from an education which her birth tho not her fortune intitled her to. That in the course of our acquaintance she has brought me six children, three of each sex, two of which a girl & a boy are since dead. That the eldest Girl is in France & the two boys at school at Fulham, the Mother and the youngest living in a pretty little Box situated between Fulham & Waltham Green, that till I went to Russia I never missed coming to the Fair Creature every morning even in the worst weather but that of late my visits are less Frequent, that the Lady is very retir'd & reserv'd but attends a French Chappel at Putney & during divine service is often seen with tears in her eyes. This information was given me on Saturday & I have taken since some pains to find out the Lady that is given me, & the Man who so strongly resembles me. Hitherto my Labor is in vain, but you will agree with me that it would be unbecoming not to have at least a wish to see a fine Creature who has belonged to me ten years.

Surmising that Mary Anne's continuing low spirits were caused, at least in part, by feeling that she had disappointed him, which he was adamant she had not, he advised her not "to teize yourself about what you cannot remedy, perhaps providence may have sent you a good Girl instead of a naughty Boy, in that case surely you are obliged to Providence. Besides you will by this means avoid twenty years anxiety which your constant attention to the Brat must have given you." He excused the letter for being shorter than usual, "my principal reason for not crowding in my usual nonsense is that just now you would not be allowed to read it yourself." He wrote twice more before Mary Anne left Norfolk, "I am glad you do not insist of changing your apartment, tho the pleasure it would have given me to concur with your inclination would have more than repaid me for the inconvenience it must have been to me."[15] He had unwelcome news for a young woman eagerly preparing to launch herself back into London society. "The Dauphiness of France is Dead. An event which will give you great uneasiness in many respects & in none more than that it will condemn you to three weeks mourning at your first coming to town, the time when you Country Lady's always wish to appear in your full Luster." As consolation he outlined for her delectation some future plans,

> Lady Sophia Egerton has done me the honor to invite me this evening to a Catch Concert which I wish you could partake of, but as a comfort you may be assured of having some soon in your own house. It is at present my intention, unless controverted by Your Ladyships supreme Mandate, that

you should have a party of between twenty & thirty He's and She's once a week, so that in the course of two Months you will have an opportunity of being civil to all those who notice you & deserve notice.

And regaled her with anecdotes,

> My Goodfortune like the Sun in London occasionally breaks through the clouds but never permanently shines upon me. Yesterday morning I met Miss Twist in all her glory & just as I was preparing to accost her with that mixture of pleasure & of embarrassment which ever attends real love, I perceived her own Captain with her. I faded at the Crowing of the Cock, & hastily withdrew not in the least from fear, it was only to avoid shocking her tender nature with that Scene of Slaughter which must have insued, had I indulged the dictates of my fond glowing heart.
>
> I was last night at a place it has not lately been in my power to frequent, Viz: Mrs Cornelys Assembly Without Cards, which, as you sometimes hear a Noise like the tuning of Fiddles, is called a Concert. Just as the Company were rising to scramble for Tea & Cake, a fine Woman drop'd Half her Head of hair in a Gentleman's Lap who sat behind her. It diverted the illnatur'd very much, but greatly the less for her being very plain & one of those unconsequential beings whom Nobody knows.[16]

Lady Temple invited the Buckinghams to an Assembly, "to which London is invited to meet all the Branches of the Royal Family" but it directly clashed with Miss Macklin's Benefit and this gave Buckingham pause for thought. He remonstrated with Mary Anne about teasing Hans Stanley over the new baby's name and advised her to steer clear of both Lady Dorothy and Lady Albinia with whom he was still on ill terms, "as from some fault in all our Tempers we never agree two days together." Believing he had covered the paper but then noticing he had not, he scribbled, "Turn over!"

> I thought till I began folding the Letter that the four sides had been full, but perceiving my mistake in time I must add something as you might be shock'd after so different a practice on my part to discover the nakedness of any side of a piece of paper from me. Little however remains to me to tell you, except that on Friday last, no Bishop being present in time, Lord Botetourt read prayers in the House of Lords, a circumstance which has not happened since the days of Oliver Cromwell.

Happily, Mary Anne was re-united with her husband in time to attend both Lady Temple's Assembly and Miss Macklin's benefit, and with the promise of lively social gatherings at their house in Spring Gardens ahead she threw herself back into London society, happy to rejoin the Ranelagh Romps. And at long last she decided upon a name for the new baby. She would be baptised Caroline Hans Hobart.

Notes

1. NRO MC 3/284 Letter 23.
2. Ibid. Letter 24.
3. *Grenville Papers ...*, Vol. III, p.284.
4. NRO MC 3/284 Letter 24.
5. Ibid. Letter 25.
6. Ibid. Letter 26.
7. Ibid. Letter 27.
8. Ibid. Letter 28.
9. When the King became aware of this marriage, which was not until 1772, he disapproved so strongly that he banned the couple and their children from the royal presence until 1780. Horace Walpole, Maria's uncle, described her as 'Beauty itself! her face, bloom, eyes, hair, teeth and person, all are perfect.'
10. NRO MC 3/284 Letter 29.
11. Ibid. Letter 30.
12. Pleasure gardens during the time of Charles II; just off Pall Mall near the original Charing Cross and just south of the extensive King's Mews stable yards (now Trafalgar Square).
13. NRO MC 3/284 Letter 31.
14. Ibid. Letter 32.
15. Ibid. Letter 33.
16. Ibid. Letter 34.

A Lasting Sorrow

Lady Suffolk had suffered many bouts of ill health during her long life but from the spring of 1767 the seventy-seven year old Countess was more regularly plagued by gout and often felt too unwell to welcome visitors. In May, learning that his adored aunt had taken a particularly bad turn, Buckingham immediately despatched Mary Anne to Marble Hill. He himself was immersed in business at Westminster, but planned to visit, as explained in an unusual fashion in a letter dated "Last Night"[1]

> I cannot dine with you yesterday, nor must you expect to see me last night, it is also morally impossible for you to see me today but tomorrow at eight o'clock (when you receive this tomorrow will be Friday) the Chaise will attend at Marblehill to convey yr Ladiship to London. On Saturday it is my intention to return with you to Marblehill, there to remain until Monday morning & on Tuesday we set out at all events for Blickling. The past arrangements cannot be corrected, the future depends in great measure upon your pleasure. I cannot close this part of my letter without recommending to you to remark upon the propriety & precision with which it is wrote. The House will sit very late today which will make it impossible for me to wait upon you this evening. I wanted to see Harriet last night but Mrs Betsey, for reasons of self convenience, had tumbled her out of the Stage Coach into Bed without a bate. You may tell Lady Suffolk that Lord Buckingham spoke yesterday in the House of Lords (but it was only to inform their Lordships that Earl Temple was indisposed.)

He then gave rein to an indignant rant,

> If the pens left me by Mr Gay had not been embezzled by the tea-stealing, paper blotting, Grammar scorning, eye circulating, scandal creating, children dropping, Whiting Wasting, Mop twirling, Footman seducing House Maids, this Paper would have had its four sides cover'd & cover'd with less unintelligible characters half an hour ago.

In London, Mary Anne had ambitions to move house, but her desires were thwarted. Buckingham commiserated, albeit facetiously, "Poor Woman, you once had hopes of Bushey, Norton, Hamsted, George Street & so on but thus you must now content yourself with Blickling & the good will of yr Buckingham. P.S. Ask Lady Suffolk if she thinks any Garret Scribbler could fill four sides of Paper with less materials." To his relief his aunt had recovered from her recent ailments and her spirits had risen with the arrival of warmer weather.

Over the years Charles Hotham and Buckingham kept up a regular correspondence and had become close confidantes. Sir Charles had lately returned from a long sojourn in Ireland to find his daughter grown close to womanhood. This child was Buckingham's great favourite, the niece he sweetly referred to as 'Mrs. Harriet.' Henrietta Hotham was "gifted with a cleverness which made her the spoilt plaything of some of the foremost wits of the older generation"[2] including Horace Walpole, all of whom doted upon her. However, the relationship between Harriet and her mother Dorothy was strained from early childhood and since the age of eight she had been more or less brought up, as Dorothy herself had been, by Lady Suffolk at Marble Hill. It appears their personalities were conversely too alike for mother and daughter to maintain a pacific relationship. Dorothy was described as spirited, vivacious, overindulged, lively and attractive and Harriet was certainly a precocious child as evidenced in this excerpt from a letter written to her parents when she was only nine years old,

> I hope I shall give you a most sensible pleasure by a full and true account of those improvements I have made both in Body, and mind, since my retirement into the Country. Upon my first arrival here there was placed a seat in a small building in the garden, upon which it was expected I should retire and meditate, but like the Hanoverian General (on another occasion), I prefer a tree. I am a great Friend to low Humor, I can grunt like a Hog, Quack like a Duck, sing like a Cuckoo, but old aunt observes this is only proper whilst I am a spinster. I have learnt with surprising quickness to sell my Uncle a bargain, and the droll face with which I perform gains me universal applause.[3]

It is interesting to call to mind here the episode in Dorothy's childhood when she imagined herself transformed into a pineapple.

Charles Hotham took it upon himself to write an inordinately lengthy letter to his daughter, instructing her about how to choose a husband and outlining in minute detail what was expected of a good wife. Conveniently amnesiac about his own chequered route to matrimony, the salient points being that he was ten years younger than his wife, that they had scandalously eloped, and most particularly that Dorothy had been with child before their marriage, his advice is breathtakingly hypocritical. Taking into consideration his wife's fiery character it may be that Hotham's married life had not turned out quite as he had anticipated. Glimpses into the letter reveal the following gems,

> The Natural Walk and Situation of Woman, is Marriage…it is of all others the most fiery trial you can undergo…he is your Head, your Lord, and Master…you must be Subordinate to him in all things.
>
> If he be ten years at least older than you, so much the better.
>
> If you think more highly of his understanding than your own, you will have the fairest Prospect before you; but if on the contrary you in your own

Mind give yours the preference, you are infallibly lost in his Esteem.

Trust in your Husband but distrust yourself.

Study, effect, your Husband's Temper and Disposition, (which if you do not and conform to it too minutely, you will be miserable.)

I beg you to remember you are never upon any account whatever, notwithstanding any provocation you may receive, to let a hasty word, much less an angry Passionate Expression, escape your Lips towards your Husband.

Never attempt to learn what he chooses to conceal, and never fancy yourself the Object of his displeasure till he informs you you are so.

I know many Women who imagine this perpetual Solicitude about themselves is a proof of their Affection; it is no such thing; it arises from Curiosity and Vanity, either of which are sufficient to fret, teaze, and wear any reasonable Man to Death.

Tho' you are never to have a Secret from him, you should never pry into his.

From the beginning of time to this Hour, the first Quarrel never was the last…avoid it by every possible means as you would the plague…you must infallibly be in the Wrong because it is your part, Business, and Duty, to submit.

He will no doubt have failings like other men…you must be Deaf, Dumb, and Blind to them all.

As to your own Friends, the fewer you have the better. Intimacies between Women are in general dangerous things.

Take up always the turn of the discourse, but never give it: and never suppose that in order to appear pleased you are always to talk, or always to laugh. It is a tiresome, Wearing, idle Habit and is excessively Ill bred.

Talking at random will keep him in a Fever while he loves you, and will make him despise you when he does not.

If ever you manifest towards him before any human Eye the least familiar Fondness; it would be disgusting to him, and Shocking to every body else.

I have given you the best advice I can, and I can only say the more of it you follow the happier Woman you will be.

The entire letter,[4] which might be more accurately described as a lecture, is in this vein. After reading this short excerpt it may not come as a surprise to learn that after copying out the entire document Miss Hotham (Mrs Harriet) never married. In addition to the most off-putting advice from her father she also had a prime example before her in Lady Suffolk, who demonstrated daily how it was possible to live in perfect contentment as an independent woman.

In July 1767 Lady Suffolk suffered another severe attack of gout and rheumatism all over her body and this time even in her face. She rallied enough to entertain two visitors on the evening of 26 July and after her friend Lady Dalkieth had taken her leave Lord Chetwynd escorted Lady Suffolk to her bedchamber where she planned to have a quiet supper alone. Thinking that she looked well enough to enjoy her repast and to get a good night's rest he bid her farewell. But whilst preparing for bed she suddenly clutched her side, collapsed, and died. Marble Hill had lost its architect, a most remarkable and original woman whose extraordinary story would not soon be forgotten. Poor young Harriet Hotham was inconsolable in her shock and grief and Lord Chetwynd returned to stay with her until Colonel Hotham and her mother Dorothy came down from East Yorkshire to take her away. Lady Suffolk was interred, by her express wish, next to her beloved George Berkeley in the family mausoleum at Berkeley Castle.

In her Will she left Marble Hill and its contents to her beloved nephew stipulating that if he died without male heirs it should then pass to Henrietta Hotham. She bequeathed £8,000 to Lady Dorothy and made provision of a £3,000 dowry for Henrietta together with "all my State Jewells China and Japan in whatever shall be contained in cabinets chests or Boxes under Lock and Key."[5]

The death of Lady Suffolk, who had been more a mother than an aunt to him for almost all his life, hit Buckingham hard. He had lost his champion, his closest confidante, and the person who understood him best in the world.

Notes

1. NRO MC 3/284, Letter 35.
2. *The Hothams ...*, p.93.
3. Ibid. p.94.
4. Ibid. pp.111-122 (excerpts from the letter which runs to 5,376 words).
5. NRO 8549 21 B6 (cited in Borman, T.).

Ousted

July 1767 also saw Buckingham's friend George Grenville put out of office permanently. He had been in a difficult position since the end of the Seven Years' War when Britain had been looking for ways of increasing revenue from taxes, not least because the national debt had doubled and there were 10,000 British military troops stationed in the colonies to be financed. Reluctant to inflict more taxes on British citizens, in March 1765 the King gave his assent to Grenville's doomed Stamp Tax, which meant that all American Colonies' publications, whether judicial, journalistic or educational had to pay tax on every single sheet they published. The Colonies objected to this imposition in no uncertain terms and the Act was repealed in March 1766. However, on the very same day, Parliament passed the Declaratory Acts, meaning Britain had free and total legislative power over the Colonies. The cumulative effect of these and subsequent actions which were seen as taxation without representation would in time lead to the American War of Independence.

In August Buckingham received a letter from an unnamed Lord asking for Jocosa's hand in marriage. Buckingham responded tactfully, saying that Miss Drury needed her mother's consent which would not soon be given and that "Miss Drury is at present far from encouraging any Ideas of Marriage, she is greatly influenced by her Mother who from her circumstances, which are assisted by a considerable allowance made by Chancery for Miss Drury's education, must be unwilling to lose her soon."[1] He added in confidence, "Lady Drury tho not rich has some thousands to dispose of from a compromise I made at the latter end of a late legal disruption, rather to save her vanity than secure herself" and advised his Lordship to befriend Mary Anne "as the affection and confidence of the Sisters is very great" and to pay great attention to Lady Drury herself. The anonymous Lord had heard there were rivals for Jocosa's hand but Buckingham was confident that "To the utmost of my knowledge the Young Lady's affections are unengaged." This confidence was misplaced because unbeknownst to him Jocosa was being discreetly wooed by Brownlow Cust[2] the only son of Sir John Cust, the Speaker of the House.

In August 1767 a rare letter from Mary Anne to Lucy Rochford gives a flavour of her personality and a glimpse into her social life in Norfolk,

> Dear Madam, A proper diffidence of my ability in any degree of contributing to your amusement has been a constant check to my inclination of assuring Lady Rochford with how much pleasure I reflect on the hours in which her company made me happy, how sincerely I regret that those hours are now no more & how eagerly I wish for the renewals of that social intercourse which is only to be found amongst the very

very few who in politeness in information in temper & in understanding are so fortunate as to resemble her. A cheerfull dinner & a good fire which has corrected the ungenial coldness of the season gives me at this moment something like a flow of spirits which cannot be employed any way so much to my own satisfaction as in reminding you of one who most sincerely loves you. My Winter after my escape from the Martyrdom of Lying in and the consequences was but very short. I had just time to buy a Lutestring, whisk round Ranelagh, peep at the Vauxhall Cascade and mope at the empty conclusion of the Opera before my Rural Lord dragged me to his pigs oxen sheep Turnips & Ploughboys...we stopped for two or three days with the Huntingtowers, she now is nicely virtuous and his Lordship's animaly fond, qualities which should make them mutually happy, and so indeed they are bating that occasionally irritability which long solicitude must produce when time and enjoyment have dull'd the Razor edge of affection. So we were there, we staid there and we left them and these are the most interesting circumstances of the visit. Since our arrival at Blickling we have had little company except four Generals, an Admiral, a Sea Captain and a Chief Justice. Had the Generals been Ensigns, the Admiral a Midshipman, the Captain a Cabinboy, & the Chief Justice a Templar they would have been full as agreeable to me, it is a duty as to a generous mind it is a pleasure to communicate ones knowledge & when once we have passed the still regretted teen years prudent Women had rather have Scholars than Masters. You will have heard of Lady Suffolk's death, she left a will which the world thinks rather unkind to Lord Buckingham, we are however in possession of Marblehill the doors of which will ever be open to you whether you wish to indulge reflection or seek amusement. The Earl of Thanet is at this moment revelling in new delights, his soul and body temporarily devoted to a Woman who is thinking of a Diamond Cap and a Birthday Gown when he is labouring to continue the united line of Tufton and Clifford through the Sackville Channel to posterity.* You will have humanity enough to pity poor Nellys disgrace as those ordinary women have not those sentimental resources against inconstancy which Women of Rank and education are ever prepared with. The Men neglect us more and more every day, so that we are hardly ever led into temptation and stand little in want of divine intervention to deliver us from evil, few know and fewer care whether we are virtuous or not, such indeed are the times or rather the Males who make the times that a Woman who is desirous of knowing thoroughly her own feelings may be obliged to put the question to herself. We have prayers every day and go to Church on Sunday and speaking of this excuse

---

*   Lucy Rochford's former lover Lord Thanet revelled in the name Sackville Tufton. He married Mary Sackville, daughter of Lord John Sackville, on 30 July 1767, apparently to the dismay of his current mistress, 'poor Nelly'.

my asking you a question it is a Whimsical one yet resolve it if you can. What can be the reason that we never feel ourselves so little disposed to keep the Commandments as when we hear them read.

If I ever get the better of my Stubborn Lord, & entre nous I feel myself gaining Inches towards dominion every day, we will visit France. Pray that my Reign may begin before your Embassy ends and believe me Yr ever affectionate Countess of Buckingham[3]

Mary Anne's writing illuminates her natural wit and intelligence. She exaggerated about her swift removal from London to the country as she had spent at least three months in London before returning to Norfolk and the company of those dusty old Generals and Justices, but her words were intended to convey to Lady Rochford that Mary Anne was a fellow woman of the world. The reference to Lady Suffolk's Will being in the view of the wider world 'unkind' to Buckingham, can be explained. In September 1758, when the Will was drawn up, she was in yearly receipt of George II's pension, but this ceased upon his death in October 1760. During the next seven years Lady Suffolk attempted to live more frugally, causing Marble Hill to suffer somewhat from lack of repair, but it was undoubtedly her most treasured possession and given with love to her beloved nephew.

To compound his grief over the recent loss of his aunt, Buckingham was deeply affected by his friend the Rt Hon Charles Townshend's sudden death at the age of forty-two. After attending the funeral in Swaffham on 14 September 1767 he told Mary Anne, "I paid the tribute of a sigh to my most lively, most entertaining acquaintance when I saw him laid in his Grave, His Life, His Character & his early death suggest reflections too copious, too complicated & too serious for me at this, or indeed, at any time, to enter into."[4] Charles had been the only member of the powerful Townshend family whose companionship Buckingham greatly valued and his loss was a grievous shock.

Planning his return he considerately informed Mary Anne, "The Scarf and Hatband might be damag'd in a Postillions Jacket, & therefore will travel to London & from thence in the Post Chaise with Your most devoted Buckingham." Back in London a juicy piece of gossip was circulating, "There are those that say the Lady Viscountess B—has produced a child without the intervention of her husband, and assert his Lordship's resolution

The Honourable Charles Townshend LC-USZ62-33231.

to procure a Divorce and drive immediately afterwards to Buckleberry in a new Chariot which is to return loaded with a new Wife and a great Fortune."[5] There was nothing substantial to report from Court or Parliament, "Long Audiences at St James's but my Ministering hand will not have an opportunity in the course of this week of introducing any New Subjects to high employment. No positive political intelligence can I send you, and therefore your imagination shall not have any opportunity through my means of playing with any Hypothetical arrangements." He had dined with Lady Drury "and your poor sister" where a Mr Cossyns, "whose accomplished figure, cultivated understanding and peculiar felicity in announcing his Ideas were all new to me. He ogled Miss Drury a little bit but did not seem to find favour in her sight." Mr Cossyns and Buckingham were of course innocent of the fact that Jocosa was being stealthily courted by Mr Cust. Buckingham's favourite Miss Twist had not yet made an appearance at Covent Garden but he enjoyed "fashionable theater" all the same. He encountered Lord Townshend who "talks to me in the most good humoured friendly manner but without the least allusion to Norfolk Politicks" and furnished Mary Anne with the London gossip,

> I was at Whites till four o'clock this morning, the evening was greatly above Parr, General Pernon who was one of the company inquired particularly after you. Lord George Manners who was left a Widower nine months ago with ten Children is going for their sakes to marry an Indigent Miss of fifteen, daughter of a Lincoln Pettifogger. The two Miss Sands and Mrs Archer were offended (as I Perciev'd from their Shruggs and their wriggles) at my coming into their box last Night, but I maintained my place with Stanleian resolution. Lady Dorothy and Col. Hotham have both been ill, I think Lady Dorothy rather in a declining way, she has had the Jaundice and is yellower than an Orange. Miss Hotham is just as she was, she has a French master, and waits for the return of Lady Harriet's Scotch Man to teach her to dance.[6]

When on his Grand Tour in 1761, John Ker, 3rd Duke of Roxburghe fell madly in love with Duchess Christiane of Mecklenburg and it was widely deemed to be a perfect match between two people of high rank. But when Christiane's younger sister Charlotte became engaged to King George III of England their marriage plans were thwarted as it was considered bad etiquette for Charlotte's elder sister to marry someone of lower rank. It is poignant to learn that neither the Duke nor Christiane ever married. King George recognised the sacrifice Roxburghe had been obliged to make and rewarded him with the position of Lord of the Bedchamber, "in the room of Lord Buckinghamshire."[7] Exactly why the King chose to replace Buckingham at this point is unclear, but whilst 'The English Peerage, Vol. 1' records that Buckingham "resigned his office" another source states he was "dismissed in November 1767 for having supported the Duke of Bedford's motion April 1767 for a Lord's address to the King to take into consideration a Massachusetts Bay act pardoning rioters in the Stamp Act disturbances'"[8] If the latter was the case the King had certainly taken his time to demonstrate his displeasure. Whatever the reason, the Earl of Huntingdon was apologetic,"The King has commanded me to acquaint your Lordship that he appointed the Duke of Roxburgh to be one of the Gentlemen of the Bedchamber in your Lordship's Room. I flatter myself your Lordship will forgive me the disagreeable necessity of executing the duty of my office.'[9] Buckingham replied, "I should think very ill of myself if I was not prepared upon all occasions and in every situation to submit becomingly to his Majesty's pleasure."[10] George Grenville did not hear of the matter until after the deed was done, "I was very sorry to find by your letter that his Majesty has been prevail'd upon to appoint another gentleman of the Bed Chamber in your place. Has any expression or cause of his displeasure been ever signified to you, or it is to be holden forth as a mark of the displeasure of his Ministers and avowed upon that principle? When I have the pleasure of seeing you in Town, you will perhaps be better able to answer these questions than you are by letter." Perhaps Buckingham was punished for going against the King's wishes but it is also feasible that he may have been ousted by rivals who had 'prevailed upon' the King.

As the year 1767 ended Buckingham may have found himself ejected from his position at Court but he and Mary Anne anticipated a happy event with the birth of their third child in the following Spring.

Notes

1. NRO MC 3/285 Letter 112.
2. Brownlow Cust became 1st Baron Brownlow and inherited Belton House, Lincolnshire.
3. NRO MC 3/285 Letter 119.
4. NRO MC 3/284 Letter 36.
5. NRO MC 3/284 Letter 37.
6. NRO MC 3/284 Letter 38.
7. In 1768 Roxburghe was further compensated and created a Knight of the Realm, in 1796 a Groom of the Stole and made a Privy Counsellor. In 1801 he was appointed a Knight of the Garter.
8. Dictionary of National Biography.
9. *Report on the Manuscripts of the Marquess of Lothian* p.285.
10. Ibid.

Blickling Hall, August 2022.

An Entrance...and an Exit

Buckingham sold his aunt's Savile Row house in February 1768 and took a house in fashionable Bond Street which had been developed in the 1720s on the fields surrounding Clarendon House on Piccadilly. While Mary Anne stayed in Spring Gardens to supervise the works on the new property and prepare herself for the upcoming birth, Buckingham returned to Blickling where the decision was taken to cover the roof of the new building with lead and to have a balustrade made of stone from the Cote de l'Eau. He allowed that this would be expensive but that on the other hand it would make the Grand Salon less gloomy. While the works were carried out he lodged some of the time with Mr and Mrs Hase "who have indeed made Sall much more my home than theirs, their constant civility and attention, in some sort distresses me, for they must find me troublesome tho they will not let me see it."[1]

By March 1768 campaigning for both the Norfolk County and City elections was underway. There were two seats to be won in each contest and Buckingham canvassed his influential friends on his cousin's behalf,

> The County Election to all appearances goes on exceptionally well, but we must not be too sanguine. Norwich is in the greatest confusion. At Mr Harbord's request I called this morning upon some of my Old Friends, I don't believe his Election is in danger, but he has been extremely ill used. Norwich Election will be on Friday next, the County Battle on Wednesday the 23rd. I call it improperly the County Battle, for in all probability the decision there will be carried on with much more decency and tranquillity than in the City where there is likely to be a Battle indeed.

Mary Anne told her husband about her mother's increasingly erratic state of mind and he advised, "Let her behaviour be never so absurd continue to go or send and take particular care to let the World know you are not wanting in proper attention, for that most worthy humane and charitable being Miss Comyns will neglect no opportunity of reflecting upon you." Presumably Miss Comyns was an acquaintance of Lady Drury's whose amiability did not extend to Mary Anne.

Buckingham implied that their attorney-at-law Richard Heron was so busy he had no time to sleep with his wife, "It is rather extraordinary that Mr Heron should not send one line in answer to two Letters, but don't take the least notice of it, he is a Man of business, he has a handsome Wife and that Wife is never with Child." He ended this letter in an unsympathetic manner meant in jest, "Expect me in town before you Cry out if you please; I shall return as soon as business will permit me. But if I should arrive before the great work, I must insist upon your crying out in dumb Show. My best compts to my Daughters, thank Harriet for her Letter, and much more for being good."

Buckingham's preferred candidates for the Norfolk County Election were Sir Edward Astley and Mr Wenman Coke. Despite his wife's being in the late stage of pregnancy he unburdened himself to her,

> When I tell you I am horrible cross you will say it is a very bad time for me to attempt writing to you, yet remember you have bound yourself to take me just as I am, & a bitter bad bargain you have. You must not however think me cross without some little foundation, & therefore here follows the three grievances. I learned this morning that Mr Wickes has got the Stone, that Mr Kendal has contracted a nervous fever, & that Mr Lawson has received a stroke of the Palsy, three Zealous Friends to Coke & Astley who are rendered totally incapable of serving them.[2]

His mood was not improved by inspecting the building works at Blickling. "As I was sitting yesterday in the study, one of the Gentlemen, concerned in demolishing the Old House, ran his Iron through the wall and damaged the stucco for several inches, & will unavoidably occasion a blemish till the whole is repaired for your Ladiships use. Lastly, three of your cows have calved & there is not one fair enough for your delicate taste." More positively he noted that in the green house her orange trees were in perfect health except "one Skeleton which remains from last year in your private Garden." About baby Caroline, who was prone to crying for extended periods through both the day and night, her father reported "The Tragedy Queen was not produced today after dinner" and mused, "My health is but indifferent, but with some little difficulty we eat, drink & sleep, could one eat without chewing, drink without suction, and either sleep in our breeches or never wear any, it would save a world of trouble. If you produce a Male he shall never put on Breeches till the last extremity, they are in the way upon all interesting occasions." He offered a bribe to little Harriet, "I hope my daughter Vertue continues attentive to her Masters, she should stick close to the Minuet only, except the Pas de Rigadon,[3] which she must desire Mr Slingsby to teach her against my return. Inform Madame Harriet that if she continues she will be in the greatest favour, & have admission at all times to my private apartment, in London, for to my new Apartment at Blickling no Females shall ever be indulged access, except those whose decency may introduce through the back door."[4]

The 'Pas de Rigadon': A merry lively dance involving early ballet steps.

Anticipating that the outcome of the County Election would disappoint him, he took "a medicinal jog trot to Blickling" from his lodgings in Salle and prepared himself, "to put on a becoming Countenance when the Sheriff shall declare on Wednesday next that Wodehouse and de Grey are Duly Elected." He made himself agreeable to his neighbour, "I squeezed Lord Walpole's reluctant hand in the Marketplace at Norwich on Saturday, the Little Man however looked goodhumoured and enquired after your Ladyship's health." Both Lords Walpole and Townshend were backers of Thomas de Grey's very costly campaign. However Buckingham's fears were unrealised when Sir Edward Astley took the first seat and Thomas de Grey the second, and his support for Sir Harbord Harbord was rewarded when he won the first seat in the Norwich City Election. The second seat went to a Mr Bacon, and the local skirmishes were over.

The baby continued her incessant bawling, "your Lady Caroline cried in and cried out this afternoon, which made me horribly cross" but he offered an ingenious solution, "Tell Harriet that if she continues good her sister will, next summer, be entirely put under her direction, when it will be particularly recommended to her to cure her of crying."

He commented on Val, Blickling's dairyman, "Your cows are not yet arrived, I believe your beauteous Dairy Maid is kept under lock and key, in all my walks we have never met, I have not it is true ever entered the Dairy as I suspect Val like all old Rakes of being somewhat inclined to Jealousy."

In his next he explained the poor quality of the writing paper, "I have but two sheets of gilt Paper which must be reserved for occasional circumstances of Ceremony, whilst my writing is legible, my construction grammatical, my reasoning just and the subject matter entertaining, your attention will be too much fixed upon the interior of the Paper to regard the roughness of the Edge."[5] He regretted that Blickling's farm manager Mr Bailey was "insolently Brutely and maliciously determined to leave me and seems to have a pleasure in the distress which he knows, at this moment, it must occasion" and that as he was unable to leave until the accounts were settled it would be another week after "this Letter is to kiss your hands" until he could be reunited with her. The spring weather was terrible, "The Country is grown excessively disagreeable. The Easterly Winds are set in, the Dust flies, the Grass looks Brown, the Blossoms wither, the Cattle look wretched, Men are cross and women crosser, all but my good Hosts who seem not to know what ill humour is." He wrote to her again the next day, having heard that she was downhearted,

It has been insinuated to me that you are rather doleful and therefore it is a pleasing task to me to dedicate some of my Leisure to your amusement. Yet as I wrote but yesterday and am still Obliged to communicate my thoughts upon these extensive sheets, the unbounded Prospect which spreads itself before my Pen is rather formidable. Were I to indite in Poetry

I could talk to you of the Northern Snowy Wastes and draw a comparison between my situation, when in a sledge in Pomerania and that of my Pen, upon this Paper. The Idea is far fetched, so far it has merit, if you can give it any more accept of my thanks before hand.

A scandal was unfolding at Blicking, "This morning as I walked by my Dairy, I called out Val. He answered not but a female figure with a Pale Meager Visage, a downcast eye, a loose Pet en l'air* and an exceedingly tight Belly issues forth and told me Val was not at home, it was however but too evident that Val had been THERE."

Buckingham passed responsibility for dealing with this delicate matter to Mary Anne, "I intreat you when it is proper for you to write, to entreat Mrs Laton to look a little into the interior state of things and give direction for every thing being carried on to agreement" and updated her about Caroline's bawling habits "It occurs to me that your Lady Caroline has been superiorly cross ever since the departure of Mrs Nurse, for she has not since appeared after Dinner, tho her Melody has frequently been heard upon the Stairs. You must not expect above two Letters more from the Antient Buckingham." Two days later Mary Anne gave birth to their third child, a daughter they named Sophia.

Two months later, on 5 June 1768, Lady Martha Drury died. The Annual Register mistakenly reiterated a false claim, "It is said her ladyship has left to her daughter, the countess of Buckinghamshire, 120,000l. And has likewise left a legacy of 500l. and an annuity for life of 50l year to her housekeeper" whereas she left only a few thousand pounds to various friends, relatives and loyal servants. She also bequeathed her yellow diamond ring to Buckingham, her ruby ring surrounded by diamonds to Mary Anne and various other diamond pieces to Jocosa.

---

*   a jacket that is a short version of a sack dress, considered deshabille.

Notes

1. NRO MC 3/284 Letter 40.
2. NRO MC 3/284 Letter 41.
3. A merry, lively dance involving early ballet steps.
4. NRO MC 3/284 Letter 42.
5. NRO MC 3/284 Letter 44.

Arrivals and Departures

Later in the summer of 1768 a scribbled draft of Mary Anne's 'Address to the Gentleman Usher to the Queen's Majesty' made it clear that their new London townhouse was not yet ready for occupation,

> Sir, I must intreat you, in all humility, to lay me at Her Majesty's feet
> & with my respectful Duty express the fullest sense of her Gracious
> Condescension in offering to Honor my Roof, tho at this time it is not in
> my power to avail myself of it. This House, as you see, has not space for
> the Queens dignity, but after my removal to Bond Street I flatter myself to
> be frequently in a situation to have these Offers Repeated, and to receive
> becomingly the Royal Person.

On the same page is a note, "Sir! It is a peculiar happiness to me that her Majesty's discernment has distinguished you by this Commission, a person whose judgement can correct any inaccuracy in my answer as His Elocution must adorn it." Whether the invitation was genuine and she wished Buckingham to answer it, or whether it was an imaginary jest meant to prompt Buckingham to hasten their move to Bond Street, is open to conjecture. What was true was that their new house would be also be occupied by a new member of the family, whose arrival was expected in the winter. The Buckinghams quietly hoped that after three "maids of honor" their next child might be an "Ensign."

Mary Anne's long standing desire to visit Paris was crushed when Lord Rochford resigned his Ambassadorship. She wrote to Lucy soon after enduring some ill health during her pregnancy,

> It must be something more than common good will yet tempt the most
> indolent creature in the Universe to put pen to paper, more especially
> as that Creature is but now recovering from a serious illness. It does not
> appear to me that those about me judg'd my life to be in danger, but like
> a good Christian I had prepar'd my mind to quit my body with decency
> but now it is prepar'd with decency I hope to occupy the homely dwelling
> some time longer. If Lady Rochford has not totally forgot the many hours
> which her society rendered agreeable, it is needless to tell that her absence
> has been lamented, & her return wish'd for with impatience. You will find
> me in a much better house & eager to renew the evening conferences.
> Many many things have I to tell you not absolutely undeserving of your
> observations & comments. Some of our Friends are gone one way, some
> another, & some, perhaps to their sorrow, no way at all. One of our
> intimates seems to be preparing to have her hand kissed, she looks great,
> big & melancholy, tosses up her head & curls her wrist. Our Old Beaux

go off & our young ones are a most miserable set of wretches indeed. I really pity the very young Women who must at the long run, take up with them. I hope the race will end before my three fair Daughters come to years of Indiscretion. That we may soon meet is the Zealous prayer of Dear Madam Your Ladiships most faithful and affectionate, Countess of Buckinghamshire[1]

Around this time Buckingham commissioned a portrait of Jocosa Drury which portrays her sitting on a bed next to her sleeping niece Caroline. Jocosa's right hand is raised with her index finger to her lips pointing upwards indicating 'hush! Do not wake the baby,' an elaborate representation of a Hobart family joke.

A delicious scandal delighted the Society gossips. The Duke of Grafton, who had flouted his relationship with the courtesan Nancy Parsons and then separated from his wife, had been in post as acting Prime Minister since William Pitt's illness in October 1768. His wife Anne, the Duchess who Mary Anne so closely resembled, had since fallen pregnant by her lover the Earl of Upper Ossory. As a result the Graftons divorced, freeing the Duke to marry the beautiful Elizabeth Wrottesley and Anne to wed her Earl and become Countess of Upper Ossory. (Miss Parsons had quickly taken another lover, John Sackville, 3rd Duke of Dorset.)

December 1769 found the Buckinghams at Blickling where Mary Anne's pregnancy was exhausting her so much that Buckingham considerately arranged a bedchamber and rooms for her comfort on the ground floor. On 17 December Mary Anne gave birth to their fourth child, a daughter baptised Julia the very next day. It may be that the baby had arrived early, was weak, or both, and that she was baptised immediately because she was not expected to live. But it was not baby Julia who was in danger. On the night of 2 December, thirteen days after giving birth and suffering complications following the delivery, Mary Anne did not survive to pen any more lively letters to her friends or to host the Royal family at her "much better house." Buckingham's vivacious Ranelagh Romp was dead at twenty-nine.

The funeral of the young Countess of Buckinghamshire took place on 6 January 1770 when she was interred in the Hobart family vault in St Andrews Church, Blickling.

Horace Walpole found himself unable to miss an opportunity to belittle Buckingham and wrote his most spiteful insinuation, which was not published until seven years after Mary Anne's death. "His first wife was the daughter of Sir Thomas Drury, by whom he had only four daughters, which had fretted him so much, that her apprehension of his ill-humour on the birth of the last was thought to have contributed to her death."[2] This evaluation, so far removed from the truth, is beneath contempt.

Although death following childbirth was a depressingly routine occurrence, Mary Anne's decline and demise nevertheless came as a seismic shock to Buckingham.

His daughters Harriet, now seven, Caroline who was almost three and Sophia coming up to two years old were left motherless, with the newborn Julia left in the care of a wet nurse as she gained strength. Grief-stricken, Buckingham deeply mourned the loss of Mary Anne but as the weeks and months passed, the stark reality of his situation dawned upon him. He was a widower with four small daughters, no son and heir to carry the title, and no wife as lover, companion or helpmeet. In the summer therefore he stirred himself to look about for a new bride.

At Westminster he had befriended Thomas Conolly, a man acknowledged to be the wealthiest in all Ireland and who at this time was MP both for Chichester at Westminster and for County Londonderry in the Irish Parliament. As the only son amongst eight siblings Conolly inherited his vast wealth and lands from his father William (who in his turn had inherited it from his uncle, another William Conolly, the renowned Speaker of the House and owner of the magnificent Castletown House in County Kildare). Just sixteen when his father died, at twenty Thomas Conolly fell in love with and swiftly married fifteen year old Lady Louisa Lennox. (Unlike her famously controversial sisters Caroline, Emily and Sarah, Lady Louisa led a blameless existence and, childless herself, aided hundreds of disadvantaged children through her charitable enterprises.) Of Thomas Conolly's seven sisters, by 1770 Frances had married General William Howe, Katherine, General Ralph Gore, Anne had wed George Byng and borne four out of their eventual seven children, Harriet had wed John Staples and borne three children, of Lucy there is no record so presumably she died young, and the two youngest sisters aged sixteen and fifteen would marry in that same year. It is safe to surmise that the youngest sisters had gleaned clues from their elders' experiences about what wedded life might involve, but their marital careers nevertheless took dramatically different paths. Jane impetuously and against her brother's wishes eloped with George Fitzgerald, a handsome yet deeply eccentric young blade who had ardently wooed her at the Dublin balls they both frequented. After their marriage in the early spring of 1770 Thomas reluctantly felt obliged to settle money on his errant sister, awarding Fitzgerald a generous £30,000 dowry. The happy and now extremely wealthy couple travelled first to Paris where they attended theatres, the races, and balls at Versailles, and continued their profligate lifestyle during lengthy stays in Rome, Florence and Brussels.

In the summer of 1770, with Jane a new bride gone abroad, Caroline's life took a quite different trajectory when John Hobart, 2nd Earl of Buckinghamshire arrived at her mother's residence at Stratton Hall in Staffordshire. Caroline was beautiful, intelligent and despite her extreme youth, already a poised and elegant figure. In her company Buckingham's spirits revived so much that he found himself charming the young woman and they rapidly reached an understanding. George Grenville got wind of the attachment and wrote to Buckingham on 14 July, "I should be very sorry to be deprived of the pleasure which I flattered myself with of meeting you if I had not heard from Lord Suffolk that you was more agreeably and better employed in Staffordshire. May that employment (the best at which you can be engaged) turn out as much to your happiness as your own wishes or those of your warmest friends can desire." A wedding invitation had been proffered but Grenville had a previous arrangement, "my dear Lord, nothing could give me a more cordial satisfaction than to be a witness of it, but I am engaged in the Autumn to make another excursion to Packington and Hagley, and afterwards to receive some company at home, which I fear will make it impossible, but my desire to do it is so sincere that if I can I certainly would come to you at Blickling."[3]

After a short courtship the wedding between the forty-seven year old Earl of Buckinghamshire and fifteen[4] year old Caroline Conolly took place at the fashionable St George's Church, Hanover Square, London on 24 September, 1770. Buckingham had found a step mother for his four daughters, a new mistress for Blickling, and had a pretty, clever new wife by his side with whom to face the future. As a further proof of his good fortune the great wealth of the Conolly family meant that even as one of the youngest of seven sisters Caroline brought a handsome dowry of £20,000. For her part, young Caroline was now Lady Buckinghamshire and also a step-mother to four girls, the eldest of whom, Harriet, was just seven years her junior. As Harriet and her little sisters welcomed Caroline into the Hobart family their aunt Jocosa married her faithful beau on 16 October, also at St George's Church, Hanover Square. Brownlow Cust had waited for three years to marry her and his patience was now rewarded.

An unexpected source of funds came to Buckingham when Jocosa requested that she might purchase her sister's moiety,[5] Mary Anne's share of their father's fortune, including jewellery. The acquisition meant that the entire Drury estate in Northamptonshire would be in the possession of Brownlow Cust. Buckingham acquiesced and decreed the proceeds from the transaction would go towards the completion of the building work at Blickling, the home Mary Anne had grown to love so deeply. A plaque was incorporated into the wall of the West Wing which reads,

MARY ANNE COUNTESS OF BUCKINGHAM DAUGHTER OF SIR THOMAS DRURY BARt BEQUEATH'D HER JEWELS TOWARDS THE EXPENCE OF ERECTING THIS FRONT ANNO.DOMINI.MDCCLXIX

Buckingham retreated from the tumult of politics both in London and Norfolk in order to devote all his attention to his new wife and four daughters. At Blickling he instructed his men to construct an ornamental cottage, to be known as Lady's Cottage, in a glade in the Great Wood in which Caroline and their friends could take refreshment. Francois de la Rochefoucauld, a young Frenchman who visited Blickling later, during the severe winter of 1783/84, described it thus, "you plunge into a wood of magnificent forest trees…on the edge of a steep gully…the cabin is built like a simple cottage, with straw seats, two prominent deal shelves all round

Blickling Hall, February 2007.

the walls, furnished with all the pottery necessary for milk and tea and making a simple meal, but as plain and as unadorned as you could find in the homes of the people."[6]

George Grenville's plan to visit the newlyweds at Blickling was permanently curtailed by his demise on 13 November 1770, coincidentally on the same day as the opening of Parliament. Having suffered respiratory illness for most of his life, he finally succumbed to a blood disorder, leaving his dear friend Buckingham bereft.

During the following year 'Great' Caroline as Buckingham had laughingly dubbed her, to differentiate her from his small second daughter, fell pregnant but miscarried. A letter dated 1 May 1771 from his Devon tenant Canon Snow indicates that the news was public, indicating that her pregnancy must have been fairly advanced,

> I can't help very sincerely condoling with your late disappointment in family hopes, but let not, my dearest Lord, your noble courage be cast down. I hope and trust your pious endeavours will succeed better next time. Tu ne cede malis, at contra audentius ito[*]. I quite approve and congratulate you of preferring private social happiness to noisy dependent concernment in publick affairs, at present in such confusion. Adieu my dear Lord, I have rubbed through this long winter pretty well and hope when I hear or two or three swallows flying about, to crawl out of my long imprisonment in my old residentiary Castle.[7]

---

[*] 'Do not yield to evils, by contrast venture boldly.'

The spring brought further lasting sorrow when baby Julia died, outliving her mother by only seventeen months. She was interred with Mary Anne on 3 May in the family vault at Blickling Church but the cause of her early death was not recorded. Yet more sadness arrived with the news that 'Great' Caroline's sister Katherine Gore had died on the same day as Julia and this was followed by news of her sister Harriet Staples' death on 31 May.

In September Caroline was aware that she was once more with child and the Buckinghams looked forward with renewed hope to the following spring. Twenty-two year old Jocosa was also pregnant but, like her sister Mary Anne before her, did not survive the birth of her daughter Ethelred, and died on 11 February. Pity the heartbroken Brownlow Cust.[8]

On 20 February 1772 Caroline presented her husband with his fifth child, a fine and healthy daughter they baptised Amelia but who would always be known affectionately as Emily.

Notes

1. NRO MC 3/285 Letter 117.
2. Doran, Dr. (ed.), *Journal of the Reign of King George the Third from the year 1771 to 1783 by Horace Walpole, being a supplement to his memoirs in two volumes.* Vol. II. Richard Bentley, 1859, p. 86.
3. *Report on the Manuscripts of the Marquess of Lothian*, p. 288.
4. As was so common in this era, dates of daughter's births and deaths were often incomplete, but it is believed Caroline was either 15 or 16 at the time of her marriage.
5. In August 1770 Jocosa '*the younger of those ladies purchased from the Earl of Buckinghamshire her late sister's moiety*' A Genealogical and Heraldic History of the Extinct and Dormant Baronetcies—John Burke p.171.
6. Scarfe. N., p.203.
7. *Report on the Manuscripts of the Marquess of Lothian*, p.289.
8. Ethelred died aged 17 in 1788. Brownlow married Frances Bankes in 1775. They had five sons and a daughter.

Peaks and Troughs

For the next three years the Buckinghams spent the majority of their time nurturing their young family. 'Great' Caroline quickly developed relationships with her step-daughters who before long called her 'Mama' and Buckingham threw himself into new projects at Blickling. Not least of these was the extension of the undulating racecourse which his father had caused to be laid out in the 1750s.[1]

In what became known as Tower Park after the completion in 1773 of a fine square red brick building from which Buckingham's guests watched races from its terrace and tower, there were tracks laid out for 4 and 5 furlong sprints and long distance 2, 3 and 4 mile courses. The Tower's interior contained pleasantly furnished rooms and a well stocked cellar provided refreshments. Races were attended by family, visiting friends and local gentry by invitation only and took place once or sometimes twice a year when Buckingham's fine taste in wine was no doubt appreciated by his guests.

During their stays in London the Buckinghams played their part in Society. One evening in January 1773, after dining at Lady Anne Conolly's with, amongst others, Lord and Lady Strafford, Lady Louisa Conolly told the Duchess of Leinster that, "You would not guess that I was so frisky as to go to Almack's last night. Lady Buckinghamshire tempted me to go. 'Twas very thin; so much so, that the ladies were obliged to dance together; I danced one with Lady Buckinghamshire. Afterwards it filled, but I did not stay to supper."[2]

Blickling Tower, now holiday accommodation.

In early 1773 Caroline confided to her husband that the 'French lady[3]' had not visited, meaning she was again with child, and on 30 August she was safely delivered of a son who was baptised John Edgar in London on 20 September. Buckingham's joy was unconfined and the whole family rejoiced at the arrival of the little "ensign". During the following summer Caroline found herself pregnant once more and their second son, Henry Philip, was born on 11 February 1775.

Life was sweet indeed for Buckingham. He adored his wife, whose character and temperament were a perfect match for his own, and they had four daughters and not just one, but two long awaited sons, to make their family's happiness complete. At Blickling the improvements to the Hall and its Estate gave the couple great satisfaction. Even minor local matters occupied Buckingham very little during this time although his philanthropy was still in evidence. For instance, he donated £100 towards the Discharge of Debtors confined to the City and County Gaols, covered the expense of inclosing the Norfolk and Norwich Hospital from the road, which amounted to £400, and subscribed ten guineas to a Peal of Twelve Bells at St Peter Mancroft Church in Norwich.[4]

For the Buckinghams the summer of 1775 was blissful and bucolic but this peace and perfect contentment was brought to a cruel end when in the autumn little John Hobart was suddenly taken ill. Perplexed doctors could do nothing for him and after a short while he died on 12 September aged just two. As the family reeled in shock and grief, his heartbroken father copied verses from John Milton's poem 'The Pity of It, On the Death of a fair Infant' and placed them on "the first cross on the hill next the Grass Walk"[5] in the gardens at Blickling.

To the memory of John Lord Hobart

O fairest flower; no sooner blown but blasted
Soft Silken Primrose fading timelessly,
Summer's chief honour, if thou hadst outlasted
Bleak winter's force that made thy Blossom dry
For he being amorous on that lovely dye
That did thy cheek envermiel, thought to kiss,
But killed alas! And then bewailed his fatal bliss.

Yet can I not persuade me thou art dead,
Or that thy Corse Corrupts in Earth's dark womb,
Or that thy beauties lie in wormy bed,
Hid from the world in a low delved tomb
Could Heaven for pity thee so strictly doom?
Ah no! For something in thy face did shine
Above Mortality, that shew'd thou wast divine

As Buckingham and his Countess laboured under this terrible loss they were at least able to console themselves that little Henry was perfectly healthy, and that there was surely time enough ahead to have more children. Tragically this belief did not last for long and they were crushed by a second dreadful blow when only five months later baby Henry ominously developed the same symptoms as his brother. Once again, none of the treatments the doctors prescribed could save him and after only a few days he too died, on 21 February 1776, and the one year old joined his brother to rest in the Hobart family vault.

As the couple grieved for the devastating loss of their two beloved little boys, Buckingham's friends and families rallied round to give their love and support. Caroline's sister-in-law Louisa Conolly wrote, "Mr Conolly's family are in great affliction for poor Lady Buckinghamshire's distress; who has lost her two little boys in the space of seven weeks, of the same disorder, water in their heads[6]; she is, poor thing, in the most violent affliction, and Lady Anne very unhappy upon her account. But I hope she will grow a little more calm; she is gone into the country quite by herself, and will see nobody."[7] (Lady Louisa meant 'in the space of seven months' which was more accurate.) Buckingham's brother-in-law, General William Howe, Commander in Chief of the British Land Forces in America wrote from Staten Island, "It was not without the deepest concern that I heard of the late calamitous state of your family, being sensible both your Lordship and Lady Buckingham must have suffered infinite pain. But as I have understood from Fanny, her Ladyship bore her misfortunes with a calmness and resignation that was much admired, and which arising from the purest principles no doubt it must have softened the affliction."[8] This report of Caroline's fortitude and dignity in such dreadful circumstances is remarkable. In private the couple sought to comfort each other in the face of a future without their two little boys, and after six months or so they gradually began to regain a little of their natural strength and spirits.

In August Buckingham cast around for a distraction from his distress and one appeared in the shape of a rumour that he might be asked to succeed Lord Simon Harcourt as Viceroy of Ireland. This was a prestigious and challenging position, one which Buckingham felt might suit him after his experience gained in Russia. The idea of living elsewhere after the traumas of recent months may also have been an incentive, and he made it known that he wished to be considered. Then, as other names were bandied about, Buckingham convinced himself that Lord North had determined against his appointment, and wrote despondently to Charles Hotham,

> I am going next Tuesday into Norfolk, not well either in body or mind. Lord George said nothing to me of my own affairs, which indeed might arise from his attention being entirely given to the officer (who said positively that Lord Rochford will not go to Ireland. No other person is mentioned, but I suppose Lord North has peremptorily determined against me.) Not to dwell longer upon the subject, I will only say that the whole of the transaction has been conducted as if it had been thought that my own private calamities had not rendered me sufficiently miserable. The

king was pleased to address Lady Buckingham and myself some few days since in a narrow lane. He looks very well, notwithstanding all the ill-natured reports to the contrary.[9] [10]

However, with the backing of Lords Germaine and Suffolk, the First Minister extended the invitation which Buckingham duly accepted. This was despite his brother-in-law Thomas Conolly doing everything he could to dissuade him, going so far as to say outright that he would oppose him in the Irish House. His wife Louisa felt Buckingham was "too near a relation" and that "Mr Conolly thinks the situation of England and Ireland so bad that he is very warm in opposition, to which he has been reduced so contrary to his natural inclinations that I think he must have strong reasons for being so." She referred to the increases in taxes Harcourt had made on the rich, "indeed, old Simon has fleeced us pretty handsomely, and I really believe hardly knows it himself, Blaquiere does so entirely manage everything."[11] Harcourt's five years as Viceroy had been "distinguished by social magnificence"[12] which in reality meant that many families of note, in increasingly deranged efforts to match the example set by the extravagant viceroy, made themselves bankrupt. "The Dublin ton danced, drank and gambled itself into penury whilst the Castle set, contemptuous and indifferent to public opinion, robbed and oppressed the country."[13] Harcourt appeared wholly uninterested in Ireland and left his Chief Secretary, Lord de Blaqueire, do the bulk of the political work whilst he threw sumptuous entertainments at Dublin Castle. Quite often he left Ireland altogether, vastly preferring to spend long stretches of time in England.[14]

No sooner had Buckingham accepted the position than 'Great' Caroline found that the 'French lady' had once more taken her leave and she was pregnant again. Buckingham reluctantly decided that it would be best if he went on ahead alone to Dublin and that she must stay in England to have her baby and join him in Ireland only when she was afterwards completely returned to health.

Edmund Pery, the Speaker of the Irish House wrote "Congratulations on your appointment to the Government of Ireland. It will be my duty as well as my inclination to assist you to the utmost."[15] Horace Walpole's verdict on the appointment, written years later, was venomous, "He had pined himself into illness for it, and was, perhaps of all the nobility, the least unfit for it, nay, the most unfit, for it. He was weak, proud, avaricious, peevish, fretful, and femininely observant of the punctiolio of visits; and he had every one of those defects in the extreme, with their natural concomitant, obstinacy." It is tempting to ponder whether these insults might more accurately reflect their author's character rather than his target. Making no allowance whatever for Buckingham's recent bereavements, and unable to resist a further barb, he added the back-handed compliment, "His wife had more sense with as much pride."[16]

Preparations for Buckingham's journey to Ireland were soon underway and General James Johnston advised him,

I have found it necessary to agree with Lord Harcourt for the two setts of horses, they would have been sold for more money in separates and the servants all dispersed. You had better have the Chariot and the Berlin[17] and if you tell me you will leave this extent of business to me, I will take care of it all. I can get all manner of men servants here for you except for cooks. Lord Harcourt had four. In short the fewer horses and servants you are at the expense of transporting the better. Two or three very fine black light legg'd stone horses with long tails and no whites will finish this business. If you can be at some expense to enlarge St Woolston's, that and another house for your family may hold you.[18]

Viceroys traditionally occupied apartments in Dublin Castle which provided decent enough accommodation for a single man but were not suitable for families, not least because they were adjacent to the busy Privy Council chamber and to the state rooms which frequently staged lively entertainments. Soon after Buckingham's appointment was confirmed Louisa Conolly wrote to her sister Emily, Duchess of Leinster and owner of 'Frascati' a stunningly beautiful property she had lavished a great deal of money upon,[19]

I shall recommend the Black Rock house to the King to buy a place for the next Lord Lieutenant. I should think this place would suit them very well, and if Lord Buckinghamshire should come and be the person to buy the place, why should we not try to make him take this? £1,000 for the land, £6–7,000 for the house. I can't help fancying I could get a thousand more from him than anybody else, because it would be so clever for their children, and what I imagine she would like. Selling that pretty house is like taking a physic, but if it must be done, take it in time to do you good.[20]

Then in some measure panicked she wrote to Emily the next morning, "my poor conscience which SMOTE ME SORE—with the recollection 'I could not help fancying I should get £1,000 more from Lord Buckinghamshire than any body else' and when I came to examine my reasons for thinking what I wrote, I could see no motive to induce Lord Buckingham but that of COAXING Mr Conolly, whom I know is likely to oppose him. The thought shocked me." She worried that "this appointment will create a sad TOURBILLON for us. 'Tis scarcely twenty-four hours since we received the account, and the day has not passed without several petitions from the trades people for recommendations."[21]

Louisa's misgivings about connotations of coercion over the Duchess's house were alleviated when Buckingham's First Chaplain, Dean Barnard[22] offered him St Woolstan's, which lay some fourteen miles west of Dublin in the village of Celbridge. Louisa declared herself delighted because the Conolly's magnificent Castletown House was close by thereby making her sister-in-law Lady Buckingham a neighbour. The 'tourbillon' or 'whirlwind' she anticipated manifested itself in December when she was inundated with "millions of applications that are made to me in consequence of Lord Buckinghamshire's coming to Ireland—if I had the appointing of all Lord Buckingham's family and the naming of all his tradesmen, I could not satisfy one half of the requests made to me."[23] By family she meant the team Buckingham would appoint to serve him, including the soon to be knighted Richard Heron, formerly Buckingham's attorney-at-law, who was made his Chief Secretary. Heron took a Major Brooks' house in Dublin in which he resided with his wife Anne, whose childless state Buckingham had jocularly blamed on Heron's propensity to work at all hours; a trait that would be stretched to full capacity during his tenure in Ireland. In early January 1777 Louisa told her sister, "Lord B has chosen to hire a place at his first coming" but that she would attempt to get him to buy the house at Black Rock for which the asking price had risen to no less than £12,000. She mentioned "Lady B don't come till next June, as she is to lie in in April or May. Lady Anne (Caroline's mother) is quite in *grief* at her coming to Ireland; she thinks she won't succeed, and in her own mind anticipates the many disagreeable things that may happen. To say the truth we none of us like it, but must now put the best face upon it. I naturally hope the best upon most occasions, and therefore fancy it will all go off better than the family expect."[24]

Buckingham was also beset by those seeking positions in Ireland. An unexpected request came from his friend the actor-manager David Garrick, couched in suitably dramatic style, "Tho' I have for nearly forty years faced the most formidable criticks yet I could not till this moment have resolution enough to write and send this letter to your Lordship."[25] He sought a place for an unhappy nephew, also named David Garrick, who had recently bought himself out of the Dragoons. Buckingham, having been warned of the great expenditure lying ahead of him, regretfully replied, "My taking the young gentleman with me without a prospect of making a permanent provision for him in Ireland would be only leading him and his friends into an unavailing expense."[26]

Buckingham's arrival in Ireland occurred at a time when rumblings of impending hostilities were heard from the American Colonies and there were alarming and persistent suspicions that the French were preparing to invade English shores. As the Irish military were engaged in the American conflicts Ireland itself was therefore made a weak and vulnerable target. To further exacerbate matters, England had proclaimed an embargo on Ireland's crucial linen exports without consulting the Irish Parliament. This had lasted three years thus far and the parlous financial condition of the majority of Irish people was in serious danger of leading to civil unrest. Of the two most recent incumbents in the role of Viceroy, Lord George Townshend had overseen a reduction in political corruption but this had returned and increased unabated under the administration of Lord Harcourt. In twenty years both the Civil List and the Pension List had practically doubled and the national debt stood at one million pounds, half of which sum had alarmingly been accumulated in a time of peace. It was into this challenging scenario that Buckingham sailed in some splendour from Holyhead to Dublin on board the yacht 'Dorset'.

On 25 January 1777 General Shannon[27] recorded the new Viceroy's entrance to Dublin Castle, "Lord Westmeath and I were sent by the Chancellor Lifford to meet Lord Buckingham on the great stairs to congratulate him on his arrival and conduct him to Lord Harcourt who sat covered in the presence chamber, from thence to the Council, where Lord Buckingham was sworn in. Mr Richard Heron, his Chief Secretary, waited on him." Shannon noted ominously, "Lord Buckingham is not liked by Lord North. He considers him as put upon him as a trick. His first wish was for Lord Hillsborough but the King having objected to him, his next was for Lord Townshend."[28] (Townshend had held the Viceroyalty from 1767–1772 but had declined the offer to return.)

Buckingham was only too aware of Lord North's hostility towards him, "Everything here continues to wear a pleasing aspect, but I doubt not some gentlemen who have lately left this country will not be very friendly to us. I fear Sir John Blaquiere has contrived to be well with Lord North, upon whom Harcourt has had a most unaccountable influence"[29] and felt that he could not trust North to convey his letters to the King unless North wholly approved of their contents. However he quite reasonably expected that North, even though he had wanted another in Buckingham's stead, should be obliged to support him now he was actually in post. He teased his friend Hotham that if he was ever forced to use another channel to reach the King's ear, "might not Sir Charles, prefacing with the best levee bow that ever courtier made, say, Sir, I have lately received a letter from Lord Buckingham—? The Irish all declare that, unless something very unexpected should arise, I cannot possibly have, for some time at least, any trouble. You will have heard much of the gracious reception, the great resort to the Castle, and the prejudices received in my favour?"[30] Although he was fully alive to the fluctuating political situation, in private he was beset by memories of his young sons and by current fears for his wife's health, which in combination depressed and troubled him, "This is a chearful outline, but discreet reflection must necessarily throw a large proportion of shade upon it. I am at this moment far from well, nor is it greatly to be wondered at."[31]

In England it was generally considered that the new Viceroy had inherited a healthy budget, a well disposed Parliament, a Speaker elected by a significant majority and that the "number of places, pensions and honours most lavishly bestowed must have left scarcely an individual of consequence in the country whose avarice and ambition ought not to be amply satisfied."[32] Buckingham perceived the true state of affairs was that "it was the great object of the late government to retire with eclat. The choosing of the Speaker was understood to be their last act, and every nerve was strained to carry out that one favourite point"[33] and that wholesale bribery was the sole reason their choice had been elected. He anticipated that any money in the Treasury would soon vanish in maintaining the troops currently in America and believed that previous holders of his role had been wilfully blind to the needs of the Irish people. He was quick to realise that "It will be evident to any man who obtains even a superficial knowledge of this country, that it has been little attended to and still less understood"[34] and predicted trouble from some of the newly appointed yet still discontented nobility, "barons think they should have been viscounts, and viscounts earls, and most of them conceive they are not obligated to government, as they bought their peerages in several instances with their boroughs. The number of resident Irish peers in 1751 was only 28, now there are 67."[35]

Louisa Conolly thought the new Viceroy had made a good first impression and that "everything promises fair for Lord Buckinghamshire. And his very civil, kind behaviour, both to the Duke of Leinster and Mr Conolly, incline them to think they shall support him; and you may be sure I most heartily hope they may." She noted that "nothing can be pleasanter than we all are at the moment" adding hopefully, "I am in very great hopes that Lord Buckinghamshire has no *devilish* thing to do."[36]

As he grew accustomed to his surroundings and waited most anxiously for news of Caroline's lying-in, he heard that neither English politics nor its leader were in the best of health. Hans Stanley wrote on 20 March 1777 to "remind you of my very faithful and affectionate attachment. I am as an individual a very principal sufferer by your absence. The House of Commons has been very near annihilated since you left England. Lord North's illness is a very serious one but Charles Townshend assures me he is now able to take the air." Stanley expressed grave fears about the growing hostilities in America and the threat of war looming with France but reassured Buckingham that at least on the home front some news was encouraging. "I doubt all this is but an unchearful sort of correspondence, we go on however feasting dancing marrying and giving in marriage like our ante-diluvian predecessors; as to which particulars I refer you to Lady Buckingham, adding that I know she must be to you the best consolation, when public prospects are gloomy, and that I have never seen her Ladyship enjoy a better share of health and beauty."[37] Buckingham was doubtless delighted to read the last comment, and just two weeks later, to his profound relief and joy, his darling 'Great' Caroline safely gave birth to their fourth child, a son they baptised George.

৵৵৹৻

Buckingham was well aware that causes for celebration were rare for the vast majority of the Irish people. He told Charles Hotham of his despair at the current method of dealing with the situation, "the misery of the people occasions great gaiety, expense and Shew, calculated for Charitable purposes, which in the course of this month, in different Shapes, cost me more than three hundred pounds, and I would cheerfully give as much more to produce a real, instead of a temporary, relief. It is a melancholy truth that fifteen thousand People in Dublin are at this time happy to receive five shillings worth of Oatmeal each."[38] Unless a loan from England was granted there was no money in circulation other than for payment of the troops abroad and he keenly felt the impotency of his position.

In June Caroline, Countess of Buckinghamshire, and newly titled Vicereine of Ireland, arrived in Dublin to take her place at her husband's side and to introduce baby George to his father. Once settled in, the Vicereine quite soon undertook her formal duties, which included reviewing the garrison. It was at this time the fashion for ladies to wear "enormous unnatural Periwigs" which Hotham's friend Colonel Baugh "regretted surmounted their pritty faces."[39] These elaborate pastel powdered wigs or, as Buckingham disparagingly called them, 'Towers of Babel' were on this occasion the cause of some confusion and considerable hilarity, as Buckingham related to Hotham,

> A few days after Caroline's arrival she was entertained with a very fine Review, Infantry, Dragoons & Artillery, together with about two thousand men. When they marched by they were to salute the Vice Queen. She accordingly stood forth, very beautiful and tolerably saucy; her Gentleman Usher (that Courteous Knight Sir John Haslet) stood behind her, holding a Parasol over the Babel which disgraced her head. The Crowd being great and other Ladys pressing forward to see her Excellency, the officers were told, to prevent mistakes, that they were to salute A LADY STANDING UNDER A PARASOL; but alas ! poor Sir John, whose person and arm, fully extended, could not give a suitable elevation to the Parasol, unfortunately brushed one of the Towers of Babel, and in consequence the Machine was instantly dismissed. This occasioned considerable irregularity in the salute, AS NO PARASOL COULD BE FOUND! So the entire garrison marched past, bowing first to this lady, then to that; and the handsome dame to whom they should all have paid homage, not knowing the cause of the fiasco, became more and more perplexed at finding herself one moment saluted with the respect which was her due and at the next ignored for some unimportant member of the Vice-regal circle.[40]

Buckingham was immensely proud to have his elegant, graceful young wife beside him and her launch into Irish society was universally declared a triumph. General Baugh wrote to Sir Charles,

> You would be charmed to see how well she does the honours, she does not lose the least sight of her situation &. Dignity &. is as easy and well-bred as the Queen, so much so as to please—I really believe—everybody; and as to his Lordship, I see nothing but what is exactly what it should be, as much BUCKINGHAM as he ought to be. The other night the ball-room all filled with women, exquisitely dressed, and the whole rising when their Excellencies came in was prestigiously striking. People are all astonishment to see how we outdo St James's.[41]

The Earl of Huntingdon later took credit for anticipating Caroline's success, "I hear from every quarter that the prediction I made to Lady Buckingham and to everyone else THAT SHE WOULD PLAY THE PART OF A QUEEN BETTER THAN ANY, is fully verified." These ecstatic reports confounded the earlier worries of Caroline's mother Anne, and Louisa's optimism was rewarded when Caroline's conquest of Dublin resulted in general approbation of their twenty two year old Vicereine. Furthermore Buckingham himself quickly won over many of those sceptical of his qualifications for the role of Viceroy. Louisa speculated that should Lord Germain lose his power over the American conflict Buckingham would lose his chief supporter but trusted in God that their mutual brother-in-law General Howe would "carry all his points, which I do believe will be the case, if any man on earth can carry them." She was awed by Buckingham's concerted efforts to assimilate, "Lord Buckingham seems to know the character here of the people as well as if he had lived amongst them." It seemed that his experience gained in Russia might well bear fruit in Ireland.

Caroline's joyous conquest of Dublin was suddenly overshadowed by fears for the health of baby George. Henry Fitzgerald, son of Louisa Conolly's sister Emily, Duchess of Leinster, had arrived at Castletown House and was to be inoculated against the small-pox during his stay. Louisa wrote, "Henry was inoculated yesterday evening from a little sucking child that had about twenty spots; I think one likes the idea of such an innocent subject to take the infection from."[42] Seventeen year old Henry was not in the least apprehensive about it, reassured as he had been by his aunt that, "Mr Power's has inoculated above 2000 persons, none of which were ever ill enough to keep to their beds." But Caroline was petrified that the smallpox might somehow infect her baby and told Louisa she would remove him to the house at Black Rock which conversely, according to Louisa, was "of all places the fullest in general of disorders." Louisa's good natured nephew said he would not stay at Castletown upon any account and took himself off to Maynooth, a house a few miles away. Louisa, rather than risk Caroline thinking her son had caught the small pox from Henry "perhaps three months hence" agreed that Henry should go, "I have consented to the indulging poor Lady Buckinghamshire's most unreasonable fears about her son, for whom she lives in such constant apprehensions that there is no reasoning with her about it; and her fright (when she heard of Henry's staying here) was so great that Mr Conolly tells me neither he nor Lord Buckinghamshire could possibly pacify her at all." Louisa's incomprehension of Caroline's terror at even the remote possibility of losing another child is perplexing but she had complete faith in inoculation. Louisa added "as wrong as I think she is about this, I pity her so much that I can't find it in my heart to give her the anxiety, as it is in my power to avoid it." She recalled many occasions where children had been inoculated in her home, even when the house was full of company, and also in the autumn "when you can't let so much air into the house as at this time of the year" but softening her stance wrote, "Poor creature, I pity her so much, that I don't believe I am *really* angry, and feel upon this occasion, as I do upon many others, the many blessings attending the *not* having children."

Lord Cadogan told Buckingham he hoped to visit Dublin later in the year and had "great pleasure in hearing that Irish affairs carry so good an appearance under your administration."[43] The Earl of Hardwicke was ordered by his physician to sea bathe at Brighthelmstone[44] but resolved "when I am tired of this country and my connections fall off, you will allow me to hope for a hospitable reception at Dublin Castle." Wills Hill, Lord Hillsborough, excused himself as he was "caught up in the village races and then the Assizes" but nevertheless requested favours in his letters to Buckingham. These and very many others of the great and the good were the correspondents from England, and in Ireland there was a relentless clamour for the Viceroy's attention. Buckingham mischievously told Hotham that "every Irish gentleman enters my presence with a P in his mouth - PLACE, PENSION, PRIVILEGE, PEERAGE OR PRIVY COUNSELLOR! as naturally as they would enter a lady's closet with a P in their hands."[45]

To begin with Buckingham's reign progressed relatively smoothly but he anticipated trouble, "By their tenor the French are not inclined to quarrel with us this year. My vessel continues to sail in smooth water, but we must be prepared for an equinoctial gale, though no quarter is foreseen from whence the storm may come."[46] In September he lamented the lack of support from Lord North who was derelict when it came to keeping him informed of England's intentions towards Ireland. A particular problem was that of desertion from the Irish Army which was "really epidemical: reluctantly we have begun and must continue a cruel remedy." Unprincipled men were enlisting and then immediately absconding with the clothes and equipment allotted to them in the mistaken belief that they would not be punished for a first offence. Buckingham came to the reluctant conclusion that "the punishing capitally a deserting Recruit may operate more for the only object, EXAMPLE, than the shooting the old Offenders. When an Opportunity offers I shall think it my duty to try this experiment, tho' with an akeing heart."[47] As a result of the commercial restrictions imposed upon it the whole of Ireland was suffering in dire poverty and all classes lived in fear of bankruptcy. The great majority of the population were commoners who did not have the right to vote so the only possible route to making their opinions heard was via Petitioning. Buckingham listened to the people, acknowledged their plight, and made requests of England which were repeatedly ignored, such as asking for "some relaxing of the embargo on several thousand barrels of beef and pork—or that the embargo might be continued to the provisions of a certain quality, so that the inferior kind, which is not taken by our contractors but sold to the French, for the use of their negroes and other such purposes, might be exported."[48] The linens Ireland exported were strictly limited to white and brown only, and imports to Ireland from plantations in the West Indies were confined to rum. These restrictions were mightily oppressive and, unsurprisingly, strong anti-English resentment grew as a result of this grossly unfair treatment. But in the English Parliament all eyes were turned towards America and to France, and as a consequence Ireland was sorely neglected.

In contrast, comforting news arrived from Norfolk from where John Thomlinson kept Buckingham abreast of the goings-on at Blickling. Their garrulous estate manager Copeman had got a good price for lambs at 5s 9d a head,

> To give your Lordship some idea of the cheapness at Cawston, very tolerable lambs were sold for 3s 6d, so that upon the whole you have escaped well and when you receive the account of the present crop of corn I have not the least doubt of the year's turning out well upon the farming line. Copeman would not let me be satisfied with his narrative (which was not less diffuse than usual) he insisted upon my being an eye witness of your riches. In the barns I found wheat and barley up to the roofs and two stacks of barley and one of prodigious fine beans in the yards besides, and such a crop of wheat upon the Aylsham Lawne as will fill them all again next harvest, so tho' you have received a check in your sheep, it is likely to be repaid in your crops.

Less welcome were reports of organised and persistent poachers,

> these gallants with great apparatus of dogs and servants have travelled to most pheasant repositories in this country. They even attacked your Lordships nursery by the ice house and shot very often before Tom Bell could get up with them. However, he drove them off, they threatened to come again next day, but Tom was ready with his gun and spaniels and swore they should not enter the premises till some of them DIES UPON THE SPOT which vigorous measure drove them off.[49]

The shooting season had been "a lamentable year. I hope that amusement has been more compleat in Ireland, and that your gun has performed its usual feats." A mercifully unfounded rumour had reached Blickling about baby George "the neighbourhood of Aylsham were much alarmed with a report that Lord Hobart was in a very ill state of health, which your Lordship's last letter to Copeman happily contradicted."[50]

In November Mr. Marsham, an elderly neighbour at Stratton, told him, "I am rooted here like my trees: with this difference only, that the spring gives no life to me. I know trees ought to be removed as soon as they whip each other with a moderate gale: but I love them as my children and I cannot act with my own judgement." He hoped that "Lady Buckingham and all your young family are well" and, returning to his preferred subject, added the post script "My Lord an oak I planted in 1720 is this autumn 83 feet and half of timber in the body: I believe very few under 70 can say so much but I wish your Excellency may say it in time."[51] Worse news reached Dublin of the passing of Buckingham's good friend Sir Armine Wodehouse of Kimberley Hall, whose sudden death was caused by a kipper bone that lodged in his throat.

Late November saw the return to Ireland of Caroline's sister Jane and her errant husband George Fitzgerald who had now earned the epithet 'Fighting' because of his propensity for frequent duelling. They had lived abroad for three years following their marriage but in that time managed to spend almost all of Jane's £30,000 dowry and now teetered on the verge of bankruptcy. Louisa spoke for the Conolly family "We shall all be glad to see poor Jane; but he is such a creature that he must always be a great distress to the family. However I hope that COOL, EVEN CIVILITY will keep him in some order concerning ourselves. As to others, I fear one must expect to hear of disagreeable things, as he will ever be in scrapes."[52] This proved prophetic as only weeks later she reported that Fitzgerald was "mad, and shut up in Swift's Hospital at William's[53] expense—run out of every sixpence—his wife had a miserable time of it and once narrowly escaped a pistol which he fired at her. She is a most beautiful woman with very pretty manners almost starving with a brute and my Lord Harcourt supposed to be in love with her."[54] Where this last rumour stems from is a mystery but it had no impact on the Fitzgerald's story. Jane and their small daughter Mary Anne were taken care of by members of the Conolly family until Fitzgerald's eventual release from the mental institution (which was the legacy of the satirist Jonathan Swift, Henrietta Howard's friend, who upon his death in 1745 left £12,000 to 'build a house for fools and mad' as his epitaph read.)

Elsewhere the whirl of social life continued with splendid balls thrown at Dublin Castle over which the Viceroy and Vicereine presided. Louisa told her sister that "the Castle is now quite the fashionable place" where recently a new dance was introduced, "a minuet de la cour they call it, but I don't think it a minuet neither, for there are entre chats."[55] It is likely that Buckingham, with years of dancing the nights away in Petersburg behind him and his recent learning of the pas de rigadon with young Harriet, mastered this new French dance with ease.

These pleasurable pursuits were balanced by the weighty trials of politics. He confided to Louisa Conolly that upon his appointment as Lord Lieutenant, Lord North had told him of "the richness of the Treasury here, where he would find upwards of £80,000; when alas ! It comes out that the Treasury is above £170,000 in debt."[56] Despite this gigantic discrepancy Louisa thought the Government would "go on smoothly" and that she still could not imagine that "Lord Buckinghamshire has any VILE thing to do." The quantity of applications for her assistance had increased so much that "in truth I cannot number them, but the most distressing of all are the poor wretches condemned to death, so that I quite dread the sight of a petition." As she was not able to help these desperate supplicants and it caused her so much distress to read them she felt "obliged to make the servants enquire of the nature of every petition before they bring them to me." 'Fighting' George Fitzgerald was released from Swift's Hospital and this time visited Castletown with Jane and little Mary Anne with no adverse consequences. Another frequent visitor was "Lady Buckingham who often comes to us in a comfortable way; she is really vastly agreeable and pleasing and does so well here it is delightful."[57]

1777 ended with reports from America that troops under the command of General William Howe, husband of Caroline's elder sister Frances, had taken possession of Philadelphia. Closer to home, a speech Buckingham made in Ireland had not gone down at all well at Westminster. Lord Hillsborough told him, "I fear a degree of dissatisfaction took place EVERY WHERE but I am glad to observe that it subsides; and I assure your Excellency that I have not been idle in endeavouring to soften and to justify.'[58] Lord North resolutely continued to ignore all and every plea for Irish aid.

Buckingham's correspondence with Wills Hill often dwelt upon the subject of alcohol consumption, with Hillsborough exhorting him to "think about correcting the intolerable drunkenness of the north."[59] After a murder was carried out whilst the perpetrator was "cursed by the drinking of spirits" during a riot, Hillsborough hoped "he will meet the fate he deserves and the Judge as the fittest person to determine what that may be."[60] An appeal was made to Buckingham to reduce the accused's sentence but he reluctantly declined. Hillsborough agreed with this difficult judgement, "you are quite right in not showing mercy to the unfortunate convict, as there was no foundation to it. Such mercy is cruelty to the public"[61] and the man was duly hanged. In June Buckingham fervently hoped that "the regulations to the brewery enacted in the last Revenue Bill will encourage the drinking of beer in preference to whisky."[62]

On a lighter note, it seems another pretty actress had caught Buckingham's eye and that Lady Caroline had a sense of humour to match his own. In reply to a letter from Lord Hillsborough, he wrote, "I have this moment been reading your Lordship's menacing paragraph relative to my avowed passion for Miss Corry, to Lady Buckingham, and at my own risk will communicate her speech in consequence: 'I like Lord Hillsborough vastly.' If this does not determine you incontinently to cross St George's Channel your spirit of gallantry is at the lowest ebb."[63] Buckingham, lately in a cheerful and optimistic frame of mind, informed Hotham, "My health and spirits are good. Some little ruffles I have had, but none from England, and not sufficient either to spoil my dinner or break my rest. No Sovereign in Europe has better Ministers." [64]

Nevertheless, the nightmare of trade deals and embargoes continued and must inevitably have brought to Buckingham's mind the agonies he suffered during the grindingly slow negotiations in Russia. The major difference now being that Ireland was a dominion of England and much better care and attention should have been given to a loyal and friendly neighbour. To add to his worries, in April 1778 increased threats of a French invasion rose once again. Buckingham told Westminster that the Irish people were strongly in favour of raising a new militia or independent companies of volunteers to protect their Country, but when no financial aid for this purpose was forthcoming the Irish gentry were driven to take matters into their own hands. Feudal attachments between landlords and tenants remained very strong and as a result troops were soon rallied to the cause. When official news reported that a French invasion of Belfast was imminent, associations for self-defence were formed under the direction of the leading families.

Buckingham viewed this rising movement with a disconcerting combination of admiration and dismay. Whilst he could not fault the motive of the volunteers, whose concerns were for the safety of their people and the defence of their country, he was greatly concerned that a great mass of armed men rising independently from the Government might in itself be cause for alarm. In May the Catholic Relief Bill was mooted and a month of fierce debates followed. Although the proposal that Catholics should be allowed to buy land freehold was roundly defeated, Parliament grudgingly allowed them to purchase land with 999 year leases. The Bill also deigned to abolish the hated law that forced Catholic land owners on their deaths to either divide their estates between their sons or leave the whole estate to one son on the express condition that he take an oath to convert to the Protestant Church of Ireland. Following many impassioned and acrimonious debates the Bill eventually passed in both houses and was translated into law in August 1778. General Baugh described one debate thus, "The Company opened very full for the Papists, which was carried by a much greater majority than the Castle expected. There were many eloquent speakers. Councillor Yelverton would have made a convert of me however prejudiced I had been; nothing could be more pathetically pictured than the horrid situation of a Catholic in this country from his birth to his burial."[65] He ridiculed Thomas Conolly who "made us laugh, and exposed himself by making the House merry at his expense, took a full glass too much, and at the best you know he DON'T SHINE.' Noting a common occurrence during many an overlong political debate he observed, "The Provost would have prosed til this time if the coughing of one half of the House had not awakened the other half at half past twelve o'clock."[66]

It had always been Buckingham's firm belief that Catholics should be treated equally throughout Great Britain but he recognised the complications inherent in trying to bring this about in Ireland. At a public meeting where feelings ran high and men with opposing views argued their cases for what seemed to him endless hours, Buckingham grew bored. Spotting a small man who he judged had an air of wisdom about him but who was quietly keeping his counsel, he enquired, "And you, sir, may I ask are you an Atheist or a Deist?" To which the diminutive man, considerably alarmed, replied shrilly, "Neether, Sir, - Neether! I am a dentist!"[67] In August Lord Hillsborough congratulated Buckingham for "having gotten through the longest and most difficult Session of Parliament I ever remember in Ireland. Your success is very much to your own honour, and gives very great pleasure to your friends."[68]

In September Louisa Conolly accompanied the Buckinghams to Frescati house at Black Rock and although Caroline admired the house enormously, any aspirations

Louisa may have clung to of selling it to the Buckinghams came to an abrupt end. She wrote to her sister, "Lady Caroline found a fault with it which had not struck me before, but that I doubt you will think one also, particularly as you have been used to the contrary in France; which are the low doors. Lady Caroline absolutely could not walk upright through any of them above stairs, and touched the top of most of those below."[69]

The stark contrast between the lives and happiness of the two youngest Conolly sisters was growing ever more pronounced. Caroline was thoroughly enjoying her busy role as Vicereine of Ireland, approved of by Louisa who found her "remarkably agreeable, very like her brother, with a very good temper: I don't mean an absolute lamb, for she is eager, quick, and warm in her manner, but pleasantly so.'[70] Caroline's marriage to her amusing, adoring husband was happy, their daughters were delightful, baby George was extremely bright and thriving and their future looked rosy. Jane's marriage was a different matter altogether, causing Louisa to observe sadly, "Mr Fitzgerald is hardly ever with her, and though she adores him, she takes his neglect patiently. She does move one's pity to such a degree that it's impossible not to be fond of her."[71] Expanding her thoughts she concluded "Unless one was tried, there is no judging what one would do in such a case. But I think if such behaviour did not break my heart, it would cure me of love. I could never go on loving without any return. How happy it is to have such a patient disposition as poor Mrs F, when it is one's fate to be so wretched![72]"

The summer months brought mournful news of the demise of Buckingham's adored maternal grandmother Elizabeth Britiffe. Little were the Buckinghams to know that infinitely worse news would soon follow. To their horror and incredulity George began to exhibit signs of the very same illness that had taken his elder brothers and it seemed appallingly likely that at eighteen months old he might be destined to follow them to an early grave. On 30 October Louisa wrote to her sister,

> A very melancholy scene I have in prospect on poor Lady Buckingham's account, as I think she is going to lose her third son with the same disorder that carried off the two others. I believe I told you what a promising, fine boy he was. About ten days ago he was taken ill with what we hoped was only teeth, though she saw many symptoms that alarmed her. Sir Nathaniel Berry thought it only his teeth, and sent him back into the country, better, as he thought; but in the evening there came on such terrible symptoms of sleepiness and sickness that Lady Buckingham thinks him gone, and, indeed, do I. She is gone back to town today with him, a very pitiable object indeed, that goes to my heart, and the more so from her calmness. She is naturally lively, all anxiety and warmth; and from her fears when he was inoculated showed such a disposition to be terrified beyond bounds, that it is now the most moving thing in the world to see her, all composure, and meekness, quite subdued with grief. She prefers

being alone or I would have gone to town with her. I cannot tell you how vexed I am about it.[73]

Three days later she wrote again, "Ah ! Poor Lady Buckingham, I am sure your heart aches for her! The poor little boy is not yet dead, but there are no hopes of him at all. God help the poor parents !"[74]

In a letter written from Dublin Castle dated 4 November, a devastated Buckingham told Hotham he was resigned to the impending catastrophe. The contrast between Buckingham's terrible private grief and the relentless demands of public duty is all too vivid,

> Tho' in some sort callous'd, from repeated sad experience, to family disappointments, and sensible that the probable humiliation, if not annihilation of the British Empire renders the succession to a Peerage of less import, yet the unexpectedly finding that my little boy is sinking into his Brother's grave is a severe Trial. Lady B is most completely miserable, but the violence of her Grief will spend itself, mine must be permanent—it will extinguish the little comfort derived from the fond Idea of leaving a Representative, which cheers the last closing scene, and warms the dying feelings of human vanity. My Son may continue to languish a day or two but his Recovery cannot be expected, my property therefore, all derived from female sources, must probably now be convey'd through the same channel.
>
> The Bells are ringing, the Guns are firing, and the Horses are decorated with Ribbons, and every other gay Circumstance is preparing for the accustomed Procession upon this day, and I am to do the honours of a very splendid entertainment. The wise men tell me that, as the poor Babe is not actually dead, no part of this can possibly be omitted. I struggle with my anguish—and by dint of forcing an appearance of tranquillity may almost be suspected of insensibility, but my heart akes.[75]

Buckingham somehow managed put on a brave face and was in some measure successful in disguising his desolation in public but behind the scenes his grief was overwhelming. Louisa wrote to her sister on 9 November, "I am sure you will be sorry to hear that poor Lord Hobart is dead at last. Lord Buckingham bears it very tolerably, and she is so composed, I hear, that I fear it will last the longer on her mind. I have not seen her yet; the child was buried today; I am to go to town to see her tomorrow."[76] Louisa continued her visits "as she seems to like to have me, and has nobody with her, Mrs Fitzgerald being in the north, and Lady Heron gone to England." On 20 November the Buckinghams bid a sorrowful farewell to each other and, accompanied by her brother Thomas, Lady Caroline set sail for England to seek comfort and solace in the arms of her mother Lady Anne and sisters Frances and Anne.

Notes

1. National Horseracing Museum, Palace House, Newmarket.
2. p. 62-63.
3. A euphemism for the menstrual cycle.
4. *Report on the Manuscripts of the Marquess of Lothian*, p.294.
5. MC 3/285 Letter 120.
6. "Water in their heads" strongly suggests that the boys had developed hydrocephalus which causes excessive cerebrospinal fluid to accumulate in the brain. Symptoms which closely match those of the Hobart boys were poor feeding, drowsiness, eyes turning downwards and fits. Treatments such as blood-letting were sometimes used in the18th century and were worse than useless. The disorder was successfully treated by surgical means but not until early-mid 20th century.
7. Fitzgerald, B. (ed.), *Correspondence of Emily, Duchess of Leinster*, Vol. III, 1957, p. 184.
8. *Report on the Manuscripts of the Marquess of Lothian*, p.295.
9. PRONI T3429/1/2.
10. America had declared Independence on July 1776 which will certainly have been on George III's mind.
11. Fitzgerald, B. (ed.), *Correspondence of Emily, Duchess of Leinster*, Vol. III, 1957, p. 217-218.
12. *The Viceroys of Ireland*, Charles O'Mahony, John Long Limited, London: 1962, p.179.
13. Ibid.
14. Only a few months after his final return from Ireland, having retired to his country seat at Nuneham Park in Oxfordshire, Simon Harcourt was found drowned in a well on his estate apparently after rescuing his favourite dog, which survived.
15. *Report on the Manuscripts of the Marquess of Lothian*, p.297.
16. Doran, Dr. (ed.), *Journal of the Reign of King George the Third from the year 1771 to 1783 by Horace Walpole, being a supplement to his memoirs in two volumes*. Vol. II. Richard Bentley, 1859, p.86.
17. Harness for eight £105.The Berlin £135.The Chasse Marine £60. The Chariot £330.
18. *Report on the Manuscripts of the Marquess of Lothian*, p. 297.
19. Emily Lennox married the Duke of Leinster with whom she had 17 children. After his death she married their son's former tutor Mr Ogilvie and they had a further three children together (although the last born from her first marriage was said to be his too). Emily had been a play-mate of Charles Hotham in their youth. She retained the title of Duchess of Leinster until her death. She and her second husband were facetiously referred to as the 'Duke and Duchess of Ogilvie'.
20. Fitzgerald, B. (ed.), *Correspondence of Emily, Duchess of Leinster*, Vol. III, 1957, p.240.
21. Ibid. p.239-240.
22. Thomas Barnard, later Bishop of Killaloe and then Limerick. Member of the famous Literary Club presided over by Dr Johnson.
23. Fitzgerald, B. (ed.), *Correspondence of Emily, Duchess of Leinster*, Vol. III, 1957, p.243.
24. Ibid. p.247.
25. *Reports on the Manuscripts of the Marquess of Lothian*, p.297.
26. Little, D. M. & Kahrl G. M. (eds.), *The Letters of David Garrick*, Vol. III, Letters 816-1362, 1963, p.1145.
27. Richard Boyle, later 2nd Earl of Shannon, Muster-Master General 1774 - 1781, older brother of Robert Boyle Walsingham who married Charlotte Hanbury Williams.

28. PRONI D2707/A/2/2/22.

29. PRONI T3429/1/7.

30. PRONI T3429/1/7.

31. Ibid.

32. PRONI T3429/1/8.

33. Ibid.

34. Ibid.

35. PRONI T3429/1/8.

36. Fitzgerald, B. (ed.), *Correspondence of Emily, Duchess of Leinster*, Vol. III, 1957, p. 254.

37. *Report on the Manuscripts of the Marquess of Lothian*, p.301.

38. *The Hothams...*, p.180.

39. Ibid. p.174.

40. Ibid. p.176-177.

41. Ibid. p.177.

42. Fitzgerald, B. (ed.), *Correspondence of Emily, Duchess of Leinster*, Vol. III, 1957, p.294.

43. *Report on the Manuscripts of the Marquess of Lothian*, p.306.

44. Later known as Brighton.

45. PRONI T/3100 Hobart papers.

46. PRONI T3429/1/12.

47. PRONI T3429/1/13.

48. *Report on the Manuscripts of the Marquess of Lothian*, p.317.

49. *Report of the manuscripts of the Marquess of Lothian*, p.320.

50. Ibid. p.321.

51. Ibid. p.328.

52. Fitzgerald, B. (ed.), *Correspondence of Emily, Duchess of Leinster*, Vol. III, 1957, p.257.

53. William, 2nd Duke of Leinster.

54. Fitzgerald, B. (ed.), *Correspondence of Emily, Duchess of Leinster*, Vol. III, 1957, p.260.

55. Ibid. p.258.

56. Ibid. p.262.

57. Ibid. p.263.

58. *Reports on the manuscripts of the Marquess of Lothian*, p.325.

59. Ibid. p.235.

60. Ibid. p.328.

61. Ibid. p.330.

62. PRONI D607/B/23.

63. PRONI D607/B/23.

64. *The Hothams ...*, p.178.

65. Ibid. p.181.

66. Ibid. p.181.

67. Ibid.p.182.

68. *Report on the Manuscripts of the Marquess of Lothian*, p.337.

69. Fitzgerald, B. (ed.), *Correspondence of Emily, Duchess of Leinster*, Vol. III, 1957, p. 313-314.

70. Ibid. p.321.

71. Ibid. p.321.

72. Jane died in 1780 and her husband George 'Fighting' Fitzgerald was hanged for murder in 1786. (Their daughter Mary Anne died in Lady Louisa Conolly's arms in 1794—Fitzgerald, B. (ed.), *Correspondence of Emily, Duchess of Leinster*, Vol. III, 1957, p.424.)

73. Ibid. p.323.

74. Ibid. p.325.

75. *The Hothams ...*, p.178.

76. Ibid. p.327.

1779

January began inauspiciously with the death of the actor-manager David Garrick. Hans Stanley, 'Little' Caroline's godfather, was a pallbearer at the funeral which was an extravagant affair befitting a legend of the London stage. The principal mourners travelled in thirty-five grand state coaches each drawn by six horses and the procession was watched by thousands of people who lined the streets between Garrick's home and Westminster Abbey.

In early March more dismal news arrived from Lord Hillsborough "poor Lord Suffolk has gone extremely ill to Bath, most people think not to return but I think his youth gives him a chance of recovery."[1] This hope was dashed a week later when he reported, "the melancholy account of Lord Suffolk's death, & the agreeable one of his Resurrection." Henry Howard had been Lord Privy Seal and only forty years old at his untimely death which was all the more tragic as his wife was pregnant; his son was born posthumously in August and inherited his title only to die two days later. Buckingham felt the loss of his friend deeply and told Lord Germain, "Lord Suffolk's death in both a publick and private light is a thorn in my pillow which will not easily be removed."[2] More positive news from afar had cheered him a little, "The intelligence of our most brilliant successes as well in the East as in the West Indies has give me a long

Monument to David Garrick in the South Transept of Westminster Abbey.

inexperienced flow of spirits" but he worried that "A most painful reflection too frequently occurs to me that my Administration should exist at a period when of all others England was oppressed with difficulties which this country instead of relieving was necessarily obliged to increase." He stood by the decisions he had made thus far which had been taken with dispassionate judgement. To Hotham he confided that "The melancholy state of this kingdom, transmitted repeatedly in my dispatches to England, though backed by the living testimony of Sir Richard Heron, does not as yet seem to have made the necessary impression. At present, perhaps, I may be suspected of having assumed the character of an Irish Patriot, for the selfish purpose of a moment."[3] He confessed ruefully that,

Since Lady Buckingham's departure, to fill up the void occasioned by the interruption of matrimonial endearments, a few ladies have been occasionally invited to a commerce party and supper at the Castle. It is now a month since, upon my entering the drawing room earlier than usual, I found a lady alone; her age eighteen, her face enlightened with the genial glow of health and the most animated expression of young desire; her breasts quite above her stays, slightly shaded by a net, in the meshes of which her rosy nipples played. Reclining in a chair she sat on the very extremity. A slight drapery covered half her legs, which, as her feet, formed by elegance itself and dressed by the graces, were separated and extended. Heureusement[4] just as I was forgetting all ceremony, the master of ceremonies entered.

Captain Corbet and several other aides-de-camp had been vying with each other for the attentions of a beautiful girl, a relation of the late Lady Coventry. "I have taken her under my protection, and she seems disposed to attend my advice, the object of which will be that she should never listen to any man, whatever he may offer with one hand, unless be brings his rental in the other."[5]

He asked Hillsborough to plead his cause at Westminster, "As your Lordship has frequent opportunities of seeing Lord North, your attention to the general wellbeing of the Empire at large as well as your immediate connection with Ireland, must lead you to urge the expediency of showing some indulgence to her trade."[6] In April Hillsborough suffered ill health, "I have been so furiously attacked by a cold and sore throat that I have not been able to hold my head down long enough to write a letter for these ten days. You will laugh, and yet I am sure be sorry to hear that our friend Barrington has got a smart fit of the gout. I fancy he swears a little, but our respective complaints keep us asunder."[7] Having heard rumours that he was to be appointed as the next Secretary of State for the Southern Colonies, Hillsborough protested, "My private opinion and indeed hope has been and still is that it will not come to me. I say my hope, because I think I should be weak enough to accept it, tho indubitably much happyer as I am, ARMIS HERCULIS AD. POSTEM FIXIS."[*] He ended gleefully, "I have this instant got a note from Barrington to tell me he has the gout in the other foot."

The Sheriffs of Dublin informed Buckingham that more than 19,000 people in the weaving trade were on the brink of starvation and that nothing but an extension of trade and free export of their goods could save them. In April a great meeting was held where everyone present pledged not to buy any goods from Great Britain. In May the Aggregate Body of the Citizens of Dublin, led by Napper Tandy (later a renowned Irish revolutionary) began to print the names of all importers of British goods. Buckingham condemned this action as he believed it was calculated to encourage aggrieved people to attack those individuals. Nevertheless Tandy's actions made popular politics an intrinsic part of the struggle for trade concessions

---

[*]   Hang up my arms at Hercules door (i.e. be put out to pasture).

and by doing so greatly influenced Lord North and British manufacturing cities to alter their stance. Buckingham feared that if the session of the English Parliament closed without some favour to Ireland that opposition would be fierce when the Irish Parliament convened.

He realised how much was unknown about large swathes of Ireland and how difficult it was to obtain accurate information and so, in order to get clearer picture of the country as a whole, asked leading Irishmen to write to him with their opinions. The nobles, principal office holders and revenue commissioners from all over Ireland unsurprisingly reached the unanimous conclusion that unless

Napper Tandy.

commercial restrictions were speedily removed, Ireland could no longer pay her way. England eventually consented to pay Irish troops who served out of Ireland, but Buckingham vehemently protested that the drain of money from Ireland to England was vastly out of proportion and that the one and only viable solution would be permission to export goods. Speaker Pery agreed wholeheartedly and encouraged Buckingham to redouble his efforts to be heard in London.

To Hillsborough Buckingham confided that "Our sentiments with respect to this kingdom entirely coincide" but complained that "the officious zeal of some of the friends to Ireland and the intemperate peevishness with which the solicited concessions have been opposed, have contributed equally to raise a very disagreeable clamour."[8] Whilst acknowledging that the circumstances "require abilities of a very superior order, far beyond any idea which the most flattering partiality could conceive of mine" he was nonetheless confident he could manage the situation with the proviso that, "It may, however, be better for me to cherish a little proportion of vanity, if only to arm me against despair." He explained his dilemma to Lord Weymouth, "It is not uncommon for me to receive a visit from a person who has expressed his uneasiness at the general situation of the kingdom, and for that person to be followed by another who shall dwell upon its tranquillity. Upon the whole, the numbers of armed men formed under their own regulations, cannot but be surveyed with a most anxious eye. And your Lordship's candour will allow that, delicately circumstanced as Ireland is at present, it is scarcely possible in my situation to avoid censure for having said or done either too much or too little."[9]

On a personal note he was content because even if the worst happened and France invaded Ireland, "Lady Caroline is returned in a state of beauty which in an evil hour may protect her husband against the insolence of a victorious Marshal of

France."[10] Five months spent in England with her family and friends had restored Lady Caroline's spirits to the extent that she threw herself behind the "buy Irish" campaign and boldly declared her intention to appear at a charity ball dressed from head to toe exclusively in Irish fabrics.

Throughout May and June persistent alarms were once again raised that a French invasion was underway. Even though the home Government thought these rumours well founded it stubbornly declined to arm the Irish Volunteer forces, voicing the well-worn excuse that the expense would be unsupportable. The Volunteers were loyal to the English crown, so loyal in fact that Lord Clanricarde declared melodramatically that he could "raise amongst his friends and tenants in the county of Galway 1,000 men who will swim in their own blood in defence of his Majesty, and of their native country."[11] Buckingham, whilst acknowledging Clanricarde's "peculiar zeal and attachment to his Majesty's and the public service"[12] regretted he could not give any encouragement or sanction to illegal associations. He watched the rising movement with mingled sentiments, the most prominent of which was an impotent dismay. Whilst the volunteer movement was an obvious response to the situation, a great body of armed men rising up altogether independently of the Government was also cause for disquiet, especially at this time when many other causes for discontent were emerging. His concern was entirely understandable; the paralysis of Government combined with the refusal of the English parliament to grant the free trade which was deemed indispensable for Ireland had created a cauldron of discontent. Although he described the volunteer forces as a necessary evil he was at the same time entirely confident that the troops were loyal and that the English should avoid giving them any reason to believe that they were either feared or suspected. Harbouring no illusions about the gravity of the situation he wrote, "You cannot doubt of my anxiety to reduce them into some legal shape, and that no pains shall be omitted to effect it" but remained optimistic, "Upon the whole, it is my private opinion, that barring insurrection, I shall go through the business of the session with success." Hillsborough favoured a legislative union but Buckingham begged him to "let me earnestly recommend you not to utter the word Union in a whisper or to drop it from your pen. The present temper will not bear it."

Both Ireland and England were now in daily if not hourly expectation of invasion. At one stage, a combined fleet of sixty-five French and Spanish ships was in the Channel and might easily have destroyed Plymouth. In Ireland more troops were regularly deployed to America leaving the volunteers as the only Irish defence. The Catholics showed their gratitude for the Relief Bill of 1778 and did all in their power to assist the Government in face of invasion but, as they were ironically still barred from joining the army, those powers were perforce somewhat limited. Buckingham's position was distressing and embarrassing in almost equal part. Despite his best endeavours he could not persuade England to send either money or troops and the sole defenders of the kingdom, the Irish Volunteer army, were out of his jurisdiction. A plea requesting Free Trade for Ireland, circumventing Parliament, was sent directly to the King but no answer was forthcoming. As frustration grew, rioters attacked the house of the Attorney General. Pery, the Irish Speaker of the House, wrote a lengthy letter to Buckingham in which he argued that,

> an easing of these restrictions would not only promote Irish prosperity but would encourage the development of a lucrative Irish market for British manufactures. Ireland is excluded from all direct commerce with the British colonies in Asia, Africa or America except for victuals and white and brown linens. Ireland is also prohibited under the severest of penalties from sending to any part of the world any manufacture made of or mixed with wool. Thus Ireland in effect is cut off from all commerce with the rest of the world.[13]

Pery further warned that seeds of discord had been sown which "if suffered to take root will soon overspread the land." The Speaker's mutually respectful relationship with Buckingham gave him the confidence to state, "If I have treated this subject with too much freedom, I am persuaded your Excellency's candour will impute it to my zeal for the prosperity of both kingdoms equally dear to me" adding plaintively, "The military gentlemen are tearing me to pieces for the money which they know I have not, and the appearance of their embracing too many ideas at once concerns me. A large sum ought to be remitted from England, or no defence can be made. Proposals for raising corps crowd in upon me from every side, which, very, very few instances excepted, are dictated by the ideas of military rank, county influence, or emolument." After further importations he pointed out "the great absentee proprietors—their not offering at this moment in some shape or other to assist a country in which they possess valuable stakes is certainly impolitic. This letter, which was begun on the 28th June is concluded the 4th July; you will conceive that the interruptions have been occasioned by business and that possibly, the business was not of a most agreeable cast."

Buckingham resumed the habit of writing to his friends to alleviate the stress of political life during his most challenging times in Ireland. His words stemmed from twin desires to lighten his own spirits and to amuse his reader, in this case his dearest friend Charles Hotham,

> Tents, Ammunition, Cannon, Carriages, Bread, Horses, Trumpets and Kettledrums, and every Din of War surrounds me. That, that's the Rub which makes my calamity. My amusements are Miscellaneous, and to enable you to judge of them, here follows the introduction of a few of the Letters which were found upon my table this morning:
>
> 'The Lord Chancellor desires his Warrants for four fat Bucks—
>
> 'Your Excellency's petitioner with four small children are starving, three of

my husbands have been killed in America—

'The Lord Mayor takes the liberty of forwarding this Petition from the Owners of several Colliers whose hands have been press'd—

'In my husband's absence I must beg leave to remind you of the Rev. Mr Supple whom you appointed one of your Chaplains at my request—

'Your Excellency not having condescended to take notice of my letter upon Flax Seed it shall be published at length in the Freeman's Journal—

'Your Excellency's amiable Predecessor almost three years ago gave me an office of five hundred pounds per ann. and it would be a most sensible mortification should your respectable Administration close without my being distinguished by your favour—

'Let me be excused from expressing my astonishment that in consequence of the death of two Prelates, no attention should have been paid to my family—

'Your Excellency should be inform'd of the flagrant abuse in the coal yards—

'The Independent Company at Morugher. May it please your Excellency, Dermost Kane and Rowley Macswiney, Mariners, have swore oath that sixty leagues south of Oyster Haven, Cape Finisterre, they fell in with the French and Spanish United Line and three hundred Frigates and Transports—

'It pains me to inform your Excellency that the three daughters of the Rev Mr Dogharty were carried off last Tuesday by twelve men from Tipperary—

'The scabbards of the Carbineers are no longer fit for service—

'Twelve thousand pounds will immediately be necessary for putting the Army in motion—

'Three of my cows were hough'd last night, let me request that a Party of the Military may be ordered immediately to Cloughtounohttouallobigs—

'I am sorry to inform your Excellency that by the last Abstract the Balance in the Treasurer's hands was—blank?

This will give you some idea of my situation. It is expected in England that Ireland will be invaded, our Army, including Artillery, exceeds thirteen thousand men, the Independent Companys are Zealous to resist an Enemy, and there is great reason to believe that the Roman Catholics would behave well.[14]

  As the summer wore on and still no concessions whatsoever were made from England, suspicions began to arise amongst the Irish that England actually

Irish Volunteers Flag c. 1782, celebrating the repeal of restrictive trade legislation and the establishment of legislative rights for the Irish Parliament.

wanted to see Ireland invaded so as to prevent an invasion of England. By the time Parliament met again in October tempers were running extremely high and Henry Grattan, famous for his rousing speeches, demanded a first right of import and export. Henry Flood, another brilliant orator, rose to propose that the term 'Free Trade' should be adopted. This was immediately agreed upon and carried unanimously. On the following day the entire House of Commons went in a body to present the address to Buckingham. Volunteer troops lined the route and presented arms as the politicians passed by. Menacing signs which read *'Free Trade or this!'* were strung around cannon. Buckingham, who was aghast but not at all surprised by this deputation, wrote once more to England demanding that the trade restrictions be repealed forthwith and stated in no uncertain terms that if they were not, he would not answer for the consequences. To his tremendous relief Lord North at last yielded and a Bill of Repeal was brought in.*

When news of this breakthrough reached Dublin rejoicing was universal, celebratory bonfires were lit all over the city and the Volunteers rapturously fired salvoes into the air. Buckingham himself, whilst naturally delighted at this remarkable progress, realised that this was only the first stage and that until the

---

*   In 1779-80 several Acts removed individual trade restrictions, but it was not until May
     1782 that legislative independence was achieved.

Bill was passed the matter was far from settled. Before the next crucial session in the House he took time to write to Hotham, beginning in whimsical style,

> The sea-boy slept upon the topmast Head, Alexander the Great snored the Eve of the Battle of Issus, Charles the 12th and General Washington in the first campaign deemed the whizzing of Bullets preferable to the Notes of a Lute, Sir Stephen Fox, aged ninety, marry'd a Beauty of eighteen, Curtius leaped into an unfathomable Gulph, and Sir Charles Thompson risqued a Tete a Tete with Mrs Dingley. I emulate such great examples, and tho' the Sheriff's Officers are ready to attend me to the most serious Session this Kingdom ever has experienced I shall dedicate a few Minutes if possible to the addressing you in a cheerful strain.[15]

Having assured Hotham (now also known as Hotham-Thompson) that although the numbers of Volunteers were increasing daily and that he was confident they were under the leadership of men who would not betray the King, he warned that "the existence of Troops under no Law is a Monster in a well-ordered State. The Lyon walks abroad with his chain, and tho' he wags his Tail, his Fangs may prove dangerous."

Just before news arrived of the passing of the Repeal Bill, Walter Hussey Burgh, the Prime Serjeant-at-law, resigned in protest after making an eloquent speech in which he declared, "Talk not to me of peace. Ireland is not at peace, it is smothered war. England has sown her laws as dragon's teeth, and they have sprung up as armed men."[16] Buckingham was dismayed at losing such a valuable ally, "this was rather a severe stroke, my affection for him, tho' not passing the love Men bear to Women, was great."[17] An accomplished classical scholar and something of a poet, Burgh was a legendary orator and universally liked. Friendly, honest and ambitious, his only fault was extravagance, always insisting that he must be driven to Court in a carriage with six horses and three outriders.[18] Buckingham described him thus, "his Manners are gentle and most engaging, elegantly informed, the liberality of a gentleman and the intelligence of a Scholar are happily blended in his conversation. His feelings are exquisitely sensible, a circumstance most amicable in society, but seriously inconvenient in business." This letter had been difficult to finish because of constant interruptions such as,

> the King at Arms this moment informs me that one of the Lords' sons who was to have supported my Train is seized with a whooping cough; one of the State Trumpeters has sold the Banner of his Instrument, and is mounted upon a Horse who has got the staggers; the State Kettle Drummer has a leg wrapped in Flannel; Signor Carravole has something which disqualifies him from horsemanship, and my Excellency's Body Coachman is gravelled and a Deputy cannot be found of sufficient dimensions to fill his coat.

A spectre from the past surfaced in the shape of Charlotte Boyle Walsingham,[19] the second daughter of Sir Charles Hanbury Williams, who as a girl had thrown herself at George (or possibly Henry) Hobart but was thwarted by her father. Now long married to Robert, the fifth son of the Earl of Shannon, she wrote to her father-in-law in the most disparaging terms about Buckingham, "I hear the government here is much dissatisfied with your governor, who is said to have quite forgot this country, and to affect to be the patriot on your side of the water. His Secretary is also much blamed for not dividing the House, and that I know to be true. You know most likely whether it is true that Lord B has toasted a free trade at his own table."[20] This rumour ran riot amongst Buckingham's detractors in London some of whom were of the opinion that the Lord Lieutenant of Ireland had "gone native". His Chief Secretary Sir Richard Heron's persistent advice to hand in his resignation, which he had been offering since May, fell on deaf ears, and Buckingham's perseverance was rewarded when at the close of 1779 Ireland was at long last granted Free Trade.

Buckingham wrote joyfully to Hotham, "The toast at my club yesterday was the "North of Ireland and prosperity to both Kingdoms."[21] His nephew Robert Hobart had been visiting but was leaving for England the next day "and you will therefore hear all the news of this country, and that our Queen is as beautiful as an angel. We are all mighty happy now defying all the powers in Europe." But he feared future unrest, "The great toast among the Patriots is "Old England and Young Ireland" but there are a set of seditious men in this country who will never be contented, for the best reason in the world, which is that WHENEVER IRELAND IS SATISFIED THEY MUST BE BURIED IN OBLIVION."[22]

After the rejoicing had abated Buckingham had time to reflect on the way he had been treated by his home Government which had deliberately left him in the dark regarding its policy towards the Irish and stubbornly resisted even attempting to understand Ireland's unique situation. He acknowledged that Lord North had been greatly intimidated by the fiscal power of the English manufacturers but notwithstanding this Buckingham keenly felt the pain of isolation and rejection. However, towards the end of 1779 and into 1780, measures were carried in England which exceeded those that only a few years earlier only the most optimistic Irishman could have imagined possible. The acts which prohibited Irish exports of wool and glass were wholly repealed and the great trade of the colonies were freely thrown open to them. Acts prohibiting carrying gold and silver coin were also overturned. Buckingham was most mightily relieved, but also completely exhausted in both body and mind.

Notes

1. *Report on the Manuscripts of the Marquess of Lothian*, p.347.
2. Ibid. p.349.
3. PRONI T3429/1/42.
4. fortunately.

5. Ibid.

6. PRONI D607/B/68.

7. *Report on the Manuscripts of the Marquess of Lothian*, p.350.

8. PRONI D607/B/86.

9. *Memoirs of the Life and Times of the Rt Hon Henry Grattan*, Vol.1 p.357 (books.google.co.uk).

10. PRONI D607/B/68.

11. *Memoirs of the Life and Times of the Rt Hon Henry Grattan*, Vol.1, p.354. (books.google.co.uk)

12. Ibid.

13. PRONI T3125/1/1.

14. *The Hothams ...*, Vol. II p.183-184.

15. Ibid. p.185.

16. *Report on the Manuscripts of the Marquess of Lothian*, p.xvii.

17. *The Hothams ...*, p.185.

18. Walter Hussey Burgh was re-appointed as Prime Sergeant-at-law in 1782. After his death in 1783 aged 41 money had to be raised to pay his debts and keep his family from ruin.

19. Charlotte married Robert Boyle when her father Sir Charles Hanbury Williams was, due to his dire mental state, unaware. He also never knew that his favourite daughter Frances died two days before her sister's wedding. On his death Charlotte became rich and when in October 1780 Robert went down with his ship HMS Thunderer during the Great Hurricane in the Antilles, she was left enormously wealthy.

20. PRONI D2707/A/2/4/19 Nov 15 1779.

21. *The Hothams ...*, p.186.

22. Ibid. p.187.

A Wedding Belle

On 18 January 1780 Buckingham threw a Grand Ball at Dublin Castle in celebration of Queen Charlotte's official birthday (her actual birthdate was 19 May) and declared it "most brilliant, and did not suggest the most distant idea of Ireland being undone. The scene was so peculiarly striking that I could not forebear wishing my master had been seated in my place."[1]

When his beloved eldest daughter arrived in Ireland in 1778 she was introduced to Louisa Conolly who noted "Lady Harriet Hobart is only fifteen, and on the footing of a child, so that there is nothing to be done with her but taking her to the play, which I did last night, to poor old Crow Street, where we had a very full house."[2] Harriet stayed for the next eleven months with John Rawden, Earl of Moira, his wife Lady Elizabeth and their five daughters and three sons at Castle Moira on their County Down estate and at their magnificent town house at Usher's Island in Dublin. Buckingham heard "some accounts from thence flatteringly assure me that she is improved in person and manner"[3] an indication

Lady Harriet Hobart.

that the pretty, bright and high spirited girl was growing into a fine young woman. When Harriet left to spend Christmas 1779 with her own family, Lady Moira, who had come to look upon Harriet as one of her own daughters, told her, "you shall hear from me very soon on a more minute scale to tell you what some people say of your beauty, & others of your understanding."[4]

Recalling his recent practical advice to a young lady that "she should never listen to any man, whatever he may offer with one hand, unless he brings his rental in the other" Buckingham was pleased when in January 1780 Harriet consented to receive the addresses of a suitor. He told Hotham,

> Harriet has made a conquest of Mr Corry, member for the county of Tyrone, who is, from every account, the best match in this Kingdom. His property is immense—£6,000 per annum, the lesser half settled upon a child by a former wife, to whom his behaviour was amiable to a proverb. He is universally esteemed, acknowledged to be generous without profusion, honourable upon the most correct line. He is rather well in his figure. His age, thirty-two. And, in addition to these capital points, his nose resembles mine.[5]

Armar Lowry Corry was in fact richer by more than double the amount quoted as he owned and reaped the income from over 70,000 acres in estates across the counties of Tyrone, Fermanagh, Longford, Monaghan and Armagh, together with property in Dublin. A widower, he had a son named Somerset from his four and a half year marriage to Lady Margaret Butler which by all accounts had been a happy one and, though he was not thirty-two but forty, Buckingham did not see the age gap as a cause for concern. His own marriages, to Mary Anne who had been sixteen years younger than himself, and now to Caroline who was double that at thirty-two years younger, were successful. A large age gap was not by any means an

Armar Lowry Corry (from the collection of the Earl of Belmore).

uncommon scenario and, put bluntly, the younger the wife the more time she had to produce sons in order to continue the family line.

The Earl of Shannon had introduced his friend Armar Lowry Corry to the Hobart family and had simultaneously proposed him for a peerage. Harriet voiced no objections to receiving Lowry Corry's advances as she had witnessed first-hand her young stepmother's happy experience with her own father. From Lowry Corry's point of view, if his suit was successful he would not only acquire a wealthy and beautiful young wife but also align himself with the Viceroy, an alliance that could only serve to raise his own status in society. Naturally his vast wealth gave him an allure that most men titled 'Mr' lacked and it was more than likely that his passage to a grander form of address would be expedited following a prestigious marriage to the daughter of a Viceroy. It may also have crossed his mind that Harriet, and therefore he, might in time inherit the Blickling Estate should 'Great' Caroline fail to produce another son.

It is not known how often Harriet met Mr Lowry Corry but since Buckingham told Hotham "you must not understand this to be a matter concluded but the Gentleman has made his proposal and the Lady has consented to receive his addresses"[6] this suggests that he had no particular expectations of a match.

Harriet though, flattered and perhaps also flustered by the attentions of a man who society judged to be such a good catch, impetuously accepted Lowry Corry's swiftly offered marriage proposal and before she had time to regret it their wedding was planned to take place only a matter of weeks later, in early March. Whilst she was by no means pressurised into the marriage, and there had been no need for such an immediate response, it is probable that a large part of her acquiescence was a desire to please her father. By marrying such a wealthy man her future would be secure and settled, leaving him only three daughters to find husbands for when they reached marriageable age. The many close friendships she had made during these formative years in Ireland may also have influenced her wish to remain.

In vivid contrast to the satisfaction he felt about his daughter's impending marriage, Buckingham was devastated by news from England of his dear friend Hans Stanley's sudden death. Hans' two brothers-in-law, Welbore Ellis, a fellow Privy Counsellor, and the MP Christopher d'Oyly, informed him of the tragedy as did several other friends. Lord Cadogan wrote sadly, "It is a most painful task to disturb your present happiness with an account of one of the most shocking events in private life that ever happened. Our poor friend Stanley has followed his father's example and is no more."[7] (Hans' father George Stanley had committed suicide by cutting his own throat when Hans was twelve years old.) Poor Lord Cadogan had been with Hans Stanley in Caversham only a few days before the tragic event and had thought him to be "in the greatest appearance of health and tranquillity of mind I ever saw" and was aghast and incredulous to hear that whilst visiting Earl Spencer at Althorp, Hans had disappeared into the woods and cut his own throat. Buckingham, labouring under the grief of his friend's untimely and incomprehensible death, was an Executor of his Will. His loyal companion, fellow *bon viveur* at The Catch Club and The Society of Dilettanti, was no more.

Politics carried on relentlessly despite these wildly disparate occurrences in his personal life and after a long period of delay and obfuscation a significant Bill was returned from England which released Irish Protestant Dissenters from taking the Sacramental Test. Other matters still deeply concerned Buckingham and he feared that some members of parliament would renege on their promises to use their votes to support him. In a state of high agitation he wrote "my mind does not know a moment's tranquillity."[8] Lord George Macartney, now MP for Armagh County, sought to reassure him by saying that the London administration was confident that he would "finish the Session with honour and success."[9] But he warned that if any constitutional question "should be carried against you, they will never forgive you for risking it, they will consider it as a dissolution of Government and every mischief and ill consequence that follows from it will be laid at your Excellency's door. Therefore, my dear Lord, put nothing to the hazard." Buckingham confided to George Germain, "You can scarcely conceive the various torments which I experience from jealousy, incredulity, confidence abused, distrust and inconsistency, the divisions and sub-divisions of connection; a gentleman will act in concert with one man as to a particular object, but oppose him and co-operate with his adversary in another."[10]

In early February Buckingham took a much needed and long overdue respite for his tired mind and body, travelling with 'Great' Caroline and eight-year old Emily[11] to a beach at Sea Point, a few miles to the south of Dublin. Rested and relaxed he told Hotham,

> Something more nearly resembling tranquillity of mind than I have for some time experienced, and a little leisure, induce me to write to you. My poor little Emily, who two or three days in the week breakfasts with me in this delightful spot, is playing upon the Beach of a calm sea under my eye, the sun gilds the Prospect, I feel no immediate bodily inconvenience, my conscience assures me that I have acted uniformly with honour and Integrity in a very difficult situation. Ought I not to be cheerfull?[12]

Young Emily had witnessed her three baby brothers sicken and die and Buckingham felt more protective than ever of his youngest daughter. Refreshed after their sea-side break he returned to the fray in Dublin. Reporting that he was now "more sanguine than it would be prudent for me to state to his Majesty's Ministers" he admitted that it was impossible to be sure but he was quietly confident that the 'bribes' would prove efficacious and "with very few instances excepted the accounts which reach one from different parts of Ireland breathe nothing but the fullest satisfaction for the intended favour." He speculated that although in England there were rumours of impending tumult in Ireland, "the reasonings upon this side of the water are very similar with respect to yourselves. Mischief seems to be ripening in every quarter; may those who so assiduously labour to heat the stoves be the first to gather the fruit!" The fate of Britain prayed on his mind, "You will imagine that there are moments when I wish to be quietly possessed of Blickling, Marble Hill and Bond Street, yet would the venerable dignity of the first, the amenity of the second, or the animated population of the latter situation prevent my meditating upon the impending ruin of my country?"[13]

The next knotty issue on the agenda was the contentious Mutiny Bill. In common with most others in authority, the Viceroy had taken it for granted that the army in Ireland was governed by the English Mutiny Act, but others disputed this assumption. Matters were brought to a head when two magistrates discharged deserters who were brought before them on the grounds that there was no actual Irish Act to compel them to remain in the army. When an Irish Mutiny Bill was proposed it stirred up more issues as this implied that the English Act should never have been applied to Ireland in the first place. Buckingham found the whole matter extremely trying, and plaintively told Hotham, "The fighting a duel with a man you have essentially injured, the languishing upon a bed of sickness abandoned by your physician, must be far lighter sensations than those which unremittingly affect me. Were I to perish at this hour the words *Irish Mutiny Bill* would appear engrav'd on my heart. Ce mandat sacre sera ma Mort*."[14]

Only too aware of the gravity of the situation, and recalling the wise advice from Macartney to ensure that no Bill should fail during the session, he was left with no

---

*   This blasted mandate will be the death of me.

choice but to resort to wider and more lavish bribery in order to ensure that the Bill would go through.

A welcome distraction from all this demanding and exhausting activity came with Harriet's wedding to Armar Lowry Corry at Dublin Castle on Saturday 11 March. The Reverend Thomas Barnard (later Bishop of Killaloe) presided over the ceremony and amongst those present alongside Buckingham and 'Great' Caroline were Lowry Corry's sister Anne and her husband William, Viscount Enniskillen. The newlyweds took up residence in fashionable Sackville Street, Dublin and The *Hibernian Magazine* flatteringly described Lady Henrietta Hobart as "a young lady possessed of youth, beauty, and elegance of manners. It affords a pleasing reflection that a native of this country has been destined to enjoy such supreme felicity."

Surprisingly, Lady Moira had been unaware of her erstwhile charge's change of status until the wedding was a fait accompli. She wrote to Harriet, "The Wedding Favors, that this morning have reached us, under his Excellency's cover; inform us that our beloved and admired friend has changed her name; not one of the many young hearts in this house that are cordially, and sincerely attached to my dear Lady Harriet, glows with more anxious warm affectionate wishes for her future happiness, than mine does. Mr. Corry must be so sensible of his uncommon good fortune, that your happiness cannot but be the study of his life." She offered some advice, "In regard to female friends, Husbands are generally not only dictatorial on that point but likewise very apt to particularly dislike those their wives are partial to; a person of sensibility must therefore be convinced that they are welcome to the master of the mansion, before they could hazard a visit beneath his roof." Lady Moira was concerned that married life might not be plain sailing for Harriet and did not want cause friction between the newly-weds, although having received no reply she wrote again on 17 April 1780, "Our not hearing from our beloved Lady Harriet would make us very uneasy, did we not attribute it to your being agreeably engaged and insensibly detained from giving us the indulgence of a sight of your handwriting" and assured her that "Lady Harriet has not in the World a more tenderly attached or more affectionate friend than I feel myself to be" and that she loved her as much as her own favourite daughter Selina.

At the end of March Buckingham received words of sympathy from Hans Sloane, son of the renowned physician Sir Hans Sloane, "I am satisfied no-one of Mr Stanley's friends has felt more deeply the great loss we have all had in his decease, than your Lordship—his loss is irreparable to us all"[15] and made complimentary observations about Buckingham's "wise and prudent administration during this critical period." But Buckingham felt frustrated, believing he was still being kept in the dark and told George Germain, 'No letters come to me from England, so that my conjectures from the newspapers and the communications from persons who affect to receive regular details of ministerial secrets, are my only documents for the forming any judgement of the situation of English Administration, my country and my Sovereign."[16] When the situation showed no signs of improvement he complained,

> I am also obliged continually to conceal resentment, for the purpose
> of carrying the business of Government through the Session; when
> it is concluded, divested from any resentment of my own, or any
> apprehensions of that of others, and recommend with firmness and
> impartiality such arrangements as may give a more consistent strength
> to HM Irish Government than the particular fatality of the times and the
> insanity of individuals has lately admitted of.[17]

In private life he observed Harriet spending considerably more of her time in Dublin society rather than at the Queen Anne house overlooking Lough Coole, her new husband's country seat. Although Lowry Corry had spent a considerable sum improving it for his new bride, she had declined to admire it. In an echo of her mother Mary Anne's wry comment about her "rural Lord's" penchant for turnips, Harriet soon discovered that Irish country life, at least at Lough Coole, was for her both remote and deadly dull. Even the design of the house itself displeased her as it meant living in rather closer quarters with servants than she was accustomed to. She made no secret of her dissatisfaction but deigned to choose the name for their prospective title, after a nearby mountain known as 'Belmore.' In town she was in her element as part of the Dublin ton[18] and her father noticed, "Lady Crosbie seems in great health and spirits, my daughter is happy in enjoying a considerable proportion of her society." At one particular ball in July 1780 Buckingham was moved to comment on the wild exertions of a dancing kilted gentleman,"Lady Buckingham, Lady Harriet Corry and Lady Emilia Hobart are all subdued by the naked hocks of Lord Strathaven, a blooming Highlander."[19] This same Lord also attracted the attention of the energetic Lady Crosbie about whom Buckingham observed, "she pursues pleasure to the extremity of fatigue."

In April the Mutiny Bill's progress was hampered when several gentlemen who had pledged their support reneged and instead voted with the minority. On this occasion most of the blame fell upon Sir Richard Heron, who had "failed to manage Parliament." Buckingham complained bitterly to Germain, "how can a Lord Lieutenant speak with confidence upon any point at a period when no fix'd principle directs, no obligations attach and no assurances can bind. Every inconvenience must necessarily be increased from the distracted state of the Mother country."[20] Buckingham told Hotham he anticipated disaster,

> Not to dwell too much upon subjects which render my existence a misery,
> if the Wise men of Ireland do not very soon determine to overrule these
> fools, this nation, instead of availing herself of greater advantages than
> ever fortune offered to any other, and hurrying on to almost unexampled
> prosperity under a well-modified system of Government, will form itself

into Anarchy, and, after having experienced every calamity which intestine conditions can produce, sink into a similar situation to that in which Earl Strong-Bow[21] found it. IRELAND IS, IN FACT, A FIRE-SHIP READY PRIMED, tho' to all appearance, at this moment, a Gallant Vessel sailing with gaudy streamers upon a Summer's Sea, but the touch of a Match, after a scene of horror, would render the whole a wreck, the fragments scarcely worth collecting. ENGLAND, HOWEVER, IS TOO NEAR NOT TO SUFFER BY THE EXPLOSION. The feeling strongly upon this subject has led one into the writing a few lines of Mad Prose, but the remainder of the Letter shall be composed in a more rational stile—;did my letter conclude without one light sentence, you would judge my situation to be desperate indeed.[22]

In June astonishing accounts emanated from London of incendiary riots fuelled by one who Buckingham referred to as "that superlatively wicked madman G. Gordon."[23] Lord George Gordon was a Scottish nobleman who frequently railed against the opposition but also routinely spoke out against his own leader Lord North, whom he deeply loathed. An eccentric and unpredictable character, Gordon was often considered to be rude, stupid, tiresome and intractable in the House of Commons but in private conversation could be witty, charming, gracious and polite. An accomplished highland dancer and bagpipe player, he was also a flagrant womaniser and it was rumoured he had

Lord George Gordon, LC-USZ62-45202.

proposed to a famous prostitute in Tottenham Court Road only for her to decline on the grounds that "she preferred the species to the individual."[24] Maliciously casting around for a suitable pretext for bringing down his enemy's Ministry his eye fell upon the Catholics. He started a Petition to repeal the Catholic Relief Act of 1778 which permitted priests to say Mass without being liable for life imprisonment and for Catholics to buy land and to join the Army (but which had not, incidentally, addressed many other iniquities such as giving them the right to vote). Gordon instilled and promoted a fear in the vast Protestant majority that because Catholics were now permitted and indeed encouraged to join up and fight in the American war (in which Gordon favoured the revolutionaries) they would instead turn into an armed and dangerous force which would turn against the Protestants. As a proud Scotsman he professed himself appalled in particular at the notion that severely impoverished Catholic Highlanders would too easily be persuaded to enlist. He started pernicious rumours, claiming that "20,000 Jesuits were hidden in a network of underground tunnels in the Surrey bank of the Thames waiting for an order from Rome to blow up the bed and banks of the river and so flood London"[25] and that "a gang of Benedictine monks had poisoned all the flour in the Borough" thus rendering bread inedible. Before long a great many people were even persuaded that the King himself was a closet Papist and they were incited to blame the "demonic" Pope for all manner of terrible events, large and small. After being appointed President of The Protestant Association, Gordon was granted several audiences with George III but was unable to persuade him of the dangers as he claimed to perceive them. Calling a meeting of his followers he proclaimed that "Popery when encouraged by Government has always been dangerous to the liberties of the people" and that England was threatened by "the purple power of Rome advancing by hasty strides to overspread this once happy nation." Announcing a rally on 2 June at St George's Fields where they would march en masse to the House of Commons and deliver a petition demanding the repeal of the Act, he declaimed passionately "the only way to go is in a bold manner and shew we are to defend Protestantism with our lives. I am not a man to do things by halves."[26]

As a result of this incendiary speech crowds estimated at between forty and sixty thousand souls assembled, many carrying banners with the legend 'No Popery' and almost all wearing a blue cockade ribbon in their hats, the symbol of the movement. Gordon duly presented the Petition to the House but outside the crowds began vandalising carriages and if their mission had been to cause havoc it was successful. Lord Mansfield, the Lord Chief Justice, had all his carriage windows smashed in and the wig torn off his head, arriving at Westminster "quivering like an aspen."[27] Even Bishops were attacked, their gowns torn off and covered in mud and excrement. Buckingham's friend Welbore Ellis suffered the indignities of being struck with a whip across his face and, with blood pouring from his mouth, of being chased by thirty or forty men into Westminster Guildhall where the doors were locked behind him. When the mob forced them open Ellis was forced to escape across the roof "at the utmost hazard"[28] to himself.

Lord North quickly perceived the danger surrounding him and ordered his coachman to rattle along at a furious speed causing people to jump out of its path right and left. As it slowed down on its approach to Westminster a man opened the door and snatched off his hat, but the Prime Minister arrived otherwise unscathed. (The enterprising thief later cut the hat into bits and sold them for a shilling apiece.) A great many Lords endured similar experiences of being manhandled and grossly insulted but a considerable number followed Lord Sandwich's example and turned their carriages homeward. Some of the more sober-minded petitioners were appalled at the violence and also went home, but others stayed, including those who were the most bigoted, the most ignorant, and the most drunk, and these formed a sizeable mob. When the Petition was predictably dismissed by a vote of

The Mob destroying and setting fire to the Kings Bench Prison & House of Correction in St George's Fields.

192 to 6 the remaining rioters were dispersed by a detachment of soldiers and many arrests were made. But the troubles were not over as that night, and all day and night for a week, the Embassies of several Catholic countries were attacked and their chapels destroyed, as were many houses of rich Catholic families. Newgate Prison, where many of the arrested men were housed, was almost destroyed, as were the Clink and many other gaols, and a Popish school in Hackney was burned to the ground.

George Byng, Buckingham's brother-in-law, wrote that on hearing Lord Rockingham's house was threatened he had sat up "both Tuesday and Wednesday nights as one of its weak defenders"[29] but the rioters instead stripped other houses of their furniture and burned down those of Lord Mansfield, Sir John Fielding and many others. Byng was "mortified to the greatest degree at the sight of the two most detestable extremes, a lawless mob, and a Military Government." He worried about an attack on his own property because he had been "the first in the House to attack Lord G Gordon; it would have fell an easy, undefended prey as I thought more of my friends than for myself" but fortunately for him it remained unscathed. After a week of dissension the troops were brought into town, many drawn up from the south coast where they had been on the look out for French invaders and London was effectively transformed into a garrison. On 7 June the unrest reached its peak when rioters audaciously attempted to raid the Bank of England but the troops repulsed them causing many deaths and casualties.[30] On 9 June Gordon was carried before the Privy Council and after four hours interrogation by North and several Privy Councillors he was charged with treason and committed to the Tower.

Hillsborough gravely warned Buckingham to be most attentive "lest disturbances should also break out on your side" because Gordon let it be known that he had received a letter from Protestants in and about Killarney asking for his advice as to how they should behave as they were "under great apprehensions from the Papists." Hillsborough was fearful, "I apprehend it would totally destroy poor Ireland to have a contest about Religion, superadded to those with which we are threatened about the Constitution."[31]

Fortunately for Ireland and for Buckingham no similar actions occurred there and a few days later Hillsborough reported that in England "the riots have happily subsided. Our jails are full of criminals, but they are all of the lowest rank of the people, except Lord G Gordon, who will probably suffer."[32] Within twelve days forty-four prisoners were tried and sentenced to death. The Old Bailey sessions ended on 11 July and in the Southwark sessions which followed a further twenty-four prisoners were capitally convicted. Somehow the Government were unable to find the "very great people at the bottom of the riot"[33] so the condemned rabble were a motley crew which included "two gypsies, a West Indian slave, a demented cross-eyed beggar, three abscess-covered climbing boys and a negro prostitute." Another most unlucky fellow was circus strong man Enoch Foster, who was condemned to death for demonstrating his strength by throwing floorboards through the windows of a house in Whitechapel. Lord Gordon himself did not suffer indignity for long as, after two weeks in a dark and dirty small apartment, he was moved to more comfortable rooms in the Tower where he was permitted to receive his many visitors. After several postponements his trial took place a full eight months later when Gordon was represented by his cousin Lord Erskine who against all the odds persuaded the jury to find the accused not guilty. Incredibly, Gordon was subsequently acquitted on the grounds that "he had no treasonable intent."[34] Upon hearing the verdict, Lord Erskine fainted.

Charles Hotham, aware of the severe toll that the stresses and worries of current political life were taking on his dearest friend, begged Buckingham to ask the King for his recall. Buckingham demurred, saying he would not consider leaving his post before the end of the session "at the very soonest the beginning of August but it is my intention to make it my humble and earnest request that his Majesty would permit me to close this anxious scene in January next."[35] His desire to drive through the new Bill was all consuming and his efforts were finally rewarded when on 19 August 1780 the home Government agreed to pass the Perpetual Mutiny Bill. Thus on 2 September closed "one of the most eventful sessions ever known to Ireland."[36]

Immediately after the termination of the session Buckingham wrote to North recommending eight commoners for the peerage, five appointments to the Privy Council, seventeen people for civil pensions and several more for favours of other kinds, explaining that it was with regret that he was driven to these measures, but that he had no choice. Germain asked Buckingham for his backing to elevate Townshend to a higher rank but having already put forward such a great number he declined as "adding a gentleman however honourable and respectable, whose claims were all long prior to my connection with this Kingdom, may embarrass the whole, and would, with reason, disgust many to whom I have refused that favour."[37] In a private letter to Germain he gave more personal reasons for his refusal, "to speak confidentially he (Townshend) has not the least claim upon me. We have lived upon very good terms in society, but our county politicks have ever been most adverse."[38] Furthermore he felt that his family had for thirty years been passed over in favour of the Townshend and Walpole contingents and that "repeated slights determined me to shew that I did not deserve them and was the occasion of their having two enemies Members for that County instead of two friends" and that "with respect to Norwich there scarcely exists the man whom I less esteem than Sir H ———- H——, his situation at Norwich was my act, and he has repaid me by accumulated ingratitude, it is unnecessary to add my indifference respecting his election." Sir Harbord Harbord, whom Buckingham had supported in the past but whose political stance repeatedly disappointed him, had been returned to his seat unopposed in 1774 and he would shortly stand again. Although many of his original supporters had deserted him, Harbord's personal influence led him to win the Norwich City Election with a large majority. The English Chronicle described him thus, "In private life he is a kind of rustic despot—rigid to his tenants, tyrannic and lofty to his immediate adherents, and exact to a degree of puerility, in all the GAME LAWS; but as a compensation for these defects he is in his public conduct the friend to FREEDOM, and votes invariably on the side of liberty and patriotism."[39]

Buckingham was deeply worried about his Secretary. "Sir Richard Heron continues dangerously ill. He is to be cut tomorrow for a fistula. The idea for an enemy would make humanity shudder: what must be the feelings for a friend. It makes me very unhappy."[40] Fortunately the operation was a complete success and Heron returned to his duties when recovered.

Although Buckingham successfully ensured the execution of the new Bill it was soon afterwards reported that he was to be recalled and replaced by Lord Carlisle at some point in December. Although this was only a month earlier than Buckingham had told Hotham he wished to leave, the swift manner in which his recall was executed shocked and dismayed him, and the ensuing disrespectful confusion over dates did nothing to assuage his distress. Behind the scenes in Dublin two powerful forces, Scott, the Attorney-General, and John Beresford, who was soon after made First Commissioner of the Revenue, had long been intriguing against him by writing repeatedly to Robinson, the English Secretary of the Treasury, demanding that the Viceroy be recalled.[41] Many people now took the opportunity to malign Buckingham and whilst some criticism may have been justifiable there were those who, out of ignorance, ingratitude or spite, took the opportunity to use him as a useful scapegoat. Downcast, Buckingham told Hotham,

> On ne meart pas de chagrin* or this letter would never have been wrote.
> It is futile to complain, but in truth my lot has been a hard one, and
> that summary judgement which attributes the disagreeables here to my
> misconduct is most illiberal and cruel. Lord North's behaviour has been
> so abominable that is is impossible for me as a Gentleman to notice him
> unless he seeks an explanation."[42]

To add to his misery the Government was suddenly reluctant to confirm the
various titles, privileges and pensions he had been obliged to promise. He
expressed his angst to Germain,

> One short word will fully express my present feelings, DESPAIR. Lord
> North seems determined upon no measure but that of expelling me with
> humiliation and disgrace from this kingdom. If the next mails do not bring
> me a letter from him I shall transmit every part of the business officially to
> Lord Hillsborough to be laid before his Majesty, appealing in some degree
> to him as a slighted and insulted servant.[43]

And later to Hotham,

> This is the eighth of November; Lord Carlisle as it is said, means to leave
> London on the 5th of next month, and not one line has as yet reached me
> from Lord North. You have frequently, perhaps with propriety, checked the
> vivacity of my feelings, yet in this instance you will think even a Feverish
> warmth very justifiable. The uncertainty of so many arrangements to
> which the honour of my Government is pledged, the confusion and
> dissatisfaction which necessarily follow here, and the reception at home
> which this treatment from the Cabinet must induce me to expect, are so
> very painful considerations that my resolution sinks under them.'[44]

At least on Irish soil he had supporters, including the Dean of Cork, Rev John
Erskine,

> You are now about to be delivered from a very turbulent scene, in which
> you have so prudently and worthily performed your part; and if I may
> judge of the sentiments of the nation, from what I hear in this quarter of
> it, none who have held the reins of Empire for so many years have ever left
> it with so much solid applause without the shadow of reproach. This will
> crown you with honour in the sight of all good men, and what is still more
> valuable, will be a lasting and homefelt comfort in your own breast.[45]

and amongst many others, Robert Gamble MP for Newcastle, Dublin,

> I receive the most inexpressible pleasure in hearing your Excellency

---

*   one does not die of sorrow

the subject of praise and affection among all ranks of men. When you shall be removed to the Royal Presence you will carry with you the most honourable testimony and reward of your virtuous administration, the hearts and affections of a truly grateful people, who will not fail to publish to Europe that your Excellency has been the real friend and patron of Ireland.[46]

In another private letter to George Germain, Buckingham's fears of the King's censure were increased by rumours that "four of the gentlemen upon my list of New Peers will be rejected—it will give me the fullest conviction that my slender credit in the closet is ruined"[47] although he believed that "The conclusion of my administration has however been judged to be honourable and meritorious by the world at large, and with every prospect of confusion the tranquillity of this Kingdom has been preserved." Excusing the letter in which he had described his despair, he explained that "the agitation of my mind had greatly warped my understanding, calmer moments induced me to adopt a more temperate conduct as you will observe from my official dispatches. But tho' the warmth of my feelings is smothered by discretion, yet the interior ferment is still the same. May you, my dear Lord, never experience anything similar."

Inexplicably, the crucial information that had not yet reached Buckingham was that Lord North was completely incapacitated. Capt A. Corbett, Secretary to Lord Carlisle, soothed Buckingham's anxiety with an abject apology, "I feel exceedingly for the very disagreeable situation your Excellency must be in, in not hearing from Lord North. He is now exceedingly ill."[48] Sir John Irwine strove to reassure him that "everybody pities you for this delay (but) your Excellency will find a gracious reception here."[49] Sir Joseph Yorke summed up the situation, "The last twelve months have been so full of remarkable events that one's head has been ready to turn every minute. My friend Buckingham's task has been a very difficult one, he has conducted himself nobly, and will I still think see his labours crowned with success; nobody honours him more, or wishes him better than I do."[50] Others, amongst them the Irish bureaucrat William Knox, not an admirer of Thomas Conolly, took the view that Buckingham would have been a good Lord Lieutenant were it not for his family connections and his incompetent secretary. Heron's many other detractors thought him so inept at managing the House of Commons that they dubbed him Sir Richard Wigblock [51]

A more measured reading of Buckingham's Viceroyalty later concluded,

During four of the most critical years in English history Lord Buckinghamshire contrived to maintain in some fashion the status quo. His partial success seemed attributable to personal qualities of tact and temper, which, combined with a sincere zeal for the welfare of the Irish people, created, in the opinion of his oft-time adversary Henry Grattan 'a passion in his favour approaching to love.'[52]

An impassioned panegyric titled *To a NOBLE LORD*[53] contained an inordinate amount of flattery, viz. "Imitative of none of his predecessors, his Excellency has surpassed them all" and proclaimed that Buckingham was first in "the constellation of viceroys." It continued, "he enlivened us with the true warmth and resplendence of political sun-shine." Lavishing extravagant praise for enabling prosperity to flourish and for being a sincere friend to the interest of freedom it waxed lyrically,

> He gladdens the icy region of the North, adds delight to the genial climes
> of the South, whether making the Laplander a philosopher, he instructs
> him to discover in his herd of rein deer, the all which modest Nature
> demands, or, crowning the intellectual enjoyments of the lettered Briton,
> bids him proclaim to the world that existence is a blessing.

As if that were not enough, it compared Buckingham to a powerful planet circling the King at the centre of the political universe and lauded him for his liberal approach to religious sentiments as "he fought to effect a social alliance of protestants and romanists" and, after expressing undying gratitude for the Viceroy's many other glorious achievements, the author rounded things off with a poem,

> *A BUCKINGHAM he came, to bless;*
> *A BUCKINGHAM he will retire;*
> *No sordid arts shall make him less,*
> *and Heaven alone can lift him higher!*

In stark and vivid contrast to this oleaginous tribute Buckingham described himself as "a man whose mind has been ulcerated with a variety of embarrassment for thirty weary months."[54] His nerves had been strained to their limits by combative, unruly politics and he was worn down by what he frequently referred to as the "epidemic perverseness of the times."[55] His refusal to commute a death sentence on the drunken rioter must have lain heavily on his heart and was concurrent with a profound and lasting grief over the loss of his third son George and the suicide of his friend Hans Stanley, all of which combined to leave Buckingham utterly drained and completely exhausted.

Lord Carlisle arrived in Dublin towards the close of December 1780 and shortly afterwards Buckingham took his leave of Ireland. He bade a fond farewell to Harriet who was now six months pregnant, and journeyed home, stricken in both health and spirits. The determined, vigorous and optimistic man who had arrived in Ireland three years earlier left it weighed down by the consciousness of failure, plagued by a gnawing sense of injustice and a sense of foreboding about his forthcoming reception at Court.

Notes

1. *The Hothams ...*, Vol. II, 1918, p.188 (letter dated 11 February 1780).
2. *Letters of Louisa Conolly*, Heron papers, National Library of Ireland 13039, 13047-13056.
3. *The Hothams ...*, Vol. II, 1918, p. 178.
4. Lothian papers, National Archive of Scotland GD/40/9/186/1-58.
5. PRONI T3429/1/54 1 February 1780.
6. Ibid.
7. *Report on the Manuscripts of the Marquess of Lothian*, p.360-361.
8. Ibid. p.359.
9. Ibid. p.361.
10. Ibid. p.359.
11. The whereabouts of her younger sisters Caroline and Sophie are unknown during Buckingham's Viceroyalty. They may have stayed in England or been billeted with families in Ireland.
12. *The Hothams ...*, Vol. II, 1918, p.187.
13. Ibid. p.188.
14. Ibid. p.190.
15. *Report on the Manuscripts of the Marquess of Lothian*, p.362.
16. Ibid. p.364.
17. Ibid. p.365.
18. 'ton' - elite aristocratic and fashionable society.
19. Hotham papers, PRONI T/3429/1/62.
20. Heron papers, National Library of Ireland 13034-3.
21. Richard de Clar, 2nd Earl of Pembroke, aided an invasion of Ireland in 12th century.
22. *The Hothams ...*, Vol. II, 1918, p.190-191.
23. PRONI T/3429/1/62.
24. *King Mob* by Christopher Hibbert, Longmans, Green & CO., London 1959, p.21.
25. Ibid. p.28.
26. Ibid. p.40.
27. Ibid. p.48.
28. Ibid. p.48.
29. *Report on the Manuscripts of the Marquess of Lothian*, p.367.
30. '21 people are known to have been executed and the Government admitted that 285 rioters were killed by the troops and 173 wounded. Wraxall believed that over 700 were killed ... the figure seems probably to have been not less than 850.' (cited in Hibbert, C., *King Mob*, Longmans, Green & Co., 1959.
31. *Report on the Manuscripts of the Marquess of Lothian*, p.367-368.
32. Ibid.
33. Hibbert, C., *King Mob*, Longmans, Green & Co., 1959, p.143.
34. George Gordon was excommunicated by the Archbishop of Canterbury (not the one he called 'a whore') in 1786, was convicted of defaming Marie Antoinette but escaped to Holland, was arrested again in Birmingham and spent five years in Newgate Prison, and in 1787 converted to Judaism taking the name Yisrael bar Avraham Gordon; some Jews believed he was Moses risen from the dead. He died of typhoid fever in Newgate Prison aged 42.

35. *The Hothams ...*, Vol. II, 1918, p.191.
36. Ibid.
37. *Reports on the manuscripts of the Marquess of Lothian*, p.372.
38. Ibid. p.373.
39. From History of Parliament ac.uk.
40. PRONI T3429/1/68.
41. Lecky, W.E.H., *A History of Ireland in the Eighteenth Century*, Vol. II, p.223 (ref taken from *The Hothams ...*).
42. *The Hothams ...*, Vol. II, 1918, p.192.
43. *Reports on the manuscripts of the Marquess of Lothian*, p.375.
44. *The Hothams ...*, Vol. II, 1918, p. 192.
45. *Reports on the manuscripts of the Marquess of Lothian*, p.374.
46. Ibid. p.377.
47. Ibid. p.376.
48. Ibid. p.375.
49. Ibid. p.376.
50. Ibid. p.370.
51. Heron, R. *Dictionary of Irish Biography*, www.did.ie.
52. *Report on the Manuscripts of the Marquess of Lothian*, p.xvi.
53. *A Review of the Conduct of his Excellency John, Earl of Buckinghamshire, Lord Lieutenant General, and General Governor of Ireland, during his administration in that kingdom; in a letter addressed to a noble lord.*(1781). Dublin.
54. Collins, G.E., *The Complete Peerage*, Vol. II, 1912, , p.402.
55. *The Hothams ...*, Vol. II, 1918, p.187.

Family Troubles

Hillsborough welcomed Buckingham back to London, "Congratulations on your return. If my Lady Buckingham looks as beautiful as she did on New Year's Day, I pity you."[1] 'Great' Caroline had returned to England earlier and the couple were now happily reunited. But before he could allow himself the longed for comfort of Blickling, Buckingham faced the ordeal of his audience with the King. The first meeting with his sovereign would be at the King's dressing when the dearest of those friends, his brother-in-law Hotham, would be present to lend his support. As it transpired this was not especially needed as the occasion echoed his return from Russia in that it was a much more gratifying and pleasant experience than he had anticipated. Onlooker John Foster noted "his reception at St James was entirely to his satisfaction. The labours of a difficult administration involved with the subjects of the greatest nicety and embarrassed with every distress peculiar to the times are now rewarded in the approbation of His Majesty joined with the grateful applause of a whole nation."[2] Buckingham was mightily relieved and made a concerted effort to appear dignified yet reserved to those ministers who had acted against him, rather than show naked resentment.

Gratifying reports arrived from Ireland that "nothing new has occurred since you left this kingdom but the phenomenon of public thanks following a departed Lord Lieutenant, and our newspapers are filled with applause instead of abuse."[3] Thomas Conolly sent local gossip and his "loves to Caroline and dear little Emily"[4] excusing his hurriedly written letter by explaining that "our gallery is full, some singing, some playing at chess, others at cards, in short making so much noise that I must conclude this with an apology for not digesting its contents better, but as you have excused much nonsense from me before, you will forgive me now." Given that Castletown House, in addition to its 80 ft long gallery, has literally dozens of other rooms in which he could have written in peace, Conolly had presumably been enjoying the company too much to shift himself. Captain Corbett, Secretary to the new Viceroy Lord Carlisle, was supportive of Buckingham, "Let all the enemies of Ireland say what they will. I must differ from all such and do justice to the character of the Irish in saying that they entertain the most grateful sense of the many advantages they obtained in the course of your Lordship's Viceroyalty. The country in general I am told continues everywhere in the same peaceful disposition as when you left it."[5]

Elsewhere in Ireland matters were far from tranquil. Harriet, since 6 January 1781 titled Lady Belmore, had unbeknownst to her father developed a severe antipathy, not to say a downright loathing, for her husband. What Belmore had done to precipitate her disgust is open to conjecture but whatever it was he had done or said Harriet was unable to forgive him or to conceal her revulsion. This was one thing in private but as she would not, or could not, hide her repugnance of him when they were in society, it soon became common knowledge. In December, when her father was preparing to leave Dublin, an angry and publicly humiliated Belmore told Harriet categorically that he would not tolerate such disrespect towards him any longer. When Harriet's behaviour changed not one iota, Belmore felt moved to demand a separation but Harriet implored him not to tell her father of his intention. The timing of Belmore's demand was all the more shocking because Harriet was at this point six months pregnant. The depth of emotion on both sides ran chasms deep but Belmore acquiesced to Harriet's fervent pleas and agreed that Buckingham need not be told, at least not whilst he was in the midst of preparations for his return to England. Harriet's step-mother was completely unaware of this most unhappy scenario and sailed for England in December followed by her father in early January. Harriet was left to endure the final months of her pregnancy alone, detesting her husband and knowing full well that he intended to be rid of her.

In March 1781 when the couple had been married barely a year and with Harriet within days of giving birth, Belmore intended to drop his bombshell on Buckingham via Sir Richard Heron. He went in person and announced "his determined resolution of being separated from Lady Belmore so soon as she shall recover from her lying in."[6] Heron, deeply shocked, entreated Belmore to at least wait until Harriet was completely recovered from childbirth before taking such a drastic step. He dreaded breaking this terrible news to Buckingham and, knowing how many women did not survive childbirth, also thought it a wise course to delay such an action because "if any accident should happen to her he would be sorry to have made Lord Buckinghamshire unhappy by an unnecessary communication of their disagreement."[7] In this most awkward and unlooked for position of go-between, Heron desperately tried to persuade Belmore to hope that "the affections which will naturally arise for their child may lead to a disposition more agreeable him"[8] but Belmore remained implacable, saying he had an "unalterable determination to obtain a formal separation."[9] Heron expressed his alarm on Harriet's behalf, assuming that Belmore had not warned her of his intentions but Belmore angrily countered that she knew before her father left Ireland and that "had I not been prevented by the entreaty of Lady Belmore, and by tenderness to that entreaty I would have brought this matter to a conclusion when Lord Buckingham was in the Kingdom." A few days later Harriet was confined for her lying-in and Buckingham's first grandchild arrived safely on 5 April in the shape of a little girl, baptised Mary Anne Julia Louisa Harriet, who would always be known as Louisa.

Six weeks later to the very day, Harriet received a letter from her husband stating he was firmly resolved to obtain a legal and permanent separation from her. Whilst her revulsion towards him had not dissipated in the slightest, Harriet was now the mother of a new baby and with the utmost dismay she belatedly realised the implications of such an outcome. In desperation she begged Belmore's forgiveness,

"Blameable though my past behaviour has undoubtedly been, yet love for my poor little child and my sincere and unalterable wish of convincing Lord Belmore of my gratitude towards him will enable me for the future to fulfill that duty which till the birth of my little girl all my efforts could not accomplish."[10] But Belmore, mortally offended by her past behaviour, was entirely unmoved. Heron asked Louisa Conolly to act as an intermediary and she took care to explain to the young mother that a formal separation could not be legalised without Harriet's consent. Louisa deplored the "singular and mysterious manner of his Lordship's proceeding in this affair till it came to the very crisis of the event, and left no opportunity for conciliatory advice" and urged Harriet to "assume dignity and steadiness" for the sake of her family and for her child. Harriet, fearful of the scandal she might bring upon her family and in particular of the disapproval and disappointment of her father, gave her authority for everything to be done that might persuade Belmore to change his mind. Louisa reported that Harriet, "being averse to becoming the subject of public conversation, was exceedingly anxious to avoid the uneasiness this measure would give her father."[11] Belmore, however, was immoveable. As his wife had not been unfaithful, which would have been an incontestable reason for separation, he resorted to intimidation. Aware of her dislike of his Queen Anne house he intimated that if she refused to co-operate he would insist upon her being confined there. Before long Heron realised he had no choice but to appraise Buckingham of the situation who, appalled and sorely disappointed, considered it best for Harriet to remain in Ireland where she could be with her baby and urged her to make every attempt to redeem herself in her husband's eyes. Belmore was averse to this suggestion if her location were to be anywhere in Ireland except Castle Coole where she would be closely observed.

Louisa suggested an ingenious solution to the impasse, "LET IT BE SUPPOSED that SHE goes to England to see her father & that HE stops here on account of his own private affairs. That would give time for her to reflect and to get over the aversion which she had for him, and for him to find it easier to relent and take her back."[12] Any hopes she had for this scheme were immediately squashed because Belmore stated categorically that his mind was "absolutely made up and his determination of parting irrevocable." He added irritably that he had only wanted the Conollys to "communicate and not to consult"and so they were left to "lament the melancholy prospect of a young woman."

At Castletown House Louisa advised Harriet that a formal separation seemed unavoidable, news she received with,

> a becoming concern, not AFFECTEDLY so but in a manner such as I
> expected from a person of her very good understanding and I must add,
> good heart, and she did not attempt justifying herself in any degree; on
> the contrary, she justified Lord Belmore's conduct towards her in this
> instance which she acknowledges has ever been in every respect that of an

honourable, generous and worthy man, but that she was so unfortunate
as not to have it in her power either to make HIM or HERSELF happy;
and she had tried in vain; what answer could I make to so generous a
confession?[13]

From this account it appears that Harriet took all the blame upon herself, but
Belmore must have said or done something deeply unpalatable to have caused
such a strong and lasting disgust. Soon Harriet realised that a legal separation
was inevitable and negotiations over custody and finances commenced. Belmore
stated that Harriet could have charge of their baby but only until she reached five
years of age, after which time she would be made to hand her back because "it is
the only comfort he looks for at home, as his son will be at school"[14] reasoning that
by then Somerset would be twelve and at boarding school. He further stipulated
that Harriet must live out of Ireland during this time and grudgingly agreed to
pay her 500 Irish pounds per year which, added to the pin money secured in her
marriage settlement would give her an allowance of 1,000 Irish pounds a year.
Harriet not unreasonably requested that the payments would be made in sterling
but Belmore flatly refused, adding that he would not increase her maintenance
even in the event of her father's death whilst at the same time insisting that he must
still receive the £15,000 agreed in the marriage settlement. Furthermore he totally
rejected the notion that he should give up any rights whatsoever to property or
money acquired by Harriet in her own right after the separation, which of course
might include Blickling Hall and its Estate. A statement outlining his views read,

> From the commencement of the treaty for this marriage Lord Belmore had
> reason to believe that Lady Belmore had a very great dislike to it, which he
> trusted he should be able to overcome by his obliging conduct, and it is
> certain, no man could be more attentive or indulgent than Lord Belmore
> was, from the day of his marriage until the resolution to separate. The
> truth is that Lady Belmore, who was under eighteen, shewed so evident
> a dislike to marrying Mr Corry that he proposed to her the taking upon
> himself to break it off; but the match being agreeable to her father &
> considering the time in which she ought to have been consulted as past,
> she unfortunately desired it to proceed.[15]

This reveals that according to Belmore himself Harriet had given him unequivocal
signs that she had no desire to marry him, yet he nevertheless pressed ahead with
the union. Evidently his "obliging conduct" had not been enough to win her round
but by that time he had presumably got what he wanted most, which was an alliance
with the Viceroy and the promise of a title. Within three months of their marriage
his "attentiveness and indulgence" had made him entirely repulsive to her. For her
part Harriet told Louisa Conolly that she had by no means been compelled to the
match but that "neither her Father nor Lady Buckingham knew of her dislike of it
as she had never owned it."[16] It is feasible that Harriet, witnessing her father grief
stricken by Hans Stanley's suicide, chose not to add to his woes; and that as he

and her dear step-mother had been away at the coast during February she believed she had left it too late to change her mind about the marriage. In her innocence the laudable aim of pleasing her father had condemned Harriet to marriage with a man she actively disliked.

Louisa was alarmed at Belmore's determination to keep control of Harriet's future financial income, including any and all property or monies she might inherit from any source. Following the deaths of her three small half-brothers Harriet was first in line to inherit Blickling and all her Father's estates unless her stepmother bore another son. The idea that on the 2nd Earl's death the Blickling Estate would fall to Lord Belmore struck her as unreasonable to say the least as "how hard it would be if

Harriet Hobart (from the collection of the Earl of Belmore).

Lord Belmore's family or even her own little girl (that is now so well provided for) should entirely swallow up (what she may have) to the prejudice of other children of hers by another husband?" Nonetheless Belmore stuck to his guns and grew increasingly impatient,

> I conceived it impossible that any delay could arise but from the base mechanical part of the business—I have wished only to expedite a business of so awkward a nature that I supposed every party concerned would have been pleased with bringing it to a speedy conclusion. My ideas in regard to it are fair plain and simple, and have neither been complicated by me nor will be departed from by me.[17]

Greatly aggrieved, he felt that "the consciousness of my own rectitude throughout the whole of this unhappy affair both supports me and determines me—indeed it is the only support I have left from which I can derive comfort." Louisa, their despondent intermediary, commentated upon the state of mind of the two combatants. Of the husband whose pride had been so deeply injured she wrote "poor Lord Belmore's distracted state of mind makes him SORE at every trifle" and of Harriet that "she continues to behave very properly but that whenever Belmore's name is mentioned I see her fist ready to BREAK out. Lady Belmore cannot bear the idea of Lord Belmore's GETTING ANY THING more by her."[18]

Buckingham was naturally shocked and disturbed by this turn of events, and although he emphatically disapproved of Belmore's stance and immediately perceived the threat of his estate falling to the Irishman, he trod a diplomatic line. When Belmore refused to back down Buckingham had to find another way to protect his property. He wrote, "Lady Belmore must determine for herself either to accept the terms or abide the consequence of declining them. The first will probably be her choice, but no consideration should induce me to advise."[19] Harriet found herself between a rock and a hard place. If she accepted her husband's terms she would keep her daughter and have the freedom to live outside Ireland with enough money to live independently in a place of her own choosing, and be at liberty to socialise as she pleased. But, by law, she would be forced to give Louisa up to Belmore in five years time. On the other hand, if she refused his terms she would be obliged to live wherever he dictated with no guarantee of seeing her daughter at all and certainly not after five years. Moreover she would forever be entirely dependent upon an estranged husband who loathed her and the lively social life she had so enjoyed in Ireland would be damaged beyond repair. Whatever decision she took she knew the scandal would occupy the gossips on both sides of the water and that she had brought shame on her family. Following the counsel of Lady Louisa and Sir Richard Heron, the two people whose judgement she most trusted, she reluctantly agreed to Belmore's terms. A Deed of Separation was swiftly drawn up which stated "In consequence of some unhappy differences they agreed to live separately and apart" and was duly signed on 15 June 1781. Soon afterwards Harriet left for London intending to send for her baby just as soon as she had devised a plan for their future but Belmore, to the general consternation and disapproval of everyone involved, spirited the ten week old Louisa away to the country and refused to give her up. Lady Enniskillen felt so strongly about this cruelty on her brother's part that the two acrimoniously and permanently fell out. Unfortunately, a direct result of this meant she had no more contact with baby Louisa than did her mother. Harriet, in a dreadful state of woe, lamented from England,

> my poor little girl, she needs it so much, and what you mention of the dispute between you and Lord Belmore, completes my grief at not having her with me as she is now deprived in a great measure of what alone could compensate for the care of her mother—tell me, my dearest Lady Enniskillen, is there no method in the world by which I could obtain her? Lord Belmore had promised Lady Louisa Conolly that she should remain with me, and it was not until after I left Ireland that he revoked it.[20]

Harriet's efforts proved futile in spite of universal condemnation of Belmore's vengeful and malicious action. Broken-hearted she wrote, "I make no comments on her ever having been kept from me, it needs none for everybody must consider it in the same light." Ashamed, exhausted, and heart-sore, Harriet sought to remove herself far from the reach of wagging tongues in London and Dublin and took an apartment within l'Abbaye Royale de Panthemont in the fashionable 6th arrondissement of Saint Germain in Paris. This history now leaves her there to recover her spirits.

Notes

1. *Report on the Manuscripts of the Marquess of Lothian*, p.380.
2. Ibid. p.379.
3. Dean Richard Woodward (Dean of Clogher made Bishop of Cloyne Jan 20, 1781).
4. *Reports on the manuscripts of the Marquess of Lothian*, p.381.
5. Ibid. p.387.
6. Marson, P., Ch.5.
7. Ibid.
8. Ibid.
9. Ibid.
10. Ibid.
11. Ibid.
12. Ibid.
13. Ibid.
14. Ibid.
15. Ibid.
16. Ibid.
17. Ibid.
18. Ibid.
19. Ibid.
20. Ibid.

Lincoln. Hamilton. Lafayette. Washington. Cornwallis. Tarleton. O'Hara. Clinton.

SURRENDER OF CORNWALLIS,
AT YORK-TOWN Va. OCT. 1781.

Lith. & Pub. by N. Currier, 2 Spruce St. N. Y.

Entered according to Act of Congress in the year 1845 by N. Currier, in the Clerks office of the District Court of the Southern District of N. Y.

The Surrender of Cornwallis: at York-Town October 1781, LC-USZC2-3051.

A Quiet Life

The year 1781 brought cataclysmic losses for Britain when on 19 October General Cornwallis surrendered his army of some 8,000 men to General George Washington at Yorktown, effectively giving up any chance of Britain winning the Revolutionary War. Buckingham arrived in London for the opening of Parliament and then immediately returned to Blickling from where he reported the news to the Bishop of Cloyne,

> A very material event indeed met my arrival in London but it was of such a calamitous magnitude as for a time incapacitaty'd me and every feeling man from any power of digested reasoning. I returned to this place, the tranquillity of which has restored to me some composure, tho' nothing can prevent the most painfull reflection upon the future prospects of this Empire but a partial removal, at last, of that gloom which now looms upon us from every quarter. As to the scene in London, the distress was really universal at the fashionable end of town. The countenances of Ministers, Maccaronis, tradesmen, artisans and painted ladys all expressed it. If America (especially connected with France) becomes independent, we may possibly be allowed to eat bread and beef in our little island; but imperial sway, national dignity, ostentation and luxury must with our commerce be annihilated—there needs no particular spirit of divination to foresee, that our West and East Indies, Newfoundland, fishery, commerce and naval power must be lost.'[1]

Having imagined the worst he added "there is a becoming and usefull spirit in hoping the best" and predicted that the Courts of Vienna and Petersburg would stand by Britain. He mused that it would be "an humiliating consolation, and how different from my feelings when I set out on the Russian Embassy when the name of an Englishman commanded deference in every quarter of the globe."

Living quietly in Norfolk was the perfect remedy for Buckingham's agitated state of mind and he was content to busy himself with continued improvements and additions to the Blickling estate. This included the construction of an elegant Green House, or Orangery. The location was chosen by Caroline, and Samuel Wyatt, who had previously made alterations to Buckingham's London townhouse, designed the elegant building. The Green House sported a large stage upon which were grown fifteen large orange trees, many young ones and several of the dwarf variety. A table, painted chairs, elbow chairs and stools were installed for the comfort of those who visited to admire these exotic plants. Seats and at least eight covered benches were placed around the gardens and the wider estate, including the Whispering Seat, the Aylsham Bench and the Prospect View. Other projects included an embellished seat on the Mount to the east of the serpentine lake which was fitted with sash windows and weatherboarding. Various lodges also appeared together with a deer shed and an abattoir which had a keeper's lodge attached to it. The erection of so many buildings exasperated the usually patient Copeman in whose opinion there were more than enough already.

Venison was consumed by Buckingham's friends and family and sometimes sent to his London townhouse. (By law venison could not be sold or bought on the open market but could be given and received as a mark of favour and patronage.) The proliferation of the deer herd together with the lure of partridge and pheasant during the winter months (game shooting was a major pastime) presented irresistible temptations for poachers. In December 1781 sixteen to eighteen men threatened the gamekeepers, swearing they would shoot them and "did violently assault and most cruelly beat and wound them with their guns and large clubs armed with iron spikes."[2] The terrible injuries of one most unfortunate keeper, Jacob Blyth, led to his death and others were "most dangerously bruised." As a result, along with other large estates similarly invaded, Blickling set spring guns in the plantation and by 1793 there were man traps in the pleasure grounds as well.

Buckingham settled so comfortably into rural life that the contrast between the apparel he donned in London and in the country was noticed by the Morning Herald. In 1782 an article headed 'Amusements Men of Fashion principally delight in' announced that the Earl of Buckinghamshire's chief pleasure in life was derived from wearing "an old coat."

The 1780s passed by with tranquil summers spent at Blickling interspersed with winter spells in Bond Street and at Marble Hill. Occasionally Buckingham travelled further afield as in July 1782 when he wrote en route to Bere Alston via Exeter that he had stopped for twenty-four hours on his way to an estate which his duties in Ireland had prevented him visiting for several years. The Blickling racecourse, used once or twice every year, was a source of great sport, and entertainments were enjoyed in both Norwich and London where his great love of theatre and opera was indulged to the full. He kept abreast of developments in Ireland via Thomas Conolly and through the lasting friendships he had made in the Emerald Isle, in particular Richard Woodward the Dean of Clogher, who had been Buckingham's first chaplain and in January 1781 was made Bishop of Cloyne. "I hope that your favourable opinion of your old servant will continue during your life—as my sincere friendship for my noble master and benefactor most certainly will to the last hour of mine."[3] He sent cordial and earnest enquiries as to the health of Lady Buckingham and of Lady Emily, suggesting "I might even add some expressions of love but whether they would come so decently (even from an old Ecclesiastic) through the channel of a father and a husband I am not so certain; it might be thought rather too much upon the brogue."

The Viceroyalty of Ireland changed rapidly in this decade, with no fewer than five incumbents, an indication perhaps of the difficult challenges involved in the role. One of their number was George Grenville, Earl Temple, the second son of Buckingham's dear departed friend, who enjoyed some success during his short tenure in 1782-1783 but fared less well in his second term of 1787-1789. In 1784 Grenville was elevated to the second incarnation of the title Marquess of Buckingham, which caused some confusion, not least to those charged with delivering post to two Lords Buckingham. Some while after the event, in 1788, Buckingham's old friend Alvaro de Nava, Vicomte de la Herreria, erroneously believed that the Earl of Buckingham had once again been made Viceroy of Ireland and asked him to send Irish linens for sheets, shirts and tablecloths, a request he was unable to fulfil.

Buckinghamshire in his Viceroy ermine by Thomas Gainsborough, painted 1784.

In 1784 Buckingham was elected as a Fellow of the Society of Antiquaries which was then based at Somerset House. In this same year he and Caroline sat, or rather stood, for Thomas Gainsborough at his studio in Schomberg House, Pall Mall. Their magnificent full-length portraits portray a confident, successful gentleman and a delicately beautiful, intelligent woman. The newspaper critic the Rev. Sir Henry Bate-Dudley, upon viewing the portraits in Gainsborough's studio, called the painting of Lady Buckingham "an admirable portrait, in which her ladyship has called forth all the powers of Mr Gainsborough." She is depicted in court dress, her coronet and state robes of red velvet and ermine on a table beside her, and in Buckingham's painting "His Lordship is represented in his 'Regal Portrait Robes' as Lord Lieutenant of Ireland. The likeness is strong. The

Gainsborough's companion portrait of Caroline.

drapery is finished in a rich stile, and well disposed." Buckingham's coat is made of brilliant blue ribbed silk with floral sprigs embroidered along the edge of his waistcoat, and draped around him is the gold-embroidered red velvet cloak of the Lieutenancy.

In February 1785 Buckingham was elected as a Fellow of the Royal Society. It was usual for gentlemen to be proposed, seconded and reasons given for their nomination, but of Peers there are no records of who was involved and what their motivations might have been. It is probable that the Society valued Buckingham as a Fellow for his wealth, influence and network of overseas connections rather than for any particular practical knowledge of science.

Buckingham's admiration for the fairest sex remained undiminished. In a piece entitled 'On Manners' he extolled them, "Partial to women from my earliest recollection, convinced that so long as we can be pleased and please, the connecting with them, as it is the most elegant, is the most justifiable sensuality, the tracing their progress in society is peculiarly interesting to me, especially as it will prove that the little polish which dresses our manners is derived from their delicate touch."[4]

From 1782 until 1789 Buckingham let Little Marble Hill, the small house next to Marble Hill House, to the twice married Lady Diana Beauclerk (née Lady Diana Spencer, and addressed by her friends as 'Lady Di') a woman as well known for adultery as for her considerable artistic talents. In truth she had been desperately unhappy in her first marriage to the notoriously unfaithful and abusive Viscount Bolingbroke and had on their divorce immediately married her devoted secret lover Topham Beauclerk, who then left her a widow in 1780. In 1785 a calf found its way into the grounds of Little Marble Hill and took a fancy to Lady Di's one and only cow. Alarmed, she informed Buckingham that the calf had "totally spoilt my cow, I fear for ever, it leaps over my fence. I am obliged to keep her constantly tethered which hurts her tho' it could not hurt the Calf for a time but your Lordship's Gardiner refuses to do it."[5] Buckingham responded politely "Were the Calf mine she should be respectfully tendered for your acceptance, but she is Lady Buckinghams, kept from the Butcher at her particular request, and she does not chuse to part with her or consent to her being confined." The matter was resolved when he purchased Lady Diana's cow and replaced it with another who he hoped would not develop the same habit, "for I have repeatedly seen her in my pasture. Your Ladish02ips indulgence must excuse my observing that the real grievance is the state of the Fence, which from the number of cattle in my grounds must render you liable to continual inconvenience."[6] Lady Diana had the fence repaired forthwith.

Buckingham's half-brother George Hobart and his flamboyant wife Albinia were famous for throwing extravagant parties at both their London residence and at their country seat at Nocton Hall in Lincolnshire. In 1742, after the death of Sir Richard Ellys (their father's cousin) his widow Sarah married Sir Francis Dashwood of the notorious Hellfire Club, and on her death in 1769, Nocton Hall, together with several estates in Lincolnshire, Leicestershire and Buckinghamshire and two London townhouses, fell to George. Ellys's Will was drawn up when Buckingham was seventeen and his half-brother nine and it may be that Sir William felt that as John was in line to inherit Blickling it was only fair and proper that George should inherit Nocton. Their younger brother Henry Hobart was only two when this decision was made and he was left out of the equation entirely, as was commonly the case. Although George enjoyed some success as a theatrical impresario and the estates brought him a handsome annual income, Albinia's addiction to the gaming tables became so intense and her losses so vast that by 1786 George was obliged to mortgage Nocton in order to pay off her debts. When in London their habit of hosting large parties in St James's Square every single evening, including Sundays, so irritated their next door neighbour Dr Porteus, the Bishop of London, that he was moved to send a letter of remonstrance. The couple made a partial concession thereafter that only sacred music would be played on Sundays.[7] As fond as Buckingham was of George he continued to find his outrageous sister-in-law excessively annoying and it is more than likely that he and Lady Caroline concocted excuses to decline invitations to the soirees.

By 1788 George and Albinia's son Major Robert Hobart[8] was MP for Portarlington in Ireland. He retrospectively sympathised with his uncle, "your Lordship's experience in this country must have convinced you that a patriot selling his vote is like a girl selling her maidenhead; the first deviation from virtue can only be obtained by love or money."[9] Soon to be appointed as Chief Secretary to John Fane, Earl of Westmoreland, a position he would hold from 1789-1793, Robert encountered the current Viceroy and found him to be "the most obnoxious man in England—no-one can love the Marquess of Buckingham. He was wonderfully civil to me, but as he makes use of the same words to everybody else, I do not think much of them."

In September the stage of the Theatre Royal, Norwich was graced by the presence of the celebrated actress Mrs Sarah Siddons who gave her Rosalind in 'As You Like It' to an appreciative audience. Billed to also perform in a farce, the local newspaper announced that "finding herself a good deal exhausted from her late performances, she fears she could not do justice to

Print of Gainsborough's portrait of Sarah Siddons LC-D416-657.

them both, and must therefore confine herself to the PLAY ONLY." Sir Charles Hotham, a friend and admirer of the great actress, asked Buckingham to show her 'special attention' and he obliged by inviting Mrs Siddons and her husband to "pass four-and-twenty hours with us, and to send an equipage to fetch her." The invitation was politely declined but he was able to report back that "your friend Mrs Siddons's Reception at Norwich was equal to her merit, and that her consequential Profit must have been more than £400."[10]

November brought drama of a more serious nature when the King descended into mania. Accounts claimed that George III often foamed at the mouth, that he talked without stopping for many hours at a stretch and on occasion believed himself to be the King of Prussia. The titular Prime Minister William Cavendish, Duke of Portland, urgently requested that Buckingham come to London "although there is little probability of any measure being then proposed in consequence of the calamitous and I believe desperate state of the King's mind. I am anxious to see you upon this very important and awefull subject."[11] Buckingham, although he modestly felt Portland's time could be better spent, made himself available. Portland's prediction was proved correct as it took until February for the House of Lords to pass the Regency Bill which was immediately made redundant because the King had by then recovered his senses.

In December Buckingham, knowing of Horace Walpole's penchant for such things, sent him a gift in the shape of a letter written in French by Peter III of Russia to his mistress Elizabeth Vorontsova in which he inquired about her health. Walpole was "quite confounded by your Lordship's goodness. I beg leave to return you my most grateful thanks. I should bring them myself to your Lordship's door were I not confined to the house by a great cold. You could not have honoured any man with such a present who would be more sensible of such a distinction."[12] His protestations of illness were, for once, not an excuse for avoiding Buckingham because he wrote elsewhere on December 26 that he had "the worst cough and cold I ever had in my days. I treat it as ill as possible, and do not give it a morsel; still it will not leave me. In revenge it will not let me speak."[13]

The surviving correspondence between Buckingham and his youngest daughter Emily demonstrates his particular fondness for the girl with whom he had formed an immensely strong bond during the tense and tragic years spent in Ireland. He wrote to her in May 1789 from Cheltenham where he was taking the waters in the hopes of improving the gout which plagued him. In writing, and perhaps also in person, he addressed her affectionately as My Dear Baby, "Having already wrote to the two Carolines it becomes now incumbent upon me to answer my Baby's Letter. This place is pleasant, the walking good and the views extensive and Romantick, but no company yet arriv'd, it is surmised that an apprehension of the Royal insanity having proceeded from drinking these Waters, has terrifyd the usual Patients away. This will be the ruin of many unfortunate speculators in Buildings & so on."[14]

On 18 June 1789 an arson attack was carried out at the King's Theatre when a fire was started on the roof during the evening dance rehearsals and performers were forced to flee the building as burning beams fell upon the stage. Suspicion fell upon the leader of the orchestra who was known to hold a grudge against the manager Giovanni Gallini who offered a three hundred pound reward for information, but no one was ever brought to justice. (Signore Carnivalli, a disgruntled former employee who Gallini had discharged, confessed on his deathbed to 'putting the torch to the original embarrassed theatre.') Sir Charles Hotham's friend, the sculptress Mrs. Anne Damer witnessed the blaze from atop the Pall Mall house of the miniaturist Richard Cosway and informed him "the poor Opera House is no more, people say that it is lucky & I know not what & that there will be a better, but I regret it, it was an old acquaintance & to it I owe many pleasant hours."[15] The building itself had been no great architectural jewel as it was a plain, dull structure with a red brick frontage and a roof of black glazed tiles. Miss Damer continued with ghoulish relish "I have one COMFORT however, which is that I saw it burned, & so fine a sight! It is far beyond description." The wanton destruction was an upsetting event for Buckingham and for George Hobart who had been manager and half shareholder of the theatre from 1769 until 1772. Lord Valletort, another ardent opera lover, recorded a event which took place soon after the destruction of the Opera House,

> London possessed at once the two finest singers in Italy. Once only they sung in the same room, at a private concert given by Lord Buckingham, when both exerted themselves to the utmost in friendly rivalship, and their combined efforts afforded the highest gratification. It was difficult to decide the point of *precedence* between two such great and equal performers; but both were civil and obliging men, despising the petty distinctions of which inferior performers are so tenacious, and Marchesi of his own accord yielded to his senior, Pacchierotti.[16]

ഇൗരു

In the background, rumblings of revolution were rising from France which caused considerable disquiet in England. News of the storming of the Bastille on 14 July 1789 did nothing to dissipate these worries.

ഇൗരു

In 1790 Buckingham returned to the enjoyable pastime of instructing more benches, seats and ornamental follies to be placed all over the Blickling Estate. This provoked his Estate

A song performed by one of the most famous mezzo-soprano castratos, Gaspare Pacchierotti

Manager Copeman to fret that, "When such a seat is built do you think that your Lordship shall like the appearance of it? Is there any pleasant object to be seen from the seat when so placed and if your Lordship is disposed to walk must you not leave a pleasanter to go there?"[17] Buckingham's reaction to this unsolicited advice is unrecorded but as Copeman's next missive read "If I have offended your Lordship in any way I am very sorry for it and am as innocent of the cause as them who never saw or heard of your Lordship"[18] it can be assumed that Buckingham overrode his Manager's objections and carried on regardless.

Buckingham spent most of his time happily ensconced at Blickling, exchanging visits with local gentry such as his dear old friend and exact contemporary Horatio Walpole (son of 1st Baron Walpole) at Wolterton Hall of whom he thought "it is not easy to find a family more good humoured and comfortable amongst themselves."[19] His loyal servants at Blickling included Tom Bell the Gamekeeper, Jack Bell the Farm Manager, Mrs Bell the Housekeeper and Mrs Butler, a superlative cook whose efforts were always liberally rewarded with effusive compliments. `

Peaceful days were spent alone with Caroline at Lady's Cottage in its tranquil location on a slope on the edge of the Great Wood. A fountain purchased from nearby Oxnead Hall was placed nearby, together with an urn displaying Milton's poem in memory of their first born son, and for a time a statue of Hercules stood proudly gazing over the country park where the racecourse was laid out. Lady's Cottage became a precious and private retreat for the couple's quiet contemplation of their love for each other and the poignant remembrance of their three lost boys.

Visits to Bond Street, to Marble Hill and to friends further afield interspersed this bucolic existence and if proof were sought regarding Buckingham's dedication to the operatic arts *The Gentleman's Chronicle* reported,

> This day the Earl of Buckingham, attended by a large party of persons of distinction, laid the stone on top of which were engraved these words, 'The First stone of this New Theatre was laid on the 3rd April 1790, in the 30th year of the reign of King George III by the Right Hon. John Hobart, Earl of Buckingham.' This was followed by his Lordship's motto "Auctor preciosa Facit"*

The sides of the stone were inscribed 'The King's Theatre in the Haymarket, first built in the year 1703', 'But unfortunately burnt down on the 17th of June 1789' and 'Prevalebit justitia.' (Justice will prevail.)

Gold and silver coins were placed in a recess in the stone and the Haymarket Opera House began its resurrection shortly afterwards. Unfortunately a complicated series of buyouts, disagreements between shareholders, and labyrinthian confusion with lawyers over mortgages caused the Lord Chamberlain to refuse a

---

*   The Giver Makes the Gift Precious

licence for the new theatre and it was obliged to open with a private performance of song and dance on 26 March 1791 from which the public was excluded but it is possible that Buckingham and George Hobart attended. [20]

Buckingham's surviving letters to his beloved 'Great' Caroline, who regularly visited London and her Conolly relations, and those to Emily, demonstrate he was a devoted husband and loving father. He often referred to the horses and dogs which played an intrinsic part in their family life, with an occasional calf or kitten making an appearance. A letter to Emily was written after a visit to Gunton Hall where "Miss Harbord and indeed her Mamma, in her insipid way, were very attentive to me, my Lord more ceremoniously respectfull"[21] but where the Recorder of King's Lynn, Sir George Chad Dour, although obsequious "to the ground" was ill-mannered as he was late to dinner and arrived at breakfast "'yawning and lolling in his chair with the becoming apathy of fashion." The letter reported on the health of her horse Scrub who was "very well but Caroline will neither ride him or her own horse, she has clapped her side saddle on Pegasus, and thinks it safer to gallop about the precipices of Parnassus than to ride in my Park. She will however find herself mistaken and get some cursed Tumble" and added that her mother would "write about the Puppies, which is naturally the female department." He told of his attendance at an Aylsham Navigation Meeting from which he had miraculously returned without "being choler'd or having his nose pulled." Demonstrating that "Caroline is not the only one of the family who can write verses" he informed Emily that when she reached Marble Hill she would have full leisure to contemplate, "Lady Emma as wise as her Sire, and as her Mother fair, her Granddam's talents, and her Grandpa's air."

Visiting Thetford on 4 January 1791 he was received by a Counsellor "with open arm (he had but one)"[22] who set off to dinner at Lord Petre's where, he told Buckingham, he would be "liberally entertained by Champain Punch." Caroline added mischievously, "P.S. Papa is quite a Noncompush[23], he cannot spell or write sense. C. Hobart - Secretary." In the spring Buckingham relayed that

> We have a proportion of sunshine but the Wind is cold, nothing could be finer than yesterday morning and this till eight o'clock when the Norway Blast came over the Water. We are very cheerful in our solitude, but do not breakfast till after nine o'clock when Bell comes with her eyes ajar complaining of the Rheumaticks. Caroline, more active, walks before breakfast. Your Mamma's new Walk is visited every day and forms a most agreeable communication. There are numberless Mares sporting about the Park and Woods, and many newly marry'd partridges are enjoying their Honeymoon."[24]

The important question of whether marble flooring might be too cold was posed in relation to the modern water closets which Buckingham was having installed at Blickling.

In early 1792, during one of his frequent visits to Horatio Walpole at Wolterton Hall, Buckingham noticed that a Mr. G. Anson was exchanging glances with Miss Walpole and gauged that "He seems that species of a Man who never marry'd himself, yet is liable to be marry'd by some determined Woman."[25]

In August 1792 news from Paris reported the storming of the Tuileries Palace and the imprisonment of King Louis and Queen Marie Antoinette. Whilst the French revolution raged on, Lady Harriet Belmore, last encountered having been forcibly separated from her child and settling into the Abbaye in Paris in 1781 was deeply entrenched in another drama of her own making, on both sides of La Manche.

Notes

1. *Reports of the manuscripts of the Marquess of Lothian*, p.406.
2. *Norwich Mercury*, 1781.
3. *Reports of the manuscripts of the Marquess of Lothian*, p.422.
4. NRO MC3/288, 468 x 5.
5. NRO MC 3/285 Letter 113.
6. NRO MC 3/285 Letter 114.
7. Wright T, & Evans,RH., *Historical & descriptive account of the caricatures of James Gillray : comprising a political and humorous history of the latter part of the reign of George the Third*, HG. Bohn, 1851.
8. Hobart, Tasmania was named after Robert Hobart when he was Secretary of State for War and the Colonies,1801—1804. On his father George Hobart's death Robert became 4th Earl of Buckinghamshire because his elder brother Charles, a Lieutenant in the Royal Navy, died in action in 1782.
9. *Report on the Manuscripts of the Marquess of Lothian*, p.488.
10. *The Hothams ...*, p.239.
11. *Report on the Manuscripts of the Marquess of Lothian*, p.437.
12. *Horace Walpole's Correspondence*, Vol. 42, p.232-233.
13. Ibid. p.233.
14. NRO MC 3/285 Letter 97.
15. *The Hothams ...*, 1918, p.244.
16. *Musical Reminiscences of an Old Amateur 1773 to 1823*, Second edition, W. Clarke, 1827. play.google.com
17. NRO MC 3/285.
18. NRO MC 3/285.
19. NRO MC 3/285 Letter 101.
20. It was not until 26 January 1793 that the first public opera was staged, although the Theatre Royal Drury Lane company performed there whilst its own theatre was being rebuilt during 1791-1794.
21. NRO MC 3/285 Letter 99.
22. NRO MC 3/285 Letter 98.
23. 'Noncompush' - a word invented by Tobias George Smollett (1721-1771) written for 'Humphrey Clinker'.
24. NRO MC 3/285 Letter 100.
25. NRO MC 3/285 Letter 101.

Trials and Tribulations

The Abbaye Royale de Penthemont, situated in the rue de Bellechasse and the rue de Grenelle in the 7th arrondissement of Paris, offered refuge to ladies of high standing seeking sanctuary, always provided they could afford the substantial fees. There were diverse reasons for the ladies' dilemmas; some had husbands who were simply away, some were escaping from difficult marriages and some had been cruelly abandoned. Residents of the Convent were free to employ their own live-in servants and even, if circumstances allowed, accommodate their children. The ladies had a choice between lodgings that ranged from a single room to apartments of up to six rooms and as Harriet's allowance converted to over 3000 livres per year she was able to live comfortably in spacious, elegant rooms.

A very great consolation to Harriet was the companionship of her fourteen year old sister Sophie (as she was known in the family) who had accompanied her to Paris. On their arrival in 1781 Harriet hired twenty-two year old Frenchman Francois le Duc as her footman and valet, and a maid for her sister. The residents were at liberty to entertain visitors and to come and go as they pleased, the only stipulation being that they were obliged to attend Chapel on Sundays even though many of the congregation, including Harriet and Sophie, were not Catholic. Over time the girls felt at home in Paris, the city their mother Mary Anne had for so long dreamed of visiting, and although the move had been intended as a temporary measure until the dust settled on the scandal of Harriet's broken marriage, they stayed much longer than anticipated.

Presiding over the Convent, which incorporated one of the most prestigious educational establishments in all France, was the remarkable Abbess Marie-Catherine Bethisy de Meziere, who had overseen the recent reconstruction of the buildings and who ruled for forty-five years. The school accepted Protestant pupils as well as Catholics including, a few years later, the daughters of Thomas Jefferson. Another notable resident was Marie-Josephe-Rose de la Pagerie, who arrived in November 1783 and certainly would have crossed paths with Harriet and Sophie. Marie-Josephe-Rose had separated from Alexandre de Beauharnais, her cruel and adulterous husband whose vile behaviour had resulted in the courts most unusually siding with the woman, commanding him to pay for his wife and their son Eugene's keep at the Convent. Mme de Beauharnais stayed until mid-1785 after which her story became the stuff of legend. Her husband was sent to the guillotine during the Reign of Terror and his widow became the wife of Napoleon Bonaparte, who always called her Josephine.

Paris in the 1780s was a lively, cultured, diverse city filled with radicals, writers and philosophers from all over the continent and Harriet gradually recovered some measure of her youthful spirits after the bruising ordeal of the separation from her husband and most especially of the cruelly enforced separation from her baby. There were many pastimes for Harriet and Sophie to enjoy; the Palais Royal alone consisted of two theatres, shopping arcades, cafes, boutiques and museums and in the milieu in which they moved there were many opportunities for conversation and encounters with English visitors, French aristocracy and European royalty. In 1782 Durand Neveu's classic tale of debauchery *Les Liaisons Dangereuse* was published and in 1783 the Treaty of Paris, which ended the American Civil War, was signed. In September of that year at Versailles the first hot air Balloon took flight, albeit just for eight minutes and carrying only a sheep, a duck and a cockerel. These brave creatures were hailed as heroes of the air and upon their unexpectedly landing alive, were rewarded with a well earned retirement in Louis XVI's Menagerie.

Although there is very little surviving correspondence between Harriet and her father during this period, bills from 1783 indicate that Harriet and her young sister were living far from frugally. Apart from the sizeable boarding fees at the Abbaye and salaries for Francois le Duc and Sophie's maid, the accounts speak of a Writing Master, Dancing Masters, a Harp Master, a Shoemaker, and presents for the Abbess's birthday, together with copious amounts of pin money. A bill covering 12 October 1781 to 1 February 1783 amounted to over £4,800, and given that Harriet's annuity from Lord Belmore was 1,000 Irish pounds per annum, Buckingham was obliged to fund the majority of his daughter's expenses. Most of the surviving letters from Harriet focus on her inability to remain within a budget and she often expressed sorrow at having to beg forgiveness for her regular lapses into debt. In January 1783, on returning to Paris after a spell in the south of France, Harriet explained that although she had offered to send Sophie back to England, "I shall consider her remaining with me as the greatest happiness and obligation; her other expenses will be trifling as for some time (that is, till we arrived at Nice) she could not have any Master, and there they were very cheap and I understand, good."[1] In July 1783 Buckingham made it known that he had no objection to both daughters returning to England and Harriet joyfully asked him for "a line at Dover to say where I must go on my arrival in London; if Marble Hill is unoccupied as it generally is during your residence at Blickling, your allowing me to remain there will towards Winter be some diminution of expence."[2] The implication being that Buckingham did not desire a reunion with his eldest daughter and had resolved to maintain some distance between them. But by the end of the month after his daughters had returned once more to Nice, Buckingham had had a change of heart. Harriet's reply read,

> Your strong representations against my travelling scheme my dearest
> Father have determined me to lay it entirely aside; at the same time I
> doubt not you will be sensible it is impossible for me to remain here any
> longer under the distressed circumstance of the debts which I have so very

imprudently contracted. Your proposal of my returning to the Convent
till the month of December would be punishing my indiscretion to no
purpose. If you my dearest Father will show me so much kindness as to
make me easy in this respect I will submit with cheerfulness and gratitude
to any reduction of my income till this money to be advanced at present
can be repaid, upon this plan I would return to England when I can with
less inconvenience, and more propriety, then reduce my expence to £500 a
year. I hope you will enable me to put this into immediate execution, at the
same time I cannot sufficiently lament the imprudence which has led me
into this difficulty. I must entreat an answer as each day till something is
settled increases my distress.[3]

Whether or not Harriet and Sophie remained in the south throughout the winter
is unknown but Harriet's next surviving letter dated June 19 1784 places her back
in Paris and in higher spirits. She reported to her father that,

All the people in the Convent are half mad, the King of Sweden has sent
word that he should come and see the Abbess, and we have heard nothing
else this fortnight. I wish something might happen to deprive us of the
honour of his Entre as they intend showing him all the Apartments, and
it will bore me to death to have him brought into mine. All his attendants
will likewise be admitted, & nothing looks more ridiculous than seeing a
parcel of men run about the Convent with the Nuns. The Abbess intends
to call us over and present us—if I was not afraid of their thinking it appear
epouvantable[4] I should lock myself up.[5]

This observation was followed by an altogether more plaintive and poignant
plea concerning her child. Someone in Ireland had informed Harriet that Lord
Belmore planned to send Louisa to school, despite the fact that she was only three
years of age.

Tho' I mentioned it to Lady Buckingham, I cannot help repeating to you
my dear Father how much my happiness is concerned in her obtaining if
possible my poor little girl for me. I cannot conceive that Lord Belmore
should refuse it after the scheme of sending her to School; especially as
you seem to desire it.

Harriet reiterated her feelings on the matter, as previously written to Lady
Enniskillen, "I make no comments on her ever having been kept from me, it needs
none, for anybody must consider it in the same light." Whatever efforts 'Great'
Caroline made to reunite Harriet with her daughter were unsuccessful and
Belmore remained resolute in his determination to keep Louisa to himself. The
remainder of the letter concerned English visitors to Paris including Lord and Lady
Granard and Lady Anne Rawdon (Harriet's old friend, a daughter of Lady Moira)
and ended with a request for "the Musical and Poetical Relics of the Welsh Bards
by Edward Jones, and dedicated to the Prince of Wales, and last years Annual

Register." She stated that she liked "any book in the world except those treating of Physiology & Theology" and begged that she wished "she knew of any book, or thing, you might want from here." Buckingham had evidently been eloquent in his letters to Harriet regarding his views on the current state of politics and she responded that "it grieves me very much that you should make yourself so uncomfortable about Politics, & am sorry to find there is reason for everyone to be so more or less." During 1784 Pitt the Younger had fought off Charles Fox's vote of no confidence and won another term as British Prime Minister, with all the usual brouhaha that accompanies such events.

It seems that Harriet and Sophie once again relocated to the south of France during the summer months. She wrote another appeal for more funds to allow them to find a larger house because "the one I mentioned in my last letter much too small for my sister and myself."[6] She had located one "currently occupied by Lady Euphemia Stewart where the rent was "about 60£" and that Lady Euphemia wished to include her furniture for "a remarkably cheap 20£." Whether she got her wish is unknown, but later that year Buckingham indicated that his daughters might be allowed to return to England at Christmas. However the next surviving letter from Harriet was sent from Paris on 14 August 1785 and explains why this did not come to pass.

> I wish you to be persuaded my dearest Father that there is nothing I desire more earnestly than to see you and return to England, but unassisted, the state of my Affairs will not admit of it at Xmas—supposing I continued to do without a Carriage and with bad furniture for the first Winter, at the end of that time I can foresee no periods when it will be in my power to purchase them, yet it is not very probable that I should save the wherewithal out of my income. I cannot wait buying linnen, China & co and cloathes so as to make a decent appearance as my present wardrobe is in the most lamentable state, and I am not a good enough Economist enough to be able to do all this, and pay any other expence of Life with one hundred pounds from January to April—I was very happy in the hope of having the pleasure of spending just part of the Winter with you, but as things are I fear it must unavoidably be deferred.[7]

The letter contained snippets about her "aunt Hobart," Henry's ailing wife Anne, who professed to Harriet that she did not like Paris at all yet in her letters to England altered her opinion so as not to seem "Mauvais ton" and that Mr Walpole

Queen Marie-Antoinette performed as 'Rosina' in Rossini's 'The Barber of Seville' when Harriet and Sophie were in Paris.

had sent for his daughters to return to keep him company. Harriet would sorely miss them and offered to send anything her father desired via their auspices. Most intriguingly Harriet wrote that "The Queen is at St Cloud and acted the Barber of Seville last week, she performed the part of Rosina, the Comte d'Artois that of Figaro and M. De Vaudreuil was the Comte Almaviva" without actually stating whether or not she and Sophie witnessed Marie-Antoinette's performance. By 2 October the Miss Walpoles had left Paris which was "a very great misfortune to Sophie & I, as they are very amiable, were the only people we saw constantly"[8] and that the only English lady they knew in Paris now was Lady Egremont. Harriet's cousin Maria Hobart, a daughter of George and Albinia, married the 3rd Earl of Guildford, George North after he wrangled with his family over his bride's lack of dowry. "I am vastly glad that Maria is married, it is a match that cannot turn out ill in the end and it will not only be stingy and ridiculous of Ld Guildford[9] if he is not reconciled, her want of fortune is the only objection that can possibly be made, and he is old enough to know what he is about." Harriet apologised for the shortage of gossip "I have been ill which adds to my natural stupidity and have heard no news that could be in any way entertaining or interesting. You are possibly as much bored with the Cardinal Rohan affair[10] as we are here, there is not even anything new on the subject & he still appears the Knave & Blackguard he was supposed to be."

The increasingly affectionate tone of their letters implies a softening on Buckingham's side and that he desired a reunion, but when Harriet and her father came to an agreement about her eventual return to London is clouded by lack of surviving correspondence. However it came about, in 1786, after almost six years in exile, Harriet, Sophie and Francois Le Duc set sail for England.

There is a dearth of evidence about where and how Harriet lived next. A letter of Buckingham's friend Alvaro de Nava, Vicomte de la Herreria, who spent three years in Paris under the Spanish Ambassador the Count d'Aranda, had befriended Harriet, whom he called "la belle et amiable Miladi Belmor".[11] In February 1788 he told her father that his years in Paris could not be considered unsuccessful because he had had the honour of getting to know Lady Belmore whose "beautiful qualities complemented her looks and was as the daughter of Milord Buckingham a very precious acquaintance." Buckingham thanked him and informed the Count that Lady Belmore "had often spoken well of the Vicomte and took the opportunity of assuring him of her friendship."[12] This confirms that father and daughter had been reconciled on her return and it is likely that Harriet set up house in London and that Sophie lived between there and their father's house in Bond Street. Buckingham's third-born daughter Sophie, who very seldom features in surviving correspondence, had returned from Paris a grown woman and she soon caught the eye of twenty-four year old Richard Edgcumbe. The couple were married on 21 February 1789 and June found Sophie "preparing her fine gowns against the arrival of their Majesties at Mount Edgcumbe" a magnificent country estate situated on the Rame Peninsula in Cornwall.[13] In August of the same year Richard's father was made 1st Earl of Mount Edgcumbe and the newly-weds took the titles Lord and Lady Valletort.

Harriet, meanwhile, whilst visiting friends in Scotland launched herself into a liaison of her own by falling head over heels in love with William Kerr, the eldest son of Major-General William Kerr, 5th Marquess of Lothian. Known as Lord Ancram, the charming and intelligent William had attended the University of Edinburgh and been made a Fellow of the Royal Society in Edinburgh at the tender age of twenty-three. Now twenty-five, he was equally smitten with Harriet, and as a consequence did not give a fig about her unusual marital history. On her return from Scotland Harriet established herself at an address in Welbeck Street and by the summer of 1790 William Kerr had become the most welcome and most frequent visitor to the house. Plans for their future happiness, which in the natural course of things would have led to marriage, were stymied by the seemingly insurmountable obstacle that Harriet was still married, even if in name only, to Lord Belmore. She correctly surmised that it would be pointless to ask him to bring divorce proceedings against her, not least because such a thing was not easily procured, especially in Ireland. Moreover Belmore would see no clear benefit to himself in taking such an action as for one thing he would lose the prospect of inheriting property through her. That it would also cost him a great deal of money and further public humiliation to put a Bill of Divorce through the Irish Parliament would have been further reasons for his point blank refusal. Added to which, although Harriet may not have been aware of this, Belmore had no desire to marry again. This is not to say that he had remained celibate since their separation because he demonstrably had not. His eye had fallen conveniently close to home upon Margaret Begby, a woman who lived in Derryvullen on his Estate, and with whom he had a relationship long enough for her to bear him two children, Emily Maria Lowry Corry in 1784 and John Corry in November 1787. However, although he took the children into his household to be raised alongside his son Somerset, he had no intention whatever of marrying their mother and was content to leave matters as they stood.

By now lovers, Harriet and William put their heads together and hatched a daring plot to induce Belmore to change his mind. Surely, they reasoned, if he was made aware of his wife's adultery he would have no alternative but to initiate divorce proceedings? An outrageous plan began to take shape, one they anticipated would cause a public scandal and bring ignominy on both their families, but as the alternative was to live together permanently as unmarried outcasts, desperation propelled them to take drastic action.

At the beginning of August 1791 Harriet rented a furnished house in Broadstairs, Kent taking with her her valet le Duc and a Mrs Bell (possibly Blickling's Mrs Bell) and William took an apartment nearby where his valet Augustus slept, but where William did not. After living in unwedded bliss for three months the couple dismissed Mrs. Bell and took a fortnight's reconnaissance trip to France. Having found a suitable property to rent on the road to Boulogne they sailed back to Calais in early December where their stratagem escalated. William and Harriet stayed firstly at l'Hotel d'Angleterre, a public inn kept by a Monsieur Dessein with whose assistance they hired a cook and a chambermaid, and William's valet Augustus joined them shortly afterwards. The lovers then lived as man and wife in a house named La Rocherie where they were widely known as and believed to be Lord and Lady Ancram.

'Great' Caroline was apparently in collusion with the adventurous pair and addressed her letters to "Lady H. Smith. A Calais, Post restante." One such survives, in which Harriet's London house was the subject,

> Since I wrote last we have considered about your House and beg to know if it is your wish that it should be Let and if it is whether it would not be better to leave your stores in it for the short time of the Lease & then keep all the furniture for you. Let me know the answer to this question as soon as is convenient as Lord B will take measures about letting it—and means to let it furnished as no Person will take it for a little while without. I set out for London on Wednesday morning so direct to me there.[14]

Caroline added the Post Script, "I did not tell Lord B how and where I direct my letters to you" but in his own hand Buckingham wrote a message of comfort, "My poor Harriet, You will find me in every situation attentive and affectionate, Buckingham." It is clear from this remark alone that neither he nor Caroline had abandoned or disowned Harriet and that they sought to help her.

Six weeks later William and Harriet were urgently summonsed back from La Rocherie to Scotland. According to Francois Le Duc the couple had been invited to be present at the marriage of Lord Ancram's sister, and Janet Hure the chambermaid averred that her mistress told her she had received letters from England which galvanised the couple into departing immediately. Someone was being economical with the truth because although William Ancram had five sisters, none of them married in 1791. Nevertheless, whatever the reason for their sudden departure, the couple left the very same day for Calais and sailed at three the next morning for Dover. By this time Harriet was almost six months pregnant and it was this indisputable development that inflicted the final humiliation on Lord Belmore. Although the couple had presented themselves as Lord and Lady Ancram whilst in France, on the road to Scotland they assumed the names Mr Anderson and Mrs Smith. On arrival in Edinburgh at the end of January 1792, they took private lodgings under these names for a week or so after which they moved to a house three or four miles outside the city. As the Lothian family seat of Newbattle Abbey, a former Cistercian monastery, was situated some four or five miles south of Edinburgh, it is most likely that William had been summoned home to explain

Harriet Hobart, (Lord Lothian's private collection).

himself to his father and that due to her interesting condition Harriet may not necessarily have taken part in those discussions. During their stay Francois Le Duc was instructed to address William as Lord Ancram and Harriet as 'My Lady' without adding any other name to the title. After five weeks the trio returned to London and moved into a house in Queen Street, Edgware Road, where on 8 April 1792 Harriet gave birth to a son the couple named William Drury Kerr. The illegitimate

William Kerr by Henry Raeburn (Lord Lothian's private collection).

baby's arrival had the desired effect of triggering the response his parents sought, in that it incensed and provoked Lord Belmore. However, unfortunately for them, instead of initiating divorce proceedings in Ireland Belmore formally accused Harriet of adultery and the case went through the London courts. The fact Belmore had by this time sired three illegitimate children was not considered the slightest bit relevant.

Although Harriet did not attend the Adultery Trial in person it was common for the depositions of witnesses in trials to be published for public consumption, as a consequence of which the Hobart name, and that of Ancram, were dragged through the mud. Copies of *"The Trial of Viscountess Belmore (formerly Lady Henrietta Hobart, and Daughter to John Earl of Buckinghamshire) for Adultery With The Earl of Ancram"*[15] were displayed and sold for one shilling and sixpence at 293 Oxford Street, under the Piazza in Covent Garden and "in all Booksellers in Town and Country." Purchasers no doubt relished reading testimony from Lady Belmore's servants outlining in salacious detail the sleeping arrangements enjoyed by the errant couple.

Lady Louisa Lowry Corry by Hugh Douglas Hamilton (from the collection of the Earl of Belmore).

The first deponents called were the Irishmen Rev. John Lowry and Charles King, who both stated that despite Lord Belmore having behaved "to Viscountess Belmore with the greatest love and affection, and appeared to be, and was, as this deponent does verily believe, desirous of doing every thing in his power to please her" that she had not any regard or affection whatever for the Viscount and that "every person who saw her behaviour believed that she had a total aversion to Viscount Belmore."[16] The Right Honourable William, Earl of Enniskillen, Belmore's brother-in-law, who abhorred Belmore's treatment of Harriet regarding Louisa, observed that very soon after their marriage the couple "seemed to live unhappy together"[17] and that there was a visible disgust on the part of Lady Belmore towards her husband. The testimonies then took an altogether more intimate turn. Janet Hure, the French chambermaid, said she saw Lord Ancram "and the person who was then called Lady Ancram, in one in the same bed together, naked and alone"[18] and aware as she now was of their true status, believed they had "committed the foul crime of adultery." The cook, Catherine Bassin, swore that there had only been one bed made up for the couple during their six week stay at La Rocherie and that she had walked in upon them at a delicate moment when they were "in one and the same bed, perfectly naked and alone, the bed-clothes being partly off—such was the nicety of their situation when this deponent saw them in bed together."[19] Bassin added that she had seen the couple "kiss each other" but as at the time she believed they were man and wife "did not particularly remark with what ardency they manifested their amorous tokens."

Francois le Duc provided detailed accounts of the couple's journeys through England, France and Scotland including the pseudonyms they had travelled under. He been a witness to the affair since its inception but on 2 April, after almost eleven years in Harriet's service, he left to take up another post as valet to Lord Beauchamp in Berkeley Square. His deposition also stated that Harriet "was with child, and expected soon to lie in."[20]

The Adultery Trial ran from 4 to 25 May 1792, when the last deponent, Sir Richard Heron, confirmed details of the part he had played in the Belmore's separation and swore that he did "'verily believe they have not since lived or cohabited together."[21]

Sentence was handed down by Sir William Scott, Vicar-General,

> We do pronounce, that the said Viscount Belmore, and the Viscountess Belmore, being free from all matrimonial contracts (except to each other) did contract matrimony between each other, and did solemnize and afterwards consummate the same by carnal copulation, and mutual cohabitation and procreation of a daughter, which said Viscountess being soon afterwards unmindful of her conjugal vow, and instigated no doubt by the devil, committed the foul crime of adultery with the Earl of Ancram; wherefore it is decreed and declared, that the said parties be divorced and separated from each other (until they shall be reconciled to each other) and neither of them to marry again during the life of the other.

The decree in itself did not signify a legal divorce and the condition about neither of the deponents marrying again did not hold water, so Belmore was obliged to take a petition to the Irish Parliament. He informed Buckingham that he was so scandalised by the conduct of the woman who still carried his name that he was forced to seek a divorce if only for the sake of his daughter Louisa's reputation, an assertion which undoubtedly wounded Buckingham deeply. Adultery was then the sole ground for divorce but was very rarely attempted, not by any means because of a shortage of adulterous behaviour, but because of the extremely large costs such an action incurred. But the enraged and now publicly humiliated Belmore was determined to be rid once and for all of the wife he so loathed and despised.

News reached Buckingham that Belmore planned to discontinue Harriet's annuity of £1,000 which had been agreed in the separation and that nor would he honour her jointure after his death. Buckingham wrote as tactfully as he could manage, "the forms of law are little known to me, but I conceive from recollection of several instances that my child is not to be left destitute. A proper confidence in your Lordship's noble nature would have prevented my touching upon the subject had it not seemed that you might be desirous of learning my wishes in that instance, which go no further than the continuation of her present annuity."[22] This flattering appeal to Belmore's better nature had the desired effect, although it took him a further eight months to concede to Harriet's legal right to her allowance and to draft a petition accordingly.

On 14 May Buckingham invited Belmore to spend the summer at Blickling, ostensibly to share his knowledge of architecture, but he would also have wished to discuss the impending divorce and to meet eleven year old Louisa. Unfortunately Belmore was not to be lured and he declined the offer with the excuse that he was too busy with building works "to do myself the honor of paying my respects at Blickling but hope in the succeeding summer to present your granddaughter to you."[23]

Concurrent with these events another drama was unfolding closer to home.

Notes

1. NLI 13045 Heron papers.
2. Ibid.
3. Ibid.
4. epouvantable - appalling.
5. Ibid.
6. Ibid.
7. Ibid.
8. Ibid.
9. Lord North, Prime Minister from1770-1782.
10. The notorious Affair of the Diamond Necklace involved Jeanne de Saint-Remy, mistress of Cardinal Rohan and significantly impacted Queen Marie-Antoinette's reputation.
11. *Report on the Manuscripts of the Marquess of Lothian*, p.434.
12. Ibid.
13. NRS GD40/9/196.
14. NRS GD40/9/204.
15. *The Trial of Viscountess Belmore, (Formerly Lady Henrietta Hobart, and Daughter to John Earl of Buckinghamshire) for Adultery With The Earl of Ancram*, 1793.
16. Ibid. p.5-12.
17. Ibid. p.23.
18. Ibid. p.16.
19. Ibid. p.19-20.
20. Ibid. p.33.
21. Ibid. p.26.
22. Marson, P., Ch. 5.
23. Ibid.

Caroline Hans Hobart

Lady Caroline Hobart had not thus far been inundated with marriage proposals but in 1792 the twenty-five year old found herself being avidly courted by William Assheton Harbord, her neighbour at Gunton Hall. This was an unforeseen development even though their families were already connected by both blood and politics. Buckingham's occasionally fraught relationship with William's father Sir Harbord Harbord had settled during their latter years and the cousins were now on relatively friendly terms. As MP (Second Member) for Ludgershall in Wiltshire, William Harbord was at this time best known as a keen cricketer, having made a name for himself as a member of the MCC (Marylebone Cricket Club) by playing three times in first-class matches during the 1791 season.

Harriet, continuing her habit of travelling incognito, received a letter from an excitable Caroline addressed to Mrs. H. Hudson, Post Office, Edinburgh,

> I am here for a few days for peace and a nervous cough which plagues me. Was not your astonishment at hearing about Mr Harbord beyond anything that ever happened to you? I will tell you about it, for you must wish to hear. After Lady B and Emily left Blickling—he passed two days with us—we went to Gunton for one day & afterwards were at Kimberley together. I thought him more <u>polite</u> but his Sisters watched him so much that I was <u>grand</u>, and indeed had always considered his thinking of me as a circumstance utterly out of the question. For the first week of my being in Town I did not go out having a wretched cold, but after that whenever we met he never left me—and on Friday at Lady Howes proposed to me <u>on the hearth whilst my Father was calling his carriage</u>. I agreed, looked almost as foolish as possible and just contrived to <u>hobble</u> downstairs. I think you would like him much—he is unreserved very amiable and diffident and it is certainly entirely his own wish.[1]

Caroline held such a high opinion of her own standing that, even though he was her second cousin, she had considered William beneath her, but now she found herself bowled over by his assiduous and earnest attentions. Whether or not he was motivated by the idea of profiting by such a marriage cannot be confirmed, but as matches were often arranged with such an aim, it is conceivable that he predicted any husband Caroline accepted might benefit from the fact that Buckingham's eldest daughter was currently in disgrace for the second time. However, Caroline's handsome dowry of £20,000 may have been sufficient inducement, as any husband she accepted would receive £14,000 on the marriage. Caroline herself had apparently anticipated courtship from another quarter,

> He has very good notions of <u>comfort</u>, as to magnificence we cannot

think of that now. The idea of having a House of my own transports me. He seems to be much liked—in short at this moment I am flattered and envied sufficiently.

For once my prayers were heard, I had wished to be engaged against Lord C arrived, and this was <u>declared</u> just after he came to London & everybody says how lucky I was to escape him.

The next day she added a post script about her new fiancé and revelled in her triumph, "He came this morn and was very pretty and very pleasing. You must know he was wanted for <u>Harriet Townshend</u> and I <u>hope</u> the D of Buccleagh[2] was anxious about it." The *Norfolk Chronicle* reported "It is said that the delicate and beautiful Lady Caroline Hobart, second daughter of the Earl of Buckinghamshire, is very shortly to be married to the Hon William Assheton son of Lord Suffield."

In the weeks between the engagement and the wedding a rift of cataclysmic proportions erupted between William Harbord and his future mother-in-law. The principal cause was a marriage settlement in which Buckingham took the opportunity to protect Blickling and his other property from falling into the hands of Belmore, who despite his legal separation from Harriet, had not actually divorced her. This in itself was a wise course of action, but the extent of his largesse towards the couple was to the detriment of not only Caroline's sisters but also, surprisingly, of his wife. He instructed that within a year of their marriage Caroline and William Harbord would be given lifetime possession of the Blickling estate which would then be inherited by any son or sons born to them in the future. Should they not produce a son, then a son of one of Caroline's sisters would, after the demise of both Caroline and William, inherit Blickling and continue the Hobart line. This meant that if William predeceased his wife, or vice versa, the survivor would have the right to live for their remaining lifetime at Blickling. Furthermore the executors Lord Brownlow, George Talbot, Lord Valletort and John Kipling were instructed that should the marriage take place within twelve months the couple would also be entitled to vast swathes of Copyhold[3] lands, and their corresponding incomes, around Norfolk, as well as their lifetime "use and possession of Blickling".

The Countess may have suspected that Harbord had inveigled himself into Buckingham's good books in order to coerce the Earl into drawing up a settlement which benefitted nobody more than himself. Perhaps Buckingham, appalled that Harriet was undergoing an adultery trial, lost sight of the ramifications of such measures and drew up the document in a state of high dudgeon. Although he stipulated that after his demise the Countess should have an annuity of £1,200 and the use and occupation of Hunworth Hall (his grandfather Robert Britiffe's house) she would not have a legal right to live at Blickling except in the unlikely event that she outlived both Caroline and William Harbord and "any son of the intended marriage under the age of twenty one."

Whether or not Harbord, by word or action, gave the Countess any other reason to object to him, she developed an intense loathing for him and was horrified when the marriage settlement was signed on 26 May 1792, just a day after Harriet's adultery trial ended. It is clear that the Countess had not kept her opinions about Harbord to herself and that she had confided in Harriet, who received a plaintive missive from her sister, written from Bond Street,

> I should not my dearest Harriet have been so long without writing to you, but that since my last I have been in a continual state of anxiety. I cannot say that the case is much mended, but as it is only related to my present situation I am endeavouring to bear up against it. I would not tell you this my love, but that it is shocking to me to think that you should at any time be unacquainted either with the blessings or the sufferings that fall to my share. The affairs are settled at length—and I have every reason to be satisfied and am so. He is everything I can wish, and I believe his regard to me to be sincere. My Father too is most kind to me and Emily is really sorry to lose me—but there is a person from whom I deserved everything, and where <u>gratitude</u> and regard I had undoubted claims—who has thought fit to embitter what should have been the best days of my life, with the most unmerited ill treatment. That kind of treatment which would make it impossible for me, was anything likely to break off the Match, to remain in my Father's house.[4]

It seems 'Great' Caroline had been vehement in expressing her antipathy towards Harbord and had perhaps advocated that Caroline break off the engagement, but this had not been well received. Caroline's naive view was that their Father's "mistaken kindness to me has been the cause of all and I am now the sacrifice, I am content to be so for I would not embitter his days" and she told Harriet,

> Nor will you think it likely after all I have endured for so many years I should forfeit all pretensions to her friendship, when no more sacrifices could be required & that because my prospects were grown brighter I should at once become mean and uninterested. I have indeed suffered most severely—her influence is now much weakened and distant civility is all I wish for or expect, <u>for my Father's sake</u> I <u>wish</u> for this. In a few weeks I hope to take my leave of her and the House she inhabits—without demeaning myself as far as to retaliate.

What Caroline had 'endured' and 'sacrificed' is unknown, but it appears the relationship between the two Carolines had never been fond. It is conceivable that Caroline felt their stepmother favoured her sisters and if this was the case then marrying Harbord and gaining control of Blickling would have been sweet revenge on 'Great' Caroline. She entreated Harriet to pretend not to know what was going on and not to alter her manner towards their stepmother as "it would answer no purpose and for my poor Father's sake we must excuse her as much as we can. I really believe she thinks herself ill used and perhaps she has been so, but then it was not by me or Mr H." She was certain Harriet would love Mr Harbord and considered herself "very fortunate, in spite of some unpleasant circumstances. We shall not be magnificent to be sure but I think we may be comfortable" and hoped to live a great deal in the Country. True to form she ended with a barb, "I gave the Duchess of B such a look the other day that I believe she felt it for she moved away."

Despite the length of the letter Caroline contrived to omit the crucial news that she and William would gain lifetime possession of Blickling within a year of their marriage. Eventually of course Harriet learned of the transaction and she responded with admirable diplomacy, "When I assure you on the present occasion that I most truly and sincerely rejoice at your prospects of happiness, that I as sincerely feel for all the unpleasant things you have to encounter till the affair is concluded" adding that she only hoped that her "Father's years should pass happily and undisturbed."[5] However she could not restrain herself from continuing,

> I think myself called upon to tell you (tho' I have received no information on the subject from you) that I am not disinterested enough to feel pleased at the present transactions. I am not ignorant that of all my Father's daughters, I am not the best entitled to complain of whatever disposal he may chuse to make of his property, I acknowledge that my conduct has left me no right to do so, and I at no time doubted your being his principal Heir but independent of the system which he always held out, had it merely been from his conduct or mine and Sophia's Marriages I never could have supposed that anything would have induced him to settle more than he could withhold, but I must own that on these occasions nothing more was required. Not however to digress from my subject, what I mean to say is this, that altho' I always expected my Father's Will would prove his preference of you, yet I was perfectly unprepared for the present event. It is not that he has settled more than I imagined he would leave, but his kindness to me lately had led me to encourage hopes that altho' nothing could prevent my being a disgrace to the Lothian Family, yet that Ld A would not in every view have cause to repent his behaving honorably to me.

Acknowledging her hopes of inheriting Blickling or of Buckingham bequeathing a significant tranche of his riches to her had been brought to an end, and pointing out that their father had two other daughters who had "never offended him" she was moved to say,

> you may perhaps think my dearest Caroline that the inviolable silence you have preserved towards me rendered this explanation unnecessary, but as you cannot suppose me to be in absolute ignorance of that which has passed, the sincerity of my own character and the unreserved habits of friendship, in which it has been my pride and comfort to live with you made me feel it indispensable to give you some slight idea of my

sentiments, when I now assure you that my friendship and anxiety for your happiness ever will continue the same. It makes me very happy to learn that your Business is likely to be concluded in a few weeks, for I can conceive nothing more uncomfortable than your situation just now.

Despite her kind words Harriet sympathised with their stepmother's grievances,

I should not have thought it necessary to mention the subject to you, but as you seem so unhappy at Lady B's behaviour to you and dwell so much on it in your letter to me, I must say it appears to me that she has some reason to think herself ill-used, Blickling and 400£ a year having been promised her on the Death of her Sons and nothing having occurred to effect a reasonable pretence for depriving her of them. You may be perfectly innocent of it, yet if she feels you to be the cause of her not being dealt fairly by, some allowance should be made for her.

What I have said calls for no answer from you.

Despite knowing full well the Countess's deep disapprobation of the marriage and its settlement, and the considerable hurt that it would cause to Harriet, Lady Caroline Hans Hobart married William Assheton Harbord at St. George's Church, Hanover Square on 4 June 1792. The *Norfolk Chronicle* noted that "immediately after the ceremony the parties set off to Richmond."

Notes

1. NRS GD40/9/201 Letter 1.
2. In 1795 Harriet Townshend married Charles, 4th Duke of Buccleugh.
3. Copyhold: tenants were given land in return for carrying out specific manorial duties or services.
4. NRS GD40/9/201 Letter 2.
5. NRS GD40/9/201.

John Hobart, 2nd Earl of Buckinghamshire.

Trivia and Tragedy

The remainder of 1792 found Harriet and William Ancram in Scotland, the newly-wedded Harbords at Gunton, Buckingham at Blickling, and the Countess and Emily dividing their time between Blickling and London. William Harbord's parents and sisters visited Blickling in a cold December which saw a flurry of inconsequential, affectionate letters fly from Buckingham to his 'Dear Baby' Emily in London. From The White Swan, Norwich he wrote,

> The ordering of a blue frock and other less important business brought me to Norwich this morning. Louisa & Catherine accompany'd me and this is wrote while they are amusing themselves at Mrs Brewsters, Mr Sealys, Mr Stephensons, Mr Nosworthy and so on. Lord and Lady Suffield remain at Blickling. They sleep over the kitchen and rejoice in the warmth. His Lordship bows down to the ground, and it is impossible, even for my old fashioned politeness, to meet his becomingly.[1]

Anxious to hear news from the continent, Buckingham fretted whenever the Post was delayed. Louis XVI had been indicted on 11 December and rumours of impending war with revolutionary France were running riot. In news from closer to home he told Emily that, "Mr Harbord's Gout is so far better that he walked yesterday to the Green House; such an attack is a very unpleasant circumstance so early in life, it indeed concerns me to think that neither he nor Caroline will ever enjoy vigorous health."[2] As the Green House lies at no great distance from the Hall, this was an indication of the seriousness of William Harbord's ailment and his remarks about Caroline suggest a young woman in delicate health. On a lighter note Buckingham reported that "The Miss Harbords are just come in wet and draggled. They condescend to recollect you. Knill writes that the Countess looks most beautifully. I must use the Lotion." It is not a surprise to find that when the Harbords visited Blickling the Countess was elsewhere.

The Harbord sisters, who addressed Emily as "My dear pony" were great friends with Emily and aware that she attracted many suitors. At one point she set her cap at Lord Cole, then a Captain of the 70th Foot, and her father enquired of her if the young man had given her any hopes. Evidently Lord Cole did not succumb to Emily's charm offensive, because Buckingham later commented "the genial climate of Italy does not appear to have warmed Lord Cole's heart for he certainly slighted your attraction." Buckingham often spent his days escorting the Miss Harbords to Norwich, where the young ladies strolled about the streets "with no other protection than their own discretion" and where there was "a delightful display of Captains." He complained that "Times are very hard, nothing is plenty but Bills, the Hens barren and no eggs for our mulled wine last Night."[3] Nothing of social importance occurred in late December except the Aylsham Assembly which because of bad weather was sparsely attended "but the Ladys had five Captains and Miss Harbords their proportion."

Other letters focused on trivial matters "Pray pray desire your mama not to be angry with me about the Cheese, it was eat with gratitude" and teasing threats, "I am to pay £15 and upwards for Schawl Drapery, but there is no mention in Mr Harvey's account of Ly Buckinghams Waistcoat. I hope to find you both in Cash for my demand will be considerable." Blickling residents were accounted for, "I saw two very little White Rabbits in the Garden and order'd the Bloody Bell not to hurt them. Bread was given by my own hand to the Silks and no Jays. The Greenhouse is in high Beauty." But there was sadness to relate, "I walked through all the Rooms to see that they were in order, and could not help dropping a Tear as I pass'd poor Bell's."[4] The faithful Mrs. Bell had died. More sombre news reached England of the execution by guillotine of King Louis XVI in Paris on 21 January 1793. Buckingham wrote, "The late dreadful events in France has given an Universal Shock to all the feelings of Humanity."

An unusual event had been witnessed from the Blickling Estate in December 1792, which Buckingham reported to Sir William Musgrave at The Royal Society. On 14 February 1793 "An account of a Meteor"[5] was read to the assembled Members :

My Park Keeper last night (the 7th) observed a sudden light nearly in the western quarter, where there immediately appeared a luminous body about the size of the horizontal Moon, its extreme elevation was about 70 degrees and it spent itself in the East about 40 degrees above the horizon. As it descended a sort of tail darted from it (his words) from whence flashes and sparks issued, he and his companion judged it to have been about 20 yards in length, thickest next the body, and ending in a point like a Bayonet. He thinks the first appearance to have been about a quarter after ten o'clock, and the duration one minute and a half. I could form no judgement of the elevation but from the angle to which the Keeper raised his arm. The night was very dark but this Meteor rendered the smallest objects visible, the Keeper who is remarkably resolute declares the appearance to have been most tremendous, his companion was very much alarmed. You must consider this relation as extracted by an ignorant Man from one still more ignorant.

The Latitude of Blickling is about six minutes short of 53 degrees.

On 12 February 1793 Lord Belmore's Divorce Petition was at long last presented to the Irish parliament with the terms fully agreed. On 8 March the first reading passed through the House where it was demanded that evidence be placed before them before a vote could be taken. Documents were duly produced to verify that

Lord and Lady Belmore had been separated for upwards of a dozen years, that Lord Belmore had successfully sued Lord Ancram for "criminal conversation"[6] with his wife, and that Lady Belmore had cohabited with Lord Ancram at a house near Calais. By this time the whole affair was a cold scandal and the Bill was sent to the Lords without amendment. It passed quietly through the House and on 19 March the divorce was finalised, releasing the couple from each other for ever. It pained Lord Belmore mightily that it cost him 4,187 Irish Pounds to bring an end to this most unhappy alliance.

As soon as they received the document Harriet and William had their marriage settlement, stating that Harriet's marriage to Lord Belmore was legally over, witnessed by John Kipling and signed on 13 April. Three days later they sealed their long and wildly dramatic courtship with their marriage at Marylebone Church. Sir Richard Heron, her friend and advisor gave Harriet away and, according to Henry Hobart, both he and Caroline, Countess of Buckinghamshire were present, but of her father there was no mention. Although Buckingham had sent words of affection and considerable financial support to his beloved eldest child during the troublesome years since the collapse of her catastrophic marriage to Belmore, Buckingham's disappointment apparently still ran deep. Though at some point after the wedding, with Harriet safely married to a man from a respected and long established Scottish family, Buckingham and his new son-in-law met. This meeting must have been an interesting occasion for both parties, and may be when Buckingham was introduced to his first, albeit illegitimate, grandson, William Drury Kerr.

During the spring of 1793 Buckingham wrote affectionately to Harriet, his letters featuring details of the on-going war with France and news from Prussia, mixed with updates on friends who had ailments or who had died. On 24 May he related a close encounter with the forgetful monarch whilst strolling in London,

> My quiet walk is little liable to occurrence, but yesterday, for the first time since taking leave of St James, I found myself very near his Majesty. My Bow savoured of the respectful deference of an Old Courtier, he view'd me with sternness and after important irresolution, put two Royal fingers to the point of his hat. It has often been said that tho a King creates a Lord, he cannot make a Gentleman. He has not tried the experiment upon himself. The disgrace was, in the instance, not mine, but his.[7]

He told of a less than melodic evening spent at Lady Downe's Catch. "Mrs Bates sang, but alas! invited Miss Rushout to join her, which preserved her dignity, but ruined the Glee" and sent his "Love to his Lordship" as he had rapidly developed an affection for her husband. In June, father and daughter corresponded over the Ancram family's Newbattle Seal which Buckingham was assisting Harriet to have copied at the Antiquarian Society, "You will oblige me in letting me have as accurate an impression as you can take, sending it carefully packed in your letter between two pieces of card." He also mentioned London social life including an event thrown by 'Great' Caroline,

> The Countess of Buckingham had a brilliant Assembly last night, the Ladys very much dressed and the gentlemen fashionably undressed. You could easily distinguish them from the Groom of the Chamber. There was much beauty at Market, but, no bidders stepping forward, no business was done.

> The Marblehill party commences upon the 16th, your friend Williams is becoming very Deaf, which as the interesting part of his conversation is his making ingenious observations upon what falls from duller men than himself, seriously affects our society, as we have the Dark Shades without any relief, the dough without the yeast.[8]

Later in June he told Harriet, "The impressions of the Seal have been much admired by one Virtuoso, and cannot but be apprehended by more as they usually follow like Wild Geese in the air." His opinion of Charles Fox, a defender of the French Revolution who believed that Britain's involvement in war with France was a grave mistake, was unequivocal, "He should retire for ever from Publick business and no longer labor the destruction of his Country. It is supposed that he will make a speech this day in Parliament calculated to forecast every sort of evil spirit and by every specious argument to elaborate discontent. May their own Gods damn him and his abettors." Adhering to his life-long habit Buckingham ended, "Yet, not to close my letter with a curse, may my Gods bless you and yours." He signed off these letters with "believe me, with all affection" and "All our loves to Ld Ancram."

It may be that the Countess succeeded in impressing upon her husband the unfairness of Caroline and William Harbord's marriage settlement which so strongly favoured the couple at the expense of his wife, or that he recovered from a temporary loss of perspective, but whatever the reason, Buckingham had a new Will drawn up and signed on 16 July. His twin objectives were to assuage the Countess Caroline's concerns for her own future should he die, and to compensate and reward Harriet with a more generous bequest now that she was free of Belmore and respectably married to the relatively impoverished Ancram.

Buckingham's half-brother George Hobart, who may have expected to be next in line to inherit the Blickling Estate, was overlooked, although he would automatically take the title 3rd Earl of Buckinghamshire following his brother's demise. This may be in part because Buckingham believed George and Albinia's continued devotion to gambling was too much of a risk for the future of his beloved Blickling Mansion House.

He wrote to Emily from Marble Hill on 20 July, "We visited your Grandmama yesterday, she is tolerably well. My present plan is to be at Blickling on Weds evening, but should you be disappointed of the ecstasy of seeing me, Gt Caroline is requested to order four Horses for my chaise. The Thames is nearly covered with weeds, and our Garden is the only ground which still preserves a shade of green." He rounded off with news about their pets, "Puck is become more reserved than ever and appears but with the Gardiner. My Affects compts to G: Caroline and respects to Scrub."[9]

In August Buckingham's sister wrote from Yorkshire regretting that she could not give a more favourable account of herself or of Hotham, as they were both now invalids. Dorothy reported that Charles complained that the failure of his limbs was increasing which in turn lowered his spirits, and this caused Buckingham to fret over his dear old friend's unhappiness.

Towards mid-August 1793 Buckingham himself began to feel unwell but no-one was unduly worried as it seemed as though he had a mild, common illness. Caroline Harbord had thought her father "rather dejected and shrunk"[10] on his return to Norfolk earlier in the summer, but had very soon remarked that Blickling had worked its magic and that he "seemed to recover and was in good spirits and good looks." Buckingham celebrated his seventieth birthday on August 17 1793 with a fine dinner at Blickling which was marred by his being "very far from well all night and it was quite an exertion to dine in company" but he returned to good health later in the month and was entertained by friends at Hoveton and in Norwich. Self medicating his digestive ailments with castor oil, Buckingham continued to enjoy a lively social life, but on Saturday 31 August after "dining heartily with Charles Townshend[11] & co" he returned to Blickling feeling very unwell indeed. A trusted physician was sent for who stayed with him until Monday morning. The doctor then departed, declaring that "he saw no danger and would return the next day," but as the discomfort returned and grew steadily worse the worried Countess called not one but two physicians to attend him.

The prediction of the fair lady in Petersburg that the 2nd Earl would live to be very old, but that "it would not be worth his trouble, as he would be a hypochondriac and gouty," was in part accurate. Buckingham had now lived for three score years and ten, when he fell even slightly ill would (according to his wife) declare himself to be at death's door, and he had for years occasionally suffered from gout. Buckingham felt much recovered on Monday and Caroline noted he "looked uncommonly well, and seemed to have no pain, but he had a Hiccup and a stoppage in his stomach." Towards evening his distress increased and "the physicians spoke doubtfully indeed but with good hopes." As a purgative, small doses of powdered rhubarb[12] were administered but during Tuesday afternoon everything changed very much for the worse. The physicians disclosed that "the mortification had begun" and Caroline Harbord went to take what she feared might be a last look at her father. "He was almost insensible, did not know me, and desired he might be suffered to rest. From that time he suffered little, was chiefly asleep, but uniformly calm, composed and firm to a very uncommon degree." Henry Hobart and Emily were then at Blickling and only too aware of the unfolding scene. Buckingham's devoted wife did everything she could and "showed him every attention possible" and he also had the constant presence of his faithful valet Wodehouse whose "attention and anxiety were beyond everything, above a servant."[13] But despite their combined ministrations and loving care, at half past eleven on the evening of Tuesday 3 September 1793, Lord John Hobart, 2nd Earl of Buckinghamshire, sometime Ambassador Extraordinaire and Plenipotentiary to Russia, former Viceroy of Ireland, husband to two Countesses and father of four daughters, died at his beloved Blickling Hall.

Notes

1. NRO MC 3/292.
2. Ibid.
3. Ibid.
4. Ibid.
5. The Royal Society Library, L&P/10/40, with thanks to Rupert Baker.
6. A euphemism for sexual intercourse.
7. NRS GD40/9/204.
8. Ibid.
9. NRO MC3/285 Letter 109.
10. NRS GD40/9/201.
11. Charles Townshend, 27, had been MP for Yarmouth for just two days when murdered by his brother Rev Lord Frederick during a coach trip in 1796. Although pronounced insane and sent to Hadham Place Asylum, Frederick maintained his position as Rector at Stiffkey, Norfolk from 1792-1836.
12. In late c18th England 'Rhubarb mania' led doctors to prescribe powdered rhubarb, sometimes mixed with honey or wine to disguise its bitter taste.
13. Ibid.

Consequences

Lady Caroline, thenceforth known as the Dowager Countess of Buckingham, was inconsolable at the sudden loss of her husband and in her anguish locked herself away in Harriet's apartment for almost a fortnight, allowing no-one near except her daughter.

Emily, anticipating the likely outcome of her father's illness, had considerably warned Lord Ancram of the impending calamity and Caroline Harbord sent the sad confirmation to Scotland directly after Buckingham's death, both sisters imploring him to break the news to Harriet, who was four months pregnant, as gently as possible. They also kept Sophie informed of the melancholy event. Caroline Harbord sent a lengthy letter to Harriet minutely detailing their father's last days of illness and told her that although she had visited Blickling twice since his death "to see Lady B and Emily, perhaps they have written to you, but I know but little of what they do"[1] she had been refused an audience with them. In the same letter she claimed to have no knowledge of what was in their father's Will except that "he desired Wodehouse might have £200" and hoped Harriet had not heard of "the terrible event suddenly, and that your health will not suffer." She wrote that their Father "had desired to be buried <u>behind the cottage</u>" but as no proper place could be made in time that "it will be better to lay him by our poor Mother for the present." In a post-script she added "Mr H Hobart is at Blickling, and I know not what could have been done without him."

It was extremely fortunate that Henry Hobart was on hand because he took it upon himself to deal with his half-brother's funeral arrangements and to keep Harriet, of whom he was immensely fond, abreast of developments. On 6 September he informed her that the Will was to be opened on the following day, after the arrival of Mr Kipling the lawyer. Henry explained he thought it best that he stay on at Blickling because his elder brother had declined to be present. He did not elaborate upon George's absence, but he hoped that "one or both the Valletorts will come down, or else only the Harbords and myself will be present, for the dear Countess declares she will not leave her apartment (which is the one called yours) until she goes away for London." Henry, having discovered that the executors were Thomas Conolly (in Ireland), Sir Richard Heron (in Brighton), Mr Kipling (at Overstone[2]) and Mr Knill (at Weymouth), ventured that,

> with Lady Buckingham's approbation to give more explicit orders for the
> funeral though not absolute ones, so much mourning and so many things
> required which are not so expeditiously procured in the country as in
> London, the Burial cannot take place before next Friday or Saturday; your
> good parent is to lay in a brickgrave in Blickling Church Chancel until the

mausoleum is erected in the great wood here which we understand he has ordered in his Will to be erected there.[3]

Henry shared the distressing news that Lady Buckingham was so agitated that she could not sleep for thinking of her beloved husband's death, believing that "every exertion was not made for his recovery." Henry thought Buckingham had had "gravel to vex him in the kidnies, gout in the stomach and inflammation in the bowels; this last illness has been very prevalent in Norfolk and fatal in many families." He judged that Emily was "pretty well and in tolerable spirits," that Caroline Harbord was very low and far from being well at Gunton, and that he himself could not afford to be indisposed because he had so much writing to do and attention to so many concerns to deal with. The next morning he added a tender post-script, "This charming venerable place is in very great beauty, your Father said with pleasure last week he never saw it look better. I wish from my soul Lord and Lady Ancram were with us here. Lady Buckingham without doubt stays here till after the Funeral, how long myself I cannot possibly say, but shall with great regret leave this place which as it were has long been a sort of home to your ever sincere and most affectionate uncle, H. Hobart."

On 11 September, eight days after the loss of her husband, Caroline found the strength to write to Harriet, whom she had supported so faithfully throughout her years of exile,

> The first moment I have been able to hold a pen I am sat down to write to you some of the horrid particulars of your Father's illness & death. You have known probably that for some time passed he has had Gouty attacks in his stomach & also that he most imprudently too often took castor oil & other Physick without proper care. The gout had certainly being flying about him lately—one day it appeared in his leg—which instead of encouraging he walked about with & it departed. Twice in the last week before the fatal attack he had the pain in his stomach at night & used Hot Brandy and Flannels. On the fatal Saturday he took his castor oil (unknown to me) and he set out to dine at Norwich—he appeared very well when he set off—but returned in the greatest agonies of pain in his stomach and said he thought himself dying but he often made that observation when he was ill. He continued very bad all Saturday night, at four o'clock in the morning at his request I sent to Norwich for the Physician he had last year in the same complaint. When he came he made slight of his illness, but that night & the next day, that night, Sunday, by taking Laudanum he slept very composedly & in the morning I made his breakfast & thought him partly well. He got up and came into the Study and was tolerably well only had some ugly Hiccups which I did not like but the Physician said it was only wind after the pain and weakness, his castor oil having operated 5 times on the Saturday before his illness. Towards evening on Monday his hiccups returned & this alarmed me dreadfully

and I sent again for the Physician who did not like the Symptoms.[4]

She added a post-script, "Miss Harbords now set out for Scotland to visit Lady Caroline which is a great pleasure to them." Caroline Harbord had retreated to her husband's regimental base, probably in order to avoid the Countess, whose next letter to Harriet describes her terrible grief,

> I was not hardly sensible. To convince you of it I went down stairs early the next morning to see his Body and never shall forget the sight as long as I live—to have seen him Saturday morn perfectly well—dead & laid out Wednesday morning think how shocking—it almost deprived me of reason—as from the circumstance of being here I know it must be some time before the Funeral I determined to stay till it was over—my presence would preserve decency and I thought I owed him that respect not to leave his Body. The being here has cost me much and my horrors of mind must continue while in this wretched Mansion.

Unsavoury details reveal reasons for her continuing abhorrence of William and Caroline,

> I sent to Ly C: Harbord on his first being ill and she was frequently here— but was more composed than I liked—Mr H I fancy thought of <u>his</u> gains and the sight of him was horrible to me. This <u>you</u> will conceive neither <u>He</u> nor <u>She</u> has ever offered me to stay here until I was better able to go away but I found had asked Emily <u>when</u> I went. By this cruel stroke I am deprived of all my Houses & places but I mean when the last horrible scene is closed to go to Bond Street till I can get a Town House and then I shall go some where into the country for my Health. You are very kind in offering to come but at present we should only make each other worse.

Lord Valletort had arrived but she had not seen him, and she was informed that the Will was to be opened at Blickling before the funeral took place. Promising that she would send "the earliest intelligence of the contents of it" she offered Harriet words of comfort, "One thing I must say—that your Father mentioned you to me when He thought himself dying, in a most kind and affectionate manner, which must be a satisfaction to you to know."

The Countess had at some point forced herself to communicate with the Harbords on a subject close to her heart, that of Buckingham's final resting place, "He desired to be buried in the Park in the Wood behind my Cottage—this I mentioned to the Harbords and they promised it should be done—in the mean while He is to lay under the communion table near your Mother & my children & they are to be removed with Him to the new Vault." Promising to write again once settled into a new London house she expressed her torment,

> I think I must be better any where but here—the regret and misery of

every body is great indeed. The Person who succeeds him had but a poor chance of being beloved for he was disliked by every body before and now to come in the place of so generous a benefactor to all the poor—and with the idea he turns Emily and I out. He will be detestable. I do not mean to see him but when my duty ends to your Father shall pack off - but He shall not have the pleasure of knowing it till I am gone. God bless you and believe me your most affct., Caroline Hobart[5]

As news of Buckingham's demise spread, letters flew to Emily from, amongst others, her aunt Anne Conolly, "I am in great anxiety for your poor Mama and in no less for you who have lost a father that was so Fond of you and the being so suddenly deprived of him must add to the Shock. I came to London to be nearer intelligence and to be in the way in case she comes to town, as I imagine she will. Your dear Mama knows my heart so well, she must be sure of my feelings for her now, and on every occasion."[6] Sophie, Lady Valletort wrote, "The melancholy event that has just happened has hurt me very much indeed and the idea that I shall never see my beloved Father any more is very shocking. Pray keep your spirits up my Dearest Emily. Pray give my kind love to Mama and tell her how much I join with her in her sorrow."[7]

In the notes Henry Hobart left entitled 'Family Collection' he wrote that his half-brother "had been very much indisposed for some days but in no apparent danger till the last instant" and letters written by both Carolines provided intimate details of Buckingham's illness and demise. Regardless of the facts, the ubiquitous Horace Walpole, although over one hundred and seventy miles away at the time, decided that the cause of Buckingham's death had been a heart attack. He claimed, "An account is come of the sudden death of Lord Buckinghamshire: he had the gout in his foot, dipped it in cold water, and killed himself; nobody can play such tricks with impunity but I."[8] It would be fair to suggest that these were not the remarks of a man in mourning.

In fact the only effective treatment for gout[9] was to use ice or very cold water to alleviate the excruciating pain the condition often caused. Walpole was also wildly off-kilter in his stated belief that "gout prevents other illnesses and prolongs life. Could I cure that gout, should I not have a fever, palsy, or an apoplexy?" In a final jibe Walpole noted waspishly that Buckingham's death had turned George Hobart into an Earl and his wife "Mrs. Hobart now a Countess with a coronet I believe a little gilt: Norfolk coronets scarce pay for the fashion."

Sir Richard Heron sent his deepest condolences to Harriet, lamenting that "the timing of the event has taken place before the return of Lord Buckingham's affection for you had taken full effect." As a friend and executor Heron was aware that since their reconciliation Buckingham had rewritten his Will to give Harriet a handsome trust fund for her sole use plus a generous allowance for her illegitimate son, William. But he was also convinced that had Buckingham lived longer he

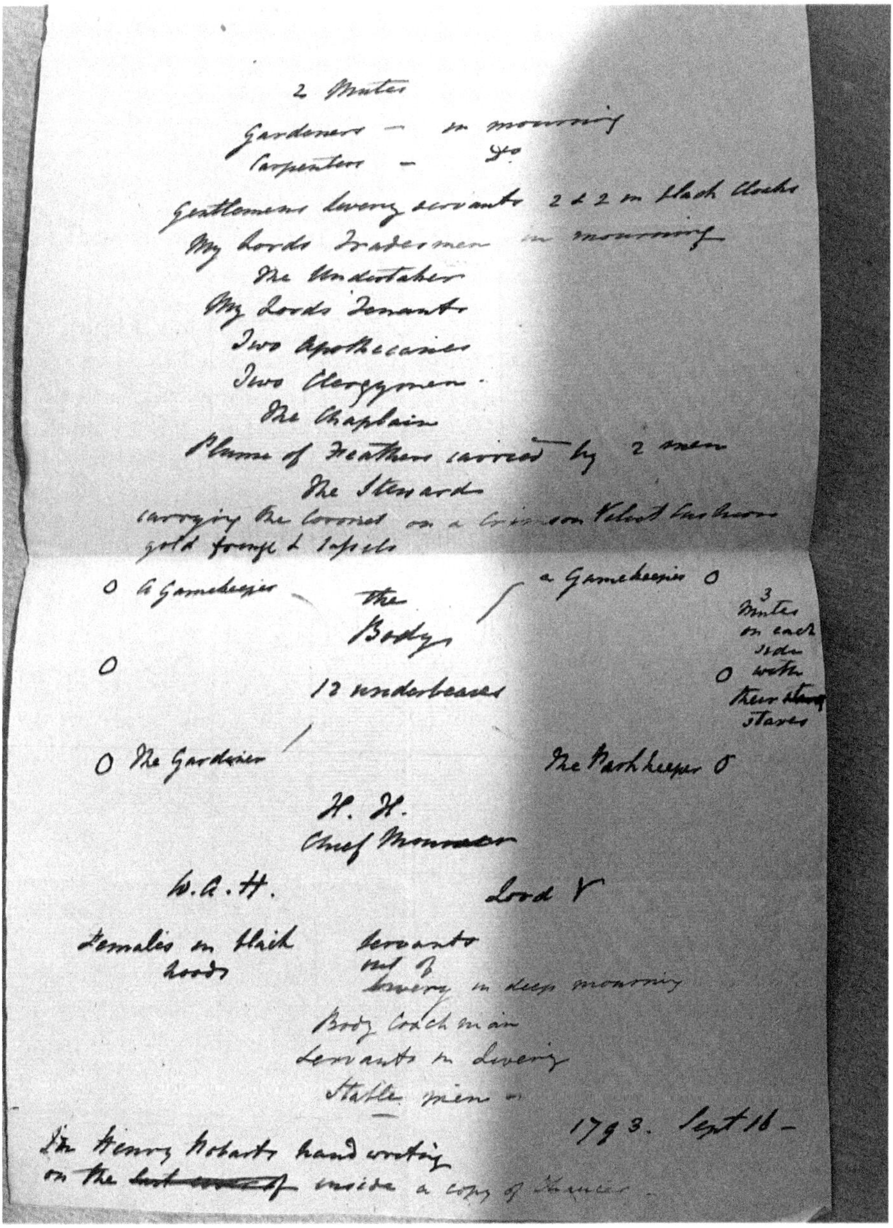

The plan for the funeral procession.

would have done much more to help his dear eldest daughter. Lord Ancram told Heron, "As we had heard of his illness yesterday Lady Ancram was in some measure prepared for the Shock, and although her spirits are at present in a state of dreadful agitation, yet as we used the precaution to have her blooded yesterday, I am not apprehensive that her health will be materially affected." On 20 September Heron wrote again to enquire after Lady Harriet's health, "I know how sincerely she loved her father, and that, all consideration of interest apart, her Ladyship is foremost in the group who mourn over his loss" and repeated his firm belief to Lord Ancram that "more favourable dispositions would most probably have taken place, if his Lordship had not been carried off so suddenly, yet Time & Chance happeneth to all, and in Time all may be well."

Henry Hobart almost single handedly arranged his uncle's funeral which took place at noon on 16 September. Large crowds of spectators watched a procession move slowly from the bottom of the great staircase in Blickling Hall, through the stone court and the great gates over the stone bridge, along the gravel walk in the courtyard and "up the Church hill into the church." At the head of the procession were two mules, followed by Labourers, Gardeners, Gentlemen's Livery Servants two by two (all in black cloaks), Tradesmen, the Undertaker, the late Earl's Servants, two Apothecaries, two Clergymen, the Chaplain, a Plume of Feathers carried by two men, and the Land Steward bearing a Coronet on a crimson velvet cushion with a gold fringe and tassels. These were followed by twelve parishioners each of whom carried silver plate and coronets.

Next, Buckingham's body was carried by twelve bearers in a crimson velvet coffin ornamented with an inscription and the corners of a black velvet pall were held by the Head Gardener, the Park Keeper and two Game Keepers. Three mutes[10] with their staves walked on each side of the coffin.

As Chief Mourner, Henry Hobart walked behind the coffin shadowed by William Assheton Harbord to his left and Richard, Lord Valletort to his right. In his later sketch of the event Henry noted that next came "Females in black hoods" and though he did not identify them they would have included the Dowager Countess Caroline, Emily Hobart, Caroline Harbord and Sophie, Lady Valletort. Male and female servants out of livery and dressed in deep mourning followed behind them. Lastly, liveried servants walked two by two, with the body Coachman and stablemen bringing up the rear.

Inside the Church the pews and pulpit were "hung with black cloth with escutcheons thereon" and the burial service was read by the Reverend Mr Thomlinson. Buckingham's coffin was solemnly deposited in a brick grave in the chancel alongside the remains of Lady Mary Anne and little Lady Julia. In an adjoining grave lay the remains of his sons Lord John and Lord Henry Hobart (George, the third born Lord Hobart, died and was buried in Ireland.)

After the funeral, which mightily tried her nerves and fortitude, not least because she was obliged to be in the company of William and Caroline Harbord, the thirty-eight year old Dowager Countess Caroline immediately left Blickling to seek solace in the company of her sisters in London, taking Emily with her. Frances, Lady Howe later reported that the Dowager Countess was "but indifferent" but that her family and friends hoped that after the first shock was over Lady Buckingham's health and spirits would gradually mend.

Henry Hobart wrote of the funeral that, "The whole was conducted with great decency under the direction, tho' I should not notice it, of H.H." He also noted with interest that in the old Hobart family vault "the coffins mostly stand up." Henry stayed on at Blickling for a further six weeks in order to act as Agent for the Executors of Buckingham's Will, namely Thomas Conolly, Sir Richard Heron, John Kipling and John Knill, which was duly recognised on 1st October 1793.

℘The Will℘

In her marriage settlement Caroline Harbord had already been given a Life Interest in the Blickling Estate which gave her the inviolable right to live there for the remainder of her life, and the same applied to William Harbord. Should the couple produce no heirs, as was widely predicted due to their ill health, Blickling would pass next to a son of Harriet, Sophie or Emily, in that order. In her father's Will, Caroline was also bequeathed all of Blickling's Household stuff, the stock of Deer in Blickling Park and a Yellow Diamond ring.

Generous provision was made for Harriet by way of income from her father's estates in Devon, Cornwall and Lincolnshire, wrapped in a trust fund for her sole use and benefit.[11] His aim was to protect Harriet's independence and the Will specified that her money should be "not subject to intermeddling by William Earl of Ancram or of any future husband in any manner or in any wise howsoever or upon any account whatsoever"[12] thus iron cladding her financial future interests from any malicious forces. Following Harriet's experience during her separation from Armar Lowry Corry it is perhaps understandable that Buckingham couched this bequest in those terms, even though he had grown fond of Ancram. He made a generous investment of £1,500 for his illegitimate grandson William to be maintained and educated until he reached twenty one. Harriet was bequeathed the Emerald Ring which had belonged to the 1st Earl and "my Snuff Box with the picture of his late Majesty King William."

Sophie and Lord Valletort were provided for by "Hereditaments and Premises in the County of Norfolk and City and Country of Norwich" and Emily was placed under the care and guardianship of her mother until she reached her majority.

George Hobart, now titled 3rd Earl of Buckinghamshire, was given £1,000 and "the right of the Church of Beerferris in the County of Devon" together with funding for his nephew Henry, Henry's son, to be educated as a Minister for the

Church and to be presented with said Church "upon the first vacancy thereof that shall happen after my decease." Henry Hobart was forgiven and released from a debt of £500 and all interest due at the time of Buckingham's demise.

His brother-in-law Thomas Conolly was charged with selling the Bond Street house and to "get the best price and translate it into Ready Money." The executors were bequeathed the "Brilliant Diamond Ring which was given to me by her Imperial Majesty the Empress of all the Russia's when I had the honor to be his Majesty's Ambassador Extraordinary and Minister Plenipotentiary to the Court of Petersburgh."

A further direction to the Executors concerned the Library to which he allotted £2,500 to buy the collection outright so that it could remain intact at Blickling in perpetuity. He stipulated that should that transaction not take place, the money should be used to purchase other books to replace those left by Sir Richard Ellys, stating that "such books be of the most general use and as well as for Information as Entertainment and that no high prices to be paid for such books as derive particular Merit only from being scarce or finely bound."[13]

In other bequests he left a yearly sum of "£30 to Leonora Hobart, Spinster Daughter of my said brother Henry Hobart," £100 yearly to John Kipling; £100 to "Robert Copeland my Land Steward in case he shall be in my service at the time of my decease: and £50 yearly to Major Robert Compton and one thousand pounds when he has the opportunity of purchasing a Commission of Lieutenant Colonel in his Majesty's army." A condition was that if or when that happened the £50 yearly would cease.

As specified in Lady Suffolk's Will, and following her nephew's death without male issue, Marble Hill passed to Henrietta Hotham, the 'Mrs. Harriet' of whom Buckingham had been so very fond. She rented out Marble Hill itself and moved into Spencer Grove, or Little Marble Hill as it was then known, the smaller of the houses on the estate. She and her maid Betty lived there contentedly for many years with their collections of fine china.

❧Caroline, Dowager Countess—the Executor's Quandary ❧

In Buckingham's Will the Dowager Countess Caroline was bequeathed all his Copyhold lands in the Manor of Isleworth Syon in the County of Middlesex and lands in the Parishes of Isleworth and Twickenham. (Their marriage settlement also provided her with £8,000, paid immediately after his demise.) In his Will she was awarded an annuity of £1,200 (this had also been specified within the Harbord's marriage settlement) together with a further £300 per annum "so long as she shall continue my widow." He bequeathed all his other rings and "also give to my said Wife such parts of Plate whereof I shall die possessed of as she shall chuse not exceeding one thousand ounces for her own use and benefit." He also left her "all the Furniture of every kind which shall belong to her own Room and her

Servants Room in my House in London."

The Harbord's marriage settlement decreed that the Countess would only have the right to use and occupation of Blickling after the demise of both William and Caroline Harbord, but his Will instructed that the Countess would be permitted to live at Blickling rent free for her lifetime, with the proviso she remained unmarried. To add to the confusion he also gave and bequeathed to his widow the use, enjoyment and occupation of "my Mansion house at Hunworth" together with "all the household Goods and Furniture Linen and China."

John Kipling was appointed Executor to both documents but he was unable in law to convert Buckingham's initial instruction within the Harbord's marriage settlement into the second instruction in his Will, which protected 'Great' Caroline's right to live at Blickling.

It is hard to fathom why Buckingham would even remotely consider depriving his adored wife of her home, a home they had shared in joy and in grief and together lavished their attentions upon. It may be that he was duped or manipulated by William Harbord who was determined to obtain Blickling for himself, and this, combined with the threat of a claim to the Estate by Belmore, provoked this very uncharacteristic overreaction. Whatever the reason, the end result of the draconian clause was that following his demise William and Caroline Harbord took possession of Blickling and the Dowager Countess Caroline left Norfolk grief-stricken and distraught.

William Assheton Harbord by/after Karl Anton Hickel.

Caroline Lady Hobart by/after Karl Anton Hickel.

Notes

1. NRS GD40/9/201.
2. Lord Brownlow transferred the Drury's house to him in 1791.
3. NRS GD40/9/207.
4. NRS GD40/9/208.
5. NRS GD40/9/208/1.
6. NRO MC3/292 Vol. III, Letter 2.
7. Ibid. Letter 3.
8. *The Letters of Horace Walpole: Earl of Orford*, Volume 9, p.410 Letter to Lady Ossory dated 6 September 1793.
9. An unwanted ramification of the realignments of alliances between the countries of Europe had directly affected British drinkers in a most unforeseen way. England's on-and-off enmity with France meant that French wines were often scarce in England. Instead, the "Port Wine Treaty" of 1703, which had cemented England's military friendship and favourable terms with Portugal, resulted in vast quantities of Port being quaffed with a consequent epidemic of gout amongst the English nobility in particular. This was because the drink was laced with lead acetate in order to sweeten it. Chronic lead exposure can cause depression, headaches, aggression and memory loss but even if Buckingham did not have those symptoms he certainly suffered a great deal of pain. In 1683 an indication of how painful a condition it can be was vividly described by the famous physician Thomas Sydenham in his Treatise on Gout, *"The patient goes to bed and sleeps quietly until about two in the morning when he is awakened by a pain which usually seizes the great toe, but sometimes the heel, the calf of the leg or the ankle. The pain resembles that of a dislocated bone and this is immediately succeeded by a chillness, shivering and a slight fever. The pain which is mild in the beginning grows gradually more violent every hour. So exquisitely painful as not to endure the weight of the clothes nor the shaking of the room from a person walking briskly therein."*
10. The mutes stood vigil outside the door of the deceased, then accompanied the coffin, wearing dark clothes, looking solemn and carrying a long stick or wand covered in black crepe.
11. Harriet's funding came from profits made on the executor's investments of £5,000 in public stocks and income from estates in Devon, Cornwall and Lincolnshire.
12. National Archives PROB 11/1237/175.
13. It took the Executors until 1802 to secure the deal which, thankfully for posterity, kept virtually all the unique collection at Blickling.

Mozarts's Piano Concerto No. 27 in B-Flat Major, Op.17,,K.595: II.Larghetto.

As with the opening Haydn piece, this is not mentioned in the text, but sums up beautifully the kind of music Buckingham was familiar with. Again, it is light, yet soft and reflective, indicative of a man in his later years contemplating his life.

Auctor Preciosa Facit

In the months following Buckingham's death Caroline and William Harbord kept their word to the Dowager Countess and put their minds towards creating a mausoleum which would reflect Buckingham's standing in the world and by association, their own, because their plan was also to be interred within it when the time came. They took inspiration from Giovanni Piranesi's print of the tomb of Cestius in Rome that Buckingham had brought home from his Grand Tour. Familiarity with Buckingham's sense of the absurd makes it easy to imagine that he teased his family about erecting such a grand monument to himself and may be a clue to where the idea originated. His widow had made no mention of a pyramid, only requesting that a 'vault' should be built to house her husband, their sons, Mary Anne, and eventually the Dowager Countess herself. His Will did not leave any burial instructions at all, but Buckingham had made it known to his wife that he desired to lie close to Lady's Cottage, that singularly peaceful place where the couple had shared their most private and contemplative times.

The appeal of a pyramidical[1] structure for William Harbord lay in the Masonic symbolism inherent in the shape itself. The Colonel was a Freemason, as were both George and Henry Hobart. Buckingham himself is not listed as a member, which could be thought an unexpected omission in one so naturally clubbable, but it is also the case that the records during this era are not complete.

Once the idea had taken root an architect was sought and there was nobody more desirable for the task than Joseph Bonomi[2], an Italian whose style was "modernised Roman" and who was usefully, together with most successful architects of the era, a Mason. Having accepted the commission to design the mausoleum, by February 1794 Bonomi had reduced his original estimate for the building from £2,500 to £1,700 "not including the painted windows, nor my Commission and drawings."[3] He had done this not by "lessening the building but by employing only Mr Wood." Henry Wood, a builder based in London, had been recommended by William Harbord, partly because Wood had previously undertaken work at Gunton Hall and was therefore familiar with employing local, cheaper, workmen than those in London.

In May, Bonomi wrote from his offices in Great Titchfield Street to Caroline Harbord. She had taken charge of the correspondence over the enterprise, largely because her husband was busy with his duties as a Colonel in the Norfolk Light Dragoons, a regiment stationed at Hamilton Barracks in Edinburgh. The couple spent much of their time there during the construction of the building, which in retrospect they may have come to regret. Bonomi had again managed to reduce the costs, this time down to £1,250, the main alteration being that the foundations would now be eighteen inches in depth rather than the original recommendation of between six and seven feet deep. This structural change meant the building would be a further five feet wide with the interior chapel 24 feet in diameter instead of 21, which Bonomi thought would make it more handsome. He ordered the brickworks at Blickling to create the moulds, which eventually produced 171,000 plain bricks and 19,000 bevelled. After further planning, additions, compromises and negotiations, in June Messrs Bonomi and Wood signed a contract in which they undertook to "erect in Blickling Park for the Right Honourable Lady Caroline Harbord a Pyramidical Monument forty feet square and high, with a circular Chapel within, twenty four feet diameter. All this to be done for the sum of eighteen hundred and fifty pounds." Fees would be paid in three stages, the first as soon as the Building was raised to the height of the inpost or the springing of the Arches, the second as soon as the brick-works of the Pyramid were in place, and the final payment would be settled when the building was complete.

For a year the plan progressed well and the Sepulchral Chapel, as it was known, began to take shape. In August 1795 Bonomi wrote to Caroline Harbord regarding a misunderstanding about the number of recesses within the Chapel and how many sarcophagi they could each contain. He explained to her that, "The centre niche opposite the door can not contain but one—the two recesses at each side can contain two large ones, or more in each, because those two recesses are considerably deeper, than the centre one."[4] He begged her to let him know her wishes in this regard, and although there is no surviving letter in reply, it may be assumed that she simply instructed Bonomi to fill in the recesses so that each recess contained space for only one sarcophagus. Mr Wood confidently informed her, "that the building will be completely finished this autumn" but this prediction proved to be far from accurate.

By January 1796 Bonomi belatedly realised how misguided he had been in putting his trust in Henry Wood despite the fact he had been engaged on William Harbord's recommendation. Upon enquiring of Blickling's Land Steward Robert Copeland "whether the iron cast door and sashes are up, whether the marble pavement is laid, and whether the veined marble sarcophagus is placed within the niche opposite the door, where the remains of the Late Lord are to be deposited" he was informed that none of these tasks had been completed. After eliciting no response whatsoever from Wood about the cause of the delay, Bonomi took the unusual step of clandestinely inspecting the shop in Sloane Square where the marble was supposed to be transformed into items for the Chapel. Wood had categorically told Bonomi that the sarcophagus was "already finished and sent" but having discovered Wood to be "not quite so true as the Gospel" Bonomi felt compelled to go to London and see for himself. He wrote to Caroline Harbord "I will next Saturday go to his shop and without any previous hint I shall surprise him, reprimand him, and inform him of your Ladyship's anxiety." The timing of Bonomi's visit was fortuitous as Henry Wood was not in the shop and therefore unable to fob him off with elaborate excuses. Instead Bonomi talked to one of Wood's sons who, innocent of his father's duplicity, showed him the exact state of progress. This did not take long because with the exception of "a part of the Pavement, the arms half and badly done, and only part of the Sarcophagus" nothing else had been accomplished. Bonomi apologised to Caroline Harbord for employing Wood and expressed sadness and regret that both he and Colonel Harbord had been deceived by him.

From this point onwards the issue of bills and payment took centre stage and Bonomi found himself in the nightmarish position of go-between. He begged Caroline Harbord not to pay any of Woods' bills until he had scrutinised them, and even then to send the money to him first. "From all these transactions I hope that your Ladyship will clearly see that the fault entirely lays on Mr Wood, and the only thing I dislike is, that I am forced to expand upon this disagreeable subject." A full eighteen months later Bonomi was still grappling with the finances and unfortunately for him the sly and elusive Wood continued to be problematic for many months more. It is therefore not until late 1797 that the building neared completion, but the wrangling over bills continued well into 1798. It is sobering to learn that the Tomb of Cestius, two thirds larger in scale and built circa 12 B.C., was completed in 330 days.

Robert Thornberry, acting for Caroline Harbord, consulted the Bishop of Norwich to enquire whether consecration could take place after the body was moved into

The Sepulchral Chapel, or Mausoleum, August 2019.

the Chapel, but the Bishop would not sanction the removal from hallowed ground to unhallowed ground under any circumstance "or let sin remain." Thornberry's advice was that "everything should be done with decency and propriety"and that removal without consecration would occasion much clamour amongst the Clergy and would place the Bishop in "an unpleasant situation." Towards the end of September, when Wood was still making minor adjustments, Thornberry informed Caroline Harbord, "I hope in this next month there will be a total end of this unpleasant business." The enterprise which had started with such promise and good intentions, was horribly soured by the petty and entirely unnecessary obfuscations of Henry Wood.

On 25 September 1797 a Petition was presented to Charles, Bishop of Norwich stating that Sir William and Lady Caroline Harbord, together with the Earl and Countess of Ancram, renounced and set apart the parcel of land on which the Sepulchral Chapel stood and requested that the Bishop "devote dedicate and consecrate" it as a place for burial and interment. The Harbords as current occupiers of Blickling and the Ancrams as next in line to inherit therefore relinquished their interests in the site of the Chapel.

The Consecration of the site took place under dark grey skies on Wednesday 18 October 1797. As instructed by Caroline, who was then in Scotland with Col. Harbord, Robert Thornberry and Robert Copeland between them contrived to keep the occasion as low key as possible. The Bishop, the Chancellor and their

Officers arrived at Blickling just before eleven o'clock and then walked in a rain shower to the Church. The rain grew steadily heavier which kept the curious away so there were only thirty people in all at the Church Service. Afterwards the chief participants took carriages to the scene of the consecration but the worsening weather meant that many of those in the Church who had intended to witness the ceremony did not even attempt the journey. Erected at the end of a mile long grassy avenue stood the magnificent Sepulchral Chapel. Flanked by Silver Fir trees it was clad in a pure white dolomite limestone hewn from a mine near Roche Abbey in West Yorkshire, giving it a most striking and dramatic effect. The site was chosen so that the pyramid could be seen from the south end of the serpentine lake Buckingham had so lovingly created.

Inscription on the mausoleum, August 2019.

Built atop the highest point on the estate amongst the glorious ancient trees of the Great Wood, and with Lady's Cottage nestled nearby, it reaches forty-five feet skywards and lies precisely in the centre of a subtle unseen circle. This discreet circle of raised earth around the pyramid may represent the Eye of Providence so often employed by the Freemasons and the interior has no religious artefacts or writings, which also corresponds with Freemasonry. Above the doors is a shield portraying a crowned Hobart star with its eight rays, flanked by a stag and a talbot, or hunting hound. On the reverse side a bull presides over an inscription which reads,

Erected
in Memory of JOHN HOBART Earl of Buckingham
who died the 3rd of September 1793
aged 70
by CAROLINE Countess of Buckingham his Widow
and by WILLIAM ASSHETON HARBORD
who married CAROLINE
his second daughter by
MARY ANNE daughter of
SIR THOMAS DRURY Bart

Within the Chapel is an elegant vaulted chamber paved with Carrera marble and there were painted windows on two sides which gave out a "warm religious glow."

Interior of the mausoleum, presently in a poor state, August 2019.

On this gloomy autumnal day Henry Hobart presented the Deed of Approbation and the Bishop carried out the brief Consecration ceremony. All was over by one o'clock when the vast iron doors, weighing half a ton each, were closed and the large key turned in the lock. Later, when the rain had stopped, other people arrived but they were too late to gratify their curiosity. The Bishop returned to Blickling Hall where he "partook of a very elegant handsome cold collation"[5] and left soon after two o'clock. Thornberry was pleased to tell Caroline Harbord that "Never was a matter conducted with less Parade and fuss—or in a more secret and private manner."[6]

Very early on the following morning the solemn and delicate task of removing the bodies from the Church and transporting them to the Chapel was undertaken. By this time Buckingham's remains had rested in Blickling Church for four years, his first wife Mary Anne for twenty-eight years, his daughter Julia for twenty-six years and sons John and Henry for over twenty-one years.

The Dowager Lady Buckingham had requested that Henry Hobart attend the removal of her children and the Bishop recommended that the Deed be presented by one of the family, so Henry's presence was, as Thornberry put it, "unavoidable". The two men dined together on Tuesday and made ready for the early hour next morning. Henry left Blickling on Thursday morning "after seeing the removal and every thing properly adjusted" and Thornberry told Caroline he sincerely hoped "with this account of the business being completed will alleviate your mind from many uneasy and unavoidable reflections on this subject. Strict orders are left that no Soul shall be admitted into the Building. In a few days all will be finished when I will see to it again and the Key shall be given to me, to whose hands none shall part with it,

The three sarcophagi, top: John Hobart, middle: Mary Anne (1st wife), bottom: Caroline (2nd wife), August 2019.

but into your own."[7] Whether her disquiet was solely caused by Henry Wood's unprofessional and devious conduct, and the considerable length of time it had taken to complete the memorial, is unclear. What is indisputable is that despite the specific written intention that she and William Harbord would be interred in the Sepulchral Chapel when their time came, they were instead buried at Gunton. The Dowager Countess Caroline's desire to be interred alongside her husband was granted. It can be surmised that the rupture between her and the Harbords never mended.

Nevertheless, the trio's ambition of creating a uniquely splendid monument to Lord Buckingham was successfully fulfilled. The Hobart family motto inscribed above the doors is, despite the grievous rift between them, an indiction of the love and respect which inspired the endeavour

AUCTOR PRECIOSA FACIT

(THE GIVER MAKES THE GIFT PRECIOUS)

Notes

1. In Freemasonry a pyramid's square base represents the base nature of mankind, made up of the four elements: earth, air, fire and water, and mankind's physical, astral, etheric and lower minds. The triangular sides also symbolise the Christian Trinity of Father, Son and Holy Spirit, or can be thought of as the higher elements of mankind: mind, soul and spirit. The construction may also be construed as symbolic, building the base on the earth which represents humans' gross nature and raising the sides which aspire to the eternal.
2. Whilst working in London during the 1770s Bonomi had befriended the celebrated artist Angelica Kauffman, a founder member of the Royal Academy, whose ward, Rosa Florini, he married. Kauffman later moved to Rome and persuaded the Bonomi family to join her, but after one of their children died there Rosa could not bear to remain. The Bonomis moved back to London permanently in 1784.
3. Correspondence on the subject of the Mausoleum read by the author at Blickling Hall.
4. Ibid.
5. NRO MC 184/4/1/15.
6. Ibid.
7. Ibid.

Key to the Mausoleum, Blickling, August 2019.

In the Aftermath

Sir Charles Hotham

In 1793 Sir Charles Hotham suffered from depression and believed that the wit and brilliant conversation which had hitherto delighted his many friends had deserted him. In September his low spirits were deeply exacerbated by the loss of Buckingham, the dearest of those friends. Horace Walpole blamed the rural solitude of Yorkshire for Hotham's mournful condition and blithely advised him to move south. Charles flatly refused, preferring "to die far from those who could contrast his present with his former self."[1] This wish was fulfilled when he died peacefully at Dalton in January 1794.

Lady Dorothy Hotham and Henrietta Hotham

In 1767, possession of Lady Suffolk's legacy made Harriet Hotham financially independent at a young age which predictably created further friction with her mother. Miss Hotham never married but she had a very long and close relationship with her maid, the nature of which caused Dorothy to refer to the maid as "that witch Betty"[2] and who was a constant bone of contention between mother and daughter. Matters did not improve in 1793 when on Buckingham's death Harriet inherited Marble Hill, and after Charles Hotham died in 1794 and left her many of his effects this made Dorothy's estrangement from her daughter complete. On her demise in 1798, aged seventy-nine, Dorothy left her entire fortune, much to his astonishment, to her brother-in-law Beaumont Hotham. Beaumont felt morally unable to accept the entirely unexpected bequest so, after settling Dorothy's affairs as her executor, gallantly made it all over to Miss Henrietta Hotham. Buckingham's "Mrs Harriet" died resolutely unmarried aged seventy three in 1816.

Henry Hobart

Henry was a kind, good humoured individual who travelled extensively and kept many detailed accounts of his experiences. On his Grand Tour he found Ostend, "a small disagreeable town,"[3] and discovered that "the most agreeable and most commodious way of travelling in Holland is in barges." In Brussels he thought the women were "in general not very handsome" and found Cologne to be a "large and dirty city with a grand cathedral." Mainz was "Large, handsome and pleasant," and Mannheim "the most agreeable town in Germany." He continued through Basle, Berne and Lausanne to reach Geneva which earned his greatest plaudit as it was "a very wealthy town with an excellent cricket ground." Henry's studies were wide reaching, including French, Latin, Greek and Italian. He also took harpsichord, dancing and fencing lessons and, like his brothers before him, threw himself into society, "hunting and running comic operas, balls and innocent conversation with the ladies." Over his two and a half years abroad he studied Euclid, Mathematics, History, Experimental Philosophy, Drawing, Architecture, Astronomy, and the Law of Motion, as well as Physics, Moral Philosophy, the Fortification and Defence of Places, and a short course in Civil Law. Somehow he also found time to amuse himself "most agreeably" with the fair ladies and there was a "certain one" in whose company he revelled. In 1759 Henry returned to England via Harwich where he encountered "a vast deal of trouble with the scoundrels of the Custom House Officers." In 1761 he married Anne Margaret Bristow of Quiddenham Hall and the couple honeymooned in Paris. Daughters Anne Catherine and Maria were born in 1762 and 1763 respectively and a third, Leonora, was born in Portugal in 1768, where Henry noted in his diary, "Lisbon roads are not very good and the city has suffered very badly from the earthquake." His growing family were presented to Portuguese Royalty, although he recorded that "ladies are only presented to the female part of the Family." En route home via Sardinia, Henry damned the islanders as "sad villains." On the good ship Lillies Henry wrote that their fellow travellers included "Mrs Bristow, Miss Mary Bristow, three servants, two large good-humoured monkeys, two Spanish pointers, one spaniel, four parrots and four Brazil birds." The ship docked at Margate where Henry was happy to report "all animals alive."

During her long illness, his mother the Dowager Countess Elizabeth repeatedly asked Henry to give her his word of honour never to sell or dispose of the Library at Blickling. In a declaration on 14 September, two days after her death in 1762, he followed the directions of her Will to "as soon as possible after her death in due form of law sign seal and execute deeds or instruments for settling and assuring the said collection of books and manuscripts in the room called the Library at the manor of Blickling for the use and benefit of my brother George Hobart and his children now promise and undertake to do so by writing under my hand."

By 1774 the family, now with the addition of a son, Henry Charles Hobart, were living between Hobart Hall in Richmond and Intwood Hall, Norfolk. At Richmond, Henry was closely involved in the creation of a bridge over the Thames and the Commissioners unanimously agreed that he should have the honour of laying the first stone. This he undertook on 23 August 1774 and a copperplate plaque commemorates the event. In Norwich, Henry was made a Freeman of the City in 1764 and was elected MP for Norwich in 1787. On 12 July 1788 Anne Hobart died; her birthdate was not recorded. In 1792 Henry became Deputy Lieutenant in the Norfolk Militia and in 1796 a further 1,992 men were formed to augment the main militia with Colonel the Hon Henry Hobart MP in command. Although he inherited his mother's estates, Henry had personal debts of around £24,000, and it was rumoured that he and other investors lost £120,000 in Portugal. The debt of £500 he was freed from in Buckingham's Will was paltry in comparison. As a Mason he was initiated into the White Swan Lodge in 1782 and in 1788 was the first person to hold the offices of Grand Superintendent for Norfolk and Provincial Grand Master simultaneously.

Henry did not enjoy the best of health during his last few years and died at Bath, where he had presumably gone to take the waters, on 10 May 1799. His obituary in the *Norwich Mercury* on 18 May was touching. "His unwearied attention to the interests of his constituents was respected and beloved by every individual. To those who were more intimately acquainted with him, and knew how to appreciate his inestimable qualities, his memory will be particularly dear." His Will read, "I the Honourable Henry Hobart being absolutely not worth one pound" and stated that his (literally) poor son should repay a £1,000 loan made by George Bristow of Ashford in Middlesex. Honouring the pledge made to his mother, Henry instructed his son on no account to sell any of Blickling's Library books "nor any of the Mahogany Tables Chairs Pictures over the doors and other ornaments," which were his sole property. Henry had been a sociable man whose main passion, shared with his brothers, was "the promotion of the Italian opera in England." Unfortunately for his son, financial acumen was not amongst his father's strengths, and the Rev Henry Hobart was left with nothing but debts. His only solace was "the living in Devonshire given me by my uncle the Earl of Buckinghamshire" and in the long run he did rather well, eventually becoming Canon of Hereford.

Armar Lowry Corry, Lord Belmore

In 1794 Lord Belmore bravely, or rashly some might say, undertook marriage for the third time. Following his long relationship with local woman Margaret Begby, he had taken up with another woman who lived even closer to home, in the gatehouse of the Belmore Estate. Miss Bowen was the daughter of Thomas Bowen, the coachman at Castle Coole, and in 1793 she gave Belmore a son he named Armar after himself. Remarkably, all three of his illegitimate children were brought up alongside Somerset and Louisa, who were by this time twenty and twelve respectively. Belmore's choice of bride was neither Miss Begby nor Miss Bowen. Instead he chose Marianne, the thirty nine year old spinster daughter of his friend Sir John Caldwell of Castle Caldwell, who although not a great beauty was said to possess a lively, even comedic personality. She brought a relatively modest dowry of 2,100 Irish pounds but she knew Belmore's history and was willing to take on the role of wife and mother to his five children. The couple married in Bath on 11 March 1794. In 1798 Marianne endured a one hundred and three hour labour only for the child to be stillborn.[4] During the winter of 1801-1802 the Belmore family stayed at No 17 Royal Crescent in Bath where Belmore developed a fever. As a remedy Marianne slipped a dose of Dr. James's Powder into his food but soon afterwards Louisa heard him fall heavily in the front parlour. She rushed to help but to her horror found her father lying dead. Dr. James's Powder was a hugely popular medication later discredited as 'quackery.' It was said to have hastened the death of the writer Oliver Goldsmith and it appears to have done the same service for Lord Belmore. Marianne, the Dowager Lady Belmore, lived at No 17 Royal

Crescent for thirty years and presided over balls held in the Assembly Rooms. She died in 1841 and is thought to have been the inspiration for 'Mrs Snuphanuph' in Charles Dicken's 'The Pickwick Papers'.

George Hobart, 3rd Earl of Buckinghamshire

and Lady Albinia Hobart

George died at Nocton Hall in 1804 and his Countess in 1816. Their son Robert Hobart, 4th Earl of Buckinghamshire was most unlike his hedonistic parents and became an accomplished statesman after whom Hobart, Tasmania was named.

The Ancram Family

William Drury Kerr

William Drury Kerr was well provided for by Buckingham's Will, financially maintained and educated until he reached twenty-one. After losing her daughter Louisa to Belmore, Harriet kept the boy close and he grew up alongside four legitimate siblings until sent to a boarding school in Yorkshire. As he was born out of wedlock William could not inherit his father's title or property and held no proper status in society. He was therefore obliged to make his own way in the world as best he could. As a young man he voyaged to India where he fell in love with Claudine Palmer, a daughter of one of the richest East Indian Merchants. Her father John Palmer was fierce in his opposition to a match between the pair as William was not only illegitimate but also a mere junior Bengal civil servant. Palmer disdainfully told his daughter that Kerr was a "silly fellow she would despise in a month."[5] However, when Claudine fell so desperately ill that her doctors advised that she risked death, but refused to return to England for treatment because of her devotion to William, her father capitulated and reluctantly gave them his blessing. A year after their marriage in 1815 Claudine gave birth to a son, and was pregnant with their second son fourteen months later, when William died in Calcutta aged twenty five, cause of death unknown. Palmer, despite his enormous wealth, callously decided he could not or would not support a separate household for Claudine and suggested that she go to England and approach her late husband's family for assistance. It appears that there she was helped by the Ancrams. Three years later, in 1822, Claudine travelled back to India and remarried. Her new husband was Captain Llewellyn Conroy of the Calcutta Native Militia but he died of cholera in 1825 leaving enormous debts and his most unlucky widow with three more sons to support. Claudine and her brood returned again to England where she threw herself at the mercy of relations of Captain Conroy.

Lady Harriet and Lord William Ancram

Following their marriage in April 1793 Harriet and William could accurately call themselves Lord and Lady Ancram. Their financial standing was not as healthy as it might have been because William's father General Kerr, although a moderate success at his army career, was not, according even to his own family, an astute manager of his Scottish estates. He was unkindly described by Henry Fox, Lord Holland as 'a vain insignificant puppy, lively but ugly.'[6] As the eldest of nine, William was in line to inherit the title, the estates and their debts. Harriet's bequest from her own father, although generous, was not altogether what she had hoped for. She had imagined that since their reconciliation, and her recent marriage, Buckingham might alter his Will in favour of his eldest child, but his sudden unexpected death put paid to that possibility. Relations with her sister Caroline were considerably strained although in later years Caroline sold portions of land which enabled her to assist the Ancrams financially. The Ancram's son John was born on 1 February 1794, five months after Buckingham's demise, followed by Robert in 1795, Isabella in 1797 and Henry in 1800. The family lived at Newbattle Abbey in Scotland but when Lord Ancram's regiment was posted to Ireland, Harriet often chose to accompany him. On those occasions he worried tremendously about her periods of extreme anxiety which rose steadily with each passing year. A letter written from Mount Stewart, the seat of his brother-in-law Lord Castlereagh, paints a picture of the situation in which he was often placed. Feeling obliged to send Harriet back to Scotland he told her "I shall not say how much it has cost me & what a heart breaking thing it was to me to feel it my duty to encourage you to do what was unpleasant for you and upsetting to myself."[7] He regretted there were no trusted physicians in Ireland to attend her should she fall ill, which,

> together with the unsettled state of this Country, would have made me half distracted, if I should be prevented from being near you at the time of your illness, of which there certainly might have been a possibility. You now have every comfort that you can expect to have about you, and I shall enjoy the satisfaction of knowing that you are in the best hands, and well taken care of. Now my dearest Harriet, out of consideration to me, if you had no other reason, I depend upon your executing all your fortitude to consider this absence as a necessary one, and that you will not allow yourself to give way to any foolish alarm about me, for if you make yourself unwell you make me miserable, and besides this you in all probability may protract the period of your return.

   William implored her to keep "her mind quiet and at ease" promising he would quit the regiment "without a moment's scruple" to attend her should her need be so great. He wrote "I know for certain that the Regt will not think I have broken my promise to them." He asked her to write to him three times a week, told her he expected to receive thirty-six letters from her and that she could bring the thirty-seventh with her. Harriet replied "for my sake my beloved we must not let me make you uncomfortable. If you are unhappy I must be wretched. I do love you so much Lord Ancram and it is hard to be absent from you under such circumstances."[8] She took solace in the company of their children, "Isabella is my nice little thing, loving and good-humoured. Schomberg is grown very like the picture of Lord Robert in the Gordon's garden. I think William ought to be sent to school, my sister says there is a school in Yorkshire where young Armytage is." (George Armytage was a nephew of Col. Harbord.) In 1798, when visiting Thomas and Louisa Conolly at Castletown during an uprising, William was again obliged to send Harriet back to Scotland, out of harm's way. On 20 June, Louisa wrote to Harriet,

> It was quite kind in you to let me hear of your safe arrival, indeed after the pleasant and satisfactory renewal of our old friendship, no situation of mind could make me forgetful of you. I felt very very miserable and wretched the last morning I saw you and my heart was so full that I could not speak to any body.

Alarmed by the latest insurgency Louisa explained,

> Thomas Conolly had determined on remaining here, thinking that if we can be serviceable in any shape to the country, it must be by staying here. We have accordingly turned our house into a Garrison. 10 soldiers sleep in our Drawing Room below stairs and the disposition every night is that of preparing against a Siege. The Insurgents are in such numbers about us within 6 and 9 miles. The Camp near the Bay of Allen is said to be very considerable however, as there are since Saturday last (since the English Regiment came to Dublin) some Troops dispersed at Hazel Hatch, Newcastle and Celbridge. We feel much greater security and I trust will not be attacked.

Louisa told her that William and his Regiment were "vastly praised for their conduct and Ancram had shown great ability as an Officer."[9]

Following the birth of Henry in 1800, Harriet asked William for permission to return to England and enjoy the society of her friends. He gave her his blessing with the greatest of pleasure but later reported the dreadful outcome,

> She went up with Lady Bath, in the full confidence that these (friends) would receive her with that kindness and affection which the many years of absence from them, and of penance to herself which she had spent in this country had quietly given her additional claims to. But alas! She found herself miserably mistaken, the generality of her friends seemed to have forgotten, and to have deserted her and this circumstance it is which I consider as the great cause of that illness which broke down her body, and which has at length reached her Vitels.[10]

William believed that it was "that decisive blow which overwhelmed her" and which continued to undermine her deteriorating constitution.

> The occasion on which we were both most alarmed for her safety was in the month of April when Lord Castlereagh sent for me express from this

country. On my arrival in London I found her very weak and very low,
and in some danger she then opened her mind to me fully, and spoke in a
manner which I can never forget, and as if she had been conscious she was
not to survive.

Survive though she did and in 1803 took a trip through France to Hamburg
and Rotterdam with their daughter Isabella whose Passport described her as
having a "malade paralysee." Harriet herself declined rapidly in body and mind,
occasionally professing she would prefer death to living with the pain she suffered.
William wrote plaintively,

with the nobleness of her mind, she never uttered a complaint, nor
excepting 3 or 4 times during an interval of more than four years, when for
the space of a few minutes at a time, nature seemed to have overpowered
her fortitude, and she would break out into involuntary agonies of grief,
and even pray for the Cruel Event.

By 1805 Harriet was in a truly pitiful condition "her faculties and feelings have
been as benumbed by malady, that she scarcely has been the same person, as we
formerly knew her." William considered himself "the only person who could truly
judge of her sentiments and wishes for these last fifteen years; I believe I knew every
thought that passed through her mind, at least till within the last 4 or 5 years."[11]
Tragically, when on 14 July forty-three year old Harriet took her last breath at their
house in New Norfolk Street, Grosvenor Square, William was elsewhere.

I do feel uneasy, very uneasy, not to have been by her in her last moments,
it would have been an everlasting consolation to me to have received
her last gasp. I do not reproach myself for my absence on that occasion,
it was unavoidable, but I do reproach myself, and always shall do so, for
not having latterly shown more indulgence to her frailties: I should have
recollected that the great change which had been effected upon her mind
during the last 4 or 5 years, was brought on by uninterrupted illness,
and sufferings. I should have borne patiently with the inequalities of her
temper, in short, I should never have quitted her side; this I shall always
feel, sorely[12].

To add to his feelings of remorse and guilt poor William also felt that his
wife had "sunk into rest before I had an opportunity of explaining to her some
circumstances in my own conduct which may have hurt her, but which I know I
could have explained to her satisfaction. I do fear much that towards her latter
end, even my name she may have added to complete the list of those who she
thought had abandoned her. Heaven knows what I have suffered on her account,
and if she herself had known all, I feel conscious she would have been more than
content with my conduct, for her heart was always ready to melt for the feelings of
others, however callous it might have been to her own: but I shall cease to torment
myself—"Upon hearing of her sister's death Caroline Harbord wrote to William

from Blickling on 19 July,

> I know not whether this will find you still in Newbattle but cannot help expressing a wish to hear from you and how you do. When I saw my poor sister about a month ago, I thought her much the same as she had been for some time past and little suspected this melancholy event was to happen as soon. I am told she wished to be buried here, to which we can have no objection.[13]

William's reply from Newbattle on 21 August explained that he had been too much occupied to respond sooner and justified his decision to bury Harriet at Newbattle,

> Your letter followed me to London and my mind has been too much occupied ever since to permit me to answer it. The remains of my beloved Harriet were interred here yesterday sennight, and I am becoming somewhat accustomed to my misfortune. I was told she had expressed a desire to be buried at Blickling, but could not trace this report to anybody but Lady Castlereagh who informed me it had been her decided wish: that she had expressed it to her long ago several times: it did not appear to me however that it had been said to her with a view of being solemnly imparted to me in the face of her death, and I know she would have mentioned it to me had the wish been at all near her heart. Altho' I never should have felt comfortable if she had been placed in any other vault than this, I should certainly not have allowed any gratification of my individual feelings to have stood in the way of her own, or even the wish of her nearest relations on this subject. I consulted most of them and should have written to you also had not your letter, in which you say that you had been told that she had wished to be buried at Blickling, and that you could have no objection to it sufficiently proved to me, but that you had never heard her mention the subject, and that personally you had no wish about the matter. I am quite confident, and am happy in that confidence, that notwithstanding the devotion she paid to her Father's memory, she would, had the question been put to her in her last moments, have requested that her ashes should be laid near mine, even tho' she had not known how much my future comfort would depend upon the circumstance: for it is, I fear, but too true, that she deserted him, and every body, and I may say every thing for my sake, and I have, thank God, by me some inestimable Relicks in her hand writing, as long as she was able to write, poor Soul, of the extent as well as of the steadiness of her attachment and affection towards me. Besides, her Will which she had in her possession till she left Scotland last, makes no mention of this subject, not did she indeed ever in the most distant manner, on any occasion touch upon it with me. Not long after Lord Buckinghams's death, drawings and sections of the Mausoleum at Blickling were sent to her: we looked them over, and admired them

together, surely this was an occasion on which she would have opened her mind to me. It always happened too, that previously to her lying in, she was uneasy and in a state of alarm, as to the Event, and at these times she more than once particularly before the birth of Henry made me different requests with as much seriousness and solemnity, as if she had been on her death bed. All these requests, however disagreeable some of them may be to me I shall endeavour to fulfill, I shall consider them as so many Laws by which my future conduct is to be governed, for I have that adoration for her memory, that even her weaknesses, if she had had any, I should feel most anxious to indulge.

Poor dear Soul! She is gone from me for ever, and with her is gone the purest, the most disinterested, the most generous, the most noble spirit that ever dwelt in woman but I do feel it as a matter not only of consolation, but even of triumph, that she retained that nobleness of spirit to the last, that she never was guilty of an act of meanness, in stooping to court the good graces of her friends, or of the world in general.[14]

This was the heart-breaking end to the love story of this remarkable couple whose highly unusual courtship had driven them to extreme measures in order to fulfil their desire to be together.

Harriet left behind a package of letters tied in pink ribbon, on which she had written, "My Father's last letters to me & their relation to his Death which happened between Eleven & Twelve o'clock on the night of 3rd Sept 1793." On a separate line she added, "I have unfortunately burnt or mislaid some of his Letters."[15]

୬୦ଓଃ

It would be romantic to imagine that William Ancram languished as a widower for the remainder of his life, but in fact he married again on 1 December in the year following Harriet's death. Twenty-six year old Lady Harriet Scott was the daughter of the 3rd Duke of Buccleuch and the couple had five sons and three daughters together. On his father's death in 1815 William succeeded to the title 6th Marquess of Lothian. In 1817 he commissioned the building of a 150 foot high Doric column in the grounds of Monteviot House near Jedburgh. It was completed ten years later and its inscription reads "To The Duke of Wellington And The British Army William Kerr VI Marquess of Lothian And His Tenantry Dedicate This Monument XXX June MDCCCXV." William was appointed Lord Lieutenant of both Roxburgh and Midlothian and was Grand Master of the Scottish Freemasons. Lady Susan Napier once declared him to be 'like his grandmother, but not so sensible, though equally red-faced, good-humoured, gentlemanlike and well made.'[16] William died in Richmond on 27 April 1824 at the age of sixty, creating his son John William Robert the 7th Marquess of Lothian. His widow died in 1833.

Sophia, Lady Mount Edgcumbe

Sophie, as she was known in the family, seems not to have caused her father any worry and was almost never mentioned in his correspondence. Sent to Paris as company for Harriet, she married soon after her return to London. A year after their wedding Lord Valletort was elected MP for Lostwithiel and Fowey. On his father's death in 1795 the couple were titled Earl and Countess Edgcumbe and took up residence at Mount Edgcumbe House, a beautiful Tudor mansion on the Rame Peninsula overlooking Plymouth Sound and the River Tamar in Devon. Sophie's first child was stillborn, but healthy daughters Emily and Caroline arrived safely in 1791 and 1792, followed by sons William in 1794, Ernest in 1797 and George in 1800. Sophie died aged thirty-eight on 17 August 1806 leaving Richard a widower until his death aged seventy-five in 1839.

Caroline, Dowager Countess of Buckingham

On Sunday 26 January 1817 Buckingham's beloved 'Great' Caroline died in London aged sixty-two, having lived as his widow for twenty-four years. The elegant, beautiful lady who effortlessly conquered Ireland and adorned English society with her natural grace and charm, who had borne the loss of her three sons with grace and dignity, had remained devoted to Buckingham's memory and to her daughter Emily. She specified in her Will that none of her family should wear mourning clothes, which was "a most singular request" according to the London newspapers, and the Norwich Mercury reported that on "Monday morning at six o'clock the remains of the Countess of Buckinghamshire were removed from her house in Grosvenor Place for interment in the family vault at Blickling, Norfolk. Her remains passed through this City on Thursday last."

Rector D. Churchill conducted the funeral on Thursday 6 February when Lady Buckingham's express wish in her Will[17] that only "Jones, Lady Caroline's principal servant, two other women and the undertaker Mr Capener" attended the service was carried out. This ensured that neither Caroline nor William Harbord were present. Also in accordance with her desire the Dowager Lady Buckingham was "buried in a very private manner in the Mausoleum at Blickling in the County of Norfolk along side the remains of my late husband John Earl of Buckingham AND MY SONS" and she requested the wording on her sarcophagus should read simply 'Caroline Countess of Buckingham.'

It was remarked upon that following Buckingham's death Lady Caroline often expressed a pronounced disinclination to "return into Norfolk." Considering the circumstances of her departure it is not beyond the bounds of possibility to suppose that her funeral in 1817 marked Caroline's first return to Blickling since 1793, although when not at her house in Grosvenor Square, or staying with friends or family, she spent time at Hunworth House. She bequeathed both houses and her Plate and other Furnishings to her beloved daughter Emily, together with the majority of her estate. Other bequests were to her niece Harriet, Countess of

Clancarty, to several friends, and she left generous amounts to loyal servants. Two in particular were bequeathed large sums; her butler Hannibal Jones received £500 plus the dividends and interest on an investment of £2,400 and her former servant Mary Morall £300 together with dividends and interest on an investment of £2,500. Mary Morall was also bequeathed Lady Caroline's "gold gowns and petticoats." A service of plate bearing the initials 'C.B.' was left to her executors William Groom and Edward Boodle.

'Great' Caroline rests next to her husband and sons, exactly as she wished.

Emily, Lady Castlereagh

Buckingham's 'Dear Baby', after a period of mourning in which the ladies were "in black gloves", resumed her attendance at balls and Assemblies towards the end of February 1794. Beautiful, slim and graceful (later she grew noticeably plump) with grey eyes and abundant wavy fair hair, she had a merry, guileless personality. Described by one admirer as "a fine, comely, good humoured, playful (not to say romping) piece of flesh as an Illyrian"[18] Emily attracted the attention of more than one eligible suitor and at least two men fell head over heels in love with her.

One of these was Prince Philipp of Lichtenstein, a minor son of Franz Joseph I, who wrote to William Ancram almost immediately after their first introduction to ask for Emily's hand in marriage. "In all the countries I have visited I have never met a woman who has made so profound an impression as Lady Amelia Hobart. Your sister-in-law to an angelic face unites, as everybody is assured, so many lovable qualities that it would be strange if I were the only one who was sensible of them."[19] He modestly claimed no good looks for himself, nor advantages of rank, of birth, or of illustrious alliances and nor did he expect to be very rich, but he offered "to undertake everything to make myself worthy of her."

Another smitten figure was Robert Stewart, Lord Castlereagh, said to be the most handsome man in the Irish Parliament and who was in London visiting his beloved ailing grandfather. Castlereagh's noble face was described as similar "to the young Augustus in its classic beauty, with sad far-seeing eyes and clear cut full-lipped mouth" and he was always exquisitely turned out with "all the grace of the French and the manliness of the English and Irish." The moment he laid eyes upon Emily at a fashionable assembly he was afflicted by what the French describe as 'a coup de foudre', a thunderbolt of love. Emily was similarly struck and before long mischievously showed him Prince Philipp's letter of proposal. This made Castlereagh realise the peril he was in and by early April he had proposed and, to his considerable relief, been accepted, leaving the Prince grievously disappointed.

Throughout their life together Robert's love and devotion to Emily was unwavering, as his many surviving letters attest. One of the first sums up the depth of his adoration, "Tell me you love me, on that my existence depends, and I can never grow tired of hearing it."[20] He had served as a Lt. Colonel in the Irish Militia under the command of Thomas Conolly, and Emily's cousin Harriet Staples congratulated her, "You know I suppose how very much my uncle and aunt approve and admire your choice, they are very well acquainted with Mr Stewart and like him as much as you know he deserves."[21] On 7 June a marriage settlement was drawn up and signed. Emily had a portion of £30,000 and would inherit income from various estates upon the death of her mother. The wedding took place on 9 June at St George's Hanover Square and the couple settled into an opulent six storey house at No 3 Cleveland Terrace overlooking St James's Park, not far from her sister Lady Valletort's London residence.

When Parliament went into summer recess the newly-weds honeymooned in the Scottish borders where they spent time with Harriet and William Ancram and their new (legitimate) son John, named after Buckingham. The Castlereagh's marriage was an extremely close and happy one. Robert rose to become a political figure of considerable stature whose opinions engendered both bitter loathing and devout admiration throughout what became an extremely demanding and eventful career. Perhaps best known in Ireland for his involvement in the repression of the 1798 Rebellion, and as one of the architects of the Anglo-Irish Union of 1800, he was vilified by many but acknowledged by all to be a consummate statesman. Castlereagh hated to be without Emily even for a day but when it was unavoidable he wrote, "I have really of late felt the deprivation with an acuteness which is only known to those who are separated from what they most love. But I find I am in danger of committing the intolerable barbarism of writing a love letter to my wife."[22] When in Ireland he often mentioned William Ancram who fought alongside him against the frequent uprisings amongst the unionist contingent, as in November 1796, "Newbattle sleeps in my room and desires me to say that he will not suffer any United Irishman to approach me,"[23] and in October 1797, "I hope Lord Ancram and I shall return together."[24]

Whenever possible Emily accompanied Castlereagh on his European tours, never complaining of the many inconveniences of foreign travel, but throwing herself into each country's society with gay abandon. She became renowned for hosting lavish soirees and was occasionally ridiculed for her ostentatious dress sense, as when she wore her husband's Order of the Garter in her hair at a re-creation of a medieval jousting tournament in Vienna. She was judged by some as flighty and over indulged but she was without exception Castlereagh's most fiercely loyal and devoted confidante. When in Britain they divided their time between London, Dublin (during Parliamentary sessions) and Mount Stewart, Lord Castlereagh's family seat situated east of Belfast.

At some point around the turn of the century Louisa Lowry Corry was sent to stay with the Castlereagh's so that her aunt Emily could oversee her coming out into Society. It is intriguing to speculate whether Louisa at this point, or indeed ever, came into contact with her mother. Lord Belmore had done his utmost to keep them apart and had certainly put his case for demonising Harriet as the villain of the piece, but Emily must surely have given Louisa her mother's side of the story during the lengthy time they spent in each other's company.

It appears that Louisa was a chip off the old block, sharing a good proportion of Harriet's good looks and high spirits. For instance, when she was nineteen years old she used to go out to look for rebels in the dark "but never saw any that were worse then her."[25] Emily guided Louisa through her coming out season and dressed her so beautifully that in 1803 the 'Ladies Magazine' singled her out for compliments when she attended the prestigious Queen Charlotte's birthday ball. Her dress was described as rich pink satin with silver draperies, black lace, and a train of black velvet with slashed sleeves, richly spangled in silver, all topped by a headdress of a handsome plume of pink feathers and a profusion of diamonds. It announced that "both the wearer and the dress were particularly beautiful." Louisa's older half-brother Somerset Lowry Corry, now 2nd Earl of Belmore, was sometimes on hand to squire her about London and occasionally she attended debates in Parliament with her aunt, where they watched from the Gallery. In April 1804 Emily took great pleasure in announcing that the vivacious and lovely Louisa was engaged to thirty-one year old George Montagu, Viscount Hinchingbrooke. Lord George was the son and heir of Buckingham's ally during his sojourn in Russia, John Montagu, 5th Earl of Sandwich. Lord Enniskillen wished Louisa every happiness "I rejoice with you that you will so soon change the NASTY name of CORRY"[26] confirming that neither he nor his wife ever forgave Belmore for severing Harriet's connection with Louisa. Their daughter Florence, now Lady Balfour, had once attempted to reunite Louisa with her mother, but Belmore fended her off saying, "I am sure your own good sense would not approve with my consenting that she should have any intercourse with her unfortunate mother during the time she is under my care—you would not recommend it to me to employ a woman to educate my daughter whose want of principle was so strongly stamped as that of Lady A."[27] Florence had to content herself by telling Louisa "I ardently hope that your happiness will last and am delighted that you are so much in love."[28] Louisa and George Montagu[29] were married from the Castlereagh's house in Upper Brook Street on 9 July 1804, and the following May brought the birth of the first of Louisa's three children, a daughter she named Harriet, two months before the death of her grandmother, Lady Henrietta Ancram.

In 1810 Castlereagh bought a forty acre estate at North Cray in Kent where Emily established her own zoo which housed merino sheep, an aviary, ostriches, llamas, kangaroos, a zebra, a Portuguese donkey, a Maltese stallion, and a lion. She also enjoyed breeding hunting hounds and mastiffs. In London Emily became a renowned Lady Patroness of the supremely fashionable Almack's where she excelled at throwing extravagant, legendary parties.

Castlereagh was a chief negotiator at the Congress of Vienna and his greatest achievement was steering the Congress towards an equitable balance of power in Europe. He also became a staunch and vociferous supporter of the abolition of slavery. Emily accompanied him on a visit to Paris in 1815 and they were for a time joined at their house at 30 rue de Faubourg Saint-Honore by her sister Sophie's twenty-four year old daughter Emma Edgcumbe. Christmas found the Castlereagh's at Blickling where Caroline and William Harbord revelled in their association with such an influential political figure as Robert Stewart. Emily may have had mixed emotions at returning to the childhood home where her beloved mother had been latterly so unhappy, but her loyalty to her husband was unwavering, and she may have taken this opportunity to pay her respects to her father at the Mausoleum. At the shoot that year, the hunters bagged five hundred head of game in one week. It may have been during this visit to Blickling that Castlereagh became aware of the letters of Henrietta, Lady Suffolk to and from her nephew Buckingham. Certainly it is thanks to him they survived because it was he who enlisted his cabinet colleague John Wilson Crocker, who was also a brilliant literary critic, to edit them for posterity.

In 1817 Emily's mother died and specified in her Will that her family should not wear mourning. This may have been principally to cause her daughter the least possible upset, knowing as she did her daughter's penchant for entertainments whenever possible. On his father's death in 1821, Castlereagh took the title 2nd Marquess of Londonderry. In 1822 a severe nervous breakdown impaired Castlereagh's mental faculties and by August he confessed that "My mind is, as it were, gone." During an audience with King George IV he became wildly distracted and ranted that he was being blackmailed for the same crime as the Bishop of Clogher, which was buggery. On hearing this the King was so alarmed he insisted that Castlereagh go straight home to rest his fevered mind. The King relayed his concern to Arthur Wellesley, Duke of Wellington who immediately followed Castlereagh to St James's Square. After a short talk in which he divined Castlereagh's troubled state of mind the Duke begged him to retire to North Cray and immediately called for his physician Dr. Bankhead to accompany him. At home Emily was so frightened by her beloved husband's behaviour that she ordered the servants to remove all knives and sharp instruments from his reach. But a few days later, in the only space of three or four minutes in which Robert Stewart was left alone, he ran to his dressing room, recovered a small knife he had somehow managed to keep hidden there, and cut his throat. Dr Bankhead caught up with him just as he fell and Emily rushed to his side, but tragically they were too late to save him.

An inquest judged that Castlereagh had been labouring under a delusion of mind and Emily's request to bury him in Westminster Abbey was permitted. Since Castlereagh's untimely death history has altered its view of Castlereagh's contribution to the welfare of Great Britain but Emily's view of him as a brilliant statesman, thoroughly honourable man and perfect husband never wavered.

The Lord Viscount Castlereagh by Charles Turner, YCBA B1977.14.9837.

Devastated by the desperate drama of his death she lived quietly in the country for the next eighteen months. She returned to something of a social life thereafter but her health gradually failed and Buckingham's 'Dear Baby' died in 1829 aged fifty-seven. The Castlereaghs had no children.

William and Caroline, Lord and Lady Suffield

Shortly after Buckingham's funeral Caroline and William Harbord made Blickling Hall their primary residence. Always preferring the countryside to the town Caroline led a less social life than her sisters and was content to live for the most part in Norfolk although she contemptuously professed, "I believe this County is more barren of pleasant people and entertaining events than most, perhaps than any."[30] She had never enjoyed particularly good health and only a year after her marriage she confided to Emily that she was inclined to "preach up solitude thrown as I am by circumstances by want of health and past anxiety into a situation bordering on retirement."[31] Evidently the rift with her stepmother had taken its toll as she was only twenty-six at this time. William's health was not much better than his wife's and over time gout plagued him more frequently, "I am still very lame and not at all well and intend seeing Dr Baillie."[32]

Despite his affliction he was an avid race goer and put the Blickling courses to good use. The *Norfolk Chronicle* of 14 October 1802 recorded, "Races held at Blickling Park. Lady Caroline Harbord gave a ball and supper for upwards of 100 guests from Aylsham and surrounding neighbourhood." On 26 August 1805 a cricket match was played at Blickling and in October a two day race meeting was held after which "a ball and supper were given by Lord Suffield." At the first meeting on 22 October 1805[33] William Harbord's horse 'Master Betty' won the Blickling Sweepstake over two miles and his mare 'Czarina' both the Norfolk Sweepstake over a mile and the Produce Two Year Old Stakes over a mile. The fourth race was won by Colonel Wyndham's horse who, oddly enough, was named 'Blickling' and all the prizes were awarded by Lady Caroline. In 1806 'Czarina' proved her mettle again by winning the 50 guinea sweepstake for horses bred in Norfolk. The couple made themselves visible at Court, as when in March 1808 Harbord wrote to his father "It will now be in my power to leave London after the Drawing Room on Thursday when I am to be presented to Her Majesty and of course Lady Caroline and Edward will be there also" and in June he reported that "Lady Caroline was last Sunday on the Terrace at Windsor and His Majesty inquired of her particularly after you."[34]

The Harbord's familial relationship with the Castlereagh's was maintained even though their politics did not align, as when in 1807 Harbord voted against the abolition of the slave trade, in which movement Castlereagh had become a most vociferous supporter. In the same year Harbord tried to persuade the Viscount to find a position for his younger brother Edward and it was hoped he would be employed by the Duke of Portland but Edward was not appointed as a Lord of the Admiralty. Later William attempted to have Edward made Lord Lieutenant of Norfolk, whilst at the same time writing to their father, "I think I would lose no time in making an application for an Earldom for should they not be decided about the Ld Lieutenancy perhaps were you created one I might have the Lieutenancy having that additional rank. I am convinced there is nobody standing in our way but Ld

Bayning."[35] No such Earldom was forthcoming but William himself was appointed Lord Lieutenant of Norfolk in 1808, a position he maintained until his demise. He also took over as Vice-Admiral of Norfolk in the following year. Harbord had been Colonel of the Norfolk Fencible Light Dragoons since 1794 and established the Blickling Rifle Volunteers in 1803, and in 1808 became Colonel of the East Norfolk Regiment of Militia. In that same year a serious fire broke out in Blickling Hall and the townspeople of Aylsham rallied to help extinguish the blaze. Afterwards the Harbords rewarded them with significant gratuities. Following the demise of Sir Harbord Harbord in 1810, William and Caroline were titled Lord and Lady Suffield but continued to reside at Blickling, condescending to use Gunton Hall only as "a shooting box."

On 1 August 1821 William Harbord, 2nd Baronet of Suffield died aged fifty-four at his house in Charles Street, Berkeley Square. Contrary to his original written intention to be interred within Blickling's Sepulchral Chapel, he was instead buried at St Andrew's Church at Gunton Hall. En route from London to Gunton the Norfolk Chronicle reported that, "The remains of his lordship arrived at Aylsham, and lay in state at the Black Boys Inn on August 12th, and the funeral took place at Gunton on the 13th" adding that as he had died without issue, he was succeeded in his title and estates by his brother, the Hon Edward Harbord, M.P. for Shaftesbury. Lady Suffield was bequeathed an annuity of £1,000 and the right to sell land. She lived quietly as a widow at Blickling Hall for almost three decades from whence she rarely travelled. Her nephew Charles Harbord later recalled, "My old aunt Caroline, Lady Suffield, who was autocratic to her finger tips, was one of those who considered railways very much beneath her dignity, and travelled in her own carriage to the end of her life rather than rub shoulders with other people in trains."[36] Lady Suffield was fond of gardening, indeed her husband had named a dessert apple grown in the Blickling Orchard the 'Caroline.' She was acquainted with the renowned landscape designer Humphry Repton from his previously commissioned work at Gunton Hall and asked his informal advice about planting at Blickling, and Repton's son John Adey consequently worked on Blickling's flower beds and garden structures. In April 1849 a second fire broke out at Blickling and Lady Suffield's loyal staff risked their lives by exposing themselves to fire and smoke to the point of near suffocation until they succeeded in extinguishing it.

Lady Caroline Hans Suffield died at Blickling aged 83 on 27 October 1850, having lived as the widow of William Harbord for twenty-nine years. As requested in her Will she was "buried very privately next to my late husband in the Family Vault at Gunton." The Norfolk Chronicle reported the "Death of Dowager Lady Suffield. Her youngest sister Amelia Ann was married to Lord Castlereagh. In consequence of this union her connection with the political world was maintained even more intimately than before. Throughout her life she continued to take a lively interest in the politics of the County, and the influence of the united houses of Gunton and Blickling in the days of contested elections was not lightly esteemed by conflicting parties."

The Lothian Connection

It had been apparent for many years that Caroline and William Suffield's marriage would produce no children and that Blickling would in due course pass through the Ancram line. Harriet was aware of this and it may have given her comfort to believe her son would regain her family home.

In due course however, it transpired that the Ancram's eldest son John William Robert, 7th Marquess of Lothian predeceased Lady Suffield in 1841 aged forty-one and as his younger brother, Schomberg Robert, died in 1825, the Estate devolved to John's son William Schomberg Kerr, 8th Marquess of Lothian.

Blickling And The National Trust

Philip Henry Kerr, 11th Marquess of Lothian left the Blickling estate to the National Trust in 1940.

Kerr Family Tree

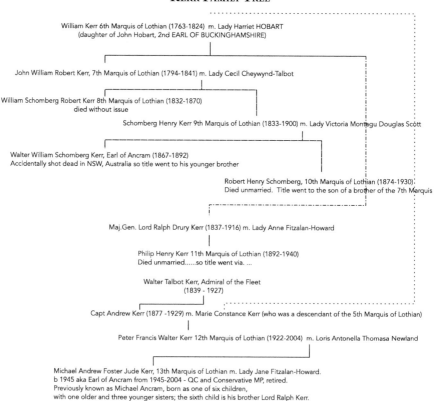

Notes

1. *The Hothams...* Vol. II, p.316n.
2. *The Hothams ...*, p.344.
3. All quotes regarding Henry Hobart come from a piece written by A.M. Greedy, M.A., December 2007. With the kind permission of Peter F. French.
4. PRONI D/1606/1/1/201.
5. Webster, A., *The Richest East India Merchant'*, 2007.
6. History of the Lothian family, monteviot.com.
7. NRS GD40/9/215.
8. NRS GD40/9/216.
9. NRS GD40/9/217.
10. NRS GD40/9/233.
11. Ibid.
12. Ibid.
13. Ibid.
14. NRS GD40/9/233/2.
15. NRS GD40/9/204.
16. *Guidebook to Monteviot House*, Jedburgh.
17. Caroline's Will dated December 29th 1813, The National Archive.
18. Leigh, I., *Castlereagh*, Collins, 1951, p.55.
19. NRO MC3/293.
20. Ibid.
21. Ibid.
22. NRO MC 3/290
23. Ibid.
24. Ibid.
25. Marson, P.
26. Ibid.
27. Ibid.
28. Ibid.
29. George Montagu died in Rome in 1818. Lady Louisa lived another 43 years as his widow.
30. NRO MC 3/290.
31. Ibid.
32. NRO GTN/5/7/15.
33. The National Horseracing Museum, Newmarket. After 1811 racing continued at Blickling up to six times a year arranged by local landowners but the results were not published in the Racing Calendar.
34. NRO GTN/5/7/15.
35. Ibid.
36. *Charles Harbord 1830–1913, My Memories*, archive.org.

Index

Printed in Great Britain
by Amazon

25993299R00176